IBM 360
Assembler Language
Programming

IBM 360
Assembler Language
Programming

Gopal K. Kapur
Associate Professor
Data Processing
San Jose State College

JOHN WILEY & SONS, INC.

New York   London   Sydney   Toronto

The author is pleased to offer thanks to the International
Business Machines Corporation for permission to reproduce
some of their copyrighted material and providing the various
photographs. The material in this book is based on the following publications copyrighted in 1968, 1967, 1966 or
1965 by International Business Machines Corporation.

A22–6821	C20–1649
A29–3427	C20–1684
C24–5037	A22–6866
C24–3414	A24–3073
C24–5036	A26–5988
C20–1685	A21–9033
C24–5030	

Library of Congress Catalog Card Number: 76-125272
ISBN 0-471-45840-6

Printed in the United States of America

10 9 8 7 6 5 4 3 2 1

To My Parents

Professor & Mrs. Bal Kishan Kapur (India)

Preface

Assembler Language is the most important language applicable to IBM System/ 360 Computers. However, the purpose, use and value of this language has been misunderstood by many people. It has been associated with compilers, assemblers and other similar usage, which is a gross misconception of the use and implementation of this language.

The objective of this book is to help the IBM System/360 student in programming the computer system in Assembler Language. The main motivation behind writing this book is to present to the student information which will teach the mechanics of Assembler Language instructions, as well as the logic and application of the language itself. It is the author's hope that the student will be able to understand the language in depth rather than in a superficial manner.

The material is presented in a form appropriate to a two-semester course. However, the chapters are largely independent and may be used in various combinations for courses that are shorter or of different duration and emphasis. I particularly desired to make the book helpful and suitable for the self-study student. To this end, the material in the text has been grouped in a building block concept. Numerous examples, exercises and programs have been included throughout the development of this material. A brief introduction to IBM System/370 has also been included.

Since none of the computer languages can be learned by merely reading about them, numerous solved problems, programs and self-evaluation quizzes have been incorporated. Although suggested solutions have been given, the student is encouraged to find and develop other ways to solve the problems. Any problem, if given to a number of programmers, will be solved in many different ways and techniques. He should also try to compile and execute on the computer as many of the programs as possible.

In general, the book is based on the Disk Operating System (DOS). It is realized that the computer manufacturer continually changes and modifies software to provide additional conveniences and improvements. This book will be of value to the programmer in adapting such modifications since it concentrates upon the most basic features of the software.

In addition to this text, the student should refer to the computer manufacturer's reference manuals for additional information whenever such need arises. The use of a flowcharting template and assembler coding form will be helpful.

My thanks go to many friends and colleagues who helped in the preparation of this text. My many thanks to Mr. Len Novak and Mr. Stan Hobbs for their faith and stimulation during the beginning periods of my career in data processing.

My sincere gratitude to my friend Mr. Massoud Khalilzadeh for many hours spent reading this text and for his professional advice and guidance.

I wish to acknowledge Gary Durbin for his assistance in developing some of the examples and exercises; and thanks to Charles Pack and Balram K. Kapur for testing most of the programs. I am most appreciative of the reviewers: Keith Carver, Sacramento City College; Louis Nashelsky, Queensborough Community College; John R. Clark, Orange Coast College; Harold Hill, San Diego City College; and Dan Thalimer, Control Data, who contributed objective comments and suggestions. Special acknowledgment is also due to Jerryn Ballard and Marilyn Rotharmal for their efforts in reading and typing of the manuscript. It has been a pleasure working with the fine editorial and production staff of John Wiley & Sons; in particular Albert R. Beckett, Gary R. Brahms, Bernard Scheier, and Barbara Newman.

Finally, my deep appreciation to my wife Indra, for her encouragement in the beginning and her loving patience throughout.

Gopal K. Kapur

San Jose, California
September 1970

Contents

x   Contents

Contents   xiii

List of Flowcharts and Sample Programs

IBM 360
Assembler Language
Programming

[1]

Introduction
to Computing

1.1 Introduction

Each day around the globe new discoveries in the scientific field and major decisions in the business world are made that improve and alter our lives. In the financial world we see transactions that affect the economics of countries around the world as well as the smaller economics of our neighbors and ourselves.

To keep abreast of these countless transactions we need more than a team of fast typists and an accurate filing system. Millions of facts are born each day that must be stored yet be at our fingertips on an instant's notice.

Important business decisions are based on information and data, such as sales and manufacturing statistics, inventory levels, supply and demand, operating costs, and market trends. Other things being equal, the person with the greatest amount of accurate information (data) at his disposal has the edge over his business competitors.

However, raw data (unorganized information) are of limited use. Only when data are examined, arranged, analyzed and treated with scientific procedures do they take on real and useful value. This is what is meant by Data Processing.

A data processing system can be defined as a group of people and machines which are organized to perform the data processing needs of an organization. The main component of this system is an electronic computer which is used to store, examine and analyze raw information to produce useful and workable data.

Within the brief span of approximately 20 years, since the introduction of medium and large scale data processing systems, the digital computers have progressed greatly. Today's third generation computers are capable of executing instructions one million to one billion times faster than a human being. The storage capacity of larger computers is counted in millions of characters and any part of this information can be

1

retrieved in a millionth of a second. However, all this complexity is mainly illusory. Despite their speed and enormous storage capacity, computers are not that much faster than a human brain in every area of intellectual endeavor. What the human brain lacks in speed of operation, it makes up for in complexity of organization. Computers are not capable of creative thinking. They serve best when called upon to do structured thinking and processing.

In data processing terminology this process is known as *programming* a computer. Programming is the act of writing instructions which, when executed by the computer, produce a desired result. This set of instructions is called a program.

This text will describe the overall functions and capabilities of the IBM—360 and will introduce the student to the concepts, methods and logic of programming using the Assembler Language.

Programming systems

In the earlier days of computer programming, the only method of programming available was to code the various commands required to solve a problem in the actual machine language. A programmer also had to perform all the routine and clerical tasks of delegating storage areas, assigning storage addresses to instructions and data, and numerous other unpleasant tasks. As the computer became more complex, the machine language became more cumbersome and the job of writing programs very inefficient. To eliminate the majority of these unnecessary and inconvenient aspects of writing in machine languages, symbolic languages were developed. A symbolic language, in essence, consists of symbols and codes and the task of translating these symbols into machine instructions is given to the computer. The translation is actually performed by machine language programs called assemblers and compilers. These translating programs are usually written, supplied and maintained by the computer manufacturers.

Several programming systems were developed, each for a different programming application. These programming systems can be grouped into four major categories.

Machine Oriented Programming System. In a machine oriented programming system the programmer uses symbols and codes to designate various operations that the computer is to perform. Symbols and codes are also used to designate storage addresses or locations of data to be used by the different instructions. When using this method, the programmer must have a basic knowledge of the characteristics and architecture of the computer hardware. Assembler Language is a machine oriented language.

Problem Oriented Programming System. In this type of programming system, the programmer uses a language in which the basic structure is conceived in terms of the problem to be solved and results to be obtained. The programmer does not need to concern himself with the technical features of the computer. The language used bears almost no resemblance to the machine language. Of course, the programmer must develop a thorough knowledge of the structure and applications of the language being used. COBOL is one of the problem oriented languages. The programmer, however, does not need to know or understand in any great depth, the application of the problem he is given to solve.

Procedure Oriented Programming System. In this type of programming system the programmer does not need any knowledge of the computer system hardware. The user generally is a scientist or a mathematician who understands and is capable of defining his problem and its procedures in complete details. He needs to familiarize himself only with the syntax and basic rules of the language being used to solve the problem. FORTRAN is one of the procedure oriented languages.

Application Oriented Programming System. There are certain symbolic languages which have been developed for very special and restrictive applications. Examples are COGO, a symbolic language of interest to civil engineers solving surveying problems, and STRESS, of interest to persons dealing with structural analysis.

Programming languages

The most commonly used symbolic languages in System 360 are:

Assembler Language.

COBOL.

FORTRAN.

PL/1.

RPG.

These symbolic languages can very well be compared to ordinary spoken and written languages as they have some very definite grammatical rules, well developed vocabulary and syntax structure. Like any other language there are changes and innovations made from time to time and periodically the manufacturers produce an updated version of a language. However, the basic rules, structure and components of a language never change.

Assembler Language. Assembler Language is one of the lower level machine oriented languages which is similar to the machine language of System 360. It is a very powerful and versatile language as it gives a programmer the ability to manipulate the basic components of System 360. Programs written in this language require the minimum of core storage and execution time. This language, unlike higher level languages, requires a great deal of documentation. Programs written in Assembler Language, if not properly documented, are very difficult to follow. Hence, great care and effort should be given by the programmer to develop proper documentation techniques, such as flow charts, record format layouts, program listing, etc.

COBOL (COmmon Business Oriented Language). COBOL is one of the higher level languages and is largely suited for commercial applications. The symbolic statements written in this language look very much like sentences in the English language. For example:

READ CARDFILE AT END GO TO NO–CARDS.

COMPUTE REG–SALARY = REG–HOURS * REG–RATE.

The COBOL compiler reads these symbolic statements and translates them into machine instructions. This language was developed jointly by the U.S. Government, computer manufacturers and some large users in an effort to create a symbolic language which was less computer oriented and more problem oriented. COBOL, unlike the Assembler Language, is very much self-documenting and requires very little additional writeups and documentations. It is quite common to see programmers code complicated problems without the use of flow charts.

FORTRAN (FORmula TRANslator). FORTRAN, a procedure oriented higher level language, is one of the oldest computer languages in use. The symbolic statements written in this language closely resemble mathematical notations. For example:

D = ABC+63.92.

3T = T+3.47.

This language is mostly employed by programmers working with scientific, engineering, and mathematical applications. FORTRAN, though not self-documenting, requires little documentation as most of the symbolic statements are interpretation and representation of mathematical formulas.

PL/1 (Programming Language/One). PL/1, a procedure and problem oriented higher level language, is one of the newest symbolic languages. This was designed to bridge the gap between COBOL (completely business application oriented) and FORTRAN (a mathematical application oriented language). PL/1 incorporates a great number of features from both COBOL and FORTRAN and provides many new features which did not exist in either of the other two languages. This language is very versatile and can adequately handle both commercial and mathematical applications. In addition, it is very suitable for semi-scientific applications such as operations research techniques and information retrieval.

RPG (Report Program Generator). RPG was developed to facilitate conversion from punched card equipment to electronic computers. The source statement in this language consists of a number of specifications regarding the input and output record formats, and computations desired. The language in turn generates a program to perform the necessary processing. This language is well suited for smaller computers and for routine business reports.

In this text we will discuss in detail the characteristics, architecture, logic and applications of the Assembler Language.

1.2 Elements of Programming

In order to execute a job correctly and efficiently, it is important for a programmer to know:

1. The definition of the problem, i.e., the given facts.
2. The form of output desired.
3. The type and extent of the system he has to work with, i.e., the hardware and the software available.

Therefore, the first step in formulating a solution is a complete analysis of the configuration and the types of machines and software available, i.e., the languages, the supervisory system and any other type of support system. This should be followed by the investigation and evaluation of the information available and the decision as to what is to be accomplished. The latter is given to the programmer in the form of a System Flow Chart by the system analyst.

System Flow Chart: This can be defined as a symbolic and pictorial representation of the data processing system in which information from the source documents is converted to final documents.

Note: The system flow chart, which shows the system flow, is not the programmer's responsibility. The chart, along with system documentation, is drawn by a system analyst and supplied to the programmer.

A system flow chart depicts the operations and procedures required to accomplish a job. In a system chart the main emphasis is on the documents to be handled and upon the machines to be used. A system chart does not show the details of the operations required to solve the problem at hand. Certain standard symbols are used to draw system charts. The use of these symbols, although not mandatory, makes it easier to understand and interpret the flow charts. Figure 1.1 is a typical system flow chart.

After the system flow chart has been analyzed, the programmer can concentrate on solving the various problems within the system.

Elements of problem solving

The various elements of problem solving can be grouped under four main categories. These are:

1. Definition of the problem.
2. Analysis and solution.
3. Implementation and debugging.
4. Documentation.

Definition of the Problem. This means locating and gathering all available information about the program. For a simple problem this may only take a few hours; however, a complex problem may require days of data gathering.

Analysis and Solution. This involves examining the information available for the particular problem at hand and then planning a logical procedure to produce the desired result. Two main steps for developing a solution are:

1. Developing program flow charts (also called Block Diagrams).
2. Translating the block diagram into a computer language (called coding).

Program Flow Chart: This is a pictorial representation of the sequence in which computer operations are to be performed. Unlike the system chart, the program flow chart, or the block diagram, shows in detail each and every step needed to arrive at the solution. Therefore a program flow chart is much more detailed.

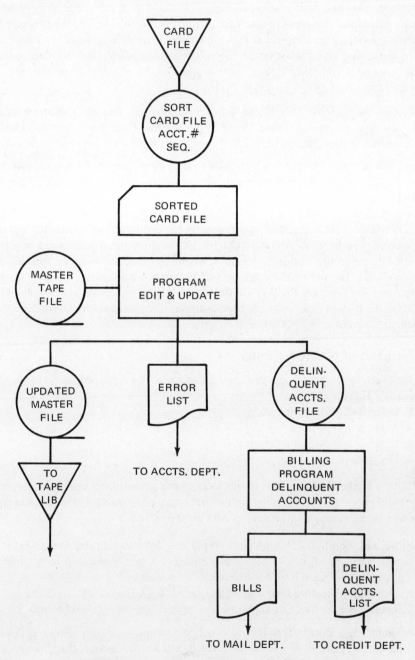

FIGURE 1.1. A Typical System Flow Chart.

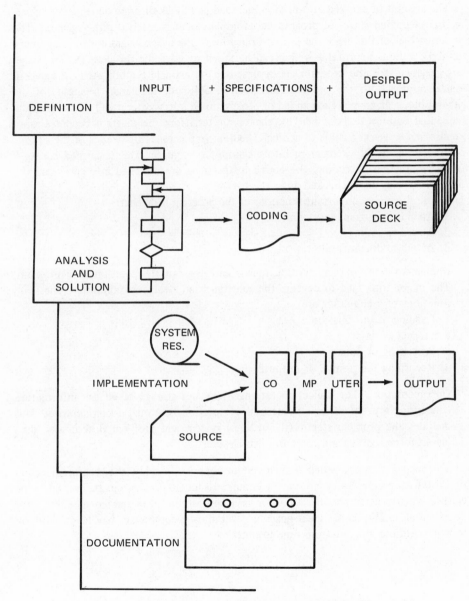

FIGURE 1.2. Steps in Problem Solving.

Standard symbols are used to represent the various computer operations. These are shown in Figure 1.3.

The amount of detailed information included in a block diagram depends on its use. At the beginning stages of program development the approach is rather general. The reason is that at this stage the primary purpose of the block diagram is to experiment with the various approaches which can be taken to solve the problem. At this stage, large segments of the program are represented by a single symbol. After the overall logical approach to the problem has been established, the larger segments of the general block diagram are expanded or broken down into greater detail showing all the individual actions to be taken by the computer. Now the diagram becomes more precise and serves as a guide to coding. The next step is to translate each of the actions portrayed in the block diagram into a computer language. This is termed *coding*.[1] Upon completion of coding, the coded instructions are punched into cards and the program is ready to be checked out.

These are three very important functions of the program flow chart:

1. An aid to program development.
2. An aid to coding.
3. An aid to documentation.

Implementation: Implementation means carrying out the solution to a problem. The major tool used to develop the solution is an electronic computer. The main functions of a computer are:

1. Reading of information.
2. Storing of data.
3. Processing of data.
4. Recording the results, or output.

Documentation: The collection, arrangement and storage of all the information concerning a problem and its method of solution is termed *documentation*. This includes the problem statement, outlines, system and problem flow charts, data layout forms, coding and computer listings, etc.

This is one of the steps which is most commonly overlooked by the programmers and the installation supervisors. Not having enough documentation means tedious and time wasting efforts when modifications or revisions of the programs are needed. Poor documentation also causes great headaches for those people who may be called upon to work with the program from time to time.

---

[1] Detailed methods of coding are discussed in Section 2.4.

PROGRAM FLOWCHART SYMBOLS	
SYMBOL	REPRESENTS
	PROCESSING A group of program instructions which perform a processing function of the program.
	INPUT/OUTPUT Any function of an input/output device (making information available for processing, recording processing information, tape positioning, etc.).
	DECISION The decision function used to document points in the program where a branch to alternate paths is possible based upon variable conditions.
	PROGRAM MODIFICATION An instruction or group of instructions which changes the program.
	PREDEFINED PROCESS A group of operations not detailed in the particular set of flowcharts.
	TERMINAL The beginning, end, or a point of interruption in a program
	CONNECTOR An entry from, or an exit to, another part of the program flowchart.
	OFFPAGE CONNECTOR A connector used instead of the connector symbol to designate entry to or exit from a page.
	FLOW DIRECTION The direction of processing or data flow.

FIGURE 1.3. Program Flowchart Symbols.

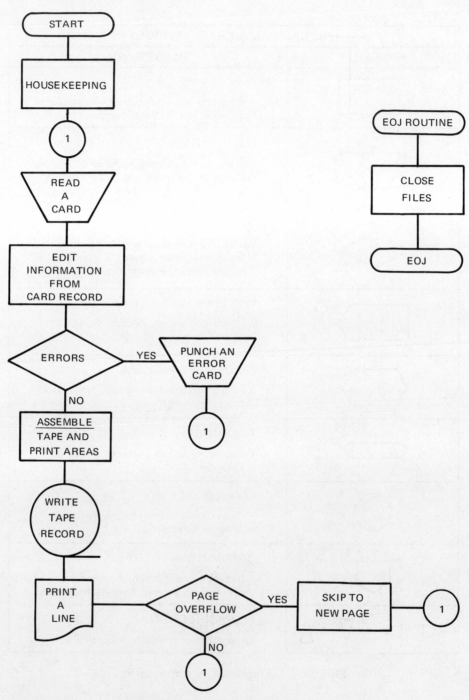

FIGURE 1.4. A Typical Block Diagram.

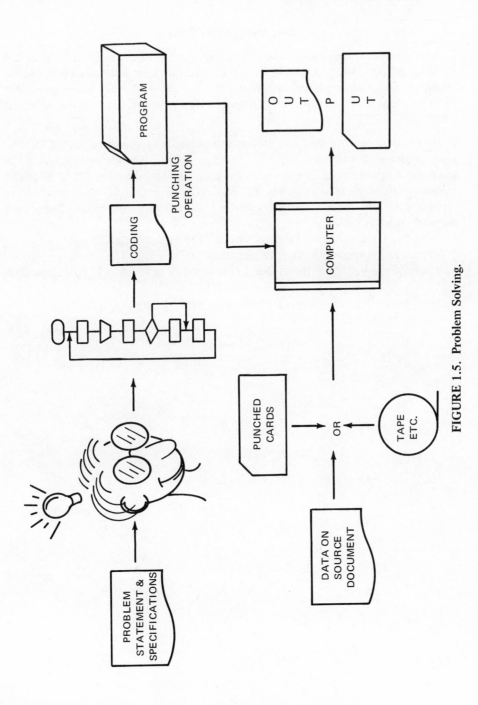

FIGURE 1.5. Problem Solving.

Self Evaluation Quiz

1. Prepare a flow chart for some day-to-day activity such as: getting up in the morning; getting ready and leaving for work; or starting a car and driving it out of the garage. Consider any unexpected action you might have to take, for example, not finding a clean shirt or perhaps an encounter with a police officer for speeding on the freeway.

2. Draw a flow chart to read and process a file containing employee payroll records. Each employee should have only one record in the file. The file has been sorted in ascending order of employee number. Your program logic should check for duplicate records and for correct sequence. In case of an error instruct the computer to terminate the job. One pay check is to be printed for every valid record. The payroll calculations are as follows:

Gross Pay = Regular Pay + Time and one-half Pay + Double-time Pay.

Regular Pay = Regular Hours * Regular Rate.

Time and one-half Pay = Hours over 35 but less than or equal to 50 * (Regular Rate * 1.5).

Double-time Pay = Hours over 50 * (Regular Rate * 2.0).

Regular Hours = 35 Hours.

[2]

Computer Components, Data Formats, and Addressing

2.1 IBM System/360 Components

There are many types of data processing systems which vary in size, speed, applications and cost. The range of these systems may vary from solutions of simple arithmetic problems to intricate scientific processes. However, irrespective of the information to be processed, all data processing involves three basic elements:

1. The INPUT entering the system.
2. Planned PROCESSING within the system.
3. The end result or the OUTPUT from the system.

All data processing systems are made up of four types of functional units:

1. INPUT DEVICES.
2. STORAGE.
3. CENTRAL PROCESSING UNIT (CPU).
4. OUTPUT DEVICES

Input devices

In order to process data, a computer must have the ability to receive these data. The elements of the computer system which enter data into the computer are known as *input devices.* Some of the most commonly used input devices are Card Read Units, Tape Units, and Disc and Drum Units. Input devices read or sense data that have been recorded on a particular medium (punched cards, magnetic tapes, etc.) and make this information available to the computer. Figure 2.2 illustrates some of these input devices. The type and number of these devices used in an installation depend mainly upon the requirements and design of the system.

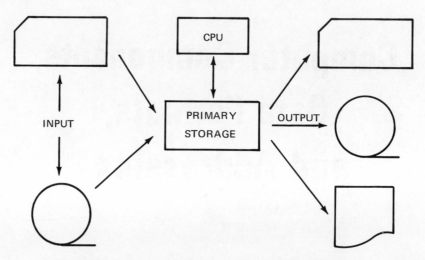

FIGURE 2.1. Basic Functional Units of a Computer System.

Storage

The purpose of a storage device is to hold data or store information. Four different types of storage devices are most frequently used with IBM systems. These are Magnetic Core, Magnetic Disc, Magnetic Drum, and Data Cell. The information can be stored in, held in, transferred, or retrieved from these storage devices. The information itself may consist of instructions and/or data.

Of all four types of storage devices available the most commonly used for the computer's main storage (memory unit) is the Magnetic Core. Although this form of storage is the most expensive the great advantage of magnetic core is that it has the fastest access time.

Access Time: The time required to locate and transfer information to and from the storage device is termed access time.

The storage or the memory unit of IBM 360 can be compared to the mail boxes in a Post Office; each box is numbered and thus identified. To identify or to locate a particular box all we need to do is to refer to its allocated number. In the same manner, the core storage is divided into cells, locations, or registers. In order to keep track of these various cells or locations, each is assigned an address. Each one of these locations is capable of holding a fixed amount of data.

Nature of Storage. A magnetic core is a tiny ring of ferromagnetic material. Each individual core is extremely small in size, a few hundredths of an inch in diameter. Aside from the fact that the core is minute in size it can easily be magnetized. Once magnetized it is capable of retaining its magnetism almost indefinitely. The core, like a

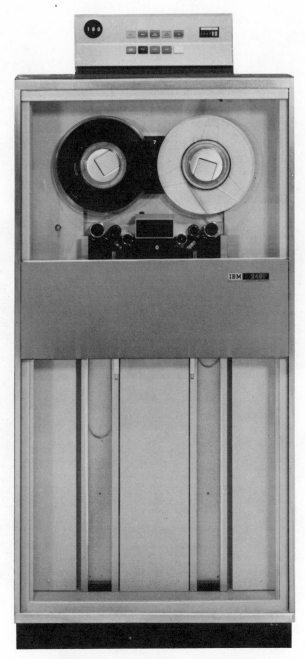

FIGURE 2.2. Some of the Input Devices.
(a) Magnetic Tape Unit

FIGURE 2.2 (continued). (b) Data Cell.

FIGURE 2.2 (continued). (c) 2540 Reader and Punch.

FIGURE 2.2 (continued). (d) Disk Storage Unit.

filing cabinet, is completely numbered and indexed. Thus, the computer has the capability of locating each and any place or position of core storage. In the case of the IBM 360 the cores are strung on a wire, like beads. Whenever a current of approximately 1/2 ampere is passed through the wire, the core is magnetized. The direction of the current being passed determines the direction of the magnetic field of the core. When this current is removed the core's magnetic field remains unchanged. Upon reversal of the direction of the current the magnetic field changes direction.

A magnetic core is capable of only two states. Thus a core can be compared to a *binary indicator.* The direction of magnetization will represent the "1" or "0".

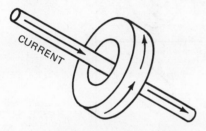

1. Current passed through the wire; core is magnetized.

2. Current removed from the wire; core remains magnetized.

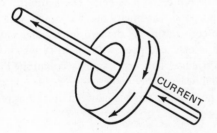

3. Current reversed; core magnetized in reverse direction.

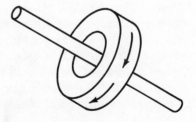

4. Current removed; core remains magnetized.

FIGURE 2.3. Effect of Current on Core.

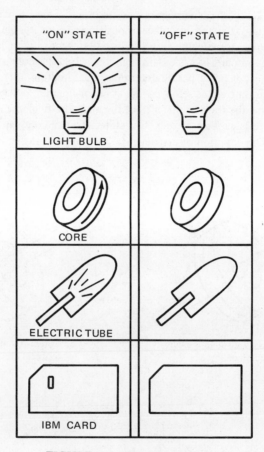

FIGURE 2.4. Binary Indicators.

These two states of magnetic core could be represented as being ON and OFF, or "1" and "0", or YES and NO. For machine purposes, the binary number system which uses digits 1 and 0 is used to represent the core status. As the two binary digits are used, a core is also termed a *bit*. The computer is equipped with circuitry which is capable of writing and reading-out the core storage. This task can be accomplished in times of the order of one millionth of a second or less. The smallest addressable unit of core in System 360 is called a *byte* (please note the difference between bit and byte). One single byte is composed of nine bits.

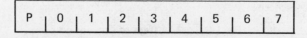

Byte: 8 data bits and 1 parity bit.

Eight of these bits are used to represent data and the ninth bit, which is the parity (P) bit, is used by the computer's internal circuitry for self-checking the storage function. The data bits, eight in all, are numbered 0, 1, 2, 3, 4, 5, 6, and 7. Depending upon the data stored in a byte, some of these bits may be ON and others OFF. The parity bit is of no concern to the programmer as it is completely controlled by the computer itself. System 360 is an odd-parity computer. By this we mean that the number of bits ON in a byte at any one time is always odd. This process is all automatic and the computer uses the parity bit to accomplish this.

A single byte, as such, is not capable of much storage capacity; however, when a large number of these bytes are grouped together, a useful and workable core storage is developed. In larger sizes of IBM computers more than one million cores are used. Various sizes available in System 360 are:

MAIN STORAGE						
Capacity			System Model			
8,192	C30					
16,384	D30	D40				
32,768	E30	E40				
65,536	F30	F40	F50			
131,072			G40	G50	G65	
262,144			H40	H50	H65	H75
524,288				I50	I65	I75
1,048,567					J65	J75

FIGURE 2.5. Various Sizes of IBM 360.

Basic Storage Function. When information is entered in a core location(s) it replaces the previously contained information in that particular core location(s). On the other hand, when information is retrieved from a core location, the contents of that location remain unaltered. In actuality, a duplicate of the information is made available. Thus, once a data item is located in storage, it may be used several times.

It is beyond the scope of this book to explain the core storage in any more detail. However, a basic understanding of the working and nature of the core storage is very helpful in understanding the overall work of the computer.

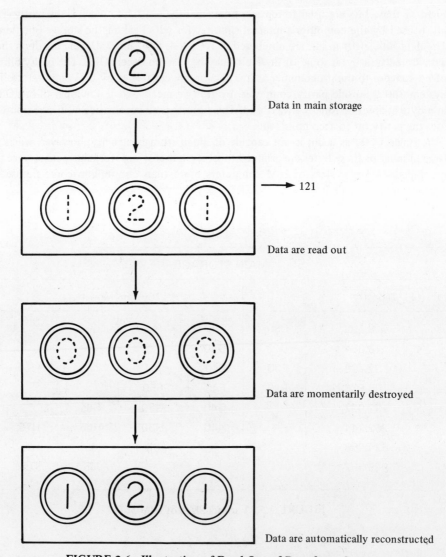

Data in main storage

121

Data are read out

Data are momentarily destroyed

Data are automatically reconstructed

FIGURE 2.6. Illustration of Read-Out of Data from Core.

Central processing unit

The word processing as related to programming means *manipulation of data according to a pre-arranged plan.* This processing in a computer system is performed by the Central Processing Unit (CPU). The CPU has three major functions:

1. To control and supervise the entire computer system.
2. To interpret the instructions or commands given to the computer by the programmer.

3. To perform (or act upon) the instructions, such as data transfer, arithmetic, etc. The CPU itself is divided into two components: the Arithmetic Logic Unit or ALU, and the Control Section.

The Arithmetic Logic Unit is responsible for such functions as arithmetic (addition, subtraction, division, multiplication), and comparing data. It can also be called upon to test various conditions that exist, and to take action depending upon the conditions tested.

The Control Section acts as an overall coordinator of the whole system. It controls the various input-output devices, and the Arithmetic Logic Unit.

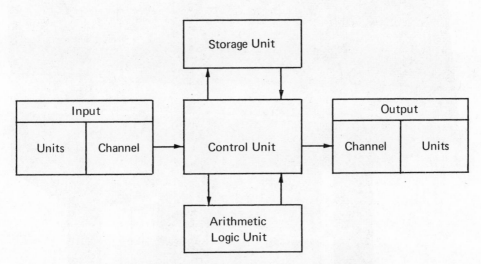

FIGURE 2.7. Functional Organization of Computer.

Output devices

After the data have been entered into the main storage and processed by the stored program, the results obtained can be recorded by the output devices for future reference. Some of the commonly used output devices are: Card Punch Units, Tape Units, Magnetic Disc and Drum Units, and Printer Units.

We can compare a computer, along with its functional units, to a human system. Various input devices can be compared to the eyes and ears of a person. The CPU, in essence, is comparable to the human brain where we store and work on various types of information. The output devices of a computer are comparable to the hands and speech organs of a person.

FIGURE 2.8. Some of the Output Devices.
(a) 1403 Printer

FIGURE 2.8 (continued). (b) Data Cell.

Stored program concept

A series of instructions pertaining to an entire procedure is termed a *program*. A program must define in complete detail the various actions a computer must take towards the solution of a given problem. The various instructions, when entered into the main storage of the computer, are translated into internal coding of the computer and stored in its memory units. These instructions are executed by the computer and an appropriate action is taken. The number of instructions contained in a program may vary from a few hundred to many thousands depending upon the magnitude of the problem. *In its normal sequence of operation the computer refers to these instructions one after another and executes them accordingly. However, a programmer may instruct the computer to modify, repeat, or skip over any instruction or set of instructions depending on various circumstances. Nonetheless, such circumstances must be anticipated by the programmer and necessary instructions included in the program.* An instruction can be divided into two main parts: an operation or command code such as add, subtract, compare etc.; an operand portion that indicates the location of the information in core or designates the device that is involved in a specific operation. There are no particular areas of storage reserved for instructions only. Generally they are grouped together and placed in the main storage consecutively in the order in which they are to be executed. This is termed *loading* of the instructions. After all the instructions are loaded, the computer locates the first instruction either by referring to a predetermined location in storage or occasionally by manual reset. After this first instruction is executed, the computer locates the next instruction, executes it, and the process continues in this manner. This process proceeds until the program is completed or the computer is directed to stop.[1]

Channel concept

Within a computer system the speeds of the various I/O devices are not only variable but are comparatively slower than the speed of the core storage. For example, the slowest speed at which the core transmits data is 1.5 μs per byte, while the fastest card reader is capable of a speed of only 750 μs per byte. This means that if a card reader is attached directly to the CPU, the CPU will have to sit idle while a card is being read into the storage, thus resulting in wastage of very valuable core time. To keep this from happening, the I/O devices in System 360 are attached to the CPU via channels.

Channels. A channel itself can be regarded as a small, independent computer. Each channel responds or is controlled by a set of commands known as Channel Command Words.[2] Channels provide the ability to read, write, and compute simultaneously.

---

[1] The manner in which instructions are executed is discussed in detail in Section 5.1.

[2] The only difference between commands and instructions is the component they are associated with. CPU responds to instructions and the channels respond to commands. CCW is the abbreviation of Channel Command Word.

Upon receiving an I/O instruction the supervisory program selects the appropriate channel and initiates the necessary CCW(s). At this time the channel program takes over the control and executes the required operations to complete the specific I/O operation, thus leaving the CPU free to perform other operations. The two types of channels in use with System 360 are: Selector Channels, and Multiplexor Channels.

Selector channels. These are used to attach high-speed devices, e.g. magnetic tapes, magnetic disc and drum units. At the maximum, six selector channels can be attached to a System 360. These are numbered 1, 2, 3, 4, 5 and 6.

Multiplexor channels. These channels are used primarily to attach low-speed devices. Some examples of these devices are card read/punch units and printers. It is possible and generally the practice to attach multiple low-speed devices to one multiplexor channel. In such cases the various I/O devices share the facilities of one channel and are able to operate simultaneously. It is possible to attach multiple high-speed devices to a multiplexor channel; however, only one device is able to operate at a time. Only one multiplexor channel can be attached to a System 360.

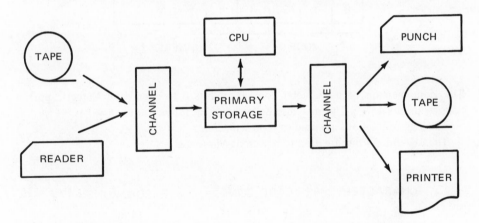

FIGURE 2.9. Illustration of CPU with Channels and Control Units.

2.2 Data Representation in System 360

The smallest addressable unit of System 360 storage is known as the *byte*. Each byte in turn consists of 9 bits. Eight of these bits are used to represent data and the ninth bit is used by the computer for internal checking of data and is known as the *parity bit.*

P	0	1	2	3	4	5	6	7

BYTE

BIT is derived from **Binary Digit**. The parity bit is of no concern to the programmer and we will not discuss it any further. Eight bits provide us with 256 possible combinations ranging from 00000000, where all of the bits are OFF, to 11111111 where all 8 bits are ON. At this time we are familiar with two methods of expressing data. These are:

1. English language characters and numerals.
2. Punched card code, where all data are expressed in terms of punched holes in a card.

In System 360 the internal code of representing data is known as **Extended Binary Coded Decimal Interchange Code** or in abbreviated form, **EBCDIC**. Not considering the parity bit, this system uses 8 bits to represent data. Let us see how this works. The bit positions in a byte are numbered 0, 1, 2, 3, 4, 5, 6, and 7. The EBCDIC code divides the byte into two parts, i.e., *Zone* and *Numeric* portion. These are shown below.

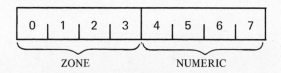

The Zone portion of a character consists of bits 0 to 3 and the Numeric portion consists of bits 4 to 7. This may also be expressed as follows:

The high-order 4 bits are used to represent *Zones*.

The low-order 4 bits are used to represent *Numerics*.

CHARACTER	CARD ZONE	EBCDIC ZONE
A to I	12	1100
J to R	11	1101
S to Z	0	1110
0 to 9	None	1111

One basic difference to be noted between the card codes and the EBCDIC codes is that the digits have a zone code in EBCDIC. As the information enters the core storage it is automatically translated to the EBCDIC format. When certain information is transferred from the main storage to an output device, such as a card punch unit, magnetic tape or printer unit, it is automatically translated from the EBCDIC format to the coding used by the particular output unit.

Note: System 360 uses EBCDIC codes to store data in core.

CHARACTER	CARD ZONE	EBCDIC ZONE
A	12 − 1	1100 0001
B	12 − 2	1100 0010
C	12 − 3	1100 0011
I	12 − 9	1100 1001
J	11 − 1	1101 0001
K	11 − 2	1101 0010
R	11 − 9	1101 1001
S	0 − 2	1110 0010
T	0 − 3	1110 0011
Z	0 − 9	1110 1001
0	0	1111 0000
1	1	1111 0001
9	9	1111 1001

S	Y	S	T	E	M
1110 0010	1110 1000	1110 0010	1110 0011	1100 0101	1101 0100

3	6	0
1111 0011	1111 0110	1111 0000

FIGURE 2.10. EBCDIC Representation of "System 360."

EXERCISE:

Convert your name into EBCDIC and show the result in hexadecimal code.

Decimal Data Format: Decimal data consists of numeric fields which represent decimal numbers. For example, decimal number 36 can be represented in two consecutive columns of an IBM card and it can be represented by two adjacent bytes in EBCDIC form.

1111	0011	1111	0110

3   6

Decimal data can appear in two forms:

Positive − Unsigned or Signed.

Negative − Always Signed.

An unsigned positive number is characterized by no overpunch in its units position. A signed positive number is characterized by a 12 zone overpunch in its units position, while a negative number is always characterized by an 11 zone overpunch in the units position of the number field. Decimal numeric fields in EBCDIC format are said to be in Unpacked or Zoned format. When characters exist in this form, one byte is needed to store one character. A typical unpacked number is illustrated below:

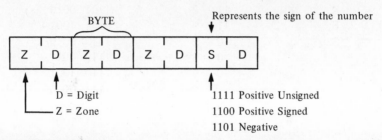

D = Digit
Z = Zone

1111 Positive Unsigned
1100 Positive Signed
1101 Negative

Packed decimal format

The Decimal Arithmetic set of instructions uses a different format of data. This format is called the *Packed* or *Unzoned* data format. Let us examine the differences. Since we need only 4 bits to store a digit (digit 9 — 0000 and digit 9 — 1001) we could save a lot of storage if 2 digits were packed together in a single byte. For example, to store decimal 12:

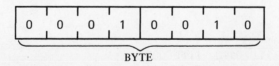

In the illustration above we used only one as opposed to 2 bytes needed to store the same information in EBCDIC. This looks fine, but what about the sign of the field? In packed decimal format, the sign of the field is contained in the 4 low-order bits of the low-order byte, while the rest of the bytes contain only numeric data.

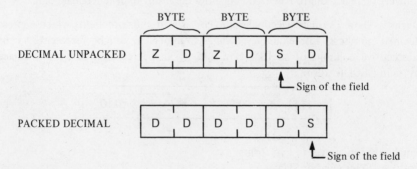

To summarize, in packed format 2 digits are packed together in a single byte except for the low-order byte itself. The low-order 4 bits of the rightmost byte contains the sign code of the field. Packed data require a less number of bytes thus resulting in conservation of core.

Let us represent + 112 in both unpacked and packed format.

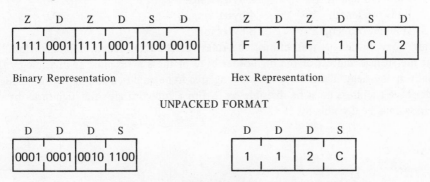

FIGURE 2.11. Packed and Unpacked Format.

Earlier it was mentioned that the decimal arithmetic set of instructions process data that are in packed format. We know that when data are entered into the core through one of the input devices, it automatically is translated into EBCDIC format. The question is, how does data get converted into packed format? There is an instruction called *Pack* which converts data from unpacked to packed format. This instruction is discussed in detail in Section 7.2. Some examples of packing are given below:

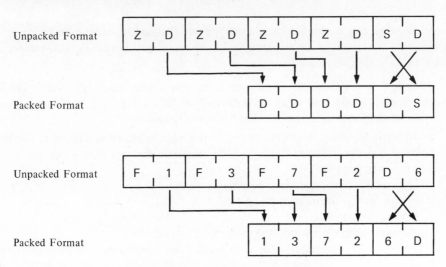

FIGURE 2.12. Packing Procedure.

Binary data

The fixed-point instructions[3] of System 360 require that the data be in fixed-point format. The fixed-point or fixed-length data in System 360 exist in three different formats:

1. Halfword length   2 bytes long..
2. Fullword length   4 bytes long.
3. Doubleword length   8 bytes long.

Apart from the length restrictions, the rules for the fixed length data also stipulate that the storage address of the high-order byte of these areas must be divisible by the length of the field. Thus, for a 2 byte long area to be qualified as a halfword, its high-order byte's address must be divisible by 2. For a fullword area the high-order byte's address must be divisible by 4.

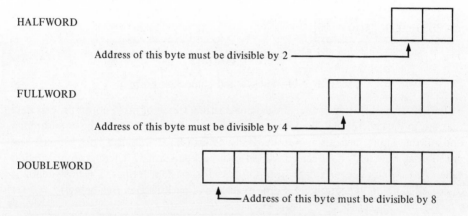

HALFWORD

Address of this byte must be divisible by 2 ———————

FULLWORD

Address of this byte must be divisible by 4 ———————

DOUBLEWORD

———— Address of this byte must be divisible by 8

Note: When an area in core is located in such a way that its high-order byte's address is divisible by the length of the area, it is said to be on Integral Boundary. This subject is further explored in Section 3.1.

Fixed Length Binary Data. The fixed-point arithmetic instructions work on data which are in binary format, and is either halfword or fullword in length. The numbers represented in this manner are termed as *fixed-point numbers.*

Fixed-point Number: A binary integer occupying a halfword or fullword. The bit position 0 or the leftmost bit is used to represent the sign of the number, also referred to as "sign bit."
If the sign bit = 0, the number is positive.
If the sign bit = 1, the number is negative.

±xxxxxxxxxxxxxxx   Halfword
±xxxxxxxxxxxxxxxxxxxxxxxxxxxxxxx   Fullword

[3]Instructions may be classified according to the type of data on which they operate as well as by their formats. Fixed-point number means a binary integer occupying a halfword, fullword or doubleword.

Summary of data formats

Character format

Description: Each 8 bit byte functions as one character: bits 0–3 (high-order 4 bits) represent the zone portion, and bits 4–7 (low-order bits) represent the numeric portion of a character.

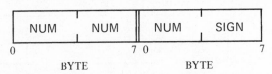

Instructions: The logical operations having operands in the main storage are normally used to manipulate data that exist in zoned format.

Length: Variable length operands can be specified, ranging from 1 to 256 bytes.

Sign: For numeric data in zoned format the zone bits of the low-order byte represent the field sign. Hex F and Hex C are treated as positive while Hex D is considered a negative sign.

Packed Decimal Data.

Description: Each byte is used to contain 2 numeric digits except the low-order 4 bits of the low-order byte; these 4 bits represent the sign of the data contained in the field.

Instructions: Decimal instructions are normally used to operate data that exist in packed format.

Length: Variable length fields can be specified, ranging from 1 to 16 bytes.

Sign: The low-order 4 bits of the low-order byte always represent the field sign. Hex F and Hex C are considered as positive while Hex D represents a negative sign.

Binary Format (Fixed-point Data).

Description: Each bit functions as binary digit.

Instruction: Fixed binary instructions are used to manipulate fixed-point data.

Length: Fixed-point data fields may exist in one of three fixed lengths. These are: Halfword, Fullword or Doubleword.

Sign: The high-order bit functions as the sign-bit and the rest of the bits are integer bits. A 0 sign-bit represents a positive number while 1 in the sign-bit position represents negative number. Negative numbers are stored in two's complement.

Note: Fixed-point data must be aligned on integral boundaries.

2.3 Addressing in System 360

Registers: Besides the magnetic core storage, the IBM 360 also uses registers. A *register* may be defined as an electronic unit which is capable of holding information during processing. In slower models of System 360, magnetic cores are used for registers, while the faster models utilize a special circuitry of film memory devices for registers. Except on slower models of 360 the registers operate at about four times the speed of the main core storage.

System 360 is provided with three different types of registers.
1. General Purpose Registers.
2. Floating Point Registers.
3. Control Registers.

Control Registers are used by the repairmen when the machine breaks down. These registers are of no interest to the programmer; thus no further explanation is provided.

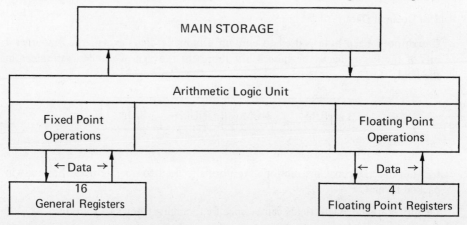

FIGURE 2.13. Registers in System 360.

General Purpose Registers (GPR). Except for model 20, sixteen general purpose registers are provided for System 360. Each of these registers is 4 bytes in length or one *word* long.

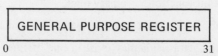

Throughout the text we will be using these GPR as index-registers, accumulators, base registers, operands for instructions, etc. System 360, model 20, is provided with eight halfword registers.

Floating Point Registers. A set of four floating-point registers is standard on faster models of 360. On slower models these are optional. These registers are doubleword or 8 bytes in length.

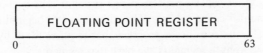

These registers are used in floating-point instructions. As this text deals only with the fixed-point binary and decimal set of instructions, we will not discuss floating-point registers any further.

The sixteen general purpose registers[4] (GPR) are numbered 0 − 15. Any of these registers can be addressed by a 4-bit binary number. For example, the general purpose register 0 can be addressed by the binary number 0000, or the general purpose register 15 can be addressed by the binary number 1111. To summarize the General Purpose Registers:

1. A set of 16 general purpose registers is standard.
2. Each register is fullword or 4 bytes in length.
3. These registers are numbered 0 − 15. Only a 4-bit binary number is required to address any of these 16 registers, such as 0000, 0001, 0010, 0011, ..., 1111.

Storage addressing

Operands of machine instructions usually refer to general registers, immediate data or storage locations. The amount of core storage required by a program is of great importance, as core is one of the most expensive components of a computer system. System 360 instructions are designed to be able to address a maximum of 16,777,216 bytes of main storage. The binary equivalent of this number is a 24-bit binary number. Let us say that in a particular program there are 500 instructions. Let us further assume that both operands of all these instructions address the main storage. As it takes a 24-bit binary number to form each of these addresses, it will take 48 bits to form addresses for both operands. Thus, it will take 3000 bytes of main storage to house these addresses. The first thing which comes to mind is, why don't we use smaller addresses for smaller models and larger addresses for larger models. This could save us some core on the smaller models. However, this address system will not be compatible for various size computers, which means that programs written for smaller size computers could not be run on bigger models. Therefore, we must look for another solution that will reduce the number of bytes taken by the instructions and still maintain the compatibility of addressing various models of System 360. Besides reducing the size of instructions, it is also desirable that any time a program is loaded into the computer, the program can be put in a different area of main storage. It would be desirable if this could be done without having to change the addresses in each and every instruction. This is known as *Program Relocation*.

The first step towards the above-mentioned goals is to check that System 360

---

[4]Model 20 is provided with 8 halfword registers.

programs are written in sections or segments, each segment being 4096 bytes in length. This does not mean that all programs must be at least 4096 bytes long. Programs that are less than 4096 bytes can be written in one segment. The beginning or the starting place of each segment is called its *Base*. The address of this beginning position is called the *Base Address*. Let us consider a program that requires 8000 bytes. By sectioning this program into 4096 byte segments, we have two segments.

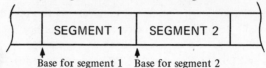

Each of the two segments has its own base address. For example, let us say that the program starts at core location 4000. Therefore, the base address for segment #1 is 4000, and the base address for segment #2 is 4000+4096=8096. The first segment has 4096 bytes in length, with the second segment having 3904 bytes in length. Now the question is, how does all of this help us to develop a better address system?

This will be illustrated later in this section.

Now then, as the maximum length of any one segment is 4096 bytes, any byte within a segment can be located by adding to the base address the displacement value of this particular byte.

Displacement: Displacement is the number of positions a particular byte is displaced (away) higher from its base address. An example is illustrated below.

In this illustration the displacement of the core location number 7034 is 3034 from the base address. Given a base address of 8000, the displacement for core location 10,033 will be 2033. Thus, we can say that the address of any core position can be obtained by adding a displacement factor to its base address. The displacement of the first byte is 0, while the last byte of a segment is displaced 4095 positions from the base.

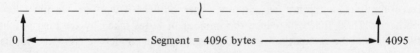

The number 4095, which is the maximum possible displacement, can be expressed in binary by a 12 bit number.

$$(4095)_{10} \equiv (111111111111)_2$$

The addressing in System 360 is handled in the following way. The base address is carried in one of the general purpose registers. The low-order 24 bits are utilized for this purpose. When a general purpose register is used to carry a base address, it is referred to as a *Base Register*. The displacement factor is carried by a 12-bit binary number. To obtain the address of a particular core position, the computer adds the base address and the displacement factor. Now we are able to search for an answer to the previously raised question, how to cut down the number of bytes used in addressing? We know that only a 4-bit binary number is needed to address these general purpose registers in which the base address is carried. The other part of the address system, the displacement factor, can be represented by a 12-bit binary number, so all we need is a 16-bit binary number. The use of 16 bits as opposed to a 24 bit direct addressing system saves us 8 bits, or one byte, every time a main storage location is addressed.

The second point in favor of the Base and Displacement Address System, is that it makes a program relocatable. Let us investigate this.

Assume two programs, X and Y, are to run together and they are located in core in the following way. Program X occupies 3000 consecutive bytes and program Y occupies the next 2000 bytes. The following 1500 bytes are unused and the rest of the available core is occupied by other data. The next day, program X, due to some modifications, requires 4000 bytes. If we were to go ahead and enter the modified version of program X, it would certainly wipe out portions of program Y. This is a

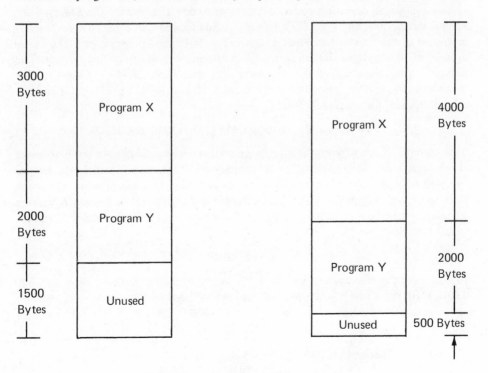

FIGURE 2.14. Program Relocation.

very undesirable act. Therefore, the question is, how to accommodate these programs in core? If we were to modify the base address of program Y so that its value is 1000 bytes higher than before, upon re-entering the program Y's starting address, and therefore all subsequent addresses, will be 1000 positions higher. This way enough positions will still be available for entering the program X. Changing the base address of a program is relatively simple and will be explained later in the text.

The use of Base Address and Displacement factor for addressing has accomplished two important objectives. These are:

1. The total number of bits required to address a core location has been reduced to 16, i.e., 4 bits to address the base register and 12 bits to specify the displacement amount. This way we still maintain the capability of addressing 16,777,216 bytes of core storage.
2. Program relocation.

2.4 Symbolic Programming

At earlier stages of computer development, the programs were written in actual machine language. This was not only very time consuming, but very tedious and unnecessary hard work for the programmers. A programmer had to remember the machine language operation codes, calculate and convert to binary the addresses for various instructions and keep track of various data locations in core. To make matters worse, all of this had to be coded in binary. For illustration purpose, let's take a look at one of the System 360 instructions in machine language coding format. The required instructions are, move the contents of core location 4143 – 4144 to core location 4514 – 4515. Assume that the register 10 is to be the base register and the base address for the program is 4002.

1101 0010 00000001 1010 0001111111111010 000010000100

This example shows why machine language coding is not desirable. In order to make the programmers' job easier other languages were developed. These languages use symbols for operation codes and core addresses. These languages appear very much like the English language and are called *Symbolic Languages*. When using Assembler Language, one of the symbolic languages, the coding for the above mentioned example would look like this:

MVC   SAVE,TEMP

In this example the operation code MVC is the symbolic code for machine code 1101 0010, the actual machine address has been replaced by two symbolic codes. You can see that it is much easier to code in symbolic rather than in actual machine language.

Symbolic statement format

Instructions written in symbolic language are called *Symbolic Statements*. A

symbolic statement may consist of the following elements:
1. NAME or SYMBOL.
2. OPERATION CODE (OP CODE) or COMMAND CODE.
3. OPERAND(S).
4. COMMENT ENTRY.
5. IDENTIFICATION AND SEQUENCE.

The OP code is the only mandatory element, all others are optional and are used depending upon the type of statement being used.

Name or Symbol. Names or symbols are created by the programmer and assigned to those statements which are to be referenced in the program. For example, if a program contains a routine to check and calculate over-time pay, you would assign a symbolic name to the beginning of this routine. From then on, whenever you needed to perform these calculations, you would only need to write a symbolic branch instruction referring to the name assigned to the first instruction of the routine. The computer, as a result, would know where to go to locate the routine.

Name	Oper	Operand	Comments
	.		
	.		
READ	GET	CARDIN	
	MVC	TEMP,ACCTNO	
	MVC	NAMEOUT,NAMEIN	
	MVC	HRSOUT,HRSIN	
	BC	15,CALPAY	BRANCH TO CALPAY
WRITE	PUT	REPORT	
	BC	15,READ	BRANCH TO READ
CALPAY	.		
	.		
	.		
	BC	15,WRITE	BRANCH TO WRITE
	.		
	.		

FIGURE 2.15. Use of Symbolic Names or Labels..

From Figure 2.15 you can see that the symbolic names are assigned to only those statements which are to be referenced.

OPERATION CODE (OP CODE). This part of the symbolic statement tells the computer what action to take, such as, add, subtract, move, compare, etc. When writing in a symbolic language, the programmer uses a symbolic OP code rather than the actual machine code. These symbolic codes are also called *Mnemonic Codes*. The word mnemonic is derived from Greek word meaning *to remember* or *aid to memory*. For example, the mnemonic code for ADD in Assembler Language is A while the actual machine code is 0001 1010. This is why they call the symbolic codes mnemonics.

Operand. The operand part of a statement is generally used to describe the location of data to be operated upon. At this time it will not be possible to discuss the operand of a symbolic statement in any more detail without bringing in specific examples. Therefore, let us put this aside temporarily.

Comments. This part of the statement has nothing whatsoever to do with the program logic. The comment entry, when written, is used to provide descriptive information about the statement. The comments are generally written on the same line as the statement. There are ways to write additional comments on the coding sheet, and we will discuss these later in this chapter under the heading Coding Sheet.

Identification and Sequence.

Identification. This part of the statement is used for writing identifying code for the program. All programs in an installation are assigned some kind of code.

Sequence. A program may run into scores of pages. As we will see later, each statement on a coding sheet is punched into a card. In order to keep these cards in sequence, it is necessary that some type of numbering system be used. The sequence number portion of the statement serves this very purpose.

The Assembler Language

Various elements that comprise the Assembler Language can be grouped into three major groups:
1. Machine Instructions.
2. Assembler Instructions.
3. Macros.
    a. Imperative.
    b. Declarative.
    c. Control.
    d. Supervisor.

In this section we will discuss the basic formats and structure of the machine instructions. Machine instructions may be represented symbolically as Assembler Language statements. The symbolic format of a machine instruction is very similar to, but does not duplicate, its actual machine format. Each machine instruction consists of a unique operation code and one or more operand fields. Comments and symbols may be appended to any instruction. Machine instructions are used to request the computer to perform various operations during program execution time.

Machine Instruction Statements. Instructions supply the following information to the computer:
1. The action to be taken, such as, add, move, subtract, multiply, etc.
2. The nature of the data, whether of variable or fixed length.
3. The location of the data, i.e., in storage or registers.

4. The length of the data affected.

In System 360 some data manipulation is done only in general registers, while other procedures require general register and storage, and still others require storage only.

In the previous section we learned that it takes 16 bits in all to address the main storage and only 4 bits are needed to address a general register. Keeping this in mind, System 360 instructions are designed in such a way that their length depends upon the general location of the data the instruction is to reference. The operation code for all instructions is one byte in length, and the length taken by the operand portion of the instruction depends upon the location of data that is to be worked on. For instance an instruction that addresses two registers needs only one byte to specify the registers.

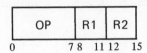

When both operands of an instruction refer to data located in the main storage, a total of 32 bits are required to specify the addresses (16 bits for each address). The instructions not only specify the addresses of the data to be worked on, but also contain codes for other informations such as the length(s) of the fields affected and additional register (called the Index register). In addition to all of this there is always the operation code.

System 360 instructions are divided into five main categories. These are:

RR   2 Bytes long   (Register to Register Operation)
RX   4 Bytes long   (Register and Indexed Storage Operation)
RS   4 Bytes long   (Register and Storage Operation)
SI   4 Bytes long   (Immediate Data and Storage Operation)
SS   6 Bytes long   (Storage to Storage Operation)

Immediate Data: A single byte of data used as an operand that is part of the instruction itself is termed immediate data.

General Information Regarding Instruction Components.

OP   Operation Code.
L   Length of the area to be affected.
D   Displacement amount.
B   Base Register assigned for the program.
X   Register to be used as the Index Register.
R   Register to be used as an operand.
I   Immediate data, always 1 byte in length.
M   Mask Value.
1   The number 1 when associated with an instruction component indicates that the component refers to the first operand.
2   The number 2 when associated with an instruction component indicates that the component refers to the second operand.
3   The number 3 identifies a component as a range parameter to be used

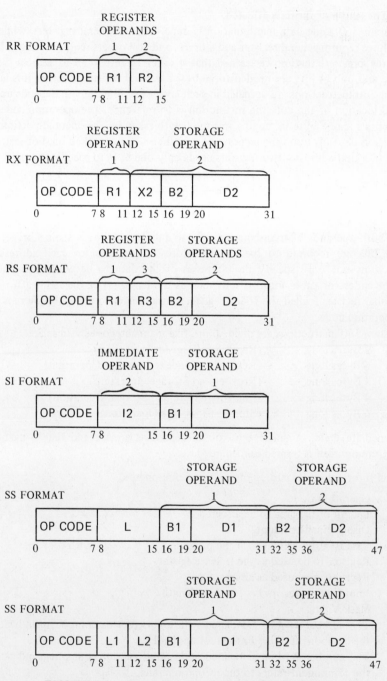

FIGURE 2.16. Instruction Formats (Machine Formats).

with multiple register instruction.

Operation Code or OP Code. The OP code of an instruction, always one byte long, supplies the computer with the following information:

1. Action to be taken, such as, add, subtract, etc.
2. Nature of data – variable or fixed length.
3. Type of data – binary or decimal.
4. The location of data – in main storage or in general registers.
5. The length of the instruction itself.

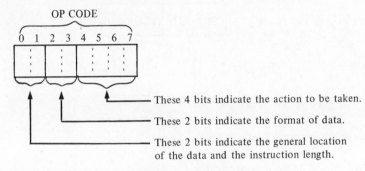

FIGURE 2.17. The OP Code.

Bits 0 *and* 1 of the OP code specify the general location of data, i.e., in main storage or in the general registers. Since the length of an instruction depends on the location of data, the instruction length is also specified by these two bits. The four different combinations possible with these two bits are, 00, 01, 10, and 11. The length of the instruction is specified by these bit settings as follows. Bit setting 00 indicates that both operands are in the general registers and the length of the instruction is 2 bytes. RR instructions come under this type. Bit setting 01 and 10 indicate that only one operand is in the main storage and the instruction is 4 bytes long. RX, SI and RS instructions come under this type. Bit setting 11 indicates that both operands are located in the main storage and the instruction is 6 bytes long. The SS type instructions come under this type.

Bits 2 *and* 3 indicate the type of data for that instruction, i.e., halfword, fullword, or variable length. The exact meaning of bits 2 and 3 depends upon the type of instruction as indicated by bits 0 and 1.

Bits 4, 5, 6, *and* 7, the last four bits of the OP code, specify the actual task to be performed such as add, subtract, etc.

RR Format. The RR type instruction, shortest of all 360 instructions, is only 2 bytes in length. Both operands are located in registers.

Example:

Write an instruction to add the contents of register 6 to register 4.

Note that the machine code for add register to register instruction is not direct translation of the mnemonic code "AR".

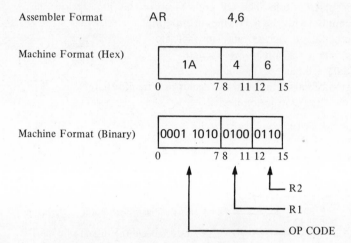

FIGURE 2.18. RR Type Instruction Format.

The instructions in the illustration above specifies that the contents of register 6 are to be added to the contents of register 4.

RX Format.

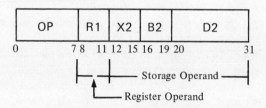

FIGURE 2.19. RX Format.

RX instructions are 4 bytes in length. This format is used when one of the operands is located in the main storage and the other is a general register. In this type of instruction the effective address is developed by adding together the contents of the Base Register, the contents of the Index Register, and the Displacement.

Index Register. This is an additional general purpose register and acts something like the base register. However, unlike the base register the contents of the index register can be modified in a program during program execution. The programmer must specify which register is to be used as the index register. If not specified, the machine inserts zero in this field and indexing is not brought into effect.

Register 0 as Index Register. Whenever this is done, the contents of this register are not used for developing the effective address.

Indexing is a very powerful tool in the hands of a programmer. The index register can be used to alter the address specification of an instruction without altering the value of the base register or the displacement. The examples that follow illustrate the use of index register in address modification.

Let us assume: Base Register=8,   Base Address=4002
                        Index Register=3,   Contents of R3=0
                        Displacement=1000

Effective address developed:

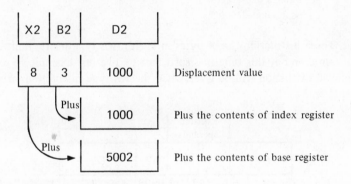

Address developed=5002

Next we add 40 to the index register so that its value becomes 40. Now the same instruction will develop an address value of 5042.

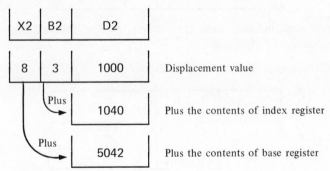

Address developed=5042

Now we will take a look at another example of RX type of instruction but in this case the index register is register 0.

Let us assume: Base Register=8,   Base Address=4002
                        Index Register=3,   Contents of R3=40
                        Displacement=1000

Effective address developed in this case:

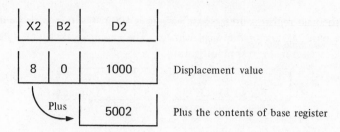

The contents of register 0 are ignored.
Address developed=5002

RS Format. These instructions are 4 bytes in length. RS type instructions are highly variable in nature and at this time it is sufficient to give one example to explain the format. Detailed discussion will be given when the RS type instructions are discussed in later chapters.

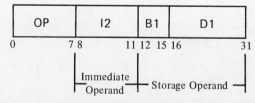

OP	R1	R3	B2	D2
0   7 8 11 12 15 16 19 20   31

LM	4	7	10	400

The above instruction will cause the contents of four fullword long areas to be transferred to registers 4, 5, 6, and 7.

SI Format. These instructions are 4 bytes in length.

OP	I2	B1	D1
0   7 8   11 12 15 16   31

Immediate
Operand — Storage Operand

Storage Immediate instructions are different from other types, in the sense that the second operand is located in the instruction itself. The receiving field which is the first operand is located in the main storage. The sending operand which is identified as I2 is also termed as immediate data. The immediate data is fixed in length and is one byte long. This type of instruction allows the programmer to insert the data in the instruction itself. The I2 field, which is 1 byte in length, may contain any of the 256 possibilities which can be represented by 8 bits.

Suppose we were to move the character "A" to core position 4010. Let's say that register 7 is the base register and the base address is 4002. The instruction will be:

Machine Format

OP	I2	B1	D1
92	C 1	7	8

I2 field contains the Hex equivalent of "A".

Assembler Format

$$MVI \qquad 8(7),X'C1'$$

SS Format. Storage-to-Storage type instructions are 6 bytes in length. SS type instructions are used when both operands are located in the main storage. SS instructions are divided into the following two sub-formats.

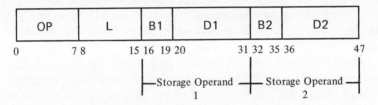

FIGURE 2.20. SS Format with One Length Code.

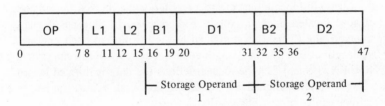

FIGURE 2.21. SS Format with Two Length Codes.

In Figure 2.20 the instruction has only one length code, identified as L, and is one byte in length. This code tells the computer the length of the first operand and the second operand is assumed to be of the same length. In Figure 2.21 the instruction has two length codes. These are identified as L1 and L2. L1 identifies the length of the first operand and L2 identifies the length of the second operand. The SS instruction with one length code can specify a maximum value of 255.

$$(1111 \ 1111)_2 \equiv (255)_{10}$$

Since all fields are at least one byte long, the length code specifies the additional bytes of data to be affected. Therefore, the maximum length of data field that can be specified by this type of SS instruction is 256 bytes. However, when the same instruction is written in assembler format, the length specified is equal to the total number of bytes in the field. Thus, the machine instruction length is one less than the Assembler Language length. The assembly program automatically subtracts one from the length specified when the instruction is assembled.

Note: The machine length is the number of bytes to be added to the field address to obtain the address of the last byte of the field.

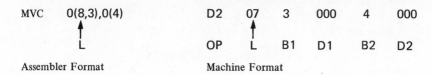

Assembler Format   Machine Format

In SS type of instruction with two length codes, each being one-half byte in length, the maximum length which can be specified is 16 bytes. When this type of instruction is encountered by the computer it assumes that the two operands are of different lengths. At this time one question should be in your mind. Why are the length codes associated with the SS type of instruction only? If this question did not arise it indicates you have not been very attentive.

RR type of instruction does not require length codes, as both operands are located in general registers. The general registers are of fixed length, each being one word in length. In the case of RX and RS type of instructions the data in the core has to be fixed length, i.e., either a halfword, fullword or doubleword in length. The operation code of the instruction designates the length itself. For example, instruction code AH means add a halfword located in core to a register, while the instruction code A means add a fullword located in main storage to a register. In SI type of instruction the sending operand, the I2 field, is contained in the instruction itself and as I2 field has an implied length of one byte, no length code is required. We can summarize by saying that, in RR, RX, RS and SI type of instructions the data is in fixed length format or that the length code is implied by the instruction itself. Thus, the length codes are used when data can be in variable lengths.

Note: A symbol may be assigned to any machine instruction. Other instructions then can use this symbol as an operand entry. The symbols assigned have the same address value as the leftmost byte of the instruction. The length attributes of the symbols depends upon the following instruction format.

Instruction Type	Symbol Length Attribute
RR	2 Bytes
RX	4 "
RS	4 "
SI	4 "
SS	6 "

Character set

The character set used in Assembler Language Programming consists of the following:

Letters	A through Z, and $, #, @
Digits	0 through 9
Special Characters	+ − , = . * ( ) ' / & blank

Coding sheet

Let us take a look at the System 360 Assembler Language coding sheet, page 50.

Space is provided at the top of the coding sheet for entering such information as the name of the programmer, the name of the program, date, punching instructions, and the card type to be used. This information is not punched into cards and serves only for identification purposes.

The remainder of the sheet contains 24 horizontal lines which are used for writing the Assembler Language Statements. The contents of these lines are punched into cards, one line to one card. Notice that columns 1 through 71 are called the *Statement*. When the symbolic program is being assembled, the assembler uses only this portion of the statement line to produce the object program. Columns 73 through 80 are used to write the identification code, page and line numbers. The entries in these columns are optional.

Upon examining the statement portion of the coding sheet, (columns 1 through 71) we see that it is divided into the following four different fields.

NAME	Cols. 1 − 8
OPERATION	10 − 14
OPERAND	16 − 71
IDENTIFICATION	73 − 80

A blank acts as a delimiting or separator character in Assembler Language coding. That is the reason that columns 9, 15 and 72 are left blank. However, there is one exception. In instances when a statement cannot be contained in one line, it can be continued onto the next line by following the two steps explained below.

1. A non-blank character must be entered in column 72 of the line to be continued.
2. The continuation portion of the statement must not begin before column 16. Any entry to the left of column 16 will be ignored by the assembler.

Note: In computer terminology, a blank, usually written as ƀ, is also termed as a character. That is why we used the word *non-blank* in statement 1 above.

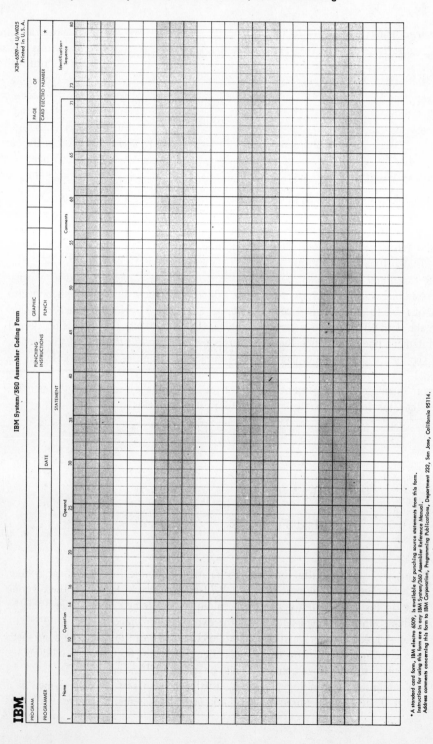

FIGURE 2.22. IBM Coding Sheet.

Name or Label or Symbol. Symbolic names are created by the programmer and are assigned to those instructions and data which the programmer wishes to address by use of symbols instead of direct addresses. For example, if your program has a routine to calculate income tax, it would be simple to assign a symbolic name to the beginning of the routine; therefore, from then on whenever you needed to perform the necessary calculations all you would have to do would be to write a branch instruction referencing that name. In the same manner, data which is to be referenced can also be assigned symbols. The use of symbols will become clearer as we proceed in the text. The Names or Symbols are usually assigned only to those statements which need to be referenced rather than to all of the statements in a program. When creating names, the programmer must follow certain rules.

1. The name must not contain more than 8 characters.
2. The first character of a name must be an alpha, however, the rest of the name may contain any character except the special characters.
3. No blanks or spaces are allowed within a name. Some examples of valid names are given below.

R10	BEGIN
AREA13	ACCTNO
START	R

4. No special characters may be used in constructing a name. Some examples of valid names are given below.

R10	BEGIN
AREA13	ACCTNO
START	ROUTINE3
F3BLOCK	SAVE

The examples given below illustrate some invalid names.

10R	First character not alpha.
ACCT NO	A blank within the body of the name.
OVERTIMEPAY	More than 8 characters.
ACCT/	Special character used.

There are two more important aspects behind the use of symbolic names.

1. All names must be defined.
2. All names must be unique.

The statement *all names must be defined,* in essence, means that if you are using a name as an operand of an instruction this name must be assigned to some statement in the program. For example, suppose you mail a letter and it happens that the address you use does not exist. Sooner or later, this letter will come back marked *no such address.* The symbolic name or label in a program acts like an address. If you, as programmers, assign addresses to the different statements of a program then you are able to reference these statements by using their respective labels. However, if you forget to assign a name and go ahead and try to reference it somewhere in the program, the computer will not be able to locate the place and will flag this as an error.

.
.
.

	MVC	SWITCH1,IN+10	040
	MVC	SWITCH2,IN+20	050
	MVC	OUT+10(4),TEMP	060
	PUT	REPORT	070
	BC	15,READ	080

.   .
.   .

IN	DS	CL80	120
OUT	DS	CL133	130
SWITCH1	DS	CL1	140

.
.

FIGURE 2.23. Coding Showing Undefined Labels.

In the coding, example three labels have not been defined. These are SWITCH2, TEMP and READ. On line 080 is an unconditional branch instruction asking the computer to branch to a symbol READ. As this symbol has not been defined, the computer will be unable to take a branch and will flag this as an error.

The second condition, *all names must be unique*, means that you should not assign the same name or label to more than one statement. You can very well imagine the confusion it will cause if two different houses on the block had identical numbers. Exactly the same situation would arise if you were to spell two or more symbolic names exactly the same way. Thus each name must be different from all other names in the program.

Operation Code. Each instruction must have an operation code. The OP code tells the computer what action to take. All instructions have been supplied with a specific OP code and a programmer has to make sure that he does not misspell it, nor create his own OP code. When writing in Assembler Language, the programmer uses symbolic codes also known as the mnemonic codes. The OP codes are written in columns 10 through 14. The entry must be left justified in this field, i.e., the first character of the OP code is to be entered in column 10.

Operand. The operand entry is written beginning in column 16. This part of the statement is used to describe the location of data to be operated upon. If an instruction has more than one operand, these must be separated by comma(s) and no blanks may appear between the operands.

IBM

IBM System/360 Assembler Coding Form

| PROGRAM | EXAMPLE OF SYMBOLIC STATEMENTS | | | PUNCHING INSTRUCTIONS | | GRAPHIC | | PAGE 1 OF 1 | X28-6509-4 U/M025 Printed in U.S.A. |
| PROGRAMMER | G.K.K. | DATE DEC. 9, 1969 | | | | PUNCH | | CARD ELECTRO NUMBER | * |

Name	Operation	Operand	Comments	Identification-Sequence
EXAMPLE	START			EXM01010
BEGIN	BALR	10,0		EXM01020
	USING	*,10		EXM01030
	OPEN	FILEIN,FILEOUT	OPEN FILES	EXM01040
READ	GET	FILEIN,INWORK	READ INPUT FILE	EXM01050
	CLC	INWORK+52(2),=C'17'	COMPARE RECORD CODE	EXM01060
	BH	OUT		EXM01070
	B	CHECK		EXM01080

*A standard card form, IBM electro 6509, is available for punching source statements from this form.
Instructions for using this form are in any IBM System/360 Assembler Reference Manual.
Address comments concerning this form to IBM Corporation, Programming Publications, Department 232, San Jose, California 95114.

FIGURE 2.24. Symbolic Statements.

```
        MVC       SAVE,ACCTNO
        LM        3,7,AREA
```

Not all instructions have operands. For example:

```
        EOJ
```

In others the operand entry is optional

```
        START
```

or

```
        START     256
```

Comments. These may be written to give descriptive information regarding the statement being used, or a series of comments may be used to explain special programming techniques. The comment(s), if used, are usually written on the same line as the statement. At least one blank space must be left between the last character of the operand entry and the first character of the comment.

```
        MVC       SAVE,ACCTNO       SAVE ACCT NUMBER
        PUT       REPORT            PRINT A LINE
```

You may leave more than one blank space if you so desire and any valid IBM character may be used in writing comments. Comments appear in the program listing produced by the assembler and do not appear in the object deck. One other method of writing comments is to write an asterisk (*) in column 1 of the coding sheet. When this is done the entire line is treated as a comment entry. Of course the comment entry must be contained within columns 1 through 71. *See* Figure 2.24.

Identification and Sequence. This field is self-explanatory. Each program in an installation is assigned an identification code. At the same time, it is a good idea to have some sort of sequencing method for the source deck. The sequencing of a source deck would avoid a lot of frustrations, feet stomping and hot tempers if someone happened to be a butterfingers (or margarine fingers if the person happened to be on a diet) and dropped a deck of cards which had a program punched in it.

Important coding points

Now that we have discussed the coding sheet and the ways to write the symbolic statements, the importance of printing clearly cannot be over-emphasized. So many people are used to writing in strange, confusing and fancy ways. This habit can affect the efficiency of an installation to a great extent. The keypunch operators punch the source program into cards. A badly written program will lead to too many keypunch errors which becomes very time consuming when a program is being assembled. For better efficiency, it is very important that you develop good printing habits. Some of the common points to watch while coding are:

1. Everything must be printed. Never write any part of a statement in longhand.
2. Try to use lead pencils of such weight that it is easy to read the material.
3. Always correct your errors by erasing the wrong entry and not by writing over it.
4. Make sure that some of the look-alike characters are written distinctly. For example:[5]
   Numeric 1 and Alpha I
   Numeric 2 and Alpha Z
   Numeric 0 and Alpha O

Also watch your Q's and 7's. Some people write a very fancy 7 which might be confused for Alpha Z.

Self Evaluation Quiz

1. Briefly explain, in your own words, the advantages of Base and Displacement type of address system.

2. Which of the following symbols are valid?

    123   F1F $F3   3$F   R   WAGE PAY   FF#   RATE/HR

3. Does a symbol assigned to a data field refer to the leftmost or the rightmost byte of the field?

4. Does a symbol assigned to an instruction refer to the leftmost or the rightmost of that instruction?

5. Where is the sign of the field located in the packed decimal, zoned decimal, and fixed-point data format?

6. Is it correct to use general register 0 as the base register? Please explain your answer briefly.

7. What is the maximum number of bytes that can be manipulated by an instruction of the following type?

OP	L1	L2	B1	D1	B2	D2

8. How many different bit configurations can be represented by the 8 bits of a byte?

9. What is the purpose of the parity bit?

10. Convert the following into EBCDIC:

    A 9 7 M V b 1 1

11. What does EBCDIC stand for?

[5]Unfortunately the notation conventions vary from installation to installation and programmer to programmer.

12. Explain briefly the advantages of having five different types of instruction formats, i.e., RR, RX, SI, RS and SS.

13. Is it possible and valid for a programmer to alter instructions during program execution?

14. Given a data field containing F1 F2 F3 F4 F5, what would the data look like if packed and placed in a 3 byte long area?

15. How many base registers are needed by a program requiring 8014 bytes of core storage?

16. What is the maximum value that can be specified by the displacement field of an instruction operand?

17. What storage locations will be addressed by an instruction which uses register 4 as the index register and register 5 as the base register? Assume that the base address is $(802)_{10}$ and the contents of the index register are as follows:
   a.   0
   b.   4
   c.   10
   d.   37
   e.   42

18. Considering problem 17, what address values will be developed if the index register is changed to register 0?

19. What is the smallest addressable unit in System 360?

20. What are the three formats possible with fixed-point data?

21. In a fixed-point number which bit is used to represent the sign?

22. How many bits are needed to address a general-purpose register?

23. Give a brief definition of Base Address.

24. Give a brief definition of displacement as used in System 360 address system.

25. What is the maximum value of the displacement that can be specified in System 360 address method?

26. How many bits are required to address a location in the main storage?

[3]

Storage Allocation, Assembly Process

3.1 Storage Allocation

Earlier, it was pointed out that a program consists of a set of instructions. These instructions are of no use unless there are some data to work on. While discussing the various elements of a computer system in Section 1.2, you learned that the input devices are used to enter data into the core storage. Core storage per se is an uncharted territory. It is necessary now to become more specific and pinpoint the particular area of core storage. It is necessary to learn to set aside specific areas in core where data are to be accommodated. Before learning the methods of reserving storage, it is important to define the types of data which need to be stored in the core.

In general three types of areas needed are:

1. Areas to receive data from input devices and areas to transmit data to the output devices.
2. Areas to accumulate totals, etc., generally termed accumulators or counters.
3. Areas to store information during problem program execution.

To define storage or to set aside areas in core the assembler instruction DS (Define Storage) is used.

DS statement

Instruction Name	Define Storage
Mnemonic OP Code	DS
Instruction Type	Assembler Instruction
Machine OP Code	None

This instruction directs the assembler program to reserve areas in core. The format of this instruction is:

    Label   OP   Operand

The basic format of the DS instruction's operand is DTLn, where D, stands for the number of consecutive areas to be reserved (also known as the Duplicating Factor); T, stands for the type of area to be reserved, such as character type, halfword, fullword, etc.; and, Ln, indicates the length of the character type area.

            DS   DTLn

Label or Symbolic Name. If an entry is made in the label field of the DS statement, the assembler will assign this label to the *high-order* byte or the leftmost byte of the area reserved. The label used is also assigned a length value equal to the value represented by the length entry (Ln).

Duplicating Factor (D). This part of the operand of a DS statement is written as an integer and indicates the number of identical areas to be reserved. In case only one area is desired, the programmer may leave this part of the operand entry out and the assembler will reserve only one area. However, if a duplicating factor of 0 is used, no area is reserved. At this time, we will not go into any further discussion of 0 duplicating factor. A detailed explanation of this is given later in this chapter.

Type (T). This part of the operand tells the assembler the nature of data which will occupy the area set aside by the DS statement. Some examples of Type are:
    C — Character Type (EBCDIC)
    F — Fullword
    H — Halfword
If this part of the entry is omitted by the programmer, the assembler assumes the area to be of C type. Various possible types are given below.
    C — Character type, 8 bit EBCDIC characters.
    H — Halfword aligned on halfword integral boundary.[1]
    F — Fullword aligned on fullword integral boundary.
    D — Doubleword aligned on doubleword integral boundary.

Length Code (Ln). When reserving more than one byte long *character* type area, a numeric integer representing the number of bytes required is entered. As the C type data have an implied length of 1 byte, no length code is needed when reserving a single byte of core storage.

    Let us look at some examples of DS statements. First, note the C type.

    AREA   DS   CL4

The assembler will set aside a 4 byte long area and will assign the label AREA to the high-order byte of this area.

---

[1]Integral Boundary: This feature is explained in detail later in this section.

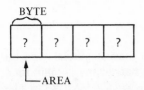

BYTE

? means that contents are unknown.

AREA

Length value assigned to the symbol AREA=4 bytes.

AREA2   DS   4CL1

In this case a duplicating factor of 4 has been assigned. The assembler will set aside four character type areas, each being one byte in length. The symbolic name AREA2 will be assigned to the leftmost byte.

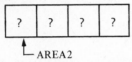

AREA2

Length value assigned to the label AREA2=1 byte. This is an important factor to note. The following DS statement

INAREA   DS   CL80

will set aside 80 bytes and the high-order byte of the area set aside will be labeled INAREA.

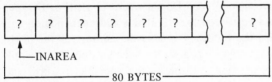

INAREA

80 BYTES

Length value assigned to the label INAREA=80 bytes

WRKAREA   DS   4CL3

The assembler will set aside four consecutive areas, each being 3 bytes long.

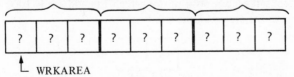

WRKAREA

Note that the label is assigned to the leftmost byte only. Although the total number of bytes set aside is 12, the length value assigned to the label WRKAREA=3 bytes.

Note: The length value assigned to a symbol of a DS statement is always equal to the value represented by the Ln part of the DS operand.

The following example will also set aside 12 bytes but the length value assigned to the label will be 12 bytes.

CONST   DS   CL12

The maximum length value that can be specified with C type is 65,535 bytes. In

Section 2.2 it was pointed out that fixed-point instructions require that the data be in fixed-length format.

In addition to this, there is one more restriction on fixed-length data and this is Boundary Alignment. A variable-length data field may start at any core location. A fixed-length data field of 2, 4, or 8 bytes, on the other hand, must have an address whose decimal equivalent is a multiple of 2, 4, or 8 bytes, respectively. For example, the address of a fullword must be divisible by four.

Note: The address of a field refers to the leftmost byte of the field.

        CONST   DS   F

will reserve a 4 byte long area located on integral boundary. The high-order byte of the area will be labeled CONST.

                DS   H

will reserve a 2 byte long area located on integral boundary.

                DS   D

will reserve an 8 byte long area located on integral boundary. The question now arises, how does an area get on an integral boundary? The assembler program is provided with facilities that automatically position the required boundary alignment. When the assembler encounters a DS statement of H, F or D type, it investigates the address of the core position available. If this address is not on an integral boundary, the assembler skips the byte and checks the address of the next byte. This process continues until an appropriate address has been located. For example, suppose that the address of the core position available to the assembler is 1001, and it encounters the following statement:

        HALF   DS   H

The core address 1001 is not divisible by two, therefore, the assembler skips this position and checks the next position for which the address is 1002. This address is divisible by two and the area set aside will be

Let us try one more.

The next instruction encountered by the assembler is:

        DOUBLE   DS   D

The next byte available to the assembler is 1004, this particular address is not divisible by eight. Addresses 1005, 1006, 1007 are all skipped until the assembler gets to the address 1008. This is divisible by eight and, as such, is on an integral boundary. The area set up will be,

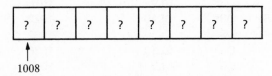

1008

The contents of this area are unknown.

Note: Boundary alignment restrictions were designed to place fixed-point data fields at consecutive integral boundaries. This is to ensure efficient machine operation when programs written for one model of System 360 are to be executed on another model. The labels or symbolic names are optional for the DS statements. If assigned, the label is associated with the highorder byte of the area, and length value equated to the label is always equal to the Ln value. Any bytes skipped to align DS statements are not zeroed.

Subdefining of storage areas

Sometimes a programmer may wish to assign symbols to the various fields within a record instead of using relative addressing. For example:

Employee Number	c.c.	1 – 5
Employee Name		10 – 30
Address		35 – 50
City		55 – 67
State		70 – 74

A programmer may want to assign symbols to each of these fields. This can be done by using a zero duplicating factor with the DS statement for this record and then writing additional DS statements to actually reserve the core storage.

A zero duplication factor can be used to assign a symbolic name to a core location without actually stepping up the location counter. Assume that the whole area (card area) is to be assigned the symbolic name IN and that each field is also to be given a symbolic name. The area-defining statements required are shown below. Assume that the location counter is initially set at hexadecimal 1000.

Name	Oper	Operand	Location Counter (Hex)
IN	DS	0CL80	1000
NUMBER	DS	CL5	1000
	DS	CL4	1005
NAME	DS	0CL21	1009
FINIT	DS	CL1	1009

(continued)

MINIT	DS	CL1	100A
LAST	DS	CL19	100B
	DS	CL4	101E
ADDRESS	DS	CL16	1022
	DS	CL4	1032
CITY	DS	CL13	1036
	DS	CL2	1043
STATE	DS	CL5	1045
	DS	CL6	104A

The first DS statement names the entire 80 position long area, the symbol assigned is IN and its length attribute is 80 bytes. However, this statement *does not* reserve any core area. The next DS statement reserves 5 bytes and the symbol assigned to the highorder byte of this area is NUMBER.

IN = 80 Bytes

NUMBER = 5 Bytes

EXERCISE:

How many bytes of core will be reserved by the following DS statements?

CARD	DS	0CL80
NAME	DS	0CL16
FINIT	DS	CL1
MINIT	DS	CL1
LAST	DS	CL1

At times when reserving storage for data records, it is advantageous to obtain storage overlay to save core. Overlay structure can be achieved by the use of ORG assembler instruction.

Instruction Name	Set Location Counter
Mnemonic OP Code	ORG
Machine OP Code	None
Type	Assembler (Program Control)

This assembler instruction is used to alter the setting of the location counter. The format of the ORG instruction is:

Name	Oper	Operand
	ORG	a relocatable expression or not used

If the operand entry is omitted, the location counter is set to a value which is one byte higher than the highest location previously assigned. In case a symbol is specified in the operand field, the location counter is set to the address value of the symbol. This symbol must be a previously defined symbol. An example of ORG instruction is:

```
          ORG        CARD1
```

The location counter will be set to the address value assigned to the symbol CARD1.

```
          ORG        *+200
```

In this case the location counter will be set to a value which is equal to the current location counter setting plus 200. One use of this assembler instruction is to obtain area overlays. This technique is illustrated by the following example.

Example:

Consider a card file containing Master and Detail records for customer charge accounts. The file has been sorted and merged in such a way that all the detail cards for a customer follow the master card. The card record formats are as follows:

Master Card

c.c.	1–5	Account Number		
	6–20	Name		
	21–41	Street Address		
	42–54	City		
	55–59	State		
	60–64	Zip Code		
	65–74	Telephone Number		
			65–67	Area Code
			68–70	Prefix
			71–74	Suffix
	75–79	Balance		
	80–80	Card Code		

Detail Card

c.c.	1–5	Account Number
	6–10	Amount
	11–79	Not used
	80–80	Card Code

With the following sequence of commands, the DETAIL sub-area will overlay the MASTER area and the various instructions in the program can reference either set of symbols.

```
MASTER     DS        0CL80
MACCTNO    DS        CL5
NAME       DS        CL15
ADDRS      DS        CL21
CITY       DS        CL13
STATE      DS        CL5
```

(continued)

```
ZIP        DS      CL5
TELNO      DS      OCL10
AREACD     DS      CL3
PREFIX     DS      CL3
SUFFIX     DS      CL4
BALLNC     DS      CL5
MCODE      DS      CL1
           ORG     MASTER          SET LOCATION COUNTER
DETAIL     DS      OCL80
DACCTNO    DS      CL5
AMOUNT     DS      CL5
           DS      CL69
DCODE      DS      CL1
```

Note: At this point it should be clearly understood that we are setting aside areas in storage and that we are not defining the values of data which will be contained in these various areas. The value of data, at this point, is unknown as it will be coming from some input device or developed as a result of processing or entered within the source program by the use of constants.

Constants

Constants may be defined as a quantity whose value usually does not change during program processing. The constants enter the storage as part of a program. What we mean by this is that the constants are not a part of the data entered into the core. Constants are used for many purposes. A constant could be used to increment the contents of an accumulator. For example, to count the number of cards read by a program, you would need to add 1 to some accumulator every time an instruction to read a card was given. This number 1 will be set up as a constant. The mnemonic code for the instruction to define constants is DC.

Instruction Name	Define Constant
Mnemonic Code	DC
Type Instruction	Assembler
Machine Code	None

The format of the operand for a DC statement is:

```
Symbol      DC      DTLn 'constant'
```

D   The duplication factor. It informs the assembler of the number of identical areas to be defined. If only one area is desired, this part of the operand is left out.

T   The type of constant desired.

C   Character type (EBCDIC format).

H   Halfword, fixed-point binary data.

F   Fullword, fixed-point binary data.

D   Doubleword, fixed-point binary data.

B   Binary data.

X   Hexadecimal data.

P   Packed data.

Z   Zoned data.

Ln   The length value for character type data.

('Constant' is the constant itself. Please note that the constant *must* be enclosed between single quotation marks.)

The length value can be explicit or implied.

Explicit Length Value: This is when the programmer specifies the actual length in the DC statement.

Implied Length Value: This is when the programmer omits the length value from a DC statement and the assembler calculates the length of the area needed. The implied length is calculated by the assembler by analyzing the type of the constant, and the constant itself.

Note: Whenever the explicit length assigned to a 'C' type constant is less than the implied length, the assembler truncates, or drops, the extra right hand side characters of the constant. In case the explicit length assigned to a DC statement is greater than the implied length (the number of bytes required to house the constant), the low-order extra positions of the area reserved are padded with blanks.

Character Type.

AREA   DC   CL5'1234'

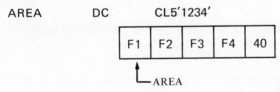

As a result, the EBCDIC code for blank is 0100 0000, thus the Hex 40.

Note: In case of C type constants, the extra low-order bytes are always padded with blanks.

Therefore, to establish a field containing all blanks, it is not necessary to define the blanks for the entire length of the field.

The following are two examples which establish identical constants.

BLANKS   DC   CL5'bbbbb'

or

BLANKS   DC   CL5'b'

Some examples of DC statements are as follows:

AREA   DC   C'0000'

In this case the programmer has left the length code out, thus the assembler will calculate the number of bytes required by itself. This is one example of implied length. As each C type character needs 1 byte each, the assembler needs 4 bytes to accommodate the constant. The constant will be assembled as follows:

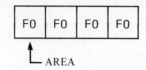

Note: F0 is hexadecimal representation of EBCDIC 0 (zero).
The same result could be obtained by specifying the explicit length of 4 bytes.

AREA   DC   CL4'0000'

In both cases, the symbolic name will be assigned to the leftmost byte of the constant. The length assigned to the symbolic name will be 4 bytes. If an explicit length is specified, it overrides the implied length of the DC statement. For example:

CONST   DC   CL3'1234'

In this case, the explicit length is 3 bytes. Thus, the number of bytes set aside by this statement will be only 3 bytes and into these bytes the assembler will enter the constant, starting from left to right. The result in this case will be:

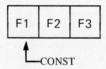

This technique becomes very helpful if the length of a blank field is large.

DC   CL80'b'

This statement will set aside an area 80 bytes in length and each byte will contain a blank. If a programmer needs to establish a number of constants containing identical sets of data, he may do so by using an appropriate duplicating factor.

REPEAT   DC   4CL3'XYZ'

The assembler will reserve four areas, each 3 bytes in length. Each of these areas will contain the constant XYZ, thus the result will be:

$$\text{X Y Z X Y Z X Y Z X Y Z}$$
REPEAT

The label or symbolic name REPEAT will be assigned to the leftmost byte and the length value of the label REPEAT will equal 3 bytes.

Some more examples of DC are as follows:

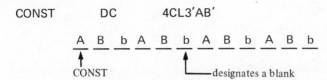

Note that the explicit length is 3 bytes while the constant itself requires only 2 bytes, thus the third (low-order) byte of each area is padded with a blank.

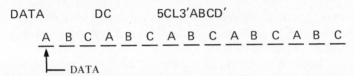

In this case, the explicit length was less than the implied length. The explicit length = 3 bytes, and the implied length = 4 bytes.

As mentioned earlier, the explicit length always overrides the implied length, thus the assembler reserves five areas, each being 3 bytes in length. The extra low-order character D of the constant is truncated. The maximum length for C type constants is 256 bytes.

H and F Type: These types are used to establish fixed-point binary constants. H and F type constants are identical except for their implied length. The implied lengths of these are H = 2 bytes and F = 4 bytes.

If the constant is written as a decimal number, the assembler converts this into binary format. For example:

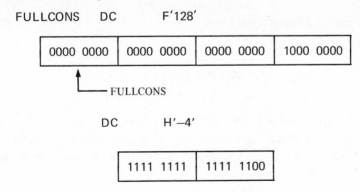

Note: Negative numbers are stored as two's complement. When the length operand is not specified, the H and F type constants are assembled and stored on integral boundaries. If the programmer specifies a length operand, the boundary alignment is not performed.

The method by which the assembler handles the boundary alignment is the same as discussed in DS statements. The maximum values which can be specified for halfword and fullword constants are:

Halfword	+32,767	−32,768
Fullword	+2,147,483,647	−2,147,483,648

If the value of the constant specified exceeds the maximum possible, the leftmost bits are truncated.

Note: Bytes skipped to align a DC statement are zeroed. The maximum length for H and F type constants is 8 bytes.

B Type. This type is used to establish true binary constants. The constant is written in binary digits and is enclosed in single quotation marks. Binary constants may be written with explicit or implied length.

If the explicit length is specified and it disagrees with the length required to store the constant, truncation or padding occurs on the left. The padding character used in binary 0.

Binary constants are established by the assembler in multiples of 8 bits. If the number of digits specified in the constant is not a multiple of 8, high-order binary zeros are added until the number of bits is a multiple of 8.

BINCONS   DC   B'01101011'

CONST   DC   B'1101'

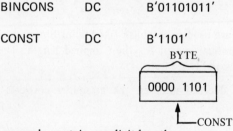

The next example contains explicit length.

BINCON   DC   BL2'110101010111'

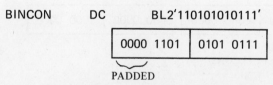

The assembler will set aside 2 bytes and in these bytes the assembler will enter the binary constant starting from right to left. As the constant is only 12 digits in all, the high-order 4 bits of the area set aside will be padded with binary zeros. Another example is:

DC   2BL2'1111'

0000 0000	0000 1111	0000 0000	0000 1111

The assembler will reserve two binary constants each being 2 bytes long.
Note: The maximum length of binary type constant is 256 bytes.

X Type. A hexadecimal constant consists of one or more hexadecimal digits, 0–F, contained within single quotation marks. The assembler translates each pair of hexadecimal digits into 8 binary digits. If the number of hexadecimal characters specified is odd, the assembler pads the high-order 4 bits of the high-order byte with hex zero.

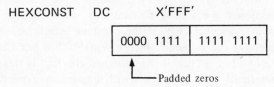

The length value assigned to the label HEXCONST is 2 bytes. If no explicit length is specified, the assembler calculates the implied length by determining the number of bytes required to contain the hexadecimal digis.

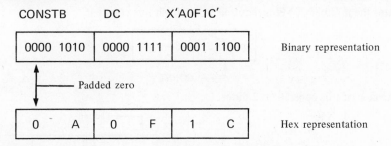

Implied length = 3 bytes.

In case an explicit length is specified and it disagrees with the implied length, padding, or truncation, is performed on the high-order digits. The padding character is hexadecimal 0. For example:

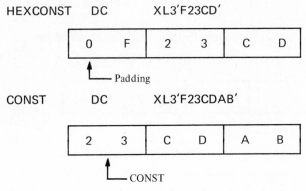

Truncated digit is F.

DC   2XL2'C4'

0 0	C 4	0 0	C 4

The maximum length of Hexadecimal Constants is 256 bytes, or 512 hexadecimal characters.

P Type. This type is used to establish packed decimal constants. In this type each pair of decimal digits is packed into one byte except the rightmost byte. The low-order 4 bits of the rightmost byte represent the sign of the constants, while the high-order 4 bits of the same byte contain a decimal digit. If the constant is positive, signed or unsigned, the assembler generates the standard positive sign 1100 or hex C; while a negative sign is translated into 1101 or hex D. An unsigned constant is treated as a positive number. Packed constants may be written with implied or explicit length values.

CONST   DC   P'123'

This constant does not contain an explicit length value and as such, the assembler calculates the number of bytes required to establish this constant.

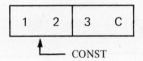

Length value of this constant = 2 bytes.

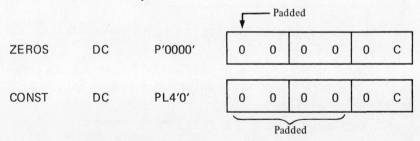

ZEROS   DC   P'0000'

CONST   DC   PL4'0'

Padding or truncation occurs to the left. Padding character is packed zero.

CONST   DC   PL4'312473'

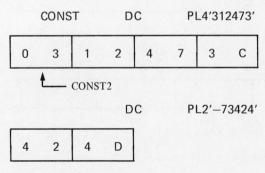

DC   PL2'−73424'

4 2	4 D

Note: Hex C represents the standard positive and Hex D represents the negative sign.

In this case, the explicit length of 2 bytes is specified. As all the digits cannot be accommodated within 2 bytes, truncation occurs to the left of the constant.

Multiple constants are allowed with P type. If more than one constant is specified, they are separated by commas. In case an explicit length is specified, it applies to all of the constants.

DC   PL3'46,−4,+7434'

In this case, three constants are specified. The explicit length of 3 bytes applies to all three constants.

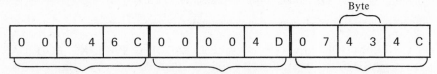

The result is three constants occupying 9 bytes.

DC   P'46,−4,+7434'

0	4	6	C	4	D	0	7	4	3	4	C

The result is three constants occupying 6 bytes. The maximum length of P type constant is 16 bytes.

Z Type. The Z type constant is identical to the P type except that the constant is assembled as a zoned decimal.

DC   Z'7734'

F	7	F	7	F	3	C	4

DC   ZL3'46,−4,+7434'

DC   Z'46,−4,+7434'

The maximum length for Z type constant is 16 bytes.

Note: A decimal constant (P or Z type) may be written with or without a sign. In case the sign is omitted, the assembler assumes a plus sign. For the sake of clarity, a decimal point may be written in the body of the constant. For example:

CONST   DC   PL3'+172.34'

The presence of a decimal point does not affect the assembly of the constant, i.e., the decimal point is not converted to its binary equivalent and as such does not get assembled into the constant. The constant coded above will be assembled as:

$$17 \quad 23 \quad 4C$$

We could have written this constant as:

	CONST	DC	P'172.34'

or

	CONST	DC	P'17234'

EXERCISE:

Write DC statements to store the following as Z and P type constants.

+7, +304, 144, −73.294, 1.111 and −17

Show the contents of storage, in hexadecimal, for these constants.

TYPE	DUPLICATION FACTOR	LENGTH VALUE	MAX.LEN. BYTES	PADDING CHAR.	PADDING	BOUNDARY ALIGN.
C	optional	optional	256	b	to right	No
H	optional	optional	8	——	——	Yes*
F	optional	optional	8	——	——	Yes*
B	optional	optional	256	binary 0	to left	No
X	optional	optional	256	hex 0	to left	No
P	optional	optional	16	pack 0	to left	No
Z	optional	optional	16	zoned 0	to left	No

*Boundary alignment performed only if no length value is assigned.

An exception exists when establishing ampersand (&) or an apostrophe (') in a constant of C type. For each ampersand or apostrophe desired in the constant, one additional ampersand or apostrophe must be written.

For example, to establish the statement

IN & OUT

the constant would have to be set up as

	DC	CL8'IN && OUT'

The space taken by the extra ampersand is not counted when specifying the explicit length to the constant. If you wished to use − THE NUMBER IS '8' − in print out, the constant itself would have to be set up as

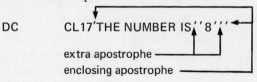

| | DC | CL17'THE NUMBER IS''8''' |

extra apostrophe ──────

enclosing apostrophe ──────

The spaces taken by the extra apostrophe are not counted.

Note: Since the computer can not differentiate between instructions and data, the programmer should make sure that the constants and area defining statements are not located within an instruction stream, that is, they should not be coded between those instructions which will be executed in sequence.

3.2 Assembly Process

Symbolic language programs use mnemonic codes, symbolic labels and symbolic addresses. The great advantage of writing in symbolic languages is that the language elements are very similar to the English language and thus are easy to remember and write. However, one disadvantage is that the computer is not capable of executing the symbolic language programs. The next step is to translate the symbolic language program into the machine language. This is accomplished by the ASSEMBLER PROGRAM.

Assembler program

This program, usually supplied by the equipment manufacturer, is a set of instructions which read and translate the symbolic language program (source program) into the machine language (object program).

Source Program: A program written in a symbolic language.

Object Program: A program in machine language.

The assembler can handle four different types of statements.

1. Each *machine statement* produces or is translated into one instruction in the object program and is used to request the computer to perform an operation during program execution time.
2. A *macro statement* is a pseudo OP code which causes several machine instructions to be generated and inserted in the object program.
3. *Assembler statements* are sometimes referred to as Assembler Control Statements. In contrast to machine instructions these statements do not always produce instructions to be included in the object program. Assembler instructions in fact direct the assembler to take certain actions during assembly time. They may be used to specify the starting point in main storage where the instructions are to be placed, to set aside work areas and input/output areas, to enter constants in the object program, etc.
4. *Comments* where used, provide descriptive information about the statement they are associated with. Comments are printed in the program listing but are not otherwise processed. Comments should be used freely to make the program listing more readable.

Assembly procedure

To obtain an object program from your source program, an assembler program must first be loaded into main storage. The assembler program in turn will read in the source statements and convert these into machine language statements.

IBM 360 uses a two-phase assembler. During the first phase, the source program is read in and the output is a symbol table and partially assembled statements. During the second pass, the output from the first pass serves as the input data and the output now consists of the Object Program and the Program listing.

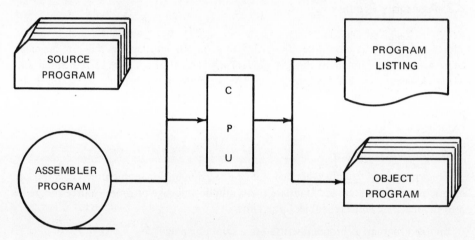

FIGURE 3.1. Assembly Process.

One of the functions of the assembler is to calculate and assign machine addresses to the various symbols used in a program. The assembler uses an area called the *Location Counter* to keep track of the addresses of various statements of the source program. The location counter is given some initial setting and then as each symbolic statement is being assembled, the counter is incremented by the length of the instructions, by the length of the constant (DC statement) or the length factor of the DS statement, etc.

For example, assume that the location counter contains a decimal value of 4000 when the following symbolic statement is encountered by the assembler.

        MOVE   MVC   SAVE,CARD

As this instruction is of SS type, the location counter will be incremented to 4006. Whenever the assembler encounters an entry in the label field of a statement, the current setting of the location is assigned to that label (the setting of the location counter before incrementing). In the example above, the assembler will assign an address of 4000 to the label MOVE. Further, suppose that the setting of the location counter is 6000 and the assembler encounters the following statements.

        AREA   DS   CL30

In this case the address assigned to the symbolic name AREA will be 6000 and then the location counter will be incremented to 6030. Consider that the next statement encountered is,

DC   CL4'DATE'

The location counter will be incremented to 6034.

Note: When bytes have to be skipped to obtain boundary alignments, the location counter is advanced accordingly. The location counter always indicates the address of the next free byte.

Location Counter: An area in the assembler which serves as a counter, used to keep track of the storage locations assigned to the various symbolic statements.

Symbol Table. The assembler uses the location counter to assign addresses to symbols. As there may be a large number of symbols in a program, there must be some way for the assembler to keep track of the various addresses assigned to the symbols.

For this purpose an area called *Symbol Table* is used. This area is set aside by the assembler.

During the first pass of the assembly, the assembler calculates and assigns addresses to all of the symbolic names. The symbolic names, along with their respective addresses, are placed in the symbol table. Assume that the initial setting of the location counter is 4002. Let us see what type of symbol table will result when the following instructions are encountered.

Name	Oper	Operand	Length in Bytes
ADDONE	AH	3,ONE	4 Bytes
	BC	8,OUT	4 Bytes
MOVE	MVC	SAVE,CARD	6 Bytes
	A	8,CONST	4 Bytes
CHKNEG	BC	4,NEGATIVE	4 Bytes
	BC	15,MOVE	4 Bytes

SYMBOL TABLE	
SYMBOL	ADDRESS*
ADDONE	4002
MOVE	4010
CHKNEG	4020

*A simplified example by using decimal numbers.

During the second pass, whenever the assembler finds a symbol in the operand field, it searches the symbol table. When a match is made, it gets the corresponding address from the symbol table and places it in the assembled machine instruction.

From this you can see why all symbols must be defined. If a symbol appears in an operand but is not defined in the label field, the assembler will not be able to make a match during the symbol table search. In such cases the error is flagged in the program listing.

In actual program listing, the symbol table addresses appear in hexadecimal format. Given below is an example of a program and its symbol table.

PAGE   1

```
    SOURCE STATEMENT                                           DOS CL2-4 03/23/69

EXAMPLE  START                                                           DBG01010
         PRINT NOGEN
CARDIN   DTFCD BLKSIZE=80,TYPEFLE=INPUT,DEVADDR=SYS008,                 CDBG01010
               EOFADDR=NOCARD,RECFORM=FIXUNB,IOAREA1=CARD               DBG01030
REPORTS  DTFPR DEVADDR=SYSO10,BLKSIZE=132,CONTROL=YES,IOAREA1=LINE,     CDBG0104C
               WORKA=YES,RECFORM=FIXUNB,PRINTOV=YES                     DBG01050
BEGIN    BALR  R9,0                                                     DBG01060
         USING *,R9                                                     DBG01070
         OPEN  CARDIN,REPORTS          OPEN  FILES                      DBG01080
         SR    R3,R3                   CLEAR   REG 3, ACCUMULATOR        DBG01090
READ     GET   CARDIN                  READ  A  CARD                    DBG01100
         PACK  DW,CARD+74(5)           PACK  AMOUNT  COL 75 - 79         DBG01110
         CVB   R2,DW                   CONVERT  AMOUNT TO BIMARY         DBG01120
         AR    R3,R2                   ACCUMULATE  AMOUNT                DBG01130
         BC    15,READ                 BRANCH  UNCONDITIONAL             DBG01140
NOCARD   MVC   LINE+10(5),TOTAL        POSITION CONSTANT IN PRINT AREA   DBG01150
         CVD   R3,DW                   CONVERT TOTAL TO DECIMAL          DBG01160
         UNPK  LINE+16(7),DW+4(4)      UNPACK TOTAL                      DBG01170
         MVZ   LINE+22(1),LINE+16                                       DBG01175
         PUT   REPORTS                 PRINT LINE                        DBG01180
         CLOSE CARDIN,REPORTS          CLOSE FILES                       DBG01190
         EOJ                                                            DBG01200
CARD     DS    CL80                                                     DBG01210
LINE     DC    132C' '                                                  DBG01220
TOTAL    DC    C'TOTAL'                                                  DBG01230
WORK     DS    CL132
R9       EQU   9
R3       EQU   3
R2       EQU   2
DW       DS    D
         END   BEGIN                                                    DBG01240
               =C'$$BOPEN '
               =C'$$BCLOSE'
               =A(CARDIN)
               =A(REPORTS)
```

FIGURE 3.2. Symbolic Program.

CROSS-REFERENCE

SYMBOL	LEN	VALUE	DEFN						
BEGIN	00002	000068	0045	0095					
CARD	00080	0000D4	0C87	0017	0019	0062			
CARDIN	00006	000000	0006	0053	0059	0081	0098		
DW	00008	000238	0094	0062	0063	0067	0068		
EXAMPLE	00001	000000	0001						
IJCX0001	00008	000020	0019	0009					
IJJC0006	00004	0C00C4	0080						
IJJ00003	00004	000C70	0052						
IJJZ0001	00001	000032	0C23						
IJJZ0002	00001	0C0068	0044						
LINE	00001	000124	0088	0038	0043	C066	0068	0069	0069
NOCARD	00006	00009C	0066	0018					
READ	00004	000080	0059	0065					
REPORTS	00006	000038	0027	0C54	0072	0082	C099		
R2	00001	000002	0093	0063	0064				
R3	00001	000003	0092	0056	0056	0064	0067		
R9	00001	000009	0091	0C45	0046				
TOTAL	00005	0001A8	0089	0066					
WORK	00132	0001AD	0090						

NO STATEMENTS FLAGGED IN THIS ASSEMBLY

FIGURE 3.3. Symbol Table.

The extent and type of program listing generated depends upon the control card statements[2]. In general, the program listing contains the following:

Machine Language instructions.

Source program statements.

Symbol table.

Diagnostic messages.

Diagnostic messages inform the programmer of the various mistakes made while writing the program. These could be: Undefined Names; Not Unique Names; Invalid Names; Invalid OP Codes, etc.

Note: During the assembly time, only the assembler instructions are executed. All other instructions are translated or assembled into machine language format. Assembler instructions do not result in machine instructions and as such do not take any space in the core storage.

To summarize, during assembly time only the assembler instructions are executed. The input data is the source program and the output is program listing, and object program.

System 360 uses at least a two-phase assembler. During the first pass, or phase, the

---

[2] Control Cards discussed in Appendix 2.

```
0000EC  C201 C347 C326 CC347 CC326  E7      MVC  IANK+2C(2),TYFE-2
C000F2  47FC C17A          C017A    88 *    B    PUTREC
                                    89 *
0000F6  0000 0000 0CCC CCCC CCCCC   9C MVOP MVC  TANK+15(5),1(5,R3)  MCVE CP CCCE FRCM TABLE IO OUTPUT
        *** ERRCF ***
CCCFC   CCCC CCCC  CCCCC            91      CLI  NAME,=C'*'          IS THIS A COMMENT CARD
        *** ERROR ***
000100  0000 0000  CCCCC            92      BNE  MVC
        *** EFFCF ***
CCC1C4  4122 CCC1   CCCC1           93      LA   R2,1(R2)
C00108  9540 2CC0   CCCCC           94 MVC  CLI  C(R2),X'40'         POINT PAST ASTERISK
CC010C  478C C144   CC144           95      BE   MV3                 IS THIS STATEMENT NAMEC

STMT  ERRCR CCCE   MESSAGE
9C    IELC35       NEAR OPERANC CCLMN 15--INVALIC CELIMITER
91    IEU020       NEAR OPERANC COLUMN 11--INVALID IMMEDIATE FIELC
92    IELC24       NEAR CPERANC CCLUMN  1--UNCEFINED SYMBCL
```

FIGURE 3.4. Program Listing (with some mistakes).

assembler builds a symbol table and the symbolic statements are partially assembled. The outcome of the second phase of the assembly run is the object program and the program listing.

A *location counter* is used to keep track of the instruction addresses and compilation of the symbol table.

A *program listing* without any diagnostic messages is called a clean assembly. Please note that during assembly time the program logic is not checked. The mistakes flagged are only those which have resulted due to violation of some rule pertaining to the writing of instructions. Program logic has to be checked out separately.

Note: During the assembly time, the assembler instructions are executed, while machine and macro statements are translated into machine instructions. During the object time the machine instructions are first loaded into the main storage and then executed.

Execution: At this time the input data is read and output data is produced. In case of program logic error no output or incorrect output will result.

The following are some important points to keep in mind.
1. During assembly time, the assembler statements are executed using the source program as input.
2. For System 360, the two-phase assembler is used.
3. During phase 1, the assembler reads the source program and a symbol table is compiled, as well as, source statements are partially assembled.
4. A location counter is used to keep track of the storage locations.
5. When the assembler encounters a symbolic name in a source statement, the current setting of the location counter is assigned to that label.
6. Every label and its address is stored in the symbol table.
7. During phase 2, a complete assembly is made and the output is: object program, and, program listing.

Note: For a complete discussion on interpretation of assembly listing see Appendix 3.

Thus far we have discussed Programming System, Assembly Program, Symbolic Language, Source Program, Object Program, Assembly Process, etc. The relationship of these various segments of a system is illustrated by Figure 3.5.

Program checkout

After a clean assembly has been obtained by conversion of a source program into an object program, the program is ready to be checked out. This is done to insure that the program does not have any logic errors (bugs) and that it is capable of producing the correct and desired results. More often than not, the test run does not function properly. This may be due to many factors. Mistakes in coding are more difficult to avoid than might be expected. It is, in fact, a rare occasion that a program works correctly the first time it is checked out. Usually several test runs have to be made before all the bugs are traced and corrected. Test runs are usually made with specially created test data which is designed to test for most, or all, of the possible conditions

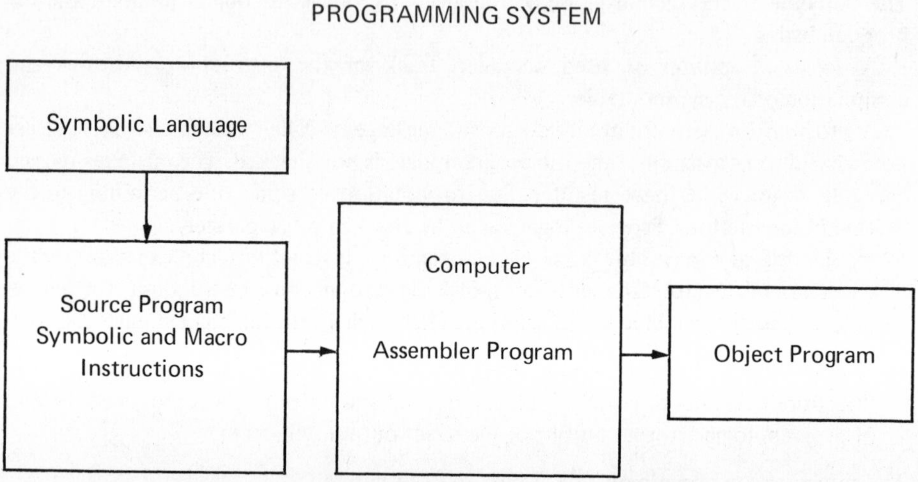

PROGRAMMING SYSTEM

FIGURE 3.5. **Programming System and its Basic Components.**

and specifications of the program. After a successful run with the test data the program is ready to be used with regular input for the problem. However, it is not unusual to use regular data for testing a program.

A common trait of programmers is to react in the following ways when a program blows up during testing or otherwise.

1. "This could not be my program."
2. "Oh! Those computer operators must have goofed."
3. "I am sure this is due to some keypunch error."
4. "Is it true that our system has not been functioning well lately?"
5. Finally, he may say: "It could be my mistake."

Self Evaluation Quiz

1. Which of the following instruction types do not usually get converted into machine format during assembly time?

 a. Machine Instruction Statements.
 b. Assembler Instruction Statements.

2. Write DC assembler instructions to store +32 as: packed decimal constant; packed decimal constant using 3 bytes; zoned decimal constant; and, fullword fixed-point constant.

3. What is the main difference between a DS and a DC?

4. Consider the coding given below and assume that the symbol CONST1 has been

assigned an address value of $(190)_{16}$. Build a symbol table showing the addresses assigned to the rest of the symbols.

CONST1	DS	H
CONST2	DS	F
CONST3	DS	D
CONST4	DC	CL3'0000'
CONST5	DS	D
CONST6	DC	CL5'ABC'
CONST7	DS	2H

5. How many bytes (total) will the following constants require?

DC	C'ABC'
DC	3C2'XYZ'
DC	3PL4'4'
DC	3CL3'A'

6. What are the length attributes of each of the following symbols?

FLDA	DS	2C120
FLDB	DC	3PL4'0'
FLDC	DC	PL4'0'
FLDD	DS	0CL80
FLDE	DS	0D

7. Show the storage layout for the constant coded below:

$$\text{DC} \qquad \text{4CL3'1A'}$$

8. Assume that the location counter is set to hex 200 when the assembler encounters the following constant:

CONST	DC	4FL2'3'

What would be the address value assigned to CONST?

9. What is meant by integral boundary?

10. As a programmer, how can you make sure that a particular DS or DC causes necessary boundary alignment?

11. Given an assembler instruction   DC   5CL70, which of the following is true?
    a. Generates one area 350 bytes in length.
    b. Generates 70 areas each 350 bytes in length.
    c. Is not a valid DC.
    d. None of the above.

12. State the various rules that must be followed when creating a symbol.

13. What is meant by undefined symbol, and unreferenced symbol?

14. Which of the two categories of symbol in the question above is most likely to cause bugs in a program?

15. Show the storage layout (with addresses) for the following DS and DC instructions. Assume that the symbol A has been assigned an address of hex 100.

```
A           DS          CL3
B           DS          D
CONST       DC          3PL2'0'
            DS          F
LAST        DC          CL3'AB'
```

16. Under what conditions is the boundary alignment not performed for H and F type of constants?

17. Given

```
CONST       DS          0CL20
```

    a. How many byte long area is reserved by this DS?
    b. What is the length attribute of CONST?
    c. What is the effect of this DS on the location counter?

18. How many bytes of data (maximum number) can be manipulated by a SS type of instruction with one length code?

19. Do the comments have any effect on program execution?

20. A symbol assigned to a DS statement refers to the: High-order byte, or, Low-order byte.

21. How many bytes will be reserved by each of the following?

```
DS          0D
DC          X'000'
DC          3CL2'A'
DS          2H
```

22. Show the storage layout for each of the following.

```
DC          PL3'12'
DC          XL4'102C'
DC          F'15'
DC          PL2'14,-10,156'
DC          ZL3'268'
```

23. Indicate the type of boundary alignment that will be performed for each of the following.

```
DS          H
DS          D
```

```
              DC      F'+3'
FULL          DC      H'−2'
              DS      0H
              DC      FL3'−18'
              DC      BL2'010111'
```

24. What is the maximum length that can be specified with a 'C' type constant?

25. Explain briefly the main function of the location counter.

[4]

Operating Systems, Macros and IOCS

4.1 Operating Systems

In earlier computers each job had to be set by the operator and when a job was finished, the operator had to reset the system to start a new job. Some of the routine tasks performed by the operator were to: reset (clear) the system for the next job; mount ·and dismount disks and tapes; and, set up the new program for loading into the core storage.

This method of computer operation was slow and wasted valuable time. As the computers became more complex and faster, frustrated operators could still go no faster than with the slower computers, and now even more costly hours of computer time backed up. Along with this human factor there were other delay-causing characteristics in the older computers. In the second generation computers, every time an unusual and/or error condition arose, the computer would halt as there were no error recovery methods available to handle such occurrences. In order to reduce the element of human intervention and to provide certain standard error handling routines, operating systems were designed. The main objective of an operating system is to provide, as much as possible, a non-stop and efficient computer operation. An operating system consists of a comprehensive collection of control and service programs. Some of the more commonly used operating systems for System 360 are:

Operating System	(OS)
Disk Operating System	(DOS)
Tape Operating System	(TOS)
Basic Operating System	(BOS)

Some of the main tasks of an operating system are outlined below.

1. Initializing system execution, commonly known as Initial Program Load (IPL).
2. Translation of the symbolic programs into a form that can be executed by the computer. This is done by the compilers, assemblers and the link editor.
3. Aiding the programmer in diagnosing program errors.
4. Interfacing with the computer to coordinate all Input/Output operations and to provide error handling routines for various machine and program alerts.
5. Performing some of the routine and commonly needed services (utilities), such as transferring data from an input/output device to another.

Discussion of operating systems is a subject in itself and to avoid detailed and unnecessarily complicated discussion on the subject we will give a brief coverage to Disk Operating System which requires at least 16K core with system residence on disk. An operating system has many components; the three major categories are: Processor Programs; System Control Programs; and, System Service Programs.

Processor programs

IBM supplies several processing programs to perform the task of translating the symbolic language programs into machine language programs, also known as object modules. The DOS provides translators for Assembler Language, COBOL, FORTRAN, PL/1 and RPG.

Control programs

Some of the major functions of the control programs are to handle Initial Program Load (IPL), machine alerts (interruptions), various input/output operations, transition between various job steps or between different jobs, and symbolic I/O device assignments. These functions are further divided and handled by the following three separate programs.

IPL Loader. When the computer system is initiated, the hardware IPL reads in the IPL loader which performs certain housekeeping routines and then reads in the supervisor program from the system residence unit, an on-line disk file in case of DOS.

Supervisor. The supervisor program acts as a super clerk and resides in the lower core when a job is being run. The size of the supervisor depends upon the machine configuration and the functions it is asked to perform. The supervisor controls the overall functions of the computer system.

Job Control. This component of the control program system functions like an internal computer operator. The job control is read into the core by the supervisor when the end of a job is signalled (usually by the EOJ macro written in the problem program by the programmer). The job control, in turn, reads in the next job from the system input device (usually the card reader) and after the new job has been loaded it turns control over to the new problem program. Thus, all the operator has to do is to stack a number of jobs in the card reader and from then on the computer, with the help of the control programs, will handle all job set-ups with a minimum of operator intervention. The job control does not reside in core at all times as it is needed only at the beginning of a new job. In case of DOS, it resides on the system residence disk pack along with other control programs.

System service programs

System service programs edit the machine language programs (obtained by translating symbolic programs) into executable form and maintain and service the system resident libraries. For DOS, the system service programs are the Librarian and the Linkage Editor.

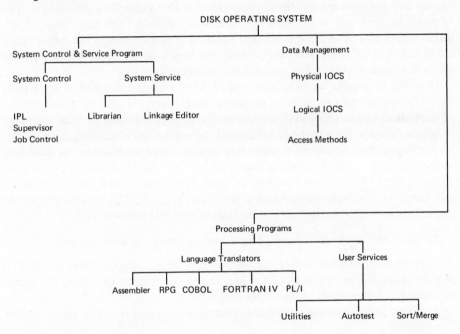

DISK OPERATING SYSTEM

Librarian. The librarian services and maintains the system libraries. Its duties are to place new programs into the libraries, to replace, delete or alter existing programs and certain other housekeeping functions. There are three libraries maintained by the librarian. These are the core image library, relocatable library, and the source statement library.

Core image library contains all the IBM-supplied processor and control programs and other application programs written by the user himself. The programs contained in this library are in executable form and are loaded directly into the main storage for execution by the supervisor.

Relocatable library contains object modules that can be combined with other program modules at link edit time without recompiling or reassembling. This allows the installation to keep frequently used routines in residence and include them in as many phases as desired without going through the time-consuming steps of reassembling or recompiling.

Source statement library contains IBM-supplied and user-written macro definitions, which can be incorporated into a program to provide some special function.

The preceding chart shows an overview of the different components of DOS.

4.2 Introduction to Macros

In most of the programs certain functions, represented by a sequence of instructions, appear over and over again without many changes. One example of this is the routine required to read and write data for various I/O devices. The basic logic of the instructions required to perform the I/O function does not change. The only changes are in the type of I/O devices to be used, the length of I/O areas and perhaps the symbolic names identifying the various files, records and devices.

It would be a great waste of time and effort if a programmer had to write these instructions repeatedly in different programs. Keeping this in mind, the manufacturers of computers began to include pre-written generalized routines in their assembler programs. These various routines, which may be resident on a magnetic tape or disc, are maintained in a library on the assembly program. All a programmer has to do is to refer to the appropriate routine. He also supplies to the assembler specific information regarding the I/O device and the areas involved. The assembler will, in turn, generate and insert the necessary instructions in the object program. This substitution of one instruction instead of writing many is the basis of MACRO instructions.

MACRO: One of the definitions of macro is *of or involving large quantities.*

For one macro instruction written in the source program, many machine instructions may be generated by the assembler. Thus, the system derives its name. The macro instruction system consists of two major parts:

1. Macro Definitions are generalized routines written and stored in the Assembler Library.
2. Source Program Macro Instruction consists of pseudo OP codes used to inform the assembler which operation is desired and also of operand entries giving specific details regarding the operation(s) to be performed.

Note: In case of macro instructions, the operand entries are generally referred to by the word parameter(s). From now on, when discussing macros, the word *parameter* will be used instead of the conventionally used term *operand entry.*

Macro definitions, also known as macro library, contain numerous sets of generalized routines. These routines are designed to meet many requirements and as such have many optional parameters. Each routine on the library is identified by a symbolic name.

Source Program Macro Instructions are the instructions written by the programmer in his source program to activate the appropriate macro library routines. The OP code of the instruction identifies the name of the routine in the macro library. The parameters of the macro instruction contain the information needed by the assembler

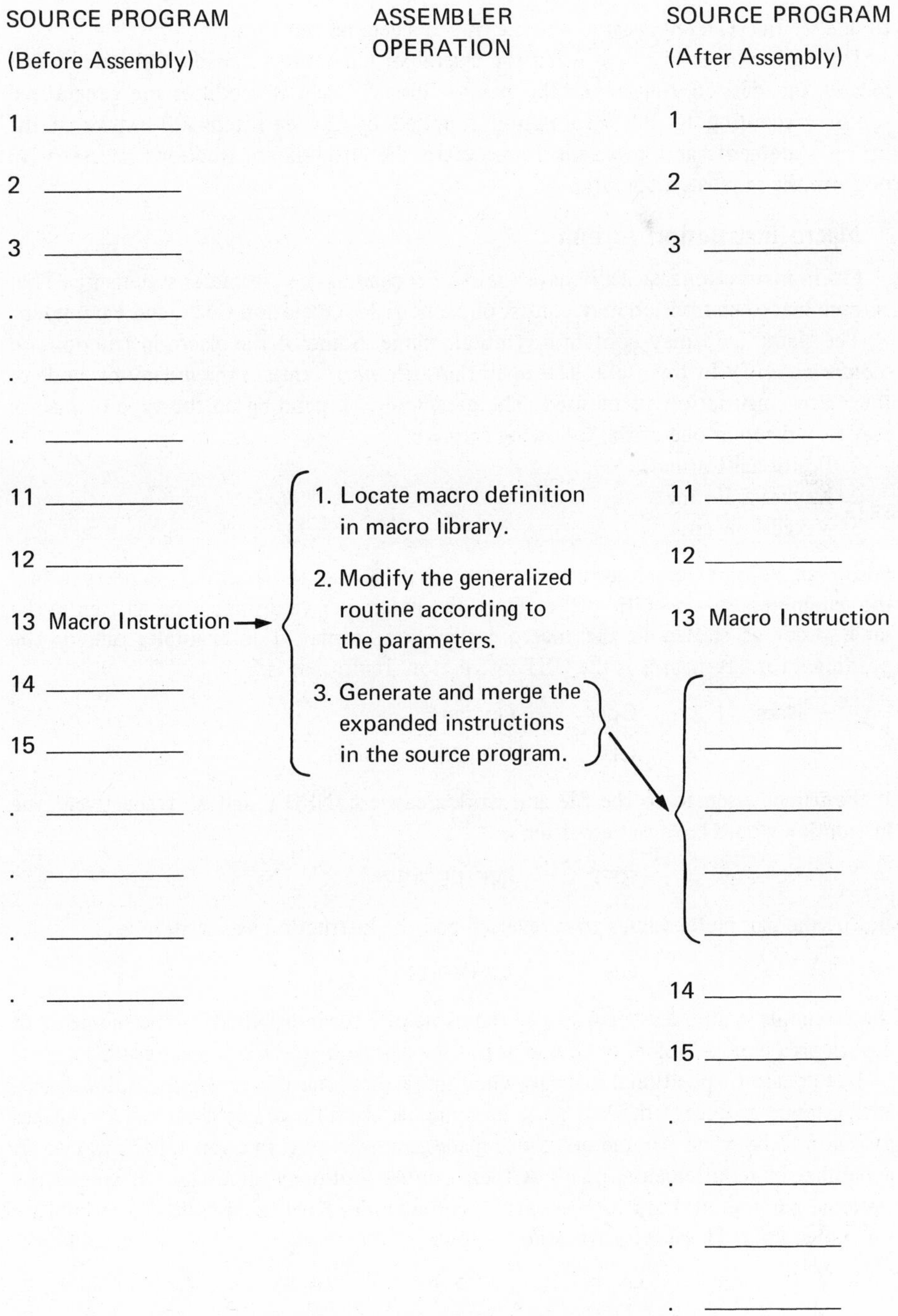

SOURCE PROGRAM
(Before Assembly)

ASSEMBLER
OPERATION

SOURCE PROGRAM
(After Assembly)

1 _____

2 _____

3 _____

. _____

. _____

. _____

11 _____

12 _____

13 Macro Instruction →

14 _____

15 _____

. _____

. _____

. _____

. _____

1. Locate macro definition in macro library.

2. Modify the generalized routine according to the parameters.

3. Generate and merge the expanded instructions in the source program.

1 _____

2 _____

3 _____

. _____

. _____

. _____

11 _____

12 _____

13 Macro Instruction

_____

_____

_____

_____

14 _____

15 _____

. _____

. _____

. _____

. _____

FIGURE 4.1. Macro Processing (Expansion).

to modify the selected routine which exists in a generalized form.

During the assembly time when the assembler encounters a macro OP code, it first locates the desired routine in the macro library. Then it modifies the generalized routine according to the information supplied by the parameters(s) entries of the macro statement, and proceeds to generate the machine instructions necessary to perform the requested operation.

Macro instruction format

Macro instructions basically have the same format as the assembler statements. That is, each macro instruction may consist of Name field, Operation Code, and Parameters.

The Name field may contain a symbolic name. Some of the macro instructions *do require* an entry in this field. The operation field *must* contain the mnemonic code of the macro instruction to be used. The parameters, depending on the type of macro, may be written in one of the following formats:

1. Positional Format.
2. Keyword Format.
3. Mixed Format.

Positional Format Parameters. In the positional format, the assembler expects to find the parameters in a specific order. Thus, the parameter values must be written in the same order as shown in the macro instruction format. For example, one of the positional format macros is the GET instruction. Its format is:

Name	Oper	Operand
	GET	filename,workarea

If the names assigned to the file and work area were INFILE and A2 respectively, the instruction would have to be written as:

GET   INFILE,A2

In case the parameter values were reversed and the instruction was written as:

GET   A2,INFILE

the assembler would expect A2 to be the name of a file and INFILE to be the name of a work area in core which, of course, is not the case and an *error* would result.

In the case of positional macros, when more than one parameter definition exists, each parameter except the last must be immediately followed by a comma. No spaces are allowed between parameters. Since macro routines exist in a generalized way to fit a number of requirements, many of them contain optional parameters. If any of the optional parameter(s) are to be omitted, certain rules have to be followed to indicate the omission(s). These rules are:

1. If the omitted parameter(s) is to be followed by another parameter, an additional comma(s) has to be inserted in place of the omitted parameter(s).
2. If the omitted parameter(s) is not followed by another parameter, the remaining

comma(s) is not necessary.

Continuation of Parameters. Column 72 must contain a continuation character[1] if the parameters fill the operand field and overflow into another line. The last line containing parameters does not need a continuation character.

Keyword Format Parameters. In the keyword format type of macro statements, parameters are equated to fixed keywords. These keywords are a part of the assembler language itself. The parameter format being:

Keyword = Parameter

In this type of macro-statement, the keywords may appear in any position and any that are not needed may be omitted. No commas are needed to indicate the omissions. Different keyword parameters may be written on the same line, each followed by a comma, or if the programmer so desires he may write each keyword parameter on a separate line. In the latter case, a continuation character must be entered in column 72 of each line except the last.

Mixed Format Macros. In this type of macro the operand portion contains both the positional and the keyword parameters. The positional parameters are written first and are followed by keyword parameters.

Input–Output Control System (IOCS)

Instructions required to accomplish any I/O operation are generally quite involved and lengthy. Yet for different devices, instructions needed to accomplish the I/O operations are identical. To simplify a programmer's work, standardized routines are provided by the manufacturers. These routines are collectively called IOCS and perform such functions as:
1. Opening and Closing of data files.
2. Reading and Writing of records.
3. Blocking and Deblocking of records.
4. Error condition checking, etc.

The IOCS consists of two parts: Physical IOCS (PIOCS); and, Logical IOCS (LIOCS).

Physical IOCS controls the actual transfer of records between the external medium and the main storage, i.e., the actual reading and writing of records. Physical IOCS consists of the following routines:
1. Start I/O routine.
2. Interrupt routine.
3. Channel schedular.
4. Device error routines.

These routines are part of the supervisor, which is permanently located in lower main storage while problem programs are being executed.

---

[1] Any non-blank character may be used. Detailed methods of writing macros are covered later in this section.

Logical IOCS perform those functions that are needed to locate and access a logical record for processing. A logical record can be defined as one unit of information in a file of like units, for example, one employee's record in a master payroll file. One or more logical records may be included within one physical record, for example, a physical tape record. The logical IOCS routines perform the following functions:

1. Blocking and deblocking of records.
2. Switching between I/O areas when two areas are specified for a file.
3. Handling end-of-file and end-of-volume conditions.
4. Checking and writing labels.

Logical IOCS uses physical IOCS to execute I/O commands whenever it determines that a transfer of data is required. For example, if a file consists of blocked records and a block has been read into main storage, logical IOCS makes each record in succession available for processing until the end of the block is reached. No physical IOCS is required. When logical IOCS determines that the last record in the block has been processed, it requests physical IOCS to start an I/O operation to transfer the next physical record into main storage.

Logical IOCS macros, GET, PUT, READ, WRITE, etc. and physical IOCS macros (such as EXCP and WAIT) are available for handling of records. The logical IOCS macro routines cause all the functions of both logical and physical IOCS to be performed for the programmer. Registers 0, 1, 14, and 15 are used by logical IOCS routines.

The physical IOCS routines are completely distinct from the routines used by logical IOCS to perform functions such as blocking and deblocking. They permit the problem program to use physical IOCS functions directly. To transfer a physical record the problem program uses an EXCP macro instruction. When the record is needed for processing, the problem program must test to determine if the transfer has been completed. This is accomplished by the use of WAIT macro instruction. Physical IOCS uses registers 0 and 1. IOCS consists of three types of macro instructions:

1. Declarative DTFxx Macro Instructions.
2. Declarative Logic Module Generation Macro Instructions.
3. Imperative Macro Instructions.

During assembly time, depending upon the macro instruction specified, the appropriate macro definition is called from the macro library. It is then modified and inserted into the program. In the subsequent phases of the assembly process, the entire program is processed to produce the object program.

Register Restriction with Macro & IOCS. General registers 0, 1, 13, 14, and 15 serve special purposes and are available for the programmer's use only under certain restrictions.

Registers 0 and 1. These two registers are used by the IBM-supplied macros and may be used without restrictions if macro instructions are not used in a program. If the manufacturer-supplied macros are used, the programmer must save their contents before a routine containing macros is executed and then reload the registers after completion of the routine.

Register 13. Logical IOCS, along with the control program subroutines may use these registers.

Register 14 and 15. These two registers are used by LIOCS for linkage. Register 14 contains the return address (to the problem program) from DTF generated routines and other subroutines. Register 15 contains the address of entry point into these routines and is also used as a base register by certain macro instructions. If a programmer wishes to use these registers, he must save their contents (and reload the same later).

Safe registers. Registers 2 through 12 are available without restrictions, and to avoid any errors these should be the registers used in a program.

Entry Cards for Declarative Macros. The parameters for the declarative macros (DTF and Logic Modules) are divided into two main parts: header card; and, detail card (optional).

The first entry card containing declarative macros is known as the header card. If all of the parameters cannot be contained in this one card, continuation card(s) known as detail cards may be used. The header card contains the following information:

1. In the Name field, the symbolic name[2] of the file to be processed. The programmer should avoid symbolic names beginning with IJ since these may conflict with the IOCS generated symbols. In DTF, the symbolic name assigned to files *may not exceed seven characters.* All other rules for symbolic names still apply. In case of logic module macros, the file name is optional.
2. The mnemonic code for the macro instruction is entered in the operation field.
3. The operand portion of the statement contains the keyword format entries.
4. If a detail card(s) is necessary, card column 72 contains the continuation character.

The detail cards follow immediately after the header card. The detail cards must be left blank in the name and operation fields. The detail card entries are made beginning in column 16. All detail cards except the last one must contain a continuation character in column 72.

4.3 DTF Entries For Card, Printer, and Console Files

Six different DTF (Define The File) macros are supplied for use with sequential processing. These are:

DTFCD	for	Card files
DTFPR	for	Printer files

---

[2]When using IOCS to process data, each data file is assigned a symbolic name and from then on the programmer refers to this name in his I/O instructions for the particular file.

DTFMT[3]	for	Magnetic Tape Files
DTFCN	for	Console Typewriter
DTFPT[4]	for	Paper Tape Files
DTFOR[4]	for	Optical Reader

These six declarative macros are subsets of the inclusive declarative macro DTFSR. The DTFSR macro is provided as a compatibility aid to users of BPS (Basic Programming Support). Assembly time is considerably improved if the subsets are used instead of the DTFSR when programming with TOS and DOS.

When using IOCS to process data, each file used in the program *must* be defined by the DTFxx macro instruction. A list of keyword entries for card and printer files is given below. Not all of the entries listed below are mandatory.

	DTFCD (Input/Output)	DTFPR
Req'd	DEVADDR=SYSnnn	DEVADDR=
	IOAREA1=	IOAREA1=
Opt'l	BLKSIZE=	BLKSIZE=
	CONTROL=YES	CONTROL=YES
	CRDERR=	CTLCHR=
	CTLCHR=	DEVICE=
	DEVICE=	IOAREA2=
	EOFADDR=	IOREG=(nn)
	IOAREA2=	MODNAME=
	IOREG=(nn)	PRINTOV=
	MODNAME=	RECFORM=
	RECFORM=	RECSIZE=(nn)
	RECSIZE=(nn)	WORKA=YES
	SSELECT=	
	TYPEFLE=	
	WORKA=YES	

FIGURE 4.2. **Keyword Entries for Card and Printer Files**

Symbolic unit addressing

One of the required keyword entries in DTFxx macro is DEVADDR=SYSnnn. This parameter is used to assign a file to a particular I/O unit. The SYSnnn part of the parameter indicates the I/O device to be used. When writing DTF entries the I/O devices are referred to by symbolic names and not by their actual addresses. A list of

[3]DTF macros for magnetic tape files are discussed in Section 14.2.

[4]This text does not include processing of paper tape and optical reader.

symbolic unit names is supplied by the manufacturer and a programmer must select his entries from this list. The list of symbolic unit names is:

SYSRDR	System Control-Card Reader.
SYSIPT	Main System Input Device.
SYSPCH	Main System Output Device.
SYSLST	Main System Printer.
SYSLOG	Printer-keyboard used for logging Job Control Statement and operator messages.
SYS000–SYS244	Any other device in the system.

The first five symbolic names are more or less permanently assigned to specific devices. The supervisor program maintains a list of these symbolic unit names along with their actual device addresses. Thus, we can say that each device is assigned two names; a symbolic unit address and an actual device address.

Usually, a programmer employs the symbolic unit address in his program instead of the actual unit address. Since System 360 has been designed to be able to execute more than one program at a time if actual device addresses were assigned, a situation could arise when more than one program referenced the same device.

In such a case, the program execution would have to be delayed until the required unit became available. On the other hand, if symbolic names were used the operator could assign[5] the available I/O device to the program and the program execution would not be delayed. In case of a single unit installation, i.e., one card read-punch unit, one printer, etc., it makes no difference whether actual or symbolic names are used.

Now we will discuss the various keyword entries associated with DTF macro for card files. The various entries are listed in alphabetical order.

Declarative file definition macros

Card File (DTFCD)   Declarative Macro

In the name field of the header card, the programmer must enter the symbolic File Name and the mnemonic code DTFCD is entered in the operation field. The keyword entries are written in the operand field and may appear in any order.

BLKSIZE=n

This entry specifies the length of the I/O area (IOAREA1), where n indicates the maximum number of characters that will be read into or written (punched) from the area. If the record format is variable or undefined, enter the length of the largest record. If this entry is omitted, the length is assumed to be 80.

CONTROL=YES

[5] Job Control Statements are used to assign actual unit addresses to symbolic names at object time. These statements are discussed in Appendix 2.

This entry is used if a CNTRL macro is to be issued to the file. The CNTRL macro is used to specify pocket selection for the cards in a file.

CRDERR=RETRY

This operand applies to card output on the IBM 2540 and 2520. This entry specifies the action to be taken if an error is detected during punching.

In case this entry is omitted and a punching error occurs, it is usually ignored and operation continues. The error card is stacked in pocket P1 and correct cards are stacked in the pocket specified by the programmer. If the CRDERR=RETRY entry is included and an error occurs, IOCS notifies the operator and then enters the wait state. The operator can instruct the IOCS to either terminate the job, ignore the error, or direct the IOCS to repunch the card.

$$CTLCHR=\begin{Bmatrix} ASA \\ YES \end{Bmatrix}$$

This entry is required if first-character control is to be used on an output file. The ASA denotes the American Standard Association set, YES denotes the System 360 character set. No further discussion of this entry is included in this text.

DEVADDR=SYSnnn

This entry is used to assign a data file to a symbolic unit name. The symbolic name is later equated to the actual device address by a job control statement. Depending upon the number of card-read units in an installation, this entry might be: DEVADDR= SYSRDR; DEVADDR=SYSIPT; DEVADDR=SYS000; DEVADDR=SYS008; etc.

DEVICE=

This entry is used to specify the type of I/O unit associated with the card file. The valid specifications are: 2540, 1442, 2501, and 2520. If this entry is omitted, 2540 is assumed.

EOFADDR=Name

This entry must be specified for an input file. The parameter of this keyword entry specifies the symbolic name of the end-of-file routine. The IOCS will cause an automatic branch to this symbolic name when all the records of the file have been read. In the end-of-file routine, the programmer can perform any operation(s) required for the end of file. An example of this entry is:

EOFADDR=NOCARDS

IOCS detects end-of-file conditions in the card reader by recognizing /* punched in card columns 1 and 2. If cards are allowed to run out without a /* trailer card (and a /& card if end-of-job) an error condition is signaled to the operator.

IOAREA1=Name

This entry is used to supply to the IOCS the name of the input and output area to be used by this file. In case of an input file, when a GET instruction is given a record is read into this area and in case of an output file a PUT instruction will transfer the contents of the IOAREA1 to the output device. An area defining statement must be included in the program using the same symbolic name as specified with the IOAREA1 entry. The length entry of the area defining statement specifies the size of the record involved. The reason for having to actually reserve the area in core is the fact that the IOAREA1 entry only specifies the name of the I/O area and a separate area defining statement is needed to reserve the positions.

Name	Oper	Operand	
CARDIN	DTFCD	IOREA1=IN,	X
	.		
	.		
	.		
	.		
	.		
	.		
	.		
IN	DS	CL80	
	.		
	.		

IOAREA2=Name

This entry specifies a *second* I/O area for the file. As with IOAREA1, an area defining statement is required to set aside the positions in core.

IOREG=(r)

In case work areas are not used to process records and two input or output areas are used, the programmer may use any one of the registers (2–12) as IOREG. In case of input files the IOCS puts the address of the first byte of the record in this register. For output files, IOCS puts the address where the user can build a record.

MODNAME=name

This entry may be used to specify the name of the logical module that will be used to process the file. If this operand is omitted, standard names will be generated for calling the logic module. If two DTF macro instructions call for different functions that can be handled by a single module, only one module is called.

$$RECFORM = \begin{cases} FIXUNB \\ VARUNB \\ UNDEF \end{cases}$$

This operand specifies the record format of the file. If the record format is fixed-unblocked, this entry may be omitted.

RECSIZE=(r)

If the record size is undefined, this entry is used to specify a register that will contain the actual length of the output record. The programmer must load the length of each record into this register before issuing a PUT for the record.

SSELECT=n

This entry is used to specify the pocket into which *all* the cards in a file are to be selected. If this entry is omitted, the cards will be selected into normal read (NR) or normal punch (NP).

TYPEFLE=

This entry specifies if the file is input or output. For input files the entry is always TYPEFLE=INPUT, and for output files the entry is TYPEFLE=OUTPUT.

WORKA=YES

If a programmer chooses to process I/O records in work areas instead of the I/O area, this entry is used.[6] An area-defining entry to set aside the area must be included in the program. If WORKA entry is specified, IOREG entry cannot be included.

Printer File(DTFPR)   Declarative Macro

For printer files, a DTFPR macro code is entered in the operation field. The name field of the header card contains the symbolic file name. The detail entries follow the DTFPR header entry. The keyword (detail) entries may be written in any order. The various keyword entries associated with DTFPR are discussed below.

BLKSIZE=

This entry is used to specify the length of the output area. If this entry is omitted, 121 is assumed.

Example:
BLKSIZE=132.

CONTROL=YES

This entry is used if a CNTRL macro is to be issued to the file. In case of printer files CNTRL macro is used to specify spacing and skipping.

$$CTLCHR=\begin{Bmatrix} YES \\ ASA \end{Bmatrix}$$

---

[6]In such cases each GET or PUT instruction associated with the file must use the work area option format. The explanation is given later in this section.

This entry is included if first-character control is to be used. The parameter ASA specifies the American Standard Association set while YES specifies the System 360 character set. No further discussion of this entry is included in this text.

DEVADDR=SYSnnn

This entry is used to specify the symbolic unit name to be associated with the printer used in the program.

Example:
  DEVADDR=SYSLST

DEVICE=Unit Number

This entry specifies the type of the printer unit to be used for the file. The unit may be any one of the following: 1403; 1404 (continuous form only); 1443; or, 1445. If this entry is omitted the 1403 unit is assumed.

IOAREA1=Name

This entry specifies the output area. An area-defining statement must be included to set aside the positions in core.

Name	Oper	Operand	
REPORT	DTFPR	IOAREA1=LINE,	X
	.		
	.		
	.		
	.		
	.		
	.		
LINE	DS	CL132	

IOAREA2=Name

This entry is used to specify a second I/O area. As with the IOAREA1 entry, an area-defining statement must be included to set aside the actual area in core.

IOREG=(r)

If no work area and two I/O areas are used, this entry is used to specify the register which will contain the address of an area where the programmer can build his record.

MODNAME=name

This parameter entry may be used to specify the name of the logic module that will be used with the DTF table to process the file. If this entry is omitted, standard names are generated for calling logic modules. If two DTF macro instructions call for different functions that can be handled by a single module, only one will be called.

PRINTOV=YES

This entry is included if a PRTOV macro is to be used in the problem program. PRTOV macro is used to check for channel 12 (form overflow) condition.

$$RECFORM=\begin{Bmatrix} FIXUNB \\ UNDEF \\ VARUNB \end{Bmatrix}$$

In case of FIXUNB record format this entry may be omitted. In case of undefined record format enter RECFORM=UNDEF and, if the records are variable and unblocked, enter VARUNB.

RECSIZE=(r)

This operand for undefined records, specifies the general register (2—12) that will contain the length of the output record. Length of each record must be loaded into the register before issuing a PUT instruction.

WORKA=YES

In case output records are to be processed in a work area instead of the I/O area, this entry is included. An area-defining entry to set aside the area must be included in the program. If this entry is included, IOREG entry cannot be used for the same file.

Console File (DTFCN)   Declarative Macro

DTFCN is used to define a file that is to be processed on an IBM 1052 printer keyboard. The various parameter entries follow.

BLKSIZE=n

This entry is used to specify the length of the I&O area for the file. In case of undefined records, this entry must specify the length of the largest record. Input/Output records must not exceed 256 characters.

$$DEVADDR=\begin{Bmatrix} SYSLOG \\ SYSnnn \end{Bmatrix}$$

The DEVADDR entry specifies the symbolic unit that is associated with the logical file.

IOAREA1=Name

This entry is used to specify the symbolic name of the I/O area for the file.

$$RECFORM=\begin{Bmatrix} FIXUNB \\ UNDEF \end{Bmatrix}$$

This entry is used to specify the record format of the logical file to be processed. If omitted, the system assumes FIXUNB.

RECSIZE=(r)

In case the record format is undefined, this entry is used to specify a register (2–12) that will contain the length of the record. The programmer must load into this register the length of each record before issuing a PUT for the record on an output file.

$$\text{TYPEFLE=}\begin{Bmatrix} \text{INPUT} \\ \text{OUTPUT} \end{Bmatrix}$$

If INPUT is specified the system will generate coding for both input and output files. On the other hand, if OUTPUT is specified, coding for an output file only is provided.

WORKA=YES

In case the logical records from the file are to be processed in a work area instead of an I/O area, this entry must be included. On a GET or PUT to the file, IOCS moves the record to or from the work area.

There are certain combinations of I/O areas and work areas that are possible. These are:

1. One I/O area with no work area.
2. One I/O area with a work area.
3. Two I/O areas with no work area.
4. Two I/O areas with a work area.

IOCS modules

Several hundred IOCS routines, more commonly known as IOCS logic modules, are available with System 360. These modules provide the necessary instructions and support to accomplish the input/output functions of the problem program. For example, these modules may test for unusual input/output conditions, building logical records in a work area, flip flop of buffers, etc. An installation could include every one of these several hundred IOCS modules in the relocatable library to support every possible IOCS function. This technique will severely tax the system's efficiency and will also require a great amount of storage. Instead, each installation, at system generation time, includes a set of those IOCS modules which are based on the equipment being used, installation's standards for record formats, processing methods and most commonly used techniques, etc.

When this is done, the Linkage Editor automatically searches the relocatable library to locate the module(s) necessary to support the I/O operation requested. If and when a specially tailored module (which does not exist in the relocatable library) is needed to process a special condition, it can be generated by using the logic module macro instructions and its parameters.

IOCS Modules Generation. There are several methods of generating a given IOCS module which have not been included in the relocatable library at system generation time. Two of thes methods are: by the use of xxMOD macro; and by entering the actual IOCS module name as one of the parameter entries of the DTFxx macro for the file.

1. XXMOD Macro: A specially tailored IOCS module can be generated by specifying xxMOD (CDMOD for card files and PRMOD for printer files[7]) macro. The rules for the header and detail card entries are the same as discussed for DTF macro.

2. CDMOD (Card Module). Listed below are the various parameters for this macro.

CONTROL=YES

CRDERR=RETRY

$$CTLCHR = \left\{ \begin{array}{c} ASA \\ \\ YES \end{array} \right\}^{8}$$

$$DEVICE = \left\{ \begin{array}{c} 1442 \\ 2501 \\ 2520 \\ 2540 \end{array} \right\}$$

IOAREA2=YES

$$RECFORM = \left\{ \begin{array}{c} FIXUNB \\ VARUNB \\ UNDEF \end{array} \right\}$$

SEPASMB=YES[8]

$$TYPEFLE = \left\{ \begin{array}{c} INPUT \\ OUTPUT \\ CMBND^{8} \end{array} \right\}$$

WORKA=YES

Thus, depending upon the logic modules not included and the program's requirements, a programmer will have to specify some or all of these parameters in the CDMOD macro. An example of this is:

```
        CARDIN      DTFCD    DEVADDR=SYS008,IOAREA1=IN1,     X
                             WORKA=YES,                      X
                             EOFADDR=END,IOAREA2=IN2,        X
                             RECFORM=FIXUNB
                    CDMOD    IOAREA2=YES,WORKA=YES
```

[7]DTFCN macro does not require xxMOD entries.

[8]These entries are not discussed in this text.

This illustrates the coding for a card input file for an installation which does not have IOAREA2 and WORKA modules included in the relocatable library. The CDMOD macro above will generate a module which will support the DTFCD for the card file. The name of the module generated will have the following format:

I J C abcde

Where:

a = F, V, or U depending upon record format.

b = A if CTLCHR=ASA.

   = Y if CTLCHR=YES; C if CONTROL=YES; and Z if neither is specified.

c = I, O, or C depending on TYPEFLE entry.

d = Z if neither WORKA nor IOAREA2 is specified.

   = W if WORKA=YES.

   = I if IOAREA2=YES.

   = B if both WORKA=YES and IOAREA2=YES.

e = 0 if DEVICE=2540.

   = 1 if DEVICE=1442.

   = 2 if DEVICE=2520.

   = 3 if DEVICE=2501.

   = 4 if DEVICE=2540 and CRDERR is specified.

   = 5 if DEVICE=2520 and CRDERR is specified.

The CDMOD macro as coded in the example above will generate a module name which would look like this:

IJCFZIW0

The second method of informing the system of a special logic module is to write the module name as one of the parameters of the DTF for the file. For example, the previously illustrated coding for the card file could have been written as follows:

```
CARDIN        DTFCD    DEVADDR=SYS008,IOAREA1=IN1,        X
                       WORKA=YES,                         X
                       EOFADDR=END,IOAREA2=IN2,           X
                       RECFORM=FIXUNB,                    X
                       MODNAME=IJCFZIW0
```

PRMOD (Printer Module)

Listed below are the various possible parameters for PRMOD macro.

CONTROL=YES

$$CTLCHR = \begin{Bmatrix} YES \\ ASA \end{Bmatrix}^9$$

[9] These entries are not discussed in this text.

IOAREA2=YES

PRINTOV=YES

$$RECFORM= \begin{cases} FIXUNB \\ VARUNB \\ UNDEF \end{cases}$$

SEPASMB=YES[9]

WORKA=YES

The module that will be generated will have the following format:

IJDabcde

Where:

a = F, V, or U depending upon record format.

b = A if CTLCHR=ASA.

= Y if CTLCHR=YES.

= C if CONTROL=YES.

= Z if neither CTLCHR nor CONTROL is specified.

c = P if PRINTOV=YES.

= Z if PRINTOV=YES is not specified.

d = I if IOAREA2=YES.

= Z if IOAREA2=YES is not specified.

e = W if WORKA=YES is specified.

= Z if WORKA=YES is not specified.

4.4 Input-Output Operations

Imperative Macro Instructions

These macros initiate such functions as opening and closing of files, making records available for processing, writing records that have been processed, checking for end of form condition (in case of the continuous form printers), etc. Imperative macros discussed in this text can be classified in three major groups:

Group Classification	Macros
Initialization of files	OPEN
Processing records	GET,PUT,PRTOV,CNTRL
Completion of processing	CLOSE,EOJ

Note: PRTOV and CNTRL macros are discussed in Section 7.1. EOJ is a supervisor communication macro.

---

[9]These entries are not discussed in this text.

Initialization

Before the first record can be read from an input file or written to an output file, the file must be readied for use by an OPEN macro instruction. This instruction activates the file(s) referred to in the operand portion of the statement. For card and printer files, OPEN simply makes the file available to the problem program. In case of magnetic disk and tape files, OPEN macro generates routines to perform several additional functions (complete coverage given in Section 14.2).

OPEN Macro   Imperative Macro

The format of this macro is:

OPEN   filename1,filename2,....

The symbolic name of the file(s) to be OPENed is entered in the operand field. The symbolic filename(s) must be the same as assigned to the DTF macro for the file. A maximum of 16 files may be opened with one OPEN macro. The filenames may be entered in any sequence and will be opened in the order specified.

Example:

Name	Oper	Operand
	OPEN	CARDIN,CARDOUT,REPORT

or

	OPEN	CARDIN
	OPEN	CARDOUT
	OPEN	REPORT

Processing of records

Two imperative macros are used for processing of records. These are GET and PUT macros.

GET Macro   Imperative Macro

GET macro makes available to the problem program the next sequential logical record from an input file. This record is either available in an input area or a work area depending upon the format of the GET macro used to obtain the record. The two formats of the GET macro are:

Name	Oper	Operand
	GET	filename
	GET	filename,workname

Filename. This is the first parameter of the GET macro. The filename must be the same as specified in the header entry of the DTF macro for the file from which the record is to be read. The routine generated by the GET macro will cause the next available record to be placed in the area specified by the keyword parameter IOAREA1= of the DTF macro for this file.

Example:

Name	Oper	Operand	
CARDIN	DTFCD	IOAREA1=IN,	X
	.		
	.		
	.		
	.		
	GET	CARDIN	
	.		
	.		
	.		
IN	DS	CL80	
	.		
	.		

In this case, when the GET instruction is executed, the IOCS will retrieve the next logical record from the file named CARDIN and will place the same in the 80 byte long area named IN.

Workname. This is an optional parameter for GET macro and, if specified represents the name of the work area into which a logical record is to be read. This parameter is used if records are to be processed in a work area which the programmer must define; for example, using a DS statement. The result of the GET instruction, when this option is used, is to move each individual record from the input area to the work area.

Example:

GET   INCARD,TEMP

Note: If work area option is specified, all GET instructions to the file must use the work area name. Only one file can be referenced with one GET instruction.

PUT Macro   Imperative Macro

This macro is used to write or punch logical records that have been built in a work area or directly in the output area for the file. It is used for an output file in the system. The PUT macro is identical to the GET macro in its logic, although its operation is opposite. The two formats of the PUT macro are:

PUT   filename
PUT   filename,workname

Filename. This is the first parameter of the PUT macro. The filename must be the same as specified in the header entry of the DTF for the file. In the following example, the record from the I/O area specified for the file named CARDOUT will be punched into a card (we are assuming that the name CARDOUT has been assigned to an output card file).

PUT   CARDOUT

Workname. This is an optional parameter and, if specified, represents the name of the work area from which a logical record is to be punched or written on the output file. This parameter is used if the programmer wishes to process (build) the records in a work area instead of the I/O area. When this option is used, it causes PUT instruction to move each record from the work area to the output area specified for that file.

PUT   CARDOUT,WORKAR

Note: 1. If the workname option is specified, all PUT instructions to the file must use the workname parameter. Only one file can be referenced with one PUT macro instruction.

2. Whenever a PUT instruction is executed it transfers the data from an output area (or work area) to an I/O device. The data remains in the area until it is replaced or cleared. Therefore, ,if the programmer plans to assemble another record with a different format, he must clear the output or the work area before he builds the new record.

Completion of processing

After processing has been completed, all the files which have been previously opened must be deactivated. To accomplish this, CLOSE macro is used.

CLOSE Macro   Imperative Macro

A CLOSE macro instruction may be issued at any time and the file(s) referenced will be deactivated. No further instructions can be issued for the file unless it is OPENed again. The CLOSE macro is generally written in the end-of-job routine. The format of this macro is:

CLOSE   file1,file2,file3.......

The symbolic name(s) of the file to be closed is entered in the operand field. A maximum of 16 files may be closed by one CLOSE macro instruction.

CLOSE   CARDIN,CARDOUT,REPORTS

Note: Any file being closed must have been opened previously. The symbolic filename must be the same as specified with the DTF macro(s) for the file(s).

EOJ Macro   Supervisor Macro

The very last step (not necessarily the last line) in a program is to inform the supervisory system that the job step is finished. To accomplish this, EOJ macro is used. The format of this macro is:

Name	Oper	Operand
	EOJ	

Upon execution of this macro instruction, the control is passed to the supervisor program. The operand field entry (if any) is ignored.

Figure 4.3 illustrates the DTF macro instructions for a program which will read a card file and will produce as output, punched cards and a printed report.

Name	Oper	Operand	
	START		
CARDIN	DTFCD	DEVADDR=SYSRDR,EOFADDR=NOCARD,	X
		IOAREA1=IN1,IOAREA2=IN2,	X
		WORKA=YES,	X
		RECFORM=FIXUNB	
CARDOUT	DTFCD	DEVADDR=SYS009,IOAREA1=OUT1,	X
		IOAREA2=OUT2,WORKA=YES,	X
		TYPEFLE=OUTPUT	
PRINTER	DTFPR	DEVADDR=SYS010,BLKSIZE=132,	X
		IOAREA1=LINE1,IOAREA2=LINE2,	X
		WORKA=YES	

FIGURE 4.3. Sample DTF Macro Entries.

The symbolic file names assigned to the three files are CARDIN, CARDOUT and PRINTER. As previously stated, the filenames must not exceed seven characters each. For the card input file we have specified two input areas and the work area option has been included indicating that records from this file will be processed in a work area.

The two I/O areas for the file, CARDIN, have been named IN1 and IN2. Actual areas in core for IN1, IN2 and the work area will have to be set aside by the programmer (usually by DS statements). As the work area option has been included, each GET to this file must use the work name option. An example of this follows.

GET   filename,workname

The EOFADDR=NOCARD entry specifies that at end-of-file condition, i.e., after all the records from this file have been processed, the IOCS will cause an automatic branch to the symbol NOCARD. This symbol usually is the entry point to the programmer's end-of-file routine. We have omitted the TYPEFLE and BLKSIZE entries for this file and the system will assume the default options, i.e., TYPEFLE= INPUT and BLKSIZE=80.

The symbolic name CARDOUT has been assigned to the card output file. Two I/O areas and the work area options have also been specified for this file. The print file named PRINTER, has basically the same options.

Note: 1. The EOFADDR entry is used for the input files only and never for the output files. The reason being that we do not want to end the job if the card punch or the printer unit runs out of cards or forms. It is only when there are no more input records to be processed that we would want to end the job. At end-of-file condition, the IOCS will cause an automatic branch to symbol which has been specified with the EOFADDR entry.

2. When logical records from a file are to be processed in a work area, the I/O area(s) for that file acts as buffers. The problem program in such cases must not reference these I/O areas as these areas participate in the I/O operations. Use of buffers increases execution efficiency as it enables the IOCS to perform I/O operations at the same time as the processing in the main program. Use of buffers, however, requires additional core storage.

The EOJ macro is used to terminate a program by transferring control back to the supervisory system.

Buffering

When we use a single I/O area to process logical records from a file, the sequence of operations in the CPU is such that a great amount of time is wasted as idle CPU time. Figure 4.4, below, illustrates the basic time and processing relationship between input, processing, and output without any overlapping of I/O with processing.

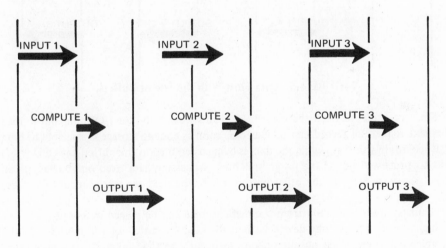

FIGURE 4.4. Data Flow Without Buffers.

In this type of data flow through the computer, the CPU sits idle during reading or writing operations. A waste of valuable time results, thus making the overall performance rather inefficient.

If the records from a file (or data set) are to be read into the storage or are to be written out in a sequential manner, the processing efficiency can be increased to a certain degree by overlapping the I/O operations with other functions of the computer system, e.g. processing of data. The technique used to accomplish this overlapping of

I/O operations is known as *buffering*.

Buffering basically involves setting of multiple I/O areas for reading in or writing out of physical records of a file. The data from the file is first read into a buffer and when instructed by the program, the contents of the buffer are transferred to the main storage. This transfer of data from a buffer to the main storage takes only a fraction of the time that would be taken to read the data directly from an input device.

Figure 4.5 illustrates the data flow through the computer system when buffering is utilized. The increased use of the CPU time is obvious.

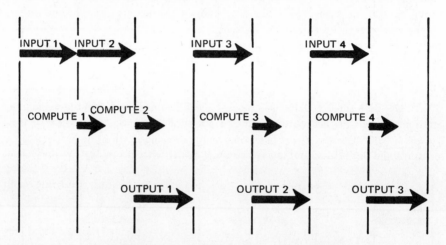

FIGURE 4.5. Data Flow With the Use of Buffers.

Since each record from the file is to be read sequentially, the I/O command to read the next sequential record can be issued as soon as enough storage is available to hold that record. In this way, while the data is being assembled in the buffer, the CPU is left free to process data. As the program is busy processing data from one buffer, it can direct the system to fill the other buffer(s) with the next sequential record from the file.

Similarly, processed data from the main storage can be placed in an output buffer at high speed. The output device is then directed to write out the contents of the completed buffer. While output operations occur, the CPU is free to continue other processing.

Note: When the program is finished using the data from one buffer, it initiates an I/O operation for it and then begins to process data from the next buffer, alternating through the buffers or a set of buffers. The IOCS of System 360 provides for *automatic* buffering when a programmer specifies *two* I/O areas for a file.

Processing Without Buffers. The following illustrations explain the sequence of events that take place when a card file is read using a single input area.

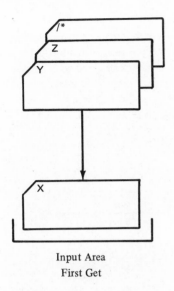

Input Area
First Get

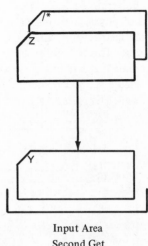

Input Area
Second Get

Upon executing a GET to the input file the IOCS causes the first card, X, to be read into the input area designated by the IOAREA1= entry for the file. A delay is caused as the I/O module checks to see if the card has been successfully read into main storage. At this time data is available for processing. These events are repeated till the end-of-file condition is recognized.

From this illustration it is clear that while a record is being read into the input area the CPU is not free to perform any other function, thus resulting in considerable loss of time. Efficiency of a program can be improved when multiple I/O areas are used to process records. The diagram on page 112 illustrates this process.

The first GET to the file causes the first record, X, to be read into INPUT1. Upon completion of the read operation the data is transferred from INPUT1 to the storage area designated by WORK. At this time the IOCS issues a command to read the second record, Y, into INPUT2. However, it does not wait until the reading operation has been completed before returning to the next sequential instruction in the problem program. At this point and time the record X is available for processing from the area named WORK. It is important to note that while the processing of data from WORK continues, the next record, Y, is being read into INPUT2. The next GET to the file causes the IOCS to transfer the data from INPUT2 to WORK. In addition to this the IOCS initiates the reading of the next record, Z, into the first IOAREA, the INPUT1. The effect is shown in the drawing on page 112.

These steps are followed through the reading of all of the records in the file until the I/O module senses the /* card. At this time the IOCS causes a branch to the routine designated by the EOFADDR= entry for the file.

Use of IOREG Entry. When IOREG= entry is specified in the DTF for the file, the sequence of events is as follows: Assuming IOREG=(3), see page 113 for sequence.

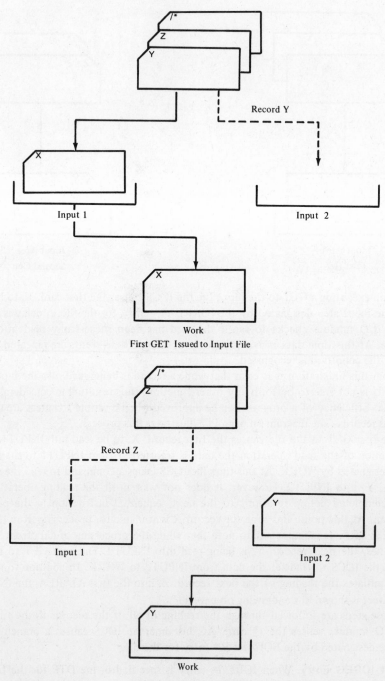

First GET Issued to Input File

Second GET Issued to Input File

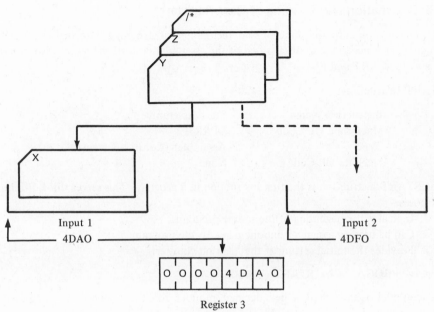

Register 3
First GET Issued to Input File

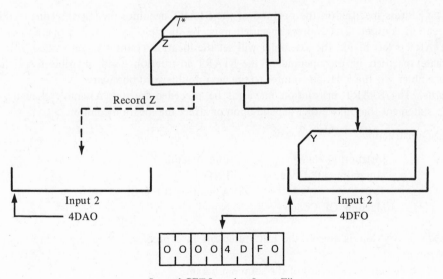

Second GET Issued to Input File

This process continues until the end-of-file condition is reached.

4.5 Designation and Loading of Base Registers

Before we look into the concept and techniques of assigning base register(s) for a program, it is necessary to discuss two of the assembler control statement instructions. These are START and END.

START Instruction

Instruction Name	Start Assembly
Mnemonic OP Code	START
Type	Assembler (Control Statement)
Machine OP Code	None

The START instruction is the first instruction in a program. This serves three different purposes:

1. Indicates the beginning of the source program.
2. Can be used to assign a symbolic name to the program.
3. Provides the initial setting of the location counter.

```
PROGA       START     4000
```

We could also have used a hexadecimal number for the operand of the START instruction.

```
PROGA       START     X'FA0'
```

The address specified in the operand of the START becomes the initial setting of the location counter. The address specified must be divisible by 8. If the operand of a START is left blank, the assembler will set the location counter to zero value. If the value specified in the operand of the START instruction is not divisible by 8 the assembler sets the location counter to the next doubleword boundary.

Note: The START instruction may not be preceded by any Assembler Language statement that may either depend upon or affect the location counter.

END Instruction

Instruction Name	End Assembly
Mnemonic OP Code	END
Type	Assembler (Program Control)
Machine OP Code	None

END instruction is always the last statement in a program. This serves three main purposes:

1. Indicates the last card of the source program.
2. Signals to the assembler to terminate assembly.
3. May also designate a point in the program, or in a separately assembled program, to which control is to be transferred after the program is loaded in core.

The END instruction usually contains in its operand field the symbolic name given to the *first machine* instruction of the program.

Name	Oper	Operand
	START	4000
	.	
	.	
BEGIN	BALR	7,0
	USING	*,7
	.	
	.	
	END	BEGIN

The operand portion of the END instruction could be left blank. In such a case, the control would be passed back to the first byte of the program. (The control goes to the first byte of the program and not the first byte of the core). We could have written:

Name	Oper	Operand
	START	4000
	.	
	.	
	.	
	BALR	7,0
	USING	*,7
	.	
	.	
	.	
	END	

Therefore, the question arises, why not leave the operand portion of the END instruction blank at all times? The answer to this should be clear after looking at this example.

Sometimes a programmer may wish to reserve I/O areas, for various files being used in a program, ahead of the processing instructions. To do this, the coding required would be:

Name	Oper	Operand
	START	4000
INA	DS	CL80
INB	DS	CL132
GO	BALR	7,0
	USING	*,7
	.	
	.	

(continued)

.

.

.

.

.

        END   GO

In the coding shown above, if the last instruction was written without any entry in the operand portion, at object time after the program load time, the control would be passed to the first byte of the program. In actuality, after the program has been loaded we would like the control to be passed to the first machine instruction so that the program execution can begin. As the first machine instruction is the BALR instruction, we have specified GO for the operand entry for the END statement.

START

1. START instruction is the first statement in a program.
2. START instruction is used to assign the initial setting to the location counter.
3. In case the operand entry of the START statement is omitted, the location counter will be set to zero value by the assembler.
4. If an entry from another program is desired, the START statement should be assigned a symbolic name.

END

1. END instruction is the last statement in a program.
2. END instruction terminates the assembly process.
3. If the END instruction contains an operand entry, the loader will pass control to that location after loading the program.
4. If the operand entry is omitted, the control is passed to the FIRST BYTE of the program.

EQU — Equate Symbol: This instruction is used to define a symbol by assigning to it the length, value, and relocatability attributes of an expression in the operand field. The expression in the operand field may be absolute or relocatable. Any symbol appearing in the expression must be previously defined. This instruction can be used to equate symbols to register numbers, immediate data, and other arbitrary values.

Name	Oper	Operand
R2	EQU	2
OUTNAME	EQU	LINE+10
ALPHA	EQU	BETA—GAMMA

Note: LINE, BETA and GAMMA must all be previously defined.

It is a good practice to equate all registers used in a program to some symbol, such as Rn or REGn, where n stands for the register number. When this is done the cross-reference dictionary of the object listing gives the register usage at a glance.

Designating and loading of base registers

In Section 2.3, we discussed one of the important programming features of System 360, i.e., use of the base register and displacement for addressing. This addressing method provides us with two significant advantages. These are:

1. Compatibility between smaller and larger systems for core addressing and, at the same time, saving of core by reducing the length of certain instruction operands.
2. Relocatability of assembled programs.

When writing Assembler Language instructions, a programmer may choose to write explicit addresses, i.e., specify base register and displacement amount, or he may delegate to the assembler the tedious and routine task of assigning base registers and calculating displacements. The latter method, the easier of the two, involves writing of symbolic addresses. In order to be able to use symbolic addresses, the programmer must inform the assembler of the following:

1. Which general register(s) is to be used as the base register.
2. What address[10] will be in the base register(s) at the object time.
3. Write the necessary instruction(s) to place the base address in the base register(s).

The first two objectives are accomplished by the USING instruction. While there are many ways of accomplishing the third objective, the most common one is to use the BALR instruction.

USING (Use Base Address Register: The USING instruction informs the assembler which general register(s) is available for use as the base register(s). This instruction also indicates to the assembler the address values these registers will contain at *object time.* Note, that this instruction does not load the registers specified with the specific address values. It is the programmer's responsibility to load the specified base addresses into these registers. The format of the USING instruction is:

Name	Oper	Operand
	USING	v,r1,r2,r3,....r16

The first operand entry, v, is an address value which can be either a symbolic name or an asterisk. When the v operand is an asterisk (*), it tells the assembler it may assume that the current value of the location counter will be in the base register at object time. The operand entry r1 specifies the general register that will contain the address indicated by the operand v. Operands r2,r3,r4... (if present) refer to additional base registers that are needed by this program. When these additional base registers are specified, the assembler assumes that the r2 register will contain an address value equal to the current value of the location counter + 4096, r3 register a value equal to the current location counter setting + 8192. Each register designated is assumed by the assembler to hold a value 4096 greater than the previous register.

[10]This address is known as the base address.

Example:

Name	Operation	Operand
	USING	*,10,11

This tells the assembler that it may assume that the current value of the location counter will be in general register 10 at object time, and that register 11 will contain a value equal to the current value of location counter + 4096.

Note: 1. Register numbers specified as r1,r2,r3....may appear in any order. The values of the operands r1,r2,r3,r4....r16 must be between 0 and 15.

2. The using instruction is an assembler instruction and, as such, takes no space in the object program.

3. If register 0 is used as the base register, the program is not relocatable. The program can be made relocatable if the programmer: replaces register 0 in the USING statement with another register; loads the new base register with a relocatable value; and, reassembles the program.

Branch and Link

There are two types of Branch and Link instructions. These are:

BALR	RR Type
BAL	RX Type

In this section we will discuss only the BALR instruction, since the BAL instruction is discussed in Section 6.1.

Mnemonic OP Code	BALR
Machine OP Code	05
Type	RR
Length	2 Bytes

Machine Format:

OP	R1	R2
0 7	8 11	12 15

Symbolic Format: BALR   R1,R2

The net effect of this instruction is to store the address of the next machine instruction in the register specified as R1, and then branch to the address specified as R2[11]. For example, let us assume that register 7 contains a value of $(4000)_{10}$ and the instruction is:

[11]This is done by loading the rightmost 32 bits of the PSW in the register specified as R1. This portion of PSW, as previously mentioned, contains the next instruction address. Although the instruction address is made up of only 24 low-order bits in the PSW, the extra 8 high-order bits do not cause any trouble.

Name	Oper	Operand
	BALR	5,7

The BALR instruction will first load the address of the next available instruction in register 5 and then a branch will be taken to the core address $(4000)_{10}$.

Let us look at another example.

Name	Oper	Operand
	START	256
	BALR	5,7
	MVC	SAVE,CARD
	.	
	.	
	.	
	.	

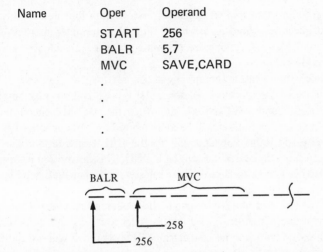

In this case, the BALR instruction will load the address of the next machine instruction. The address value loaded into register 5 will be $(258)_{10}$, and then a branch will be taken to core address $(4000)_{10}$. There is one important variation of this instruction. In case the R2 register operand is specified as zero, the next machine address (also known as link information) is stored without branching.

Let us now look at the USING and BALR instructions to see how the loading of the base registers is handled.

Name	Oper	Operand
	START	256
BEGIN	BALR	5,0
	USING	*,5
	GET	CARDIN
	MVC	SAVE,CARD
	.	
	.	
	.	
	.	

(Continued)

.

.

.

.

.

END   BEGIN

At this time, it is very important to distinguish between what is done at assembly time and what is done at execution time. At *assembly* time, the assembler instructions are executed and the machine instructions are assembled. During the object time, the machine instructions are executed.

At assembly time, the location counter will be set to 256 by the START instruction. As the START instruction is an assembler type, it will not take any space in core and the location counter will stay at 256. When the assembler encounters the BALR instruction, the location counter will be incremented by 2, the length of BALR, and it will assign core positions 256 and 257 to the BALR instruction. The next instruction encountered by the assembler will be USING. This instruction informs the assembler: that register 5 is to be used as the base register; and, that the assembler is to assume 258 to be the base address.

From this step on, the assembler will assign the base register and will calculate displacements of symbolic addresses. These base register numbers and displacements become part of the assembled machine instructions. The assembler will not, however, load the base address into the base register during the assembly time, since that can be done only when the program is executed. The actual loading of the base address takes place at object time and is accomplished by the BALR instruction. It has probably been noticed that the *starting address is not the same as the base address.*

For the next few chapters, it will be assumed that the programs in the text and also those we write require only one base register. Use of multiple base registers is discussed in Chapter 11.

Relocatability & relocation

Let us assume that after assembling a program we were to decide on a new starting address. This may be to avoid conflict with other programs in core. The use of the base and displacement method of addressing allows us to do this without having to reassemble the whole program. For example, let us assume that a program assembled with a starting address of 256 had to be relocated to a starting address of 1200. With an appropriate control card, we can inform the relocatable loader that the first byte of the program is to go into address 1200. When the program is loaded and execution begins the first instruction will be assigned core location 1200. The address assigned to the next instruction (*see* illustration below) will be 1202. When BALR instruction is executed, the value loaded into the base register will be 1202 and it will become the base address. The displacements in the assembled instructions have not been affected, thus the effective addresses calculated will always be displacement value + 1202.

Thus, a complete relocation of a program after assembly is possible with a simple control card.

Note: For the next few chapters we will assume that the programs in the text and also written by you, as programmer, require only one base register. Use of multiple base registers is duscussed in Chapter 11.

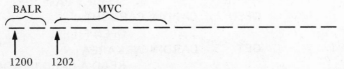

A problem with a suggested solution

We are to read a card file and for each card read, we are to punch out a duplicate card. Assume a 2540 card-read-punch unit. Figure 4.6 contains the block diagram and Figure 4.7 is the coding.

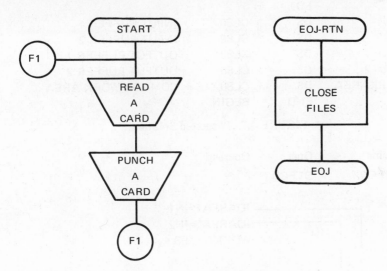

FIGURE 4.6. Suggested Flowchart.

Name	Oper	Operand	
	START		
CARDIN	DTFCD	DEVADDR=SYS008,IOAREA1=IN1,	X
		DEVICE=2540,	1
		EOFADDR=PROGEND,IOAREA2=IN2,	X
		WORKA=YES,	2
		TYPEFLE=INPUT	

(continued)

```
CARDOUT    DTFCD     DEVADDR=SYS009,IOAREA1=OUT1,       X
                     DEVICE=2540,                       1
                     IOAREA2=OUT2,TYPEFLE=OUTPUT,       X
                     WORKA=YES
BEGIN      BALR      2,0         LOAD BASE REGISTER
           USING     *,2         SPECIFY BASE REG
           OPEN      CARDIN,CARDOUT
*                                OPEN FILES
F1         GET       CARDIN,WRKAREA
*                                READ A CARD IN WORK AREA
           PUT       CARDOUT,WRKAREA
*                                PUNCH CARD FROM WORK AREA
           BC        15,F1       SEE NOTE BELOW
PROGEND    CLOSE     CARDIN,CARDOUT
*                                CLOSE FILES
           EOJ
IN1        DS        CL80        INPUT BUFFER 1
IN2        DS        CL80        INPUT BUFFER 2
OUT1       DS        CL80        OUTPUT BUFFER 1
OUT2       DS        CL80        OUTPUT BUFFER 2
WRKAREA    DS        CL80        COMMON WORK AREA
           END       BEGIN
```

FIGURE 4.7.   Suggested Solution.

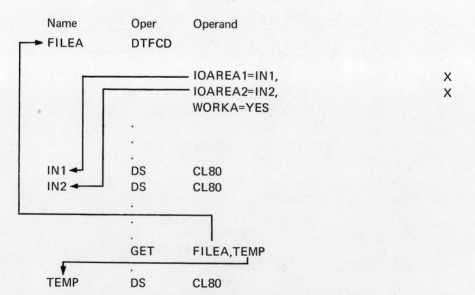

Name	Oper	Operand
FILEA	DTFCD	
		IOAREA1=IN1, X
		IOAREA2=IN2, X
		WORKA=YES
IN1	DS	CL80
IN2	DS	CL80
	GET	FILEA,TEMP
TEMP	DS	CL80

FIGURE 4.8.   Relationship Between I/O and Work Areas.

Note: The BC 15,F1 is an unconditional branch instruction, at program execution time this instruction will cause a branch to the label F1. This instruction is explained in Section 5.2.

Figure 4.8 illustrates the basic relationship between the I/O areas, work area and the DS statements required to set aside I/O and work areas in core.

Dummy section

A dummy section represents a control section that is assembled but is not part of the object program. This is a convenient means of describing the layout of an area of storage without actually reserving the storage. The coding example that follows illustrates the use of a dummy section.

```
Name        Oper     Operand

            START
CARDIN      DTFCD    DEVADDR=SYSRDR,IOAREA1=IN1,          X
                     IOAREA2=IN2,                         X
                     EOFADDR=NOCARD,IOREG=(3)
PRINTFL     DTFPR    DEVADDR=SYSLST,IOAREA1=OUT 1,        X
                     IOAREA2=OUT2,                        X
                     BLKSIZE=97,IOREG=(4)
BEGIN       BALR     2,0
            USING    *,2
            OPEN     CARDIN,PRINTFL
            USING    CARD,3   USING FOR INPUT DUMMY SECTION
            USING    LINE,4     USING FOR OUTPUT DUMMY SECTION
            MVI      LINE,C' '
            MVC      LINE+1(96),LINE
READ        GET      CARDIN
            MVC      NUMBERPR,NUMBERCD
            MVC      NAMEPR,NAMECD
            MVC      ADDRSPR,ADDRSCD
            PUT      PRINTFL
            BC       15,READ
NOCARD      CLOSE    CARDIN,PRINTFL
            EOJ
IN1         DS       CL80
IN2         DS       CL80
OUT1        DS       CL97
OUT2        DS       CL97
CARD        DSECT            DUMMY SECTION FOR INPUT
NUMBERCD    DS       CL5
```

(continued)

```
NAMECD      DS        CL20
ADDRSCD     DS        CL45
            DS        CL10
LINE        DSECT               DUMMY SECTION FOR OUTPUT
            DS        CL10
NUMBERPR    DS        CL5
            DS        CL9
NAMEPR      DS        CL20
            DS        CL8
ADDRSPR     DS        CL45
            END       BEGIN
```

There are two important points to remember when using DSECT to achieve symbolic addressing of this type. These are:

1. Programmer must write USING statement specifying both a general register that the assembler can assign to the machine instructions as a base register, and a value from the dummy section that assembler may assume the register contains.

2. Programmer must also make sure that the register stated in the USING statement is loaded with the actual address of the storage area. In the case of the problem coded above, this particular function is performed by the I/O module each time a GET is issued to the input file and a PUT is issued to the output file.

Self Evaluation Quiz

1. Draw a flow chart and write the necessary coding to read a card file and to produce the following outputs:

   a. For each card read, punch out two cards. Output cards to have the same format as the input cards.

   b. List each input card on the printer.

Assume a 2540 card read-punch unit and a 1403 printer.

[5]

Introduction to Data Movement and Branching

5.1 Self-Defining Terms

A self-defining term is one whose value is inherent (explicit) in the term. A self-defining term is not given any value by the assembler. For example, a self-defining term "10" represents a value of ten. There are four types of self-defining terms:

1. Decimal.
2. Hexadecimal.
3. Binary.
4. Character.

Decimal self-defining terms

A decimal self-defining term is an unsigned decimal number and is written as a sequence of decimal digits. Use of high-order insignificant zeros is allowed. A decimal self-defining term may not exceed 8 digits, nor have a value which is greater than 16,775,215. A decimal term is translated into its binary equivalent by the assembler. Some examples of the decimal terms are 1, 10, 007, 1100, etc.

Hexadecimal self-defining terms

A hexadecimal self-defining term is a sequence of hexadecimal digits. The maximum value allowed is six hexadecimal digits. The terms must be enclosed between single quotation marks and preceded by the letter X, for example X'FF', X'123', etc. Each hexadecimal digit is assembled into a 4 bit binary equivalent. The maximum value of a hexadecimal term is X'FFFFFF'.

Binary self-defining terms

A binary self-defining term is composed of a series of binary digits, i.e., 1's and 0's. The term must be enclosed within single quotation marks and preceded by the letter B, for example, B'1001', B'11001'. The maximum length of a binary term is 24 bits or 3 bytes.

Character self-defining terms

A character self-defining term consists of one through three characters enclosed in single quotation marks and preceded by the letter C, for example, C'ABC'. Any of the 256 possible punch combinations may be used in a character self-defining term. For example:

```
C' ' (blank)
C'/'
C'ABC'
C'12C'
```

Because of the use of ampersand[1] in the macro language and the apostrophes in the Assembler Language as syntatic characters, special rules must be observed when these two characters are used in a self-defining term.

For each apostrophe or ampersand written in the body of a character-type self-defining term, two must be written. For example, if the term IT'S was desired, it must be coded as:

```
             DC          C'IT''S'
```

To obtain the term C'# the constant must be coded as:

```
             DC          C'C''#'
```

Each character written in a character self-defining term is assembled as its 8-bit EBCDIC equivalent. Each pair of ampersands or apostrophes is assembled as a single ampersand or apostrophe.

Instruction execution and branching

A logical series of instructions, used to solve a problem on a computer, is known as a *program*. System 360 programs are also referred to as *stored programs* because of the fact that a program is kept in the core storage during execution. The stored instructions are read out of the core storage one at a time and decoded in the control section of the CPU. The next phase is the actual execution of the instruction and this phase takes place in the ALU (Arithmetic Logic Unit) section of the CPU. Instruction execution can be divided into I-Time, and E-Time.

I-Time. During I-time of the instruction execution, the instruction is fetched from the main storage and brought into the control section for decoding.

---

[1] Written as &.

E-Time. During E-time the operation specified by the instruction is performed.

When execution has been completed, the next fetch cycle begins which is in turn followed by an execution cycle and this process is repeated. In System 360, there is no clear distinction between the I and E time. That is, before an instruction has been completely fetched and decoded by the control section, the execution cycle has already begun, thus giving an overlapping effect. However, for all practical purposes the two cycles can be treated as being separate and distinct.

Instructions are located in adjacent bytes and are normally executed in a sequential manner. This sequential manner of instruction fetching and execution can be interrupted by special instructions known as branch instructions. Thus, when the next instruction is read out from a non-sequential location, we say that branching has occurred. The question arises as to how the computer (CPU) keeps track of the address of the next sequential instruction, or how a branch is taken. In order to understand this clearly, we need to investigate the functions of the Program Status Word (PSW).

PSW. In System 360, there is a doubleword area which is used to control and indicate the status of the "current" program. The PSW, which is being used with the program, is not kept in either the main storage or the general registers. It is part of the internal machine circuitry and, as such, is not easily changed. The PSW consists of seven different fields which indicate the status of the program *currently* being executed. For this reason, it is often referred to as the *current* PSW. The different fields of a PSW indicate such status information as: the location of the next instruction to be executed; the result of a compare instruction; and, the result of an arithmetic operation, etc.

The PSW being a doubleword contains 8 bytes.

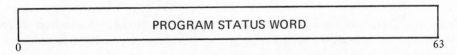

Of all the seven fields of a PSW, we are presently concerned with only one field which occupies bit locations 40 through 63. This 24-bit long area is known as *instruction address* portion. This particular field contains the location of the next instruction to be fetched from the core storage.

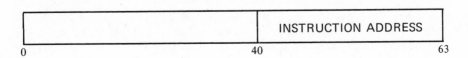

When a program is loaded into the core storage the last card of the object program, the END card, informs the CPU of the address of the first machine instruction of the program.

Name	Oper	Operand
	START	256
	DTFCD	....
	.	
	.	
	.	
	.	
BEGIN	BALR	3,0
	USING	*,3
	.	
	.	
	.	
	.	
	END	BEGIN

The CPU places this address into the address portion of the current PSW and the first fetch cycle begins. To fetch an instruction from the core, the CPU obtains its address from the instruction address portion of the PSW. This instruction address portion of the PSW is automatically updated for each instruction fetched and executed. That is, the length value of the instruction is added to the instruction address portion. After updating this portion of the PSW the address will indicate the address of the next instruction to be fetched. Let us assume that an RX type of instruction is fetched from location 3000, and the instruction address portion of the PSW will be incremented by 4^2 which makes it 3004. The instruction address portion now indicates the location of the next instruction.

We have seen how sequential instructions are fetched and executed. What happens when a branch instruction is encountered by the CPU? When a branch instruction is executed, the instruction address portion of the PSW is replaced by the address of the instruction being branched to. To illustrate, let us assume that an RX type of branch instruction is fetched from core location 4000. Under normal circumstances, the instruction address portion of the PSW will be updated by a value of 4, the length of the RX type of instruction. This, however, being a branch instruction, the instruction address portion will be *replaced* by the branch address contained in the branch instruction. Let us take a look at Figure 5.1 which explains the fetching and execution of instructions.

The actual sequence of events which takes place when the CPU encounters a branch instruction depends upon the instruction type and also the model of System 360. Figure 5.2 shows that the instruction address portion of the PSW is first updated by the instruction length and then is replaced by the branch address. On the other hand, Figure 5.1 indicates that the instruction address portion is replaced by the branch address directly. For us, as application programmers, the important step to note is that

[2] The length value of an instruction is obtained by the CPU by analyzing the high-order byte of the instruction.

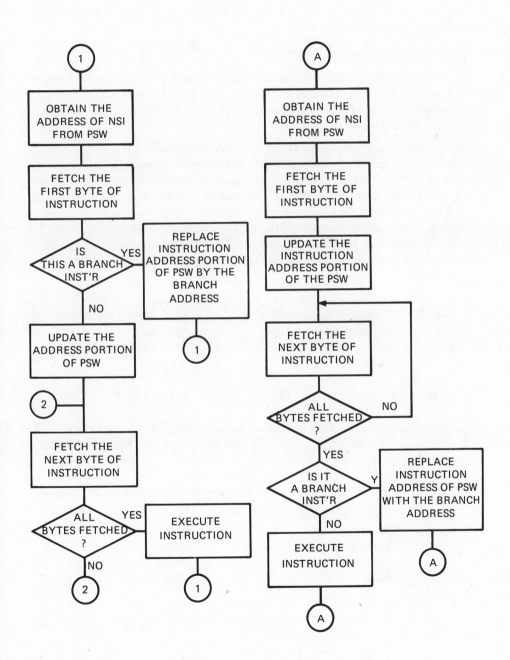

FIGURE 5.1. and FIGURE 5.2. Fetching and Execution of Instructions.

when the CPU decides to take a branch, the address of the *branch to* location is placed in the instruction address portion of the PSW. This field as you know is located in bits 40 through 63 of the PSW.

Relative addressing

Relative Addressing is the technique of addressing undefined (un-named) areas in core in relation to the location counter or to some symbolic location. The area or location being referenced may be an instruction or data area. This type of addressing is always in bytes, never in bits.

Relative Addressing of Data Areas. The Relative addressing method is generally used to reduce the number of symbols in a program. The assembler program has a limit on the number of symbols[3] that can be used in a program. When too many symbols are used, the assembly time increases because of the need to look up symbols in the symbol table. Thus, whenever a need arises to refer to locations just a few bytes away, relative addressing can be used to increase efficiency. Nonetheless, symbols are still needed to refer to locations that are quite far apart. To illustrate this discussion, let us take a look at an employee's name and address card. The card record contains the following fields.

Employee Number	c.c.	1 – 5
Employee Name		10 – 30
Street Address		35 – 50
City		55 – 67
State		70 – 74

IN   DS   CL80

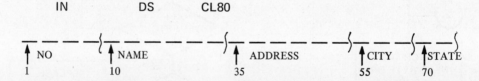

Using the relative addressing method we could reference the various fields as follows:

Employee Number	IN
Employee Name	IN+9
Street Address	IN+34
City	IN+54
State	IN+69

A + sign following a symbol means that the byte being referenced is located to the right of the symbol. Use of a – (minus) sign is also permitted. A minus sign indicates that the data is located to the left of the symbol.

---

[3] This is mainly dependent on the storage capacity of the computer.

Relative Addressing of Instructions. In order to relatively reference instructions, the programmer can use either a symbol or an asterisk as the referencing point. The example that follows illustrates this technique.

Name	Oper	Operand
BEGIN	SR	1,1
	MVC	FLDA,FLDB
	AR	1,7
	LH	3,FLDC
	BC	15,*−14

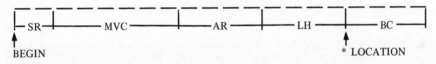

(Remember, * indicates the current location counter setting.)

In the above sequence of instructions, if you were to write a branch instruction to branch back to the MVC instruction with reference to a symbol, the instruction would be:

BC   15,BEGIN+2

Introduction to data movement

MOVE CHARACTERS

Mnemonic Code	MVC
Machine Code	D2 (HEX)
Type	Storage to Storage (SS) with one length code
Length	6 bytes
Symbolic Format:	MVC D1(L,B1),D2(B2)

Note: Only one length code is associated with this instruction.
Functions: To move data from one core location to another. To transfer the contents of the second operand to the first operand location.

Program Interruptions Protection, Addressing[4].
Condition Code   Not affected.

As this is a storage-to-storage type of instruction, the movement of data occurs within the storage. The first operand is the receiving field and the second operand is the sending field.

[4]For explanation of interrupts, refer to Appendix 1.

Various characteristics of this instruction are:
1. The movement of data occurs from left to right, i.e., high-order to low-order.
2. Data are moved one byte at a time.
3. The number of bytes moved is governed by the length of the first operand. The assembler assumes that the sending field is the same length as the receiving field.
4. A maximum of 256 bytes can be moved with one MVC instruction. (The reason for this is since the length code is one byte long, the maximum number which can be specified is $(1111\ 1111)_2 \equiv (255)_{10}$. As all operands are at least one byte in length the maximum number of bytes affected is 255+1=256.)
5. The contents of the second operand are copied and moved to the first operand location. The contents of the second operand location *do not alter*.

Let us look at some examples of MVC instruction.

Example:

A   B   C   D   1   2   3   4
└──FLDA   └──FLDB

MVC   FLDA,FLDB   MOVE FLDB TO FLDA

Result: Four bytes from FLDB will be moved to FLDA, as the implied length of the receiving field is 4 bytes.

1   2   3   4   1   2   3   4
└──FLDA   └── FLDB

The sending field does not alter.

Example:

A   B   C   D   1   2   3   4
└── FLDA   └──FLDC

MVC   FLDA(2),FLDC

In this case, an explicit length of 2 bytes has been specified for the first operand. At this point it is necessary to recall that when explicit length is assigned, the implied length of the field is ignored. By writing an explicit length of 2, the length of the receiving field has been reduced to 2 bytes. Thus, the instruction now means, move to the two high-order bytes of FLDA the contents of the two high-order bytes of FLDC. The result will be:

$$\underset{\uparrow}{\underline{1}} \quad \underline{2} \quad \underline{C} \quad \underline{D}$$

└── FLDA

$$\underset{\uparrow}{\underline{1}} \quad \underline{2} \quad \underline{3} \quad \underline{4}$$

└── FLDC

Example:

Original contents:

$$\underset{\uparrow}{\underline{1}} \quad \underline{2} \quad \underline{3}$$

└── FLDA

$$\underset{\uparrow}{\underline{A}} \quad \underline{B} \quad \underline{C}$$

└──FLDB

MVC FLDB(1),FLDA

The first operand of this instruction specifies an explicit length of one byte; thus, the number of moves made will only be one. The result will be the transfer of the high-order byte of FLDA to the corresponding byte of FLDB.

Result:

$$\underset{\uparrow}{\underline{1}} \quad \underline{2} \quad \underline{3}$$

└──FLDA

$$\underset{\uparrow}{\underline{1}} \quad \underline{B} \quad \underline{C}$$

└──FLDB

Example:

Original contents:

$$\underset{\uparrow}{\underline{1}} \quad \underline{2} \quad \underline{3} \quad \underline{4} \quad \underline{5}$$

└── FLDA

$$\underset{\uparrow}{\underline{X}} \quad \underline{Y} \quad \underline{Z} \quad \underline{C} \quad \underline{D} \quad \underline{E}$$

└── FLDB

Move the 2 bytes containing Y and Z to the high-order 2 bytes of FLDA.

MVC FLDA(2),FLDB+1

Result:

$$\underline{Y} \quad \underset{\uparrow}{\underline{Z}} \quad \underline{3} \quad \underline{4} \quad \underline{5}$$

└──FLDA

$$\underset{\uparrow}{\underline{X}} \quad \underline{Y} \quad \underline{Z} \quad \underline{C} \quad \underline{D} \quad \underline{E}$$

└──FLDB

Example:

Let us see what the result would be if we were to write our instruction without any explicit length for the first operand.

Original contents:

$$\underset{\uparrow}{\underline{1}} \quad \underline{2} \quad \underline{3} \quad \underline{4} \quad \underline{5}$$

└── FLDA

$$\underset{\uparrow}{\underline{X}} \quad \underline{Y} \quad \underline{Z} \quad \underline{C} \quad \underline{D} \quad \underline{E}$$

└──FLDB

MVC FLDA,FLDB+1

This instruction does not specify any explicit length; thus, the number of moves made would be equal to the implied length of the first operand. In all, five moves would result.

Result: $\underline{Y \quad Z \quad C \quad D \quad E}$ $\underline{X \quad Y \quad Z \quad C \quad D \quad E}$
⬆——FLDA   ⬆——FLDB

It is important to note that the first byte moved from FLDB is the one that contains the character Y.

Example:

Original contents: $\underline{A \quad B \quad C \quad D \quad E \quad F \quad G \quad 1 \quad 2 \quad 3 \quad 4 \quad 5 \quad 6 \quad 7 \quad 8}$
FLDA—⬆   ⬆——FLDA+2   ⬆—FLDB   ⬆—FLDB+3

MVC   FLDA+2(3),FLDB+3

In this case, the receiving field, FLDA, starts from 'high-order plus 2' and the sending field, FLDB, starts at 'FLDB plus 3'. The first operand has an explicit length of three bytes so only three moves will be made.

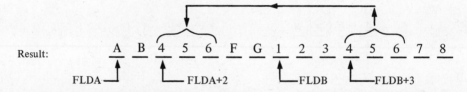

Result: $\underline{A \quad B \quad 4 \quad 5 \quad 6 \quad F \quad G \quad 1 \quad 2 \quad 3 \quad 4 \quad 5 \quad 6 \quad 7 \quad 8}$
FLDA—⬆   ⬆—— FLDA+2   ⬆—FLDB   ⬆—FLDB+3

Only 3 bytes of the receiving field are replaced by the 3 bytes of the sending field.
Note: If a character adjustment is specified for the first operation, it is important that you specify the length of the remainder of the field.

Overlapping of Fields. With MOVE instruction we can overlap the sending and the receiving field. This method is generally used to propagate the same character throughout a field. Let us say we have a DS and a DC statement as follows:

```
FLDA        DS        CL10
BLANK       DC        C' '
```

The first statement will set aside ten positions in core and the high-order position of the area set aside will be labeled FLDA. At this time, the contents of this area are unknown. The second statement will set aside one position in core storage and a blank will be entered into this byte by the assembler. This particular byte will be labeled BLANK.

To set FLDA to blanks, first move the blank character to the high-order position of the FLDA by the following instruction.

MVC   FLDA(1),BLANK

The result will be:

$$b \quad ? \quad ? \quad ? \quad ? \quad ? \quad ? \quad ? \quad ? \quad ?$$

⬆
└─ FLDA

"?" means that the contents are unknown.

"b" denotes the presence of a blank character.

Now we can use the MVC instruction to propagate the blank character throughout the length of FLDA. To do this, write the MVC instruction so that the first operand starts one position to the right of the second operand. The instruction will be:

MVC   FLDA+1(9),FLDA

The blank character will be propagated throughout the length of FLDA.

Note: We have to specify an explicit length of 9 bytes for the receiving field as we need to move only 9 blanks. The first blank has been moved to the high-order byte of the field by the previous instruction.

As an explanation, let us assume that FLDA is located from position 6000 to 6009. The instruction above will first move the contents of byte 6000 to 6001 as follows:

FLDA = 6000   and   FLDA+1 = 6001

Now, as the receiving operand has an explicit length of 9 bytes, 9 cycles in all will be taken. In the second cycle the instruction will move the contents of byte 6001 to 6002 and so on, until 9 moves have been made.

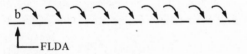

⬆
└─ FLDA

It is important to note that the explicit length specified is only 9. If the instruction was written without any explicit length, it would be as follows:

MVC   FLDA,BLANK

The result would be in all, 10 moves, equal to the implied length of FLDA. This would be wrong as the instructions would take us outside the boundaries of FLDA.

MVC instructions can be written with implicit length or explicit length and/or addresses.

Example:

Implicit address and implicit length for both operands.

MVC   FLDA,FLDB

The addresses of both operands are implied and taken from the area-defining statements as is the length code of the first operand.

Example:

Implicit addresses for both operands but explicit length assigned to the first operand:

MVC   FLDA(4),FLDB

Example:

Explicit addresses and length value for both operands, the format followed is:

D1(L1,B1),D2(B2)

The programmer specifies actual base register(s), the amount of displacement of each field, and a length code for the first operand.

MVC   436(4,8),408(8)

To calculate the core storage address of the first operand, the assembler will add the contents of the base register 8 and the displacement amount of 436. The length specified for the first operand is 4 bytes. The location of the second operand will be calculated by adding together the contents of the base register 8 and the displacement amount of 408.

Note: An explicit length *cannot* be specified for the second operand of MVC instruction, thus:

MVC   FLDA,FLDB(2)

would be wrong.

Example:

Given two areas IN and OUT, the area named IN contains name and address information. Move this information to the area named OUT. The format of these two areas is as follows:

	IN	OUT
I.D. Number	1 − 4	11 − 14
Name	6 − 26	20 − 42
First Init.	6	20
Middle Init.	7	22
Last Name	8 − 26	24 − 42
Street Address	30 − 50	50 − 70
City	55 − 67	75 − 87
State	70 − 73	90 − 93
Zip Code	75 − 79	96 − 100

Name	Oper	Operand	
	MVC	OUT+10(4),IN	MOVE NUMBER

(continued)

```
        MVC     OUT+19(1),IN+5      MOVE FIRST INITIAL
        MVC     OUT+21(1),IN+6      MOVE MIDDLE INITIAL
        MVC     OUT+23(19),IN+7     MOVE LAST NAME
        MVC     OUT+49(21),IN+29    MOVE STREET ADDRESS
        MVC     OUT+74(13),IN+54    MOVE CITY
        MVC     OUT+89(4),IN+69     MOVE STATE
        MVC     OUT+95(5),IN+74     MOVE ZIP CODE
```

EXERCISE

What will be the contents of FLDA after the execution of the following instructions?

```
        MVC     FLDA,FLDA
        MVC     FLDA+2,FLDB
        .
        .
FLDA    DC      CL4'ABCD'
FLDB    DC      C'12XYZ'
        .
```

MOVE IMMEDIATE

Mnemonic Code	MVI
Machine Code	92
Type	Immediate data and Storage (SI)
Length	4 bytes
Symbolic Format	MVI D1(B1),I2

Function: To move 1 byte of immediate data to a storage location.

Program Interruptions	Protection, addressing
Condition Code	Not affected

One byte of immediate data is moved to the first operand location. Immediate data is stored in the instruction and is identified as I2.

As the I2 field is only 1 byte in length, we can move only 1 byte long data or we could say:

MVI INSTRUCTION HAS AN IMPLIED LENGTH OF ONE

The I2 field could be any character as long as it can be contained in 1 byte, i.e., 8-bit binary number, 2 hexadecimal characters, 1 EBCDIC character, or, any decimal number as long as its value does not exceed 255.

The data to be moved, which is the I2 field, is specified as a self-defining term. During assembly time, this data is translated into 8-bit binary format and inserted into the I2 field of the instruction. The programmer may specify the self-defining term in any one of the following ways:

1. An 8-bit binary self-defining term. Eight binary digits must be specified.
2. A hexadecimal self-defining term may be specified. In this case 2 hex digits must be included. Each of the hex digits is translated into its 4-bit binary equivalent.
3. A one-character self-defining term may be used. Only one character may be specified. The character specified will be translated into its 8-bit EBCDIC equivalent.
4. A decimal self-defining term may be used as long as its value does not exceed 255.

These restrictions imposed on self-defining terms apply only to the I2 field of SI type instructions.

Example:

Suppose we are required to move an EBCDIC character 'B' to the high-order position of an area named HOLD. The instruction would be:

Original Contents   1   2   3   4   5
                     └── HOLD

          MVI   HOLD,C'B'

Result: B   2   3   4   5
                     └── HOLD

Example

Required to move character 'A' to the low-order position of a field named SAVE.

Original contents   Y   X   Z   3
                     └── SAVE

          MVI   SAVE+3,C'A'

Result: X   Y   Z   A
                     └── SAVE

Example

Move a blank to the high-order position of an area named HOLD.

Original contents   A   B   C   D   E   F   G
                     └── HOLD

          MVI   HOLD,C' '

Result:

```
  b  B  C  D  E  F  G
  ↑
  └─HOLD
```

The I2 field can be specified in binary, hex, decimal or EBCDIC format. For example, to move character 'B' to an area named HOLD, we could write our instruction in any one of the following methods.

Name	Oper	Operand	
	MVI	HOLD,C'B'	EBCDIC FOR B
	MVI	HOLD,X'C2'	HEX FOR B
	MVI	HOLD,B'11000010'	BINARY FOR B
	MVI	HOLD,194	DECIMAL FOR B

Note: MVI instruction has no length code, so an explicit length cannot be specified. The instruction has an implied length of 1 byte. Following is an *invalid* instruction:

MVI   HOLD(1),C'B'

The combination of MVI and MVC instructions can be used to propagate the same character throughout an area. This combination is usually used to set an area to blanks. For example, the following DS statement will set aside 80 positions in core. The contents of this area are unpredictable.

CARDOUT   DS   CL80

```
  ?  ?  ?  ?  ?  ?  ?  ?  ?  ──────────  ?  ?
  ↑
  └─ CARDOUT
```

To clear this area we could write the following instructions:

MVC   CARDOUT,C' '
MVC   CARDOUT+1(79),CARDOUT

The first instruction moves one blank to the high-order position of the area named CARDOUT. MVC instruction then moves the high-order byte to the next byte to its right. As we have overlapped the sending field, the blank will be moved to the rest of the field. Another method of clearing storage areas without the use of a MVI instruction is illustrated below.

```
              .
        MVC       CARDOUT,CARDOUT−1
              .
        DC        D' '
CARDOUT DS        CL80
              .
```

Example:

At times we may be required to clear storage areas which are more than 256 bytes long. For example, consider a 600 bytes long area named LONGAREA. To set this area to blanks a sequence of instructions somewhat like the following could be used.

Name	Oper	Operand
	.	
	.	
	MVI	LONGAREA,C' '
	MVC	LONGAREA+1(199),LONGAREA
	MVC	LONGAREA+200(200),LONGAREA+199
	MVC	LONGAREA+400(200),LONGAREA+399
	.	
	.	

EXERCISE:

Register 3 contains the address of a symbol DATA, write program steps to move the alpha character A to a location which is 10 bytes away from DATA.

EXERCISE:

Using register 3 as the base register, write program steps to move numeric 1 to core location 5006. Base register 3 contains 4002.

5.2 Branch Instructions

Branching was briefly discussed in Section 5.1 in regard to the instruction address portion of the PSW. In this section we will discuss the logic and methods of branching in greater detail. The term branch or branching can be defined as departing from a given sequential instruction execution to another instruction or set of instructions. Branching instructions provide a programmer a tool with which to direct his logic through one or more separate paths based on factors encountered during the problem program execution. The execution of a branch instruction is usually, though not always, activated by the result of some previous instruction or decision. Branch instructions can be grouped into two main categories. These are: Conditional and Unconditional Branches; and, Program Linkage Branches.

Conditional branches are used to direct the program logic path through one or more paths, while program linkage branch instructions are used to establish linkage between the main program and subroutine(s), subroutine to subroutine, etc.

Conditional branch instructions

Before proceeding with the discussion of the various branch instructions in this category, it is necessary to discuss another field in the PSW called the *Condition Code*.

The condition code field occupies bits 34 and 35 of the PSW. These 2 bits are used to reflect the status of the CPU after certain instructions have been executed. The

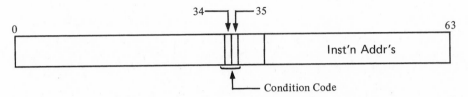

FIGURE 5.3. Program Status Word.

condition code field, 2 bits in all, is capable of assuming 4 different bit combinations: 00, 01, 10 and 11 (Binary bit configuration). The execution of the majority of the Assembler Language instructions, although not all, effects the condition code setting[5]. The two main uses of the condition code are: to indicate the result of a compare instruction; and, to indicate the result of arithmetic instructions.

At this point we will discuss in detail various condition code settings and their relationship with the branch instructions. In System 360 Assembler Language, a compare operation is used to compare the contents of the first operand with those of the second operand. Depending upon the result of the compare instructions, the condition code is set to one of the four possible settings. The condition code setting indicates whether the first operand is equal to, less than, or greater than the second operand. The relationship between the compare instructions and the condition code settings is shown below.

Comparison Result	Condition Code
Equal	00
Low	01
High	10

(Notice that a condition code setting of 11 is not possible after a compare instruction.)

Another use of the condition code setting is to indicate the result of arithmetic operations. Whenever a binary or decimal arithmetic is performed, the result could be a zero balance, a positive number, a negative number or an overflow. The relationships of these results and the condition code settings are illustrated by the chart below.

Arithmetic Result	Condition
Zero Balance	00
Negative or <0	01
Positive or >0	10
Overflow	11

The question now arises, how does it help us to know the various condition code settings?

---

[5]From now on, whenever you read about an instruction, one important point you should make note of is, its effect on the condition code.

In System 360, there is a type of instruction called *branch on condition*. This instruction, when executed, directs the CPU to examine the condition code setting of the PSW and if the setting matches that of a code specified in the *branch on condition* instruction, a branch takes place to address specified by the instruction. In case a match is not made, normal sequential processing continues.

Branch on Condition Instructions

Instruction Name	Branch on Condition
Mnemonic OP Codes	BC and BCR
Machine OP Codes	47 and 07
Type	RX and RR
Condition Code	remains unchanged
Program Interruptions	none

BC Instruction

Symbolic Format   BC   M1,D2(X2,B2)   RX Format

On examining the machine format of the BC instruction you will notice that it represents a departure from the standard RX format. In its standard format the operand portion of the RX type instructionss is represented as:

R1,D2(X2,B2)

However, in the case of the BC instruction the R1 operand is called a *mask* and is designated as M1. The condition code is tested by matching it against the M1 field of the branch instruction. If the condition code setting matches with the mask specified, a branch is taken to the address specified by the second operand of the branch instruction. In case the condition code setting does not match with the mask, the control is passed to the next sequential instruction.

Note: 'Branch on Condition' instruction's branch address must always refer to another instruction in the core and not to a data field.

The mask field of the BC instruction occupies bit positions 8 through 11 and is 4 bits in length. These 4 bits of the mask are tested against the condition code setting of the PSW. Depending upon the mask value specified by the programmer, the result of the condition tested would be to:

1. Branch if one of the four conditions is present.
2. Branch if one or another of the conditions is present.
3. Always branch.
4. Never branch.

The mask bit setting (value) is tested against the condition code setting according to the following chart. .

Mask Field Bin. Value	Mask Field Dec. Value	Condition Cd. Bin. Value	Condition Cd. Dec. Value
1000	8	00	0
0100	4	01	1
0010	2	10	2
0001	1	11	3

Note: The relationship between the 4 mask bits and the 4 condition code settings is completely arbitrary. There is no logical or mathematical correspondence.

Let us investigate how this relationship works. If the mask value, i.e., the mask bit setting, was $(1000)_2$ a branch would occur only if the condition code of the PSW was set to $(00)_2$. Similarly, if the condition code setting was $(10)_2$, a branch would occur only if the mask specified was $(0010)_2$ or a decimal value of 2. When writing a branch instruction, the programmer usually specifies the desired mask value as a decimal number. The assembler will convert it to a 4 bit binary number during assembly time.

Name	Oper	Operand
	BC	8,OUT

A branch would be taken to a symbolic name OUT only if the condition code setting were $(00)_2$.

	BC	4,F1

A branch would be taken to the symbolic name F1 only if the condition code setting were $(01)_2$.

We have seen how to write a branch instruction to test any one of the condition code settings. A programmer may, however, combine the various mask values to set 2 or more mask bits ON. In this case, a branch would occur on either of the respective conditions. For example, suppose that we were to branch to a location named OUT if the result of a compare operation was equal or less. We know that the mask value which tests for equal compare is 8 and, the mask value used to test for less is 4. To turn both these bits on in the mask field of a branch instruction, you must specify a mask of $(12)_{10}$. The instruction would be written as:

	BC	12,OUT

Let us look at another example. If we were to write an instruction to test the result of addition for zero balance or positive number, the mask value would be: 8 for zero balance; and, 2 for positive number. Thus, the instruction would be:

	BC	10,ZEROPOS

Unconditional branches

There are times when the program logic requires a branch, regardless of the condition code setting. For example, after completing a series of instructions of a routine, we may wish to go back to the first instruction in the series to repeat the routine again. To accomplish this, an unconditional branch instruction is needed. This is done by setting all 4 mask bits ON, i.e., a mask value of $(1111)_2$ or $(15)_{10}$. The use of mask value of 15 relies on the fact that during a program execution one condition code value or another will always be present, i.e., either 00, 01, 10, or 11. Thus, whatever the condition code setting, a branch will occur.

```
       F1              GET      CARDIN
                        .
                        .
                        .

                       BC       15,F1             UNCONDITIONAL BRANCH
```

By contrast, a branch instruction can be made inoperative by setting all of the mask bits to zeros, i.e., $(0000)_2$. In this case, no branch will occur and the control will flow to the next sequential instruction. The reason for this is the fact that the mask setting of 0000 does not test any of the condition code settings of the PSW. This type of branch instruction is also known as no-operation instruction[6].

BCR Instruction

Symbolic Format   BCR   M1,R2

The only difference between the BC and the BCR instruction is the method of specifying the branch address. In the case of BCR instruction, the branch address is specified by a general purpose register identified as R2. For example, in the following instruction a branch is specified with the help of a register. Register 7 points to the branch address.

```
                       BCR      8,7
```

In this case a branch will be taken (to the address specified by register 7) if the condition code setting was $(00)_2$.

Note: The programmer must, however, load the branch address in the R2 register (in this case register 7) before the branch instruction is executed.

The logic of execution of a branch instruction can be interpreted as in Figure 5.4.

Note: A branch must always be taken to another instruction and never to a data field.

Note: When several branch instructions are coded in sequence, it is advantageous to put at the top of the list that branch instruction which is most likely to occur, followed by the next most likely to occur, and so forth. This approach of coding branch instructions will result in efficient program processing as fewer unsuccessful conditions will be tested.

[6]Application of no-op instruction is discussed in Section 8.2.

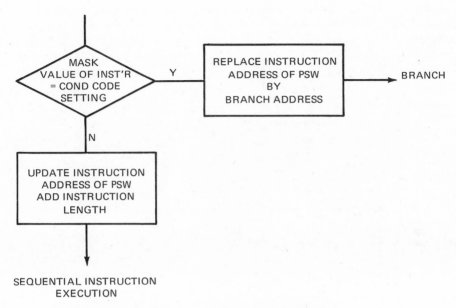

FIGURE 5.4. Execution of a Branch Instruction.

A sample problem with suggested solutions

In this section we will program the problem of reading a card file and listing the records on a printer. The input and the output record formats are as follows:

Field Name	Input Record		Output Record	
Employee Number	c.c.	1 – 5	p.p.	11 – 15
Employee Name		6 – 25		25 – 44
Employee Address		26 – 70		53 – 97

In the pages that follow, four different solutions are presented with the emphasis on the use of different I/O and work area combinations. There are other such combinations which can be used to solve this problem and such possibilities should be explored by the student.

Figure 5.6 represents a solution where we are using one input and one output area only. In this case, each GET to the file will place one logical record into the area named IN. The MVC instructions that follow assemble the input data into the output area named OUT. Each PUT to the file named PRINTFL (output file) will transfer the contents of the output area for the file to the appropriate output device, in this case a 1403 printer. Figures 5.5 and 5.6 depict a suggested solution to this problem.

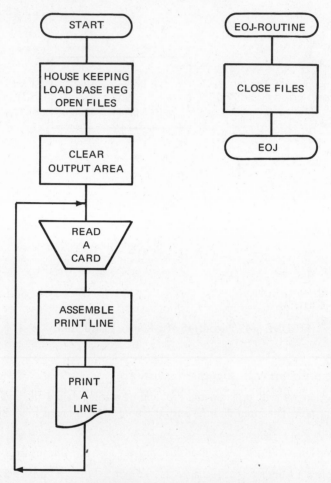

FIGURE 5.5. Suggested Flowchart.

One Input Area and One Output Area.

Name	Oper	Operand	
	START		
CARDIN	DTFCD	DEVADDR=SYSRDR,IOAREA1=IN,	C
		DEVICE=2540,	C
		EOFADDR=NOCARD,TYPEFLE=INPUT	
PRINTFL	DTFPR	DEVADDR=SYSLST,IOAREA1=OUT,	C
		BLKSIZE=97,	C
		DEVICE=1403	

(continued)

```
BEGIN       BALR    2,0                  LOAD BASE REGISTER
            USING   *,2                  SPECIFY BASE REG
            OPEN    CARDIN,PRINTFL       OPEN FILES
            MVI     OUT,C' '             CLEAR
            MVC     OUT+1(96),OUT        PRINT AREA
READ        GET     CARDIN               READ A CARD
            MVC     OUT+10(5),IN         MOVE NUMBER
            MVC     OUT+24(20),IN+5      MOVE NAME
            MVC     OUT+52(45),IN+25     MOVE ADDRESS
            PUT     PRINTFL              PRINT A LINE
            BC      15,READ              UNCONDITIONAL BRANCH
NOCARD      CLOSE   CARDIN,PRINTFL       CLOSE FILES
            EOJ
IN          DS      CL80                 INPUT AREA
OUT         DS      CL97                 OUTPUT AREA
            END     BEGIN
```

FIGURE 5.6. Suggested Solution.

In Figure 5.7 we see that aside from one I/O area for each file we have also specified a separate work area for each file. The work areas, INAREA and OUTAREA, must also be defined in the program (see DS statements) and the programmer must make sure that their use corresponds to the use assigned to these areas in the DTFs' for the files. When buffers are used, the I/O operations take place at the same time as the processing in the problem program, thus increasing the program efficiency.

Figure 5.8 illustrates the use of IOREG= entry for processing the logical records from a file. In this problem, general register 3 has been specified as the IOREG for the input card file. Each time a GET is issued to the file, the IOCS places the address of the logical record available for processing in this register. The data from the record can then be retrieved by using this register as the base register for data manipulating instructions, for example, the MVC instructions in Figure 5.8.

Note: In case IOREG entry is used, the WORKA entry can not be specified for the same file.

One Input, One Work; One Output and One Work Area Options.

```
Name        Oper    Operand
            START
CARDIN      DTFCD   DEVADDR=SYSRDR,IOAREA1=IN,              C
                    DEVICE=2540,                            C
                    EOFADDR=NOCARD,TYPEFLE=INPUT,           C
                    WORKA=YES
PRINTFL     DTFPR   DEVADDR=SYSLST,IOAREA1=OUT,             C
                    (continued)
```

```
                              BLKSIZE=97,                              C
                              DEVICE=1403,WORKA=YES
BEGIN         BALR            2,0
              USING           *,2
              OPEN            CARDIN,PRINTFL
              MVI             OUTAREA,C' '
              MVC             OUTAREA+1(96),OUTAREA
READ          GET             CARDIN,INAREA
              MVC             OUTAREA+10(5),INAREA
              MVC             OUTAREA+24(20),INAREA+5
              MVC             OUTAREA+52(45),INAREA+25
              PUT             PRINTFL,OUTAREA
              BC              15,READ
NOCARD        CLOSE           CARDIN,PRINTFL
              EOJ
IN            DS              CL80            INPUT BUFFER
INAREA        DS              CL80            INPUT WORK AREA
OUT           DS              CL97            OUTPUT BUFFER
OUTAREA       DS              CL97            OUTPUT WORK AREA
              END             BEGIN
```

FIGURE 5.7. A Suggested Solution.

Two Input Areas, No Work; Two Output Areas, One Work.

```
Name          Oper            Operand
              START
CARDIN        DTFCD           DEVADDR=SYSRDR,IOAREA1=IN1,              C
                              IOAREA2=IN2,                            C
                              DEVICE=2540,EOFADDR=NOCARD,             C
                              IOREG=(3)
PRINTFL       DTFPR           DEVADDR=SYSLST,IOAREA1=OUT1,            C
                              IOAREA2=OUT2,                           C
                              DEVICE=1403,BLKSIZE=97,WORKA=YES
BEGIN         BALR            2,0
              USING           *,2
              OPEN            CARDIN,PRINTFL
              MVI             OUTAREA,C' '
              MVC             OUTAREA+1(96),OUTAREA
READ          GET             CARDIN
              MVC             OUTAREA+10(5),0(3)
              MVC             OUTAREA+24(20),5(3)
```

(continued)

```
            MVC       OUTAREA+52(45),25(3)
            PUT       PRINTFL,OUTAREA
            BC        15,READ
NOCARD      CLOSE     CARDIN,PRINTFL
            EOJ
IN1         DS        CL80            INPUT BUFFER 1
IN2         DS        CL80            INPUT BUFFER 2
OUT1        DS        CL97            OUTPUT BUFFER 1
OUT2        DS        CL97            OUTPUT BUFFER 2
OUTAREA     DS        CL97            OUTPUT WORK AREA
            END       BEGIN
```

FIGURE 5.8. A Suggested Solution.

Two Input Areas, Work Area; Two Output Areas, Work Area.

```
Name        Oper      Operand
            START
CARDIN      DTFCD     DEVADDR=SYSRDR,IOAREA1=IN1,        C
                      IOAREA2=IN2,                        C
                      DEVICE=2540,EOFADDR=NOCARD,         C
                      WORKA=YES
PRINTFL     DTFPR     DEVADDR=SYSLST,IOAREA1=OUT1,       C
                      IOAREA2=OUT2,                       C
                      DEVICE=1403,BLKSIZE=97,WORKA=YES
BEGIN       BALR      2,0
            USING     *,2
            OPEN      CARDIN,PRINTFL
            MVC       OUTAREA+1(96),OUTAREA
READ        GET       CARD,
                      INAREA      READ CARD INTO WORK AREA
            MVC       OUTAREA+10(5),INAREA
            MVC       OUTAREA+24(20),INAREA+5
            MVC       OUTAREA+52(45),INAREA+25
            PUT       PRINTFL,OUTAREA
            BC        15,READ
NOCARD      CLOSE     CARDIN,PRINTFL
            EOJ
IN1         DS        CL80        INPUT BUFFER 1
IN2         DS        CL80        INPUT BUFFER 2
INAREA      DS        CL80        INPUT WORK AREA
```

(continued)

```
OUT1       DS        CL97      OUTPUT BUFFER 1
OUT2       DS        CL97      OUTPUT BUFFER 2
OUTAREA    DC        CL97' '   OUTPUT WORK AREA
           END       BEGIN
```

FIGURE 5.9. A Suggested Solution.

Figure 5.10 illustrates the use of a common work area for two different files. In this program, for each card read, a card is punched.

Name	Oper	Operand	
CARDIN	DTFCD	DEVADDR=SYS008,IOAREA1=IN1,	C
		IOAREA2=IN2,	C
		DEVICE=2540,EOFADDR=NOCARD,	C
		WORKA=YES	
CARDOUT	DTFCD	DEVADDR=SYS009,IOAREA1=OUT1,	C
		IOAREA2=OUT2,	C
		DEVICE=2540,WORKA=YES,	C
		TYPEFLE=OUTPUT	
BEGIN	BALR	2,0	
	USING	*,2	
	OPEN	CARDIN,CARDOUT	
READ	GET	CARDIN,COMONWOR	
	PUT	CARDOUT,COMONWOR	
	BC	15,READ	
NOCARD	CLOSE	CARDIN,CARDOUT	
	EOJ		
IN1	DS	CL80	
IN2	DS	CL80	
OUT1	DS	CL80	
OUT2	DS	CL80	
COMONWOR	DS	CL80	
	END	BEGIN	

FIGURE 5.10. A Suggested Solution – Use of Common Work Area.

Branch and link instructions

There are two types of branch and link instructions. These are BALR and BAL. The former, RR type, was discussed in Section 4.5. In this section, we will discuss the RX format instruction, i.e., the BAL instruction.

Instruction Name	Branch and Link
Mnemonic OP Code	BAL

Machine OP Code	45
Type	RX
Condition Code	Remains unchanged
Program Interruptions	None
Assembler Format	BAL R1,D2(X2,B2)

Branch and link instructions are generally used to establish linkage between the main program and subroutines, subroutine to subroutine, etc. After the subroutine is executed, the programmer can return to the instruction following that instruction which caused the branch to occur. This is illustrated by the following coding:

```
              .
          BAL      4,RTN1              BRANCH TO RTN1
READ      GET      CARDIN
              .
              .
          BC       15,READ
RTN1          .
              .
              .
          BCR      15,4                EXIT FROM RTN1
XXX           .
```

On execution of the BAL instruction the CPU places the address of the next sequential instruction in register 4. In this case, the address placed in register 4 will be the same as assigned to the label READ, and then a branch will be taken to RTN1. The last instruction of this routine is an unconditional branch instruction. Upon execution of this instruction the CPU will cause a branch to the address contained in register 4. This register, if you recall, contains the address of the symbol READ.

The coding example in Figure 5.11 illustrates the application of the branch and link instruction to write a single print routine in a program.

Name	Oper	Operand	
	.		
	.		
	.		
	MVC	LINE+4(30),HDNG	
	BAL	4,PRINTRTN	SAVE RETURN ADDRS IN R4
READ	GET	CARDIN	READ A CARD
	.		ASSEMBLE
	.		DATA

(Continued)

```
                    .                          IN
                    .                             PRINT
                    .                                AREA
            BAL      4,PRINTRTN    SAVE RETURN ADDRS IN R4
            BC       15,READ       BRANCH TO SYMBOL READ
PRINTRTN    PUT      REPORTS       PRINT A LINE
            MVC      LINE,LINE-1   CLEAR PRINT AREA
            BCR      15,4          EXIT FROM PRINT RTN VIA R4
                    .
                    .
                    .
                    .
```

FIGURE 5.11. Illustration of Basic Logic of Subroutines.

Another very interesting and rather helpful application of the BAL instruction is illustrated below.

```
            BAL      2,ERR1
                    .
                    .

            BAL      2,ERR2
                    .
                    .

            BAL      2,ERR3
                    .
                    .
                    .
ERR1        BAL      3,PRINT
            DC       C'SEQUENCE ERROR
ERR2        BAL      3,PRINT
            DC       C'DATE CARD MISSING
ERR3        BAL      3,PRINT
            DC       C'MASTER CARD MISSING
                    .
                    .
PRINT       MVC      LINE(20),0(3)
```

(Continued)

```
PUT        REPORT
BCR        15,2
   .
   .
```

Each of the first three BAL instructions stores in register 2 the address of the next sequential instruction, the return address. You can see that the last instruction, BCR, uses this register to return after printing the error message. When the BAL instruction, with the symbol ERR1 is executed, the address of the constant following this instruction gets stored in register 3 and then a branch is taken to the symbol PRINT. At the label PRINT we have a move character instruction which uses register 3 as the base register for the second operand. If you remember, register 3 at this time has stored in it the address of the constant following the BAL instruction with the symbol ERR1. Thus, the move instruction moves to the print area the following constant:

SEQUENCEbERRORbbbbbb

In the above, b represents a blank. The logic behind moving of the other two error messages is basically the same.

Note: There are two points to remember when using this approach. First, all of the error messages must be of equal length. Second, the messages must contain an even number of characters. Violation of the second rule will cause improper boundary alignment of the instructions that follow. (All instructions must be aligned on halfword boundary.)

This approach of grouping all the messages together is very helpful when a large number of messages appear in a program.

5.3 Decision Making Instructions

A frequent requirement in data processing and especially programming is the comparison of two quantities, such as account numbers or account names, for determining their relative magnitude. This may be done to establish correspondence between records in different files. For example, a record from a detail file may be matched against a record from a master file for updating purposes. Another application of data comparison is in organizing a file in an ascending or descending sequence. Comparison of this type is usually based on keys contained in the records involved.

Data as you know can exist in three distinct formats. These are: character data; packed decimal data; and, fixed-point data. In accordance with this, three types of compare instructions are provided with System 360 Assembler Language: logical compare instructions; decimal compare instructions; and, algebraic compare instructions.

In this section we will discuss those instructions which compare data logically. In this type of operation comparison is *binary*, and all codes are valid. This is in contrast to the algebraic compare instructions where a field's sign is taken into account according to the rules of algebra, by which any positive number is greater than any negative number. As a programmer, you must be well aware of this difference between the two types of instructions and also of the format of data that is to be compared. This point is well exemplified by the discussion that follows.

Consider, for example, the comparison of the following binary fields.

$$0\ 000\ 0001 \qquad \text{1st. Operand}$$
$$1\ 111\ 1111 \qquad \text{2nd. Operand}$$

First we will discuss the comparison of these fields on an algebraic basis, i.e., data is considered to be signed binary numbers. Thus, the values of these two numbers can be represented as:

$$\overset{s}{0}\ 000\ 0001 \equiv (1)_{10} \qquad \text{1st. Operand}$$
$$\overset{s}{1}\ 111\ 1111 \equiv (-1)_{10} \qquad \text{2nd. Operand}$$

This shows that the first operand represents a +1 value while the second operand's value is -1. Under these conditions the first operand has a greater value than the second operand. If, on the other hand, the same fields were compared on a logical basis, they would be treated as unsigned binary numbers and their values would be:

$$(0000\ 0001)_2 \equiv (1)_{10}$$
$$(1111\ 1111)_2 \equiv (255)_{10}$$

In this case, the first operand would be judged as the lower of the two. From this, it is clear that a programmer must be completely aware of the format of his data before deciding which type of compare instruction to use.

Note: The EBCDIC code is so arranged that under logical comparisons the numeric, alphabetic and special characters collate in pure binary sequence. The collating sequence of the EBCDIC system is as follows:

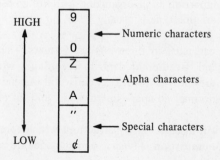

There are four logical compare instructions available to a programmer. These are: register-to-register; register-to-fullword; storage immediate; and, storage-to-storage compares.

Instruction Name	Compare Logical Register-to-Register
Mnemonic OP Code	CLR
Machine OP Code	15
Type	RR
Assembler Format	CLR R1,R2

Instruction Name	Compare Logical Register to Fullword
Mnemonic OP Code	CL
Machine OP Code	55
Type	RX
Assembler Format	CL R1,D1(X2,B2)

Instruction Name	Compare Logical Immediate
Mnemonic OP Code	CLI
Machine OP Code	95
Type	SI
Assembler Format	CLI D1(B1),I2

Instruction Name	Compare Logical Storage-to-Storage
Mnemonic OP Code	CLC
Machine OP Code	D5
Type	SS
Assembler Format	CLC D1(L,B1),D2(B2)

Program Interruptions	Protection (CL, CLI, CLC)
	Addressing (CL, CLI, CLC)
	Specification (CL)

Resulting Condition Code	Meaning
0	Both operands are equal
1	First operand is low
2	First operand is high
3	————

```
                                                          ── Both operands equal
                                                          ── First operand low
                                                          ── First operand high
                                                          ── Not used with compare
Condition Code        0      1      2      3
Mask Field Value      8      4      2      1
```

In all of the logical compare instructions, the first operand's contents are logically compared with those of the second operand and the result of the comparison is indicated by the condition code setting. The compare operation proceeds from left to right, one bit at a time. The instruction execution ends when an inequality is found or the ends of the fields are reached. Please note that the condition code setting always reflects the status of the first operand. In all of the logical compare instructions the comparison is done on binary basis and all codes are valid.

CLR Instruction

Both operands are general purpose registers.

CL Instruction

The second operand must address a fullword located on integral boundary and the first operand is always a general purpose register.

CLI Instruction

The second operand, a single byte of immediate data, is logically compared to a single byte addressed by the first operand. The second operand can be specified in any one of the permissible formats for the immediate data. For example, the instruction CLI IN+79,C'A' compares the location addressed by the first operand to the alpha character A. The second operand in this case could have been specified as X'C1' or B'11000001' or as a decimal self-defining term of 193.

EXERCISE:
Write program steps to read a card file named CARDS into an area named IN and branch to:
1. CODE1 if the character in cc 80 is a 1.
2. CODE2 if the character in cc 80 is a D.
3. Else branch to ERRORS.

EXERCISE:
Given a deck of cards with identification codes punched in column 80 of each card, we are to list only those cards which have the digit 9 in column 80.

EXERCISE:
Check positions 10, 11, 17, 20 and 30 of a record named IN for alpha character Z; if the position checked contains this character replace it with numeric 1.

CLC Instruction

This is a storage-to-storage type of instruction with one length code, L, which specifies the length of the first operand. The second operand is assumed to be the same length as the first. The comparison, as with all logical compare instructions, proceeds from left to right and may extend to a maximum of 256 bytes.

Note: Storage-to-storage type of logical compare instruction, CLC, can be used to compare unsigned packed decimal or alphameric information in any code that has a collating sequence based on binary values.

Example:
The coding below illustrates the use of logical compare instruction.

```
                    .
            CLC     FLDA,CONST
            BC      8,EQUAL
            BC      4,LOW
            BC      15,HIGH
                    .
FLDA        DS      CL4
CONST       DC      C'1434'
                    .
```

The CLC instruction above compares a field named FLDA to a character constant containing 1434, subsequent branch instructions check the condition code setting and branch to EQUAL or LOW depending upon equal or low compare. The third branch is an unconditional branch instruction. If this instruction was to be written in a different position it would have to be as follows:

```
            BC      2,HIGH
```

Example:
Suppose we were to branch to a symbol NOTEQU in case a field named AMOUNT was not equal to 100, the instructions would be:

```
                    .
            CLC     AMOUNT,CONST
            BC      6,NOTEQU
                    .
CONST       DC      C'100'
                    .
```

At times it may be necessary to validate the sequence of a file (ascending or descending) during processing. For example, in case of a card file containing multiple sales cards for sales personnel it is very important that all cards for the same salesman fall together in the file. At other times, it becomes very important to check for duplicate records in a file. For instance, in case of employee payroll file where each card repsents one employee, it is important to make sure that no one has more than one record. For processing such a file the first step is to sort the file in a given order, usually the ascending sequence and then during processing the program should check for duplicate cards. Duplicate records, if not checked, may result in two or more payroll checks for the same person. The examples that follow illustrate the logic and coding for checking of sequence and duplicate record errors.

EXERCISE:

Consider the following coding.

```
            CLC     FLDA,FLDB
            BC      8,EQUAL
            BC      4,LOW
            BC      2,HIGH
            BC      15,ANYWAY
              .
              .
  FLDA      DC      C'748'
  FLDB      DC      P'749'
              .
```

Which of the branches coded above will be taken?

Sequence error check

Figure 5.12 illustrates a typical program logic for sequence checking of a card file. All records in the file are assumed to be in ascending sequence by employee identification number, cc 1 through 7. If the file is in correct ascending sequence, each incoming record after the first should always be higher than the previous record. An error condition exists if the incoming record is lower than the record that precedes it. The action taken on such a condition varies and is programmed by the programmer according to the system specifications. The most usual action is to abort the job for resorting. On the other hand, it is not unusual to list the error record on an output device and continue the job.

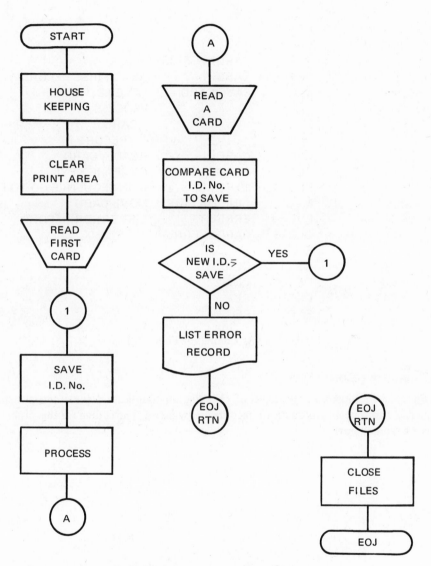

FIGURE 5.12. Sequence Checking.

Name	Oper	Operand	
	START		
	.		
BEGIN	BAL	2,0	
	USING	*,2	
	OPEN	CARDIN,ERRLIST	
	GET	CARDIN	READ FIRST RECORD
F1	MVC	SAVE,CARD	SAVE I.D. NUMBER
	.		PROCESS
	.		CARD
	.		RECORD
	GET	CARDIN	READ A CARD
	CLC	CARD(7),SAVE	COMPARE KEYS
	BC	10,F1	IF IN SEQUENCE GO TO F1
	MVC	LINE(80),CARD	MOVE CARD
	PUT	ERRLIST	LIST ERROR RECORD
NOCARD	CLOSE	CARDIN,ERRLIST	
	EOJ		
CARD	DS	CL80	
LINE	DS	CL132	
SAVE	DS	CL7	
	END	BEGIN	

FIGURE 5.13. Coding for Figure 5.12.

Duplicate record check

Figure 5.14 illustrates the logic of checking for duplicate records and also the sequence error check. All duplicate records are bypassed. The coding for this problem must be worked out.

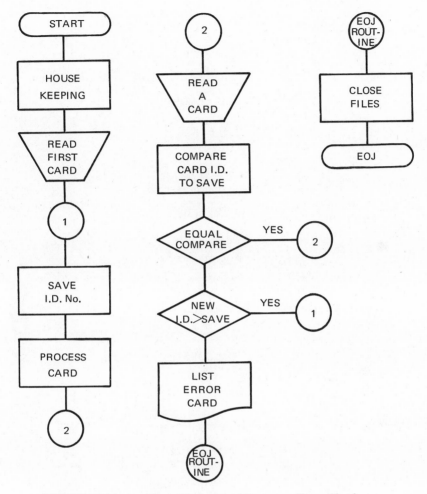

FIGURE 5.14. Duplicate Record and Sequence Error Check.

Self Evaluation Quiz

1. The length code(s) in the object instruction is:
   a. Equal to;
   b. One less than; or,
   c. One greater than; the actual number of the bytes to be dealt with.

2. The length code(s) in the symbolic instruction is:
   a. Equal to;
   b. One less than; or,
   c. One greater than; the actual number of the bytes to be dealt with.

3. What is the maximum number of bytes that can be moved from one location to another with a single MVC instruction?

4. What is meant by implied and explicit length codes?

5. How many bytes of data will be moved by the MVC instruction below:

```
        MVC     FLDA,FLDB
            .
FLDA    DS      7CL3
FLDB    DS      3CL7
            .
```

6. Express the following MVC instruction in machine format:

```
        MVC     0(9,2),3(3)
```

7. Show the contents of the receiving field after each of the following instructions:

```
        MVC     FLDA(4),FLDB
        MVC     FLDA+3(2),FLDB+2
        MVC     FLDA,FLDB
        MVC     FLDB,FLDA
            .
            .
FLDA    DC      C'ABCDEF'
FLDB    DC      C'1234'
FLDC    DC      C'XYZ'
            .
```

8. Which of the following instructions are coded wrong, if any?

```
        MVC     FLDA(2),FLDB
        MVC     FLDA+2(2),FLDB+4(2)
        MVI     FLDA+1(1),C'A'
        MVC     FLDA,FLDA
```

9. In the instruction BALR 7,6 the branch will be taken to the address specified in:

    a. Register 7
    b. Register 6
    c. Register 0

10. Consider the coding below.

```
        START   4000
        BALR    10,0
        USING   *,10
```

(Continued)

```
LOAD        BALR    6,7
            MVI     SW+1,C'1'
              .
```

a. What is the value of the base address?
b. Which register is being used as the base register?
c. What address will be loaded into register 6 by the instruction named LOAD?

11. Given a MVC instruction in machine format:

$$D2\ 06\ 30\ 00\ 40\ 02$$

a. Which register(s) is being used as base register(s)?
b. How many bytes will be affected by the instruction?

12. FLDA contains $(10101100)_2$. What will be the condition code setting after execution of the following instruction?

```
CLI     FLDA,X'AB'
```

13. Given three data fields, each 3 bytes in length containing character data, write instructions necessary to arrange these fields in ascending order.

14. Arrange the data fields described in the previous problem in descending order.

15. Indicate the condition code setting after execution of each of the following instructions.

```
            CLC     FLDA,FLDB
            CLC     FLDA(8),FLDB
            CLC     FLDA(7),FLDB
            CLC     FLDB(8),FLDA
              .
    FLDA    DC      C'WILLIAMS'
    FLDB    DC      C'WILLIAM '
              .
```

16. What will be the condition code setting after execution of the following instruction?

```
              .
            CLI     CONST+1,150
              .
    CONST   DC      X'C8C1E8'
              .    .
```

17. Given three fields containing character data (each field is 2 bytes long), write a routine to test for equality among the three data fields and branch to symbol ALLEQUAL, if all three are equal, TWOEQUAL if any two are equal, and NOT-

EQUAL if none are equal.

18. Write DS statements necessary to define storage for an 80-byte record. The record is to be sub-defined as follows:

Columns	Symbolic Name
1 – 5	IDNUM
1 – 2	DEPT
3 – 5	SERIAL
6 – 11	DATE
6 – 7	DAY
8 – 9	MONTH
10 – 11	YEAR
12 – 32	NAME
12 – 12	FINITL
13 – 13	MINITL
14 – 32	LNAME
33 – 50	Not Used
51 – 55	INVNO
56 – 60	INVAMT
61 – 79	Not Used
80 – 80	CODE

19. How many bits are there in a PSW?

20. Which part of the PSW is used to contain the instruction address portion?

21. What is meant by relative addressing?

22. What will be the contents of AREA after the following instruction has been executed?

```
        MVC       AREA-3(4),AREA+1
        .
        .
        DC        CL4'1234'
AREA    DC        CL2'AB'
        DC        CL3'XYZ'
        .
```

23. To which symbol will the branch be taken by the last instruction coded below?

```
ADD     AR      2,3
MOVE    MVC     0(3,2),0(4)
LOAD    LA      4,2(4)
        DC      15,*-10
```

24. How many characters will be moved by the MVC instruction coded below?

	MVC	FLDB-2(4),FLDA
	.	
FLDC	DS	CL6
FLDB	DC	C'ABC'
FLDA	DC	C'*167'
	.	

25. What will be the contents of FLDC when the branch is taken to the symbol OUT?

MOVE	MVC	FLDC-1(1),FLDD+1
	MVC	FLDC+3(3),FLDA
	CLC	FLDC–1(1),FLDD
	BC	8,OUT
	MVC	FLDD(1),FLDA+5
	BC	4,MOVE
	BC	15,OUT
	.	
OUT	.	
	.	
FLDA	DC	CL3'A'
	DC	XL3'E2C9'
FLDC	DC	PL3'6'
	DC	BL3'11110000'
FLDD	DC	ZL2'62'
	.	

[6]

Binary Arithmetic

6.1 Introduction to System 360 Arithmetic

Arithmetic operations performed by the System 360 fall into three categories: fixed-point arithmetic; decimal arithmetic; and, floating-point arithmetic. In this text, only the first two types, i.e., fixed-point (binary) and decimal arithmetic (because the floating-point arithmetic is mostly used in scientific programming applications) will be discussed.

Data formats

The basic arithmetic operand is the 32 bit fixed-point binary fullword. In most of the binary arithmetic operations, halfword operands may be specified for improving performance or storage utilization.

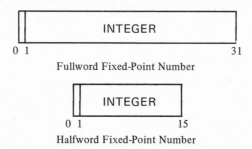

Fullword Fixed-Point Number

Halfword Fixed-Point Number

FIGURE 6.1. Fixed-Point Data Formats.

Binary arithmetic must be performed in a general purpose register. The registers, as previously stated, are 32 bits or one word in length. Fixed-point numbers occupy a fixed-length format consisting of a one-bit sign (the high-order bit) followed by the integer field. A fullword fixed-point quantity has a 31-bit integer. Some multiply, divide, and shift operations use an operand consisting of 64 bits where the integer field is contained in 63 bits and the high-order bit represents the sign. This type of operand is always located in a pair of adjacent registers, for which a special addressing technique is used. Both operands of a binary arithmetic operation must contain binary data. The first operand of all arithmetic instructions must always be a general purpose register, while the second operand may be a register or a fixed-point data in main storage. Fixed-point data in the main storage may occupy a 32-bit word or a 16-bit halfword, with a binary integer field of 31 bits or 15 bits, respectively. These data must be located on integral boundaries. A halfword operand in main storage is expanded to a fullword as the operand is fetched from storage[1]. The result of the arithmetic operations always replaces the contents of the first operand. The second operand remains unchanged.

Number representation

All fixed-point operands are treated as signed integers (no fractions). Positive numbers are represented in true binary notation with the sign bit set to zero. The negative numbers are represented in the two's complement notation with the sign bit set to one. The two's complement of a number is obtained by reversing each bit of the number and adding a one to the low-order bit position. The bits between the sign bit and the leftmost significant bit are identical to the sign bit. This so-called *sign extension* allows convenient algebraic calculations.

A halfword binary number contains one sign bit and the remaining 15 bits represent the binary integer. The maximum values that can be represented by a halfword fixed-point number are: +32,767; and, –32,768.

A fullword binary number consists of 31 data bits and one sign bit. The maximum values that can be represented by a fullword fixed-point number are: +2,147,483,647; and, –2,147,483,648.

Examples:

Halfword Binary Number	Decimal Equivalent
0 111 1111 1111 1111 ≡	+32,767
1 000 0000 0000 0000 ≡	–32,768

There are two very unique points about two's complement numbers. First, the zero has a very unique representation — there is no negative zero. Consider the reason for this. To obtain two's complement, we take the true form representation of the given number, reverse each bit and then add one to the rightmost bit position.

---

[1] The halfword operand in storage does not change and the operand participates as a fullword. The halfword is expanded to a fullword by propagating the sign bit through the high-order 16 extra bits. Expansion occurs after the halfword operand is obtained from the storage.

0 000 0000 0000 0000	true form
1 111 1111 1111 1111	Reverse each bit
1	Add 1
0 000 0000 0000 0000	resulting number

Secondly, the range of negative numbers is one greater than the largest positive number. Consider a halfword fixed-point number. In case of positive numbers, as the sign bit is occupied by a zero, the largest positive number consists of 15 one bits. The value represented in this case is equal to 2^{15} −1 or decimal 32,767.

$$2^{15} - 1 \equiv 32{,}767 \equiv \overset{s}{0} \;\; 111 \;\; 1111 \;\; 1111 \;\; 1111$$

In contrast, the largest negative number consists of an all zero integer field with a sign bit of one. Thus, the largest 16-bit negative number is:

$$-2^{15} \equiv -32{,}768 \equiv \overset{s}{1} \;\; 000 \;\; 0000 \;\; 0000 \;\; 0000$$

Two's Complement. The two's complement in binary notation is analogous to the ten's complement in the decimal notation system. The two's complement can be obtained by simply inverting (that is, a 0 bit is changed to 1 and a 1 bit is changed to 0) and adding a 1 to the low-order bit. Before this process can be illustrated, the rules for binary addition should be quickly examined.

In the binary system, there being only two symbols 0 and 1, the adding of 1 and 1 exceeds the limit of counting and, therefore, the result is 0 with a 1 carried to the next high-order digit position. The rules of binary addition are illustrated below:

$0 + 0 = 0$
$0 + 1 = 1$
$1 + 0 = 1$
$1 + 1 = 0$ with a carry of 1
$1 + 1 + 1 = 1$ with a carry of 1

The binary addition table below summarizes these results.

+	0	1
0	0	1
1	1 1	0

Consider the following examples of storing negative numbers. For convenience and brevity, we will use all halfword numbers.

To store − 72 the first step is to represent this number in its true form.

$\overset{s}{0}$ 000 0000 0100 1000	+72 in true form
1 111 1111 1011 0111	each bit reversed
+1	add 1
1 111 1111 1011 1000	two's complement

Form two's complement of 128.

```
 s
 0  000  0000  1000  0000        +128 in true form
 1  111  1111  0111  1111        each bit reversed
                       +1        add 1
 1  111  1111  1000  0000        two's complement of 128 or –128
```

Form two's complement of 0.

```
       s
       0  000  0000  0000  0000        0 in true form
       1  111  1111  1111  1111        each bit reversed
                            +1        add 1
 1     0  000  0000  0000  0000        two's complement
```

↑
└── carry is lost

Note: A zero amount is always positive and is represented in true form.

Subtraction is essentially the same as addition except for the fact that the subtrahend (the number on the bottom) is first complemented and then added to the minuend (the number on the top).

Example: (using 4 bit accumulators)

```
                 s                           s
     7           0  111         7            0  111
    -2           0  010      +(-2)           1  110
                                         _____
                +5                           0  101 ≡ +5


                 s                           s
     3           0  011         3            0  011
    -2           0  010      +(-2)           1  110
                                         _____
                +1                           0  001 ≡ +1


                 s                           s
     4           0  100         4            0  100
    -5           0  101      +(-5)           1  011
                                         _____
                -1                           1  111 ≡ -1
```

Overflow. Overflow in addition and subtraction occurs when the carry into the sign bit position of the number does not agree with the carry out of the sign bit, i.e., when one is *no carry* or 0 carry and the other is 1. This, in essence, happens when numbers which lie outside the range of a register are generated as a result of an operation. Therefore, the overflow indicator is turned ON and can be tested by the programmer. An example of an overflow condition is given below.

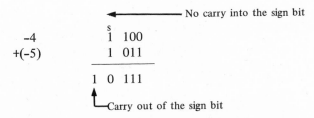

Notice that there is a carry out of the sign bit without a corresponding carry into it.

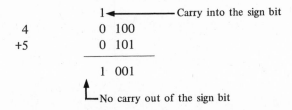

In the preceding example, an overflow will occur as there is no corresponding carry out of the sign bit for the 1 carry into the sign bit.

To summarize, all binary arithmetic is performed in general registers. The first operand of the binary arithmetic instructions must be located in a general register.

The second operand may be located in a general register or in the main storage. If the second operand is located in the main storage, it must be on an integral boundary (fullword or halfword).

The result of the arithmetic operation is stored in the first operand and the second operand remains unaltered. Positive numbers are stored in true form and negative numbers in two's complement.

One last point to note is that signs and two's complements are generated automatically by the computer.

6.2 Data Format Conversion Instructions

Normally, data enter into the computer storage in EBCDIC format. Before binary arithmetic operations can be performed, the data to be operated upon must be converted into fixed-point binary format and placed into a register or a fullword or halfword. Converting of EBCDIC data into binary format requires the following two steps.

1. Convert the EBCDIC data into packed format.
2. Convert the packed data (from step 1) into binary.

The first step involves the use of PACK instruction which converts the EBCDIC data into packed format. The second step involves the use of Convert to Binary (CVB) instruction which takes the packed data, converts it into binary format, and stores the result in a general register.

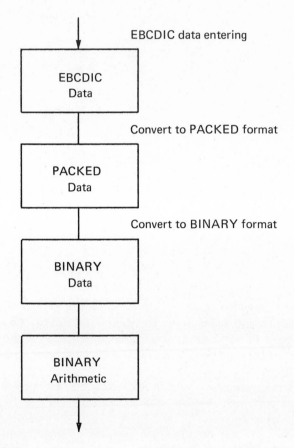

FIGURE 6.2. Steps to Convert EBCDIC Data into BINARY Format.

Pack Instruction

Instruction Name	PACK
Mnemonic OP Code	PACK
Machine OP Code	F2
Type	SS
Assembler Format	PACK D1(L1,B2),D2(L2,B2)
Program Interruptions	Protection, Addressing
Condition Code	Unchanged

This instruction converts the data from the second operand, the sending field, to packed format and the result is stored at the first operand location. The data in the sending field remain unchanged. As a result of this instruction, the original contents of the receiving field, the first operand, are replaced by the packed data. The second operand is assumed to have the zoned format. All zones are ignored except the zone over the low-order digit of the sending field which is assumed to represent a sign. During packing, the sign is placed in the rightmost 4 bits of the low-order byte and the digits are placed adjacent to each other in the remainder of the receiving field.

Note: The sign and digits are moved unchanged to the receiving field and are not checked for valid codes.

The PACK instruction addresses the high-order byte of each operand. However, bytes are fetched and stored from right to left, i.e., low-order to high-order.

Example:

FLDA contains 132 and FLDB is 2 bytes in length. Let us see the result of a PACK instruction:

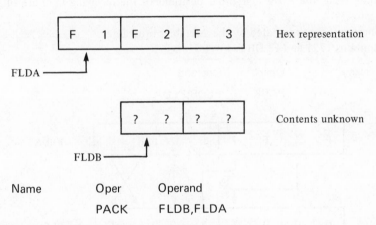

Name	Oper	Operand
	PACK	FLDB,FLDA

The result will be:

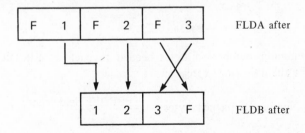

If the receiving field is too short to contain all of the significant digits of the second operand field, the extra high-order digits of the sending field are ignored. For example, FLDA contains 13724 and FLDB is 2 bytes in length. The result of PACK FLDB,FLDA is shown below:

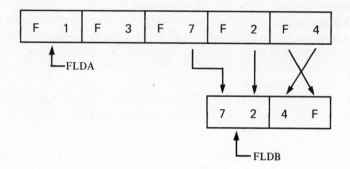

In case the receiving field is larger than the length required to contain all the digits of the sending field, the extra high-order positions of the receiving field are filled with packed zeros.

Note: These zeros are generated by the assembler program.

FLDA contains 1721 and FLDB is 4 bytes long.

Name	Oper	Operand
	PACK	FLDB,FLDA

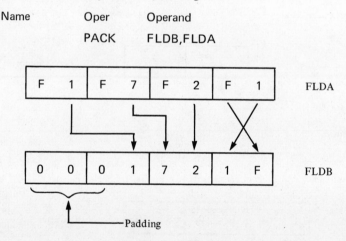

Note: The minimum number of bytes needed to pack an EBCDIC field can be calculated by the following expression:

$$\text{Number of packed bytes} = \frac{\text{EBCDIC field length}}{2} + 1$$

For example, to pack a 3 byte long EBCDIC field we need a minimum of $3/2 + 1 = 2$ bytes. (Resulting quotient +1.)

Overlapping fields may occur and are processed by storing 1 result byte immediately after the necessary operand bytes are fetched. Except for the rightmost byte of the resulting field, which is stored immediately upon fetching the first byte, 2 sending bytes are needed for each resulting byte.

EXERCISE:

FLDA contains 13243. Show the contents of the receiving field after each of the following instructions; consider these instructions independently.

Name	Oper	Operand
	PACK	FLDA+2(3),FLDA
	PACK	FLDA,FLDA
	PACK	FLDA+3(2),FLDA
	PACK	FLDA+1(4),FLDA

Example:

In case the length of data to be packed is longer than 16 bytes, packing can be accomplished by using a routine somewhat like the one illustrated below.

Given a 45 byte long data field named DATA and it is to be packed and placed into another field named PACKED which is 23 bytes in length.

.
.
.

	PACK	PACKED(8),DATA(15)
	PACK	PACKED+7(8),DATA+14(15)
	PACK	PACKED+14(8),DATA+28(15)
	PACK	PACKED+21(2),DATA+42(3)

.
.

PACKED	DS	CL23
DATA	DS	CL45

.

The first impression a person gets is that the routine will produce 4 zone (sign) fields. However, a close inspection will reveal that each PACK instruction addresses in such a manner that each time the high-order decimal digit from the source field will overlap the zone generated by the previous pack instruction.

The example below illustrates the use of explicit base register, displacement and length code in writing the PACK instruction.

Example:

Assume that storage locations 2004–2008 contain the following zoned-decimal data that is to be converted to a packed-decimal format and left in the same location. Assume also, that the base register is register 4 and it contains 00 00 20 00.

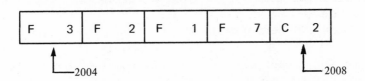

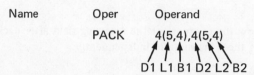

Machine Format[2]

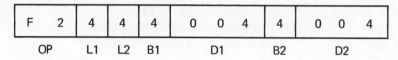

Packed Field

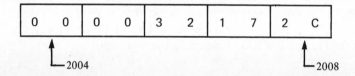

Note: 1. Two length fields (L1 and L2), each one-half byte long, are provided in the PACK instruction to allow individual length specification for each operand. The maximum length for each operand is 16 bytes.

2. The PACK instruction can be used to switch the two digits in 1 byte by specifying a length code of one and the same address for both operands.

EXERCISE:

The contents of FLDA are 172137+. Show the contents of the receiving field after each of the following instructions; consider these instructions independently.

```
PACK    FLDB(1),FLDA
PACK    FLDB(4),FLDA
PACK    FLDB(4),FLDA+1(1)
PACK    FLDB(6),FLDA
PACK    FLDA+2(3),FLDA
PACK    FLDA+1(1),FLDA+1(1)
PACK    FLDA,FLDA
          .
          .
```

Convert to Binary Instruction

Instruction Name	Convert to Binary
Mnemonic OP Code	CVB
Machine OP Code	4F

---

[2]Please note that the length code in machine format is one less than the number of bytes to be handled.

Type	RX
Assembler Format	CVB R1,D2(X2,B2)
Program Interruptions	Protection, Addressing, Specification, Fixed-point divide, Data
Condition Code	Unchanged

The radix of the second operand is changed from packed decimal to binary and the result is placed in the first operand location which is always a general register. The second operand *must* contain packed decimal data as the CPU checks the data for valid sign and digit codes. Improper codes are recognized as data exceptions and cause a program interruption. The second operand *must* be located in a doubleword which must be on an integral boundary. *Violation of this rule will cause specification exception.*

The result of the conversion is stored in the general register specified as R1. A program interruption can occur if the value of the packed decimal field being converted to binary exceeds the value that can be contained in a register. These values are: +2,147,483,647, or, –2,147,483,648. For any number outside of this range, the operation is completed by placing the 32 low-order binary bits of the number in the register. A fixed-point divide exception exists and a program interruption follows. The examples that follow illustrate the mechanism of CVB instruction.

Example:

Assume a doubleword named DOUBLE contains 00 00 00 00 00 24 57 6C, and convert this number into binary format. The receiving operand is register 10.

Name	Oper	Operand
	CVB	10,DOUBLE

As a result of this instruction register 10 would contain:

$$(00\ 00\ 60\ 00)_{16} \equiv +24,567$$

Example:

Use of explicit base and displacement. In the previous example, assume that the doubleword named DOUBLE was located in core positions 8808-880F. Also assume that the base register is register 3 and it contains $(8800)_{16}$.

The CVB instruction would be:

Assembler Format   CVB   10,8(0,3)

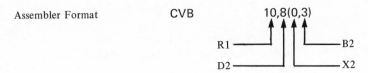

Example:

Card columns 10-16 contain some number. Convert this number into binary and place it into register 3. The necessary instructions are:[3]

```
        PACK    DOUBLE,IN+9(7)
        CVB     3,DOUBLE
         .
         .
         .
DOUBLE  DS      D
IN      DS      CL80
```

The PACK and CVB instructions give us the ability to convert zoned decimal data into binary format and place it into a register. After this has been done, binary arithmetic operations can be performed on the data. However, before data can be produced as output (for example, on printer) it must be converted to decimal form and then into EBCDIC format. We have at our disposal two instructions to accomplish this conversion. These instructions are discussed in the material that follows.

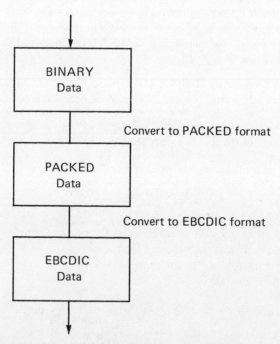

FIGURE 6.3. **Steps to Convert BINARY Data to EBCDIC Format.**

[3] As the CVB instruction requires the packed data to be contained in a doubleword on integral boundary, it is important to pack the data into a doubleword.

Convert to Decimal Instruction

Instruction Name	Convert to Decimal
Mnemonic OP Code	CVD
Machine OP Code	4E
Type	RX
Assembler Format	CVB R1,D2(X2,B2)
Program Interruptions	Protection, Addressing, Specification
Condition Code	Unchanged

The CVD instruction is one of the few instructions *where the sending field is the first operand and the receiving field is the second operand.* The sending field is always a register and the receiving field must always be located in the main storage.

The radix of the first operand is changed from binary to packed decimal and the result is stored in the second operand location. It is important to note that the second operand *must* be a doubleword located on an integral boundary. If this rule is violated, a specification exception is recognized and a program interruption occurs. If the binary number being converted to decimal is positive, the low-order 4 bits (the sign bits) of the packed field will contain the standard positive sign 1100 or Hex C. If the data in the register is negative, the sign bits of the resulting packed number will be set to 1101 or Hex D. The following are some examples of CVD instructions.

Example:

Assume that register 7 contains Hex 00 00 01 00 and we are required to convert this number into packed decimal and place the result in an area named DOUBLE.

Name	Oper	Operand
	CVD	7,DOUBLE

Result:

00 00 00 00 00 00 25 6C

Example:

Assume that register 4 contains Hex FF FF FF 80. The instruction CVD 4,DOUBLE will result in:

00 00 00 00 00 00 12 8D

Note: Even if you, as a programmer, happen to know that the binary number to be converted to packed does not need 8 bytes, it is still necessary to have the second operand, as a doubleword, located as an integral boundary.

The next step toward converting the data into zoned format is called *unpacking* the data. This is accomplished by UNPK instruction.

Unpak Instruction

Instruction Name	UNPACK
Mnemonic OP Code	UNPK
Machine OP Code	F3
Type	SS
Program Interruptions	Addressing, Protection
Condition Code	Unchanged
Assembler Format	UNPK D1(L1,B1),D2(L2,B2)

The UNPK instruction changes the format of the second operand from packed to zoned and the result is placed in the first operand location. The fields are processed right to left, even though the instruction addresses the high-order byte of both operands. Unpacking is done by supplying zone coding of 1111 for all bytes except the low-order byte of the resulting data. The low-order byte of the resulting data receives the sign of the packed data being converted to zoned format.

Note: The operand sign and digits are not checked for valid codes.

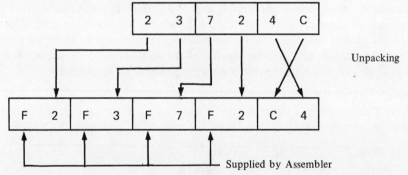

Unpacking

Supplied by Assembler

If the receiving operand is too short to contain all of the significant digits of the sending field, the extra high-order digits of the sending field are ignored. On the other hand, if the receiving field is longer than required to contain all of the digits from the sending field, the extra high-order positions of the receiving field are padded with zoned zeros. The maximum length that can be specified for either operand is 16 bytes.

Example:

UNPK   FLDB,FLDA

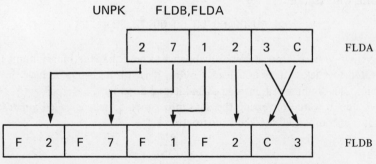

Example:

FLDA contains 12 34 2D and FLDB is 6 bytes in length. The instruction
UNPK FLDB,FLDA will result in:

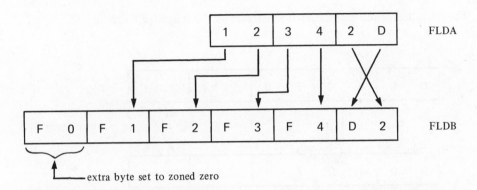

Example:

FLDA contains 71 12 34 2D and FLDB is 5 bytes in length. The instruction
UNPK FLDB,FLDA will result in:

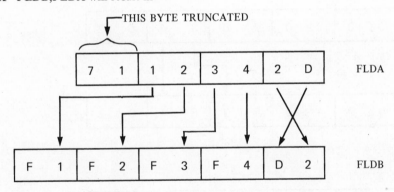

Overlapping. The first and the second operand fields may overlap and are processed by
storing the first result byte immediately after the rightmost byte is fetched; for the
remaining bytes, 2 result bytes are stored immediately after 1 byte is fetched from the
sending field.

Example:

FLDA contains 12 73 42 12 7C.

UNPK   FLDA(3),FLDA+3(2)

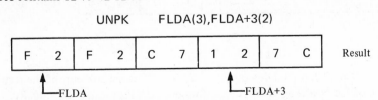

Example:
FLDA contains 00 40 70 34 2C.

UNPK   FLDA,FLDA+2(3)

The execution of this instruction is illustrated by the following diagrams:

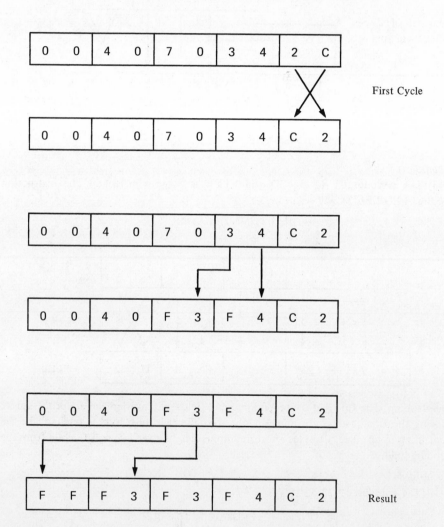

First Cycle

Result

EXERCISE:

Assume that FLDA contains 00 72 34 72 9C. Show the contents of the result field after each of the following instructions. Consider each instruction individually.

```
UNPK    FLDB(6),FLDA
UNPK    FLDB(9),FLDA
UNPK    FLDA(3),FLDA+4(1)
UNPK    FLDA(4),FLDA+3(2)
UNPK    FLDA,FLDA+2(2)
UNPK    FLDA(1),FLDA+4(1)
```

Removal of Zones. Assume that FLDA contains 255 which if represented in hex format will appear as F2 F5 F5. Consider the coding below:

Name	Oper	Operand									
	PACK	DOUB,FLDA	00	00	00	00	00	00	25	5F
	CVB	4,DOUB						00	00	00	FF
	CVD	4,DOUB	00	00	00	00	00	00	25	5C
	UNPK	FLDA,DOUB							F2	F5	C5

Upon examining the sign bits of the resulting FLDA, we see that it contains Hex C which is the same as 1100 (standard positive sign code). If this field was moved to a print area and printed, the result would be 25E instead of 255 which was the original contents of FLDA. This is due to the CVB instruction. When a positive field, signed or unsigned, is converted to binary, the sign bit of the register is set to zero. In turn, the CVD instruction generates the standard positive sign 1100 which, when unpacked, results in a signed data field. For the data which needs to be printed it is necessary to remove the zone and replace it with the zone coding of 1111 or Hex F. It is not only in case of signed positive numbers that it is necessary to remove the sign coding. This also needs to be done in case of negative numbers which are supplied with a zone coding of 1101 or Hex D.

Move Zone Instruction

Instruction Name	Move Zone
Mnemonic OP Code	MVZ
Machine OP Code	D3
Type	SS
Program Interruption	Protection, Addressing
Condition Code	Unchanged
Assembler Format	MVZ D1(L,B2),D2(B2)

This being a SS type instruction, there are no boundary alignment requirements as the instruction deals with variable length data fields. The computer assumes that the second operand is the same length as the first operand and the maximum length that can be specified for the first operand is 256 bytes.

The high-order 4 bits of each byte of the field addressed by the second operand, are transferred to the high-order 4 bits of the corresponding byte of the first operand location. The movement of data is from left to right through each field, 1 byte at a time. The two fields may overlap in any manner desired.

Example:

FLDA contains F1 F3 C2. To remove the sign C from the low-order byte and to replace it with no zone coding of F we could use the following instruction:

$$\text{MVZ} \qquad \text{FLDA+2(1),FLDA}$$

or

$$\text{MVZ} \qquad \text{FLDA+2(1),FLDA+1}$$

Note: The sending field's zone bits are not checked for valid zone codes.

Example:

FLDA contains 52 73 5C, the instruction MVZ FLDA+1(1),FLDA will result in:

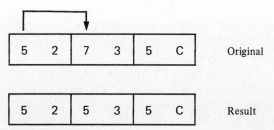

| 5 | 2 | 7 | 3 | 5 | C | Original

| 5 | 2 | 5 | 3 | 5 | C | Result

Since the instructions which provide us with the capability of radix conversion have been discussed, focus can now be put on the actual arithmetic instructions. Fixed-point arithmetic is performed in general purpose registers. A number of instructions are provided for performing binary arithmetic. The next two sections will discuss binary add and subtract instructions.

6.3 Binary Add Instructions

Binary add instructions can be grouped under two sub-headings: Algebraic Add, and, Logical Add instructions.

Algebraic Add Instructions

Instruction Name	Add Register to Register
Mnemonic OP Code	AR
Machine OP Code	1A
Type RR	
Program Interruptions	Fixed-point overflow
Condition Code	is affected
Assembler Format	AR R1,R2

The second operand contents are algebraically added to the first operand, and the sum is placed in the first operand location.

AR   7,10   ADD CONTENTS OF REG 10 to REG 7

Machine Format

1	A	7	A

0   7 8   11 12   15

Resulting Condition Code	Meaning
0	sum is zero
1	sum is less than zero
2	sum is greater than zero
3	overflow

If the carry out of the sign-bit position does not agree with the carry into of the sign-bit, an overflow occurs and a program interruption follows. A positive overflow yields a negative final number and a negative overflow yields a positive result.

Note: If the same register is specified for both operands, the result is doubling of the number.

Consider the following examples of AR instructions. In the interest of brevity, we will assume 8-bit registers.

		AR R ,R
R1:	+16	0 001 0000
R2:	+32	0 010 0000
	+48	0 011 0000

No carries–no overflow.

R1:	−32	1 110 0000
R2:	−16	1 111 0000
	−48	1 101 0000

A one is carried into and out of the sign bit, therefore no overflow results.

R1:	+ 64	0 100 0000
R2:	+ 66	0 100 0010
	+130	1 000 0010

A one is carried into the sign bit, however there is no carry out of this position, resulting in an overflow.

Note: It is important to note that the sum of the addition replaces the contents of the register specified as the first operand.

Instruction Name	Add Fullword to Register
Mnemonic OP Code	A
Machine OP Code	5A
Type	RX
Program Interruptions	Protection, Addressing, Specification, Fixed-point overflow
Condition Code	is affected
Assembler Format	A R1,D2(X2,B2)

This instruction is used to add the contents of a fullword in the main storage to the contents of the general register specified as the first operand. The resulting sum replaces the original contents of the receiving field. The second operand must address a fullword located on an integral boundary otherwise specification exception will be recognized and an interruption will occur. Both operands must contain fixed-point quantities. Rules regarding the fixed-point overflow are the same as discussed in AR instruction.

Example:

Name	Oper	Operand
	A	7,AMOUNT
	.	
	.	
	.	
AMOUNT	DS	F
	.	
	.	

In the coding above, assume that the fullword named AMOUNT is located at core position 2004-2007. Also assume that the base register is register 2 and it contains 00 00 2000. The assembler and machine formats of the instruction A 7,AMOUNT are shown below.

Assembler Formats	A 7,4(0,2)

Example:

To count the number of cards processed by a particular program the add instruction previously discussed could be used.

Example:

READ	GET	CARDIN	READ A CARD
		(continued)	

```
                A         2,ONE        ADD 1 TO REG 2
                .
                .
                BC        15,READ      BRANCH TO READ
                .
ONE             DC        F'+1'
```

Note: At this time we will assume that register 2, the count register, is originally set to zero. In the next section we will learn to clear a register.

The condition codes and their meanings (for Add Fullword) are given in the chart below.

Resulting Condition Code	Meaning
0	Result is zero
1	Result is less than zero
2	Result is more than zero
3	Overflow

Instruction Name	Add Halfword to Register
Mnemonic OP Code	AH
Machine OP Code	4A
Type	RX
Program Interruptions	Protection, Addressing, Specification, Fixed-point overflow
Condition Code	is affected
Assembler Format	AH R1,D2(X2,B2)

The halfword second operand is algebraically added to the first operand and the sum is placed in the register specified as R1. The halfword is first expanded to a fullword by propagating the sign bit through the additional 16 bits and then the addition takes place. This expansion takes place *after* the halfword operand has been fetched from storage, thus the contents of the second operand do not alter. The second operand must be located on a halfword boundary, otherwise, specification exception will occur resulting in a program interruption. The rules regarding the fixed-point overflow and the resulting condition codes are the same as discussed in the two previous add instructions.

Note: In all of the add instructions discussed so far, the resulting sum always replaces the original contents of the first operand location. The second operand remains unaltered and the condition code setting can be tested by conditional branch instructions.

Example:

The last example for add fullword instruction, illustrated coding for counting the number of cards processed by a particular program. The same could be accomplished by the following:

```
READ         GET        CARDIN
             AH         2,ONE
             .
             .
             BC         15,READ
             .
             .
ONE          DC         H'+1'
             .
```

In this case the constant ONE has been set as a halfword thus saving 2 bytes in core, which, if considering a large number of constants, could be a great saving of core storage.

Example:

Given three amount fields in a card; their locations are columns 1–4, 6–10 and 12–17. Add these three quantities into registers 2, 3 and 4, respectively, and also accumulate all three quantities into register 7.

Solution. The DTF and other housekeeping instructions will be omitted for the sake of brevity.

Name	Oper	Operand
INST1	PACK	DOUB,IN(4)
INST2	CVB	6,DOUB
INST3	AR	2,6
INST4	AR	7,6
INST5	PACK	DOUB,IN+5(5)
INST6	CVB	6,DOUB
	AR	3,6
	AR	7,6
	PACK	DOUB,IN+11(6)
	CVB	6,DOUB
	AR	4,6
	AR	7,6
	.	
DOUB	DS	D
IN	DS	CL80
	.	

FIGURE 6.4.

INST1 is used to pack the contents of the first field located in card columns 1 through 4 in a doubleword named DOUB. This area is reserved by the assembler instruction DS, which performs the necessary boundary alignment. The second instruction, INST2, converts the contents of area named DOUB into fixed-point binary format and places it into register 6. (General register 6 is being used as a work register.) The third instruction, INST3, adds the contents of register 6 to register 2 and INST4 adds register 6 to register 7. The same process is repeated for the other two amounts.

Logical Add Instructions

Instruction Name	Add Logical Register to Register
Mnemonic OP Code	ALR
Machine OP Code	1E
Type	RR
Program Interruptions	none
Condition Code	is affected
Assembler Format	ALR R1,R2

Instruction Name	Add Logical Fullword to Register
Mnemonic OP Code	AL
Machine OP Code	5E
Type	RX
Program Interruptions	Protection, Addressing, Specification
Condition Code	is affected
Assembler Format	AL R1,D2(X2,B2)

In both of these logical add instructions the second operand's contents are added to the first operand's contents and the resulting sum replaces the original contents of the first operand. Logical addition is performed by adding all 32 bits of both operands. The logical add instructions differ from the algebraic add instructions in three ways:
1. Absence of interruption in case of fixed-point overflow.
2. The meaning of the condition code settings.
3. There is no add halfword logical instruction.

Resulting Condition Code	Meaning
0	Sum is zero (no carry)
1	Sum is not zero (no carry)
2	Sum is zero (carry)
3	Sum is not zero (carry)

The logical add instructions are not very widely used. Nonetheless, they have some very important applications.

Example:

Code a routine that will add two doublewords of binary data located in registers 4 - 5 and registers 8 - 9 and place the resulting sum in registers 8 and 9.

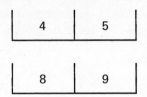

This could be accomplished by using a combination of AR and ALR instructions. First, we add logically the contents of register 5 to register 9 with an ALR instruction. The next step is to test for a carry. If a carry had resulted, we would first add a 1 to register 8 and then add the contents of register 4 to register 8 with an AR instruction. In case of no carry we would simply add register 4 to register 8 with an AR instruction. The reason for using an ALR instruction to add register 5 to register 9 is the fact that, in case of a carry, we do not want a program interruption to occur. However, when adding register 4 to register 8 we would not want an overflow to go unnoticed, thus using the AR instruction. The coding required to accomplish this is shown in Figure 6.5 below.

Name	Oper	Operand	
	.		
	.		
	.		
	ALR	9,5	ADD LOGICAL REG5 TO REG9
	BC	3,CARRY	IF A CARRY, GO TO CARRY
	BC	15,OUT	BRANCH TO OUT
CARRY	AH	8,ONE	ADD 1 TO REG8
OUT	AR	8,4	ADD REG4 TO REG8
	.		
	.		
	.		
ONE	DC	H'+1'	
	.		

FIGURE 6.5. Use of ALR Instruction.

The following problem illustrates yet another approach to the same type of problem. In this case we again have two doublewords of binary (fixed-point) data that needs to be added together. However, one of the doublewords is located in the main storage and the other one in registers 8 and 9. Consider the coding below:

```
              .
           AL      R9,DOUBLE+4 ADD LOGICAL LOW-ORDER WORD
           BC      12,NOCARRY  IF NO CARRY BRANCH
           AH      R8,ONE          ELSE ADD 1 TO REG8
NOCARRY    A       8,DOUBLE        ADD BINARY HIGH-ORDER WORD
              .
              .
DOUBLE     DS      D
ONE        DC      H'1'
              .
```

The flowchart below illustrates this logic.

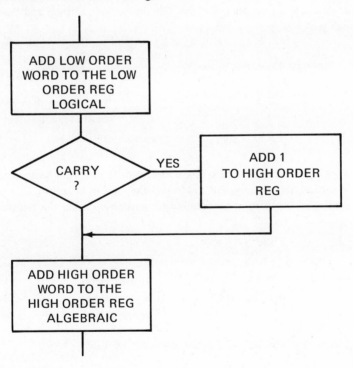

6.4 Binary Subtract Instructions

Binary subtract instructions can be grouped under two sub-headings: Algebraic Subtract; and, Logical Subtract instructions.

Algebraic Subtract Instructions

    Instruction Name   Subtract Register from Register

Mnemonic OP Code	SR
Machine OP Code	1B
Type	RR
Program Interruptions	Fixed-point overflow
Condition Code	is affected
Assembler Format	SR R1,R2

The contents of the second operand are subtracted from those of the first operand and the resulting difference is placed into the first operand location. Subtraction actually is performed by adding the two's complement of the second operand to the first operand's contents. All 32 bits of both operands participate in the instruction execution. An overflow condition will occur if the carry into the sign bit does not agree with the carry out of the sign bit. When an overflow condition is recognized, fixed-point overflow interruption follows. Condition code settings and their meanings are given below.

Resulting Condition Code	Meaning
0	Result is zero
1	Result is less than zero
2	Result is greater than zero
3	Overflow

Note: If both operands of the SR instruction specify the same general register, the result of subtraction is equivalent to clearing the register to zeros.

In the examples of subtraction that follow we will assume that the registers are 8 bit registers.

SR   R1,R2

		s		s		
R1	+64	0 100 0000		0 100 0000		+64
R2	+32	0 010 0000		1 110 0000		−32
				0 010 0000		+32

A one is carried into and out of the sign bit – no overflow.

		s		s		
R1	+32	0 010 0000		0 010 0000		+32
R2	+32	0 010 0000		1 110 0000		−32
				0 000 0000		+ 0

A one is carried into and out of the sign bit – no overflow.

		s		
R1	+64	0 100 0000	0 100 0000	+64
R2	-32	1 110 0000	0 010 0000	+32
			0 110 0000	+96

No carries – no overflow.

		s		
R1	+64	0 100 0000	0 100 0000	+64
R2	-68	1 011 1100	0 100 0100	+68
			1 000 0100	+132

A one carried into the sign position, but there is no carry out of that position – overflow.

Instruction Name	Subtract Fullword from Register
Mnemonic OP Code	S
Machine OP Code	5B
Type	RX
Program Interruptions	Protection, Addressing, Specification, Fixed-point overflow
Condition Code	is affected
Assembler Format	S R1,D2(X2,B2)

The second operand, which must be a fullword containing a fixed-point quantity, is subtracted from the contents of the first operand. The operand in storage must be located on a fullword boundary. Other than the fact that the second operand is located in the main storage, all other rules of SR instruction apply to this instruction, including the condition code settings.

Example:

Assume 2 fullword fixed-point quantities are located in core in areas named QUANTA and QUANTB; subtract QUANTB from QUANTA and place the difference in RESULT in EBCDIC Format.

```
RESULT    DS      CL6
QUANTA    DS      F
QUANTB    DS      F
DOUB      DS      D
          A       3,QUANTA
          S       3,QUANTB
          CVD     3,DOUB
          UNPK    RESULT,DOUB
```

Example:

In the above example, assume that QUANTA is located in positions 2004-2007, QUANTB in positions 2008-2011 and RESULT occupies core positions 2015-2020. Assume that the base register is register 2 and contains 00 00 20 00. We would write our coding as follows:

```
DOUB         DS        D
             .
             A         3,4(0,2)
             S         3,8(0,2)
             CVD       3,DOUB
             UNPK      15(6,2),DOUB
```

Instruction Name	Subtract Halfword from Register
Mnemonic OP Code	SH
Machine OP Code	4B
Type	RX
Program Interruptions	Protection, Addressing, Specification, Fixed-point overflow
Condition Code	is affected
Assembler Format	SH R1,D2(X2,B2)

This instruction is used to subtract the contents of a halfword second operand from the register specified as R1. The result of subtraction replaces the original contents of the first operand. Before subtraction, the second operand halfword is expanded to a fullword by propagating the sign bit through 16 high-order bit positions. This expansion takes place after the halfword has been fetched and placed in the control unit. Thus, the second operand is not altered in any manner. All other rules as explained in the SR instruction apply also to this instruction.

Logical Subtract Instructions

Two logical subtract instructions are provided. These are: Subtract Logical Register from Register (RR Type); and, Subtract Logical Fullword from Register (RX Type).

Assembler Format	SLR	R1,R2	RR Type
Assembler	SL	R2,D2(X2,B2)	RX Type

In both of these instructions, the second operand is subtracted from the first operand and the difference is placed in the first operand location.

These instructions differ from algebraic subtract instructions in three ways.

1. There is no provision for subtracting a halfword from a register.

2. In case of an overflow, program interruption does not occur.

3. Meaning of the condition code.

Resulting Condition Code	Meaning
0	———
1	Difference is not zero (no carry)
2	Difference is zero (carry)
3	Difference is zero (no carry)

Since a zero difference can not be obtained without a carry out of the sign bit, the condition code setting of 0 is of no meaning and hence not used.

EXERCISE:

Write program steps to generate 6 halfword constants and name them F1, F2, F3, F4, F5 and F6 containing +7, +10, 87, 1732, +1001, and 2017, respectively. Compute:

$$F1 + F2 - F3 + 2(F4) - F5$$

and place the result in register 6.

6.5 Load and Store Instructions

In Section 5.1, we learned two data moving instructions, MVC and MVI. MVC, being a storage-to-storage type of instruction, moves data from one core location to another. MVI instruction, a storage-immediate type, is used to move immediate data to some storage location. In programming, there are many occasions when it becomes necessary to transfer data from storage locations to register or vice versa. At times, transferring the contents of one register to another is also necessary. For example, we may need to store the result of an addition or subtraction during program processing. In the pages that follow, we will discuss various instructions which give us the capability of doing just this.

Load instructions

In programming terminology, transferring of data from storage to register is called *loading*. The load instructions essentially function as move instructions, i.e., the data from the sending operand is copied and moved to the receiving field. The receiving field is always a register and the sending field may be a core storage location or another register.

Instruction Name	Load Register into Register
Mnemonic OP Code	LR
Machine OP Code	18

Type   RR
Assembler Format   LR R1,R2

This instruction transfers the contents of the second operand identified as R2 into the first operand location, R1. The data being transferred is not altered in any sense and the second operand remains unaltered.

LR   4,7

This instruction would transfer the contents of register 7 to register 4. The condition code is not affected by this instruction.

Instruction Name	Load Fullword to Register
Mnemonic OP Code	L
Machine OP Code	58
Type	RX
Program Interruptions	Protection, Addressing, Specification
Assembler Format	L R1,D2(X2,B2)

This instruction causes the contents of the second operand to be placed into the general register specified as R1. The second operand must address a fullword located on an integral boundary. The contents of the second operand are not changed.

Example:

```
      .
L          4,FULL
      .

FULL    DC      F'17'
      .
```

The load instruction above will transfer the contents of the second operand into general register 4.

Instruction Name	Load Halfword into Register
Mnemonic OP Code	LH
Machine OP Code	48
Type	RX
Program Interruptions	Protection, Addressing, Specification
Condition Code	not affected
Assembler Format	LH R1,D2(X2,B2)

This instruction places the contents of the second operand, which is a halfword in storage, into the register specified as R1. The first operand must always be a register and the second operand must be a halfword containing a fixed-point quantity located on an integral boundary. After the halfword operand is obtained from storage and before it is placed into the register, the halfword is expanded to a fullword by propagating the sign bit through the 16 high-order bit positions. The second operand is not altered in any manner.

Example:

	LH	3,CONST
	.	
	.	
CONST	DC	H'30'

EXERCISE:

Write a DC statement to store -512 in a halfword and then load this constant into register 6. Show in hexadecimal, the contents of the halfword and register 6.

Instruction Name	Load Multiple Registers
Mnemonic OP Code	LM
Machine OP Code	98
Type	RS
Program Interruptions	Protection, Addressing, Specifications
Assembler Format	LM R1,R3,D2(B2)

This is the first of the RS instructions to be discussed, so let us review the basic format and characteristics of RS formats.

The first byte of the instruction, as always, contains the operation code. The second byte contains R1 and R3 operands. This type of register specification is also termed as *range parameters,* i.e., R1 and R3 specify the range of the registers to be affected by the instruction. In case of the LM instruction, the set of general registers starting with the register specified by R1 and ending with the register specified as R3, is loaded from the core location addressed by the second operand. The general registers are loaded in ascending order starting with R1 and continuing up to and including the register specified as R3.

The second operand must start at a fullword integral boundary and continue through as many fullwords as needed.

Consider how this instruction can be used in programming application. Assume that we need to transfer the contents of 4 fullwords of data to 4 general registers. The registers to be used are 4, 5, 6 and 7 and the areas in core are named FULL1, FULL2, FULL3 and FULL4. One way to accomplish this would be to use 4 *load fullword* instructions.

	L	4,FULL1
	L	5,FULL2
	L	6,FULL3

(continued)

```
              L            7,FULL4
                           .

FULL1         DS           F
FULL2         DS           F
FULL3         DS           F
FULL4         DS           F
                           .
```

The same objective could be accomplished by using a single load multiple instruction:

```
              LM           4,7,FULL1
```

EXERCISE:

Write program steps to store +17, -30, +40, 20, and +73 as fullword constants and then store these constants into 5 consecutive registers starting with register 3.

Any of the following combination of register addresses may be used in specifying R1 and R3 registers:

1. Both R1 and R3 specify the same register. When R1 and R3 are the same, only one word is transferred.
2. R3 register number less than R1. In this case, the register addresses wrap around from 15 to 0.

Example:

```
                           .

              LM           14,2,AREA
                           .

AREA          DS           5F
                           .
```

The LM instruction above will transfer the contents of 5 fullwords into registers 14, 15, 0, 1 and 2.

Note: The storage location specified for Load Instructions except for LR, must begin at fullword integral boundary. The second operand does not change.

Store instructions

Store instructions are used to transfer the contents of register(s) into core storage locations. The movement of data is from register to storage and the *first operand is the sending field.*

Instruction Name	Store Register into Fullword
Mnemonic OP Code	ST
Machine OP Code	50

Type	RX
Program Interruptions	Protection, Addressing, Specification
Condition Code	not affected
Assembler Format	ST R1,D2(X2,B2)

This instruction is used to transfer the contents of a general register, specified as R1, to a fullword in storage. All 32 bits of the register are copied and moved to the second operand location. The sending operand's contents remain unchanged. The second operand must be located on fullword integral boundary.

Example:

```
              ST       4,FULL
                .
    FULL      DS       F
                .
```

The contents of register 4 will be transferred to a fullword identified with the symbol FULL.

Instruction Name	Store Register into Halfword
Mnemonic OP Code	STH
Machine OP Code	40
Type	RX
Condition Code	is affected
Assembler Format	STH R1,D2(X2,B2)

This instruction transfers the rightmost 16 bits of the general purpose register, specified as R1, into the second operand location. The receiving field, the second operand, must be a halfword located on integral boundary. The data remains unchanged as it is transferred from register to storage. The high-order 16 bits of the register R1, do not participate in the instruction execution.

Example:

```
              STH      7,HALF
                .
    HALF      DS       H
```

The rightmost 16 bits of register 7 will be transferred to the halfword named HALF.

EXERCISE:

1. Write two DC statements to store +1732 and +123 as halfword binary constants. Add these together and place the result into another halfword named RESULT.

2. Write program steps to store in 27 consecutive halfwords of storage the binary numbers 0 through 26. Write any DS or DC statements required in this routine.

Instruction Name	Store Multiple
Mnemonic OP Code	STM
Machine OP Code	90
Type	RS
Program Interruptions	Protection, Addressing, Specification
Condition Code	is affected
Assembler Format	STM R1,R3,D2(B2)

The contents of the general registers, starting with the register specified as R1 and ending with the register specified by R3, are stored in storage locations starting with the one addressed by the second operand. The registers are transferred in ascending order starting with R1. Transfer of data stops after the contents of R3 have been stored.

Note: The receiving words in storage must begin on word boundary and be adjacent to each other.

With store-multiple instruction, wrap around of registers is permitted. The instruction STM 14,2 FULL will transfer the contents of registers 14, 15, 0, 1 and 2 into five adjacent words in storage.

Instruction Name	Load and Test Register
Mnemonic OP Code	LTR
Machine OP Code	12
Type	RR
Program Interruptions	None
Condition Code	is affected
Assembler Format	LTR R1,R2

This instruction causes the second operand to be placed into the first operand location, R1, and the sign and magnitude of the data being moved are tested. The resulting condition code reflects the result of the test as illustrated by the chart below.

Resulting Condition Code	Meaning
0	Result is zero
1	Result is less than zero
2	Result is greater than zero
3	———

Note: If R1 and R2 operands specify the same register, the operation is equivalent to a test without data movement. For example, LTR 4,4 will result in a specific condition code setting without the actual transfer of data.

EXERCISE:

Write program steps to test the magnitude of a quantity punched in card columns

10–15, if the amount is negative branch to a routine named NEGAMT. The card record has been read into an area named IN.

Example:

A	DS	F
B	DS	F
C	DS	H
D	DS	H
E	DS	F

Compute: $E = 2A + C + B + 2D$

.	
L	3,A
AR	3,3
AH	3,C
A	3,B
LH	4,D
AR	4,4
AR	3,4
ST	3,E
.	
.	

Example:

The following two fullwords have been defined.

WORDS	DS	2F

Reverse the order of these words.

.	
LM	1,2,WORDS
LR	0,2
STM	0,1,WORDS
.	

Example:

X	DS	F
Y	DS	H
Q	DS	F
R	DS	H

Compute: $R = 3Y + 4X + Q$

```
          LH         4,Y
          LR         3,4
          AR         4,4
          AR         3,4
          L          4,X
          AR         4,4
          AR         4,4
          AR         3,4
          A          3,Q
          STH        3,R
          .
          .
```

Note: In this example we assume that the magnitude of the result developed is not greater than a halfword fixed-point number.

EXERCISE:

Consider the coding below.

```
          LM         5,6,CONST
          LTR        5,6
BRANCH1   BC         8,OUT1
BRANCH2   BC         4,OUT2
BRANCH3   BC         2,OUT3
          .
CONST     DC         F'-32477'
          DC         F'61440'
          .
```

Which of the three branches will be taken? Also show the contents of register 5, in hexadecimal, after the execution of the LTR instruction.

A problem with suggested solution

Write a program to read a card file which has three quantities, X, Y, and Z, punched in each card. The format of the card record is as follows:

c.c	
1 − 5	X
6 − 10	Y
11 − 15	Z

For each card read, compute the value of X+Y+Z and print the result along with the three quantities. The output should have the column headings, FIELD X, FIELD Y, FIELD Z, and X+Y-Z. The heading line is to appear on the top of the first page only.

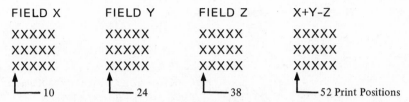

FIELD X	FIELD Y	FIELD Z	X+Y–Z
XXXXX	XXXXX	XXXXX	XXXXX
XXXXX	XXXXX	XXXXX	XXXXX
XXXXX	XXXXX	XXXXX	XXXXX
└──10	└──24	└──38	└──52 Print Positions

FIGURE 6.6. Sample Report Layout.

Figure 6.7 is the block diagram for this problem and the coding is given in Figure 6.8.

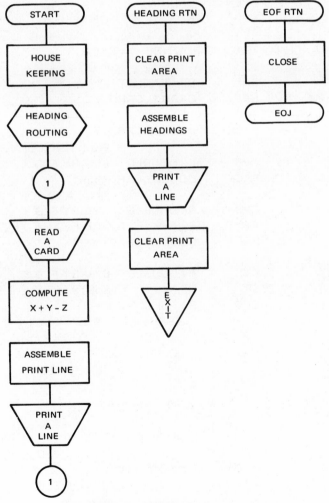

FIGURE 6.7. Suggested Flowchart.

```
Name        Oper        Operand
            START       0
CARDIN      DTFCD       DEVADDR=SYS008,IOAREA1=IN1,              X
                        IOAREA2=IN2,                            X
                        WORKA=YES,EOFADDR=NOCARD
REPORT      DTFPR       DEVADDR=SYS010,BLKSIZE=56,               X
                        WORKA=YES,                              X
                        IOAREA1=OUT1
BEGIN       BALR        R2,0
            USING       *,R2
            OPEN        CARDIN,
                        REPORT          OPEN FILES
*
*BRANCH TO HEADING ROUTINE VIA REG 3
*
            BAL         R3,HEADING
READ        GET         CARDIN,CARD
*                                       READ A CARD
            PACK        DOUBLE,CARD(5)
*                                       PACK AND CONVERT TO
            CVB         R3,DOUBLE       BINARY FLD X
            PACK        DOUBLE,CARD+5(5)
*                                       PACK AND CONVERT TO
            CVB         R4,DOUBLE       BINARY FLD Y
            AR          R3,R4           ADD FLD Y TO FLD X
            PACK        DOUBLE,CARD+10(5)
*                                       PACK AND CONVERT TO
            CVB         R4,DOUBLE       BINARY FLD Z
            SR          R3,R4           SUBTRACT FLD Z FROM X+Y
            CVD         R3,DOUBLE
            UNPK        LINE+51(5),DOUBLE+5(3)
*                                       POSITION X+Y-Z
            MVZ         LINE+55(1),LINE+51
*                                       REMOVE ZONE
*
*MOVE FIELDS X, Y AND Z TO PRINT AREA
*
            MVC         LINE+9(5),CARD
*                                       MOVE FIELD X
            MVC         LINE+23(5),CARD+5
*                                       MOVE FIELD Y
```

(continued)

```
              MVC      LINE+37(5),CARD+10
*                                         MOVE FIELD Z
  q           PUT      REPORT,LINE
*                                         PRINT A LINE
              BC       15,READ
*

*PAGE HEADING ROUTINE
*
HEADING       MVC      LINE,LINE-1  CLEAR PRINT AREA
              MVC      LINE+9(7),HDG1
              MVC      LINE+23(7),HDG2
              MVC      LINE+37(7),HDG3
              MVC      LINE+51(5),HDG4
              PUT      REPORT,LINE
*                                         PRINT HEADING LINE
              MVC      LINE,LINE-1  CLEAR PRINT AREA
              BCR      15,R3
*

*END OF FILE ROUTINE
*
NOCARD        CLOSE    CARDIN,REPORT
*                                         CLOSE FILES
              EOJ
*

*DECLARATIVES
*
              DC       C' '            BLANK SPACE
LINE          DS       CL56            WORK AREA FOR PRINTER
OUT1          DS       CL56            BUFFER FOR PRINTER
CARD          DS       CL80            WORK AREA FOR CARDS
IN1           DS       CL80            BUFFERS
IN2           DS       CL80              FOR CARDS
DOUBLE        DS       D
HDG1          DC       C'FIELD X'
HDG2          DC       C'FIELD Y'
HDG3          DC       C'FIELD Z'
HDG4          DC       C'X+Y-Z'
R2            EQU      2               EQUATE REGISTER 2
R3            EQU      3               EQUATE REGISTER 3
R4            EQU      4               EQUATE REGISTER 4
              END      BEGIN
```

FIGURE 6.8. Suggested Solution

Self Evaluation Quiz

1. The receiving field for the CVD instruction must be:
    a. Four bytes long on integral boundary.
    b. Could be any number of bytes as long as it is long enough to contain all the data.
    c. Eight bytes in length.
    d. Doubleword located on integral boundary.

2. FLDX contains 00 34 00 2C; indicate the contents of this field after execution of the instruction

$$\text{UNPK} \qquad \text{FLDX,FLDX+2(2)}$$

3. Is it valid to specify explicit length for the second operand of a MVZ instruction?

4. Given the following fixed-point quantities:

```
BALANCE    DS       F
INVAMT     DS       F
AMTPD      DS       F
CHARGES    DS       F
```

Write program steps to compute the following:

    BALANCE = INVAMT + CHARGES - AMTPD

    If BALANCE is zero, branch to ZEROBAL

    If BALANCE is positive, branch to POSBAL

    If BALANCE is negative, branch to NEGBAL

5. There are 5 fullwords named F1, F2, F3, F4 and F5 located at consecutive core locations. Write an instruction that will transfer the contents of the last 4 words into registers 14, 15, 0 and 1.

6. Given 6 fullwords in storage named F1, F2, F3, F4, F5, and RESULT, compute:

    RESULT = 2(F1 + F2 - F3) + (F4 + F5)

7. A data field named FLDA contains F3 F7 F2 F4. What will be the contents of this field after execution of the following instructions?

```
           PACK      DOUB,FLDA
           CVB       7,DOUB
           CVD       7,DOUB
           UNPK      FLDA,DOUB
             .
DOUB       DS        D
             .
```

8. General register 7 contains negative four and general register 8 contains positive five. Indicate the resulting condition code setting for each of the following instructions:

```
SR      7,8
SR      8,7
AR      7,8
ALR     8,7
LTR     8,8
LTR     7,7
SR      8,8
```

9. Write program steps to compute:

$$RESULT = (Z - A) + (X - A) + (Y - A)$$

```
A          DS      F
X          DS      F
Y          DS      F
Z          DS      F
RESULT     DS      F
```

10. Indicate what will be printed when the following instructions are executed.

```
MVI        PRINT,C' '
MVC        PRINT+1(131),PRINT
PACK       WORK,A(4)
CVB        7,WORK
PACK       WORK,B(5)
CVB        9,WORK
AR         7,9
LTR        9,7
CVD        7,WORK
UNPK       PRINT+10(7),WORK
PUT        PRINTER,PRINT
```

```
WORK       DS      D
A          DC      C'10345'
B          DC      X'F0F0F3F6F165'
PRINT      DS      CL132
           .
```

[7]

Form Control, Stacker Selection, and Editing

7.1 Form Control

The continuous form printer units of System 360 are provided with tape-controlled carriage mechanisms for high-speed feeding, spacing and skipping of continuous forms. The carriage movement, spacing and skipping, is controlled by punched holes in a carriage-control tape that corresponds in length to the length of one or more forms. Holes can be punched into the control tape to stop the form skipping operation when it reaches any predetermined position.

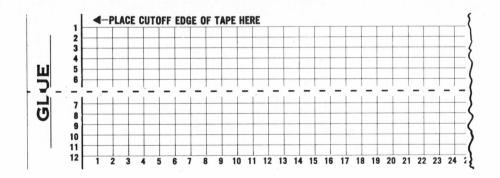

FIGURE 7.1. Carriage-Control Tape.

The carriage of the continuous form printers is capable of accommodating forms of great variety, short, medium or long, and the form can be designed to permit printing in practically any arrangement. Skipping to different sections of a form is controlled by problem program instructions in conjunction with the control carriage tape. Spacing of forms is controlled solely by program instructions.

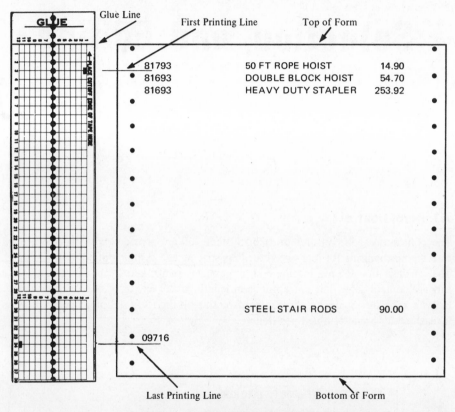

FIGURE 7.2. Use of Carriage-Control Tape.

The control tape has 12 columnar positions indicated by vertical lines called channels. Holes can be punched in each channel throughout the length of the tape. Round holes in the center of the tape are prepunched for the pin-feed device that advances the carriage tape in synchronism with the movement of the printer form.

To mark a carriage tape for punching, it is generally placed beside the left edge of the form it is to control, with the top line (immediately under the glue portion) even with the top edge of the form. Then a mark is made in the first channel on the line that corresponds to the first printing line on the form. Additional marks are made in the appropriate channels for each of the other skip stops and for the form overflow position. Usually, a punch in channel 1 is used to indicate the first printing position, while a punch in channel 12 or 9 indicates the last printing line or the overflow position. The markings for one form should be repeated as many times as the usage length of the tape allows. The line corresponding to the bottom edge of the form is marked for cutting after the tape has been punched. After punching holes in the required positions, the bottom edge is glued to the top edge marked, glue. The center feed holes should coincide when the two ends of the carriage tape are glued together.

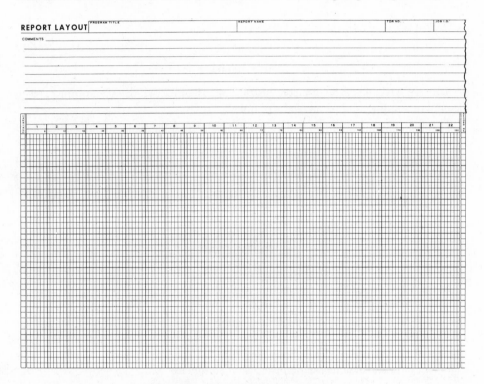

FIGURE 7.3. Report Layout Form.

Reading brushes are provided in the carriage control mechanism to sense the holes punched in a carriage tape. Now we shall take a look at the problem program instructions needed to control the spacing, skipping and the testing of the overflow conditions of a carriage tape.

Instruction Name	Print Overflow
Symbolic OP Code	PRTOV
Machine OP Code	None
Type	Imperative Macro

The PRTOV macro is used in conjunction with a logical printer file to test and perform certain action upon form overflow condition. This instruction, in fact, tests for the form overflow indicator[1]. If the indicator is ON, action specified by the instruction is performed, otherwise, the program branches to the next sequential instruction. If the PRTOV macro is used in a problem program, the DTFPR entries for the file *must* include the entry:

PRINTOV=YES

Symbolic Format of the PRTOV macro is:

Name	Oper	Operand
	PRTOV	filename,n,routine-name

This is a *positional type* of macro instruction. The first two parameters must always be present and the third parameter is optional.

The first parameter must be the same filename as assigned to the DTF macro for this printer file. The second operand, n, specifies the punch position on the carriage tape used to signal the form overflow condition. The channel most commonly used for this purpose is 12; however, channel 9 can also be used. The third parameter is optional and will be discussed later in the text. First, observe how this instruction functions when only the first two parameters are specified.

Name	Oper	Operand
	PUT	REPORTS
	PRTOV	REPORTS,12

Execution of the PRTOV instruction will direct the IOCS to test for form overflow condition, sensing of channel 12 in this case. When an overflow condition is sensed, the IOCS will restore the carriage to channel 1 punch which, if you remember, designates the first printing line and then the program control flows to the next sequential instruction. If the indicator tested is OFF, no restoration of carriage takes place and the sequential instruction execution continues.

Example:

The coding below illustrates the use of the PRTOV macro.

Name	Oper	Operand	
	START		
CARDIN	DTFCD	DEVADDR=SYS008,IOAREA1=IN1,	X
		IOAREA2=IN2,	X
		EOFADDR=END,WORKA=YES,DEVICE=2540	
REPORTS	DTFPR	DEVADDR=SYS010,IOAREA1=OUT1,	X
		WORKA=YES,	X
		IOAREA2=OUT2,DEVICE=1403,	X

(continued)

---

[1]The form overflow indicator is set when the sensing brushes on the carriage control mechanism sense a 12 or 9 punch in the carriage tape.

```
                          PRINTOV=YES
BEGIN         BALR        2,0
              USING       *,2
              OPEN        CARDIN,REPORTS
              MVC         LINEWORK,LINEWORK-1
READ          GET         CARD,TEMP
              MVC         LINEWORK+10(80),TEMP
              PUT         REPORTS,LINEWORK
              PRTOV       REPORTS,12
              BC          15,READ
END           CLOSE       CARDIN,REPORTS
              EOJ
IN1           DS          CL80
IN2           DS          CL80
TEMP          DS          CL80
OUT1          DS          CL132
OUT2          DS          CL132
              DC          C' '
LINEWORK      DS          CL132
              END         BEGIN
```

FIGURE 7.4. Program Showing Testing for Form Overflow.

Note: 1. The third parameter of the PRTOV macro is specified if the programmer prefers to branch to a routine on a form overflow condition, rather than letting the IOCS skip the form directly to channel 1. The third parameter designates the entry point to the programmer's routine. In this routine, the programmer may issue any IOCS macro except the PRTOV macro.

2. An important point is when the third parameter is used, the IOCS on sensing the form overflow condition, *does not* restore the carriage to channel 1. Instead, a branch is taken to the address specified by the third parameter.

The programmer, if he so desires, has to include appropriate instructions to restore the carriage to channel in his routine.

```
Name          Oper        Operand
              PUT         REPORTS
              PRTOV       REPORTS,12,HDGRTN
```

In the example above, the PRTOV macro will test for form overflow condition. If such a condition exists, a branch will be taken to the symbolic name HDGRTN. At the time the branch is taken to the symbolic name designated by the third parameter, the IOCS places the return address, i.e., the address of the next sequential instruction after PRTOV macro, in the general register 14. At the end of his routine, the programmer must return to the IOCS via the address in register 14. In case any IOCS macro is written in the routine, the programmer *must save and then restore* the contents of register 14.

Example:

Name	Oper	Operand	
		.	
	PUT	REPORTS	
	PRTOV	REPORTS,12,HDGRTN	
		.	
		.	
		.	
HDGRTN	ST	14,SAVE	SAVE CONTENTS OF REG 14
		.	
		.	
		.	
	L	14,SAVE	RESTORE REGISTER 14
	BCR	15,14	BRANCH VIA REGISTER 14
		.	
SAVE	DS	F	
		.	

In the coding above, the third parameter is included for the PRTOV macro and is specified as HDGRTN. When the form overflow condition, channel 12, is sensed, the IOCS will cause a branch to the symbol HDGRTN. IOCS will not, in this case, restore the carriage tape to channel 1. In his routine, the programmer may print total lines, etc., and then skip to channel 1 before returning to the main program stream. At the end of his routine, the programmer *must return* to IOCS via register 14. As previously stated, this is the register which is supplied with the return address when a branch is taken by the PRTOV macro.

In the coding example illustrated above, the first instruction of the routine with the entry point identified as HDGRTN saves the contents of register 14. The reason being the fact that, if the programmer uses any other IOCS macro instruction in his routine (such as GET, PUT, etc.) the return address stored in register 14 will be destroyed. Just before returning to the IOCS, we restore the contents of register 14.

To summarize, PRTOV macro is used to test for form overflow condition, i.e., sensing of channel 9 or 12. If the third parameter, routine-name, is omitted, the IOCS on sensing the form overflow condition simply restores the carriage tape to channel 1. If the third parameter, routine-name, is specified, upon sensing the form overflow condition the IOCS does not restore the carriage to channel 1. Instead, a branch is taken to the symbolic name specified as the third parameter.

When using the PRTOV macro in a program, the programmer must include PRINTOV=YES entry in the DTF entries for the file.

CNTRL macro

Spacing and skipping in a printer file and stacker selection in the card read-punch units can be controlled by IOCS routines. To cause the IOCS to generate the necessary instructions, the programmer has to use the CNTRL macro in his problem program. If the CNTRL macro is used in a problem program, the DTF entries for the file *must include* CONTROL=YES entry. The format of the CNTRL macro is:

Name	Oper	Operand
	CNTRL	Filename,code,n,m

This is a positional format macro and the assembler *expects* the various parameters to be in the same format as specified above. The first two parameters are mandatory and the last two are optional. If the third parameter is left out, the omission must be indicated by a comma. The first parameter, filename, must be the same symbolic name as assigned to the file with the DTF macro instruction. The second parameter, code, is the mnemonic code for the command to be performed. This code can be selected from one of a set of predetermined codes. For different possible codes see Figure 7.5.

UNIT	MNEMONIC CODE	n	m	COMMAND
2540 Card Read	PS	1 2 3		Select Pocket 1, 2, or 3
2520, 1442 Card Read Punch	SS	1 2		Select Stacker 1 or 2
	E			Eject to Stacker 1 (1442 Only)
1403, 1404, 1443, 1445 Printers	SP	See Note c	d	Carriage Space 1, 2, or 3 lines
	K	c	d	Skip to Channel c and/or d

Note: c = An Integer Indicating Immediate Printer Control (Before Printing).
       d = An Integer Indicating a Delayed Printer Control.

FIGURE 7.5. Card and Printer Codes.

The third parameter, n, is used when a stacker selection or an *immediate* carriage control is desired. By immediate carriage control, we mean that the specified action is taken whenever the instruction is encountered by the CPU. The fourth parameter, m, is used when a *delayed* carriage control is desired. By delayed carriage control we mean that the action is taken after the next print command. Please note that there is no provision made for a delayed stacker selection.

Spacing

The CNTRL macro is used when we need to obtain extra spacing, i.e., spacing not provided by the printer unit automatically. As you know, each PUT to a printer file results in only one space between lines.

Example of immediate spacing

Name	Oper	Operand	
	.		
	PUT	REPORTS	
	CNTRL	REPORTS,SP,1	SPACE 1 IMMEDIATE
	.		

In this case, the CNTRL macro will generate instructions which, when executed, will cause the printer to take a single space. It is important to point out that the PUT macro causes an automatic space after printing. Thus the net effect of the instructions coded above will be two spaces between lines.

In the CNTRL macro coded below, the third parameter has been omitted and the fourth parameter specifies delayed spacing. In such cases, the action specified is *not* taken until the next PUT instruction to the file. One other point to note is that, when delayed spacing is specified, the standard single space does not take place. Thus, the instructions coded below will cause two spaces in all and the report will be double spaced. A *maximum of three spaces* can be specified with any one CNTRL macro.

Name	Oper	Operand
	.	
	CNTRL	REPORTS,SP,,2
	PUT	REPORTS
	.	
	.	

Skipping

CNTRL macro can also be used to specify skipping to different channels punched in a carriage control tape.

	Oper	Operand
	.	
	PUT	REPORTS
	CNTRL	REPORTS,SK,1
	.	

The CNTRL macro coded above will cause an *immediate* skip to channel 1. Similarly, the instructions coded below will cause the carriage to skip to channel 4.

```
PUT        REPORTS
CNTRL      REPORTS,SK,4
```

The CNTRL macro can also be used to cause *delayed* skipping. For example, the coding below will cause a skip to channel 4 when the PUT macro is executed.

```
CNTRL      REPORTS,SK,,4
PUT        REPORTS
```

The SP and SK (spacing and skipping) operations can be specified in any sequence. However, two or more consecutive immediate skip instructions to the same printer file will have the same result as the first skip only. That is, any skip command after the first one is ignored. In the same light, two or more consecutive delayed spacing and/or skips to the same printer file result in the last space or skip only. Any other combination of consecutive space and skip commands, such as an immediate space followed by another immediate space, will cause both operations to be executed.

Note: The PRTOV macro will cause either a skip to channel 1 or a branch to the programmer supplied routine if an overflow condition is sensed on the preceding space or print command. However, an overflow condition is not recognized during a carriage skip operation. Thus, after execution of any command that results in carriage movement the programmer should issue a PRTOV macro before writing the next PUT or CNTRL macro in his program. Doing this ensures that the overflow options included in the program will be executed at the correct time.

7.2 Stacker Selection

In this text, we will consider the 2540 and 1442 card units. The 2540 card read-punch unit has 5 stackers or pockets into which cards being read and punched can be selected. The figure below illustrates the flow of cards through a 2540 unit.

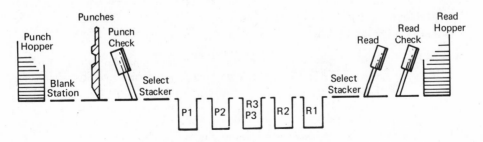

FIGURE 7.6. 2540 Read and Punch Card Flow.

The cards from the read side can be selected by the problem program into pockets R1, R2 and R3. From the punch side, the cards can be directed to go into pockets P1, P2 and P3. The middle stacker is shared by both feeds. Under normal conditions, i.e., when no SSELECT or CNTRL entry is specified, the cards from the read side fall into R1 and the punched cards fall into P1. The CNTRL macro can be used to distribute cards into any of these stackers. The format of the CNTRL macro for selecting stackers is:

Name	Oper	Operand
	CNTRL	filename,PS,n

Depending upon the pocket to be selected, the third parameter, n, could be any of the following values.

OPERATION	POCKET	n
Read	R1	1
Read	R2	2
Read	RP3	3
Punch	P1	1
Punch	P2	2
Punch	RP3	3

FIGURE 7.7.

Input Files. When selecting stackers from the read side, CNTRL macro is always issued *after* the GET to the file as in the example below.

```
GET      CARDIN
CNTRL    CARDIN,PS,2
```

The instructions coded above will select all cards being read into pocket R2.
Note: 1. If used, the CNTRL macro must be issued after the GET macro.
2. Once used, the CNTRL macro must be used with every succeeding GET instruction for the file. This, however, does not mean that all cards have to be selected in the same pocket.

Output Files. When a programmer desires to select a particular card in one of the three punch pockets, the CNTRL macro must be issued *before* the PUT for that card. However, CNTRL does not have to precede every PUT macro for the file.

Name	Oper	Operand
	CNTRL	CARDOUT,PS,3
	PUT	CARDOUT

In this case the card will be selected into pocket P3.

Cards fed into 1442 unit are normally directed to the stacker specified in the SSELECT entry for the particular file. In case the SSELECT[2] entry is omitted, the cards would be selected into pocket 1. The CNTRL macro can be used to override the normally selected pockets.

Input Files (Card Reading). To select a particular card, the CNTRL macro must be issued after the GET for that card and before the GET for the subsequent card. The CNTRL macro can only be used when one I/O area or, one work area together with one I/O area, is specified for the file.

Output Files (Card Punching). The CNTRL macro must be issued before the PUT instruction for the card to be selected. Any permissible combination of I/O and work area can be specified.

7.3 Editing Output

Until now, the amount fields have been printed without any punctuation. For example, an amount field of 001234 was printed as such. A more desirable way would be to print the field as 1234, or in case the field contained dollar and cent amounts it would be printed as 12.34 or \$12.34 or **12.34, to mention a few possibilities. This punctuation and insertion of special characters along with zero suppression can be done with the EDIT instruction, one of the features of System 360 Assembler Language. The edit instruction has a vast range of capabilities and some of these are listed below.

1. Sign control.
2. Punctuation insertion.
3. Suppression of leading zeros.
4. Check protection character insertion.
5. Floating currency sign insertion.

Two edit instructions are included in System 360 instruction set. These are EDIT, and EDIT and MARK instructions.

Instruction Name	EDIT
Mnemonic OP Code	ED
Machine OP Code	DE
Type	SS
Program Interruptions	Operation, Protection, Addressing, Data
Condition Code	is affected
Assembler Format	ED D1(L,B1),D2(B2)

The first operand, the receiving field, contains an edit pattern which indicates the manner in which the data from the second operand, the sending field, is to be edited.

---

[2]The SSELECT entry was discussed in Chapter 4 under the declarative file definition macros.

The edit pattern is constructed by the programmer following certain rules which will be discussed shortly. The length field, L, specifies the length of the edit pattern which is usually longer than the sending field. The second operand, sometimes also referred to as the source field, *must be* in packed format and *is checked* for valid digit and sign codes. The edit instruction is *executed* from left to right, one character at a time. The source field digits, when moved to the pattern are automatically expanded to zoned format, i.e., automatically unpacked. (Overlapping of source and pattern fields will give unpredictable results.) As a result of this instruction the edit pattern is replaced by the edited result. Thus, it is important to set up the edit pattern as a constant outside the output area and then to move the pattern in position before an edit instruction is issued. Due to this particular reason, a programmer usually has to write two instructions whenever editing is desired. These are: a move instruction to position the edit pattern; and, the edit instruction to perform editing.

The edit pattern is written in unpacked format and may contain any valid characters; however, three characters have special meaning to the assembler when used in editing.

Character	Hex Coding	Substitute[3] Character
Digit Select	20	d or D
Significant Start	21	(or S
Field Separator	22	) or F

When establishing patterns the usual practice is to use hex coding for the above mentioned digits. For example, a pattern containing 4 digit select characters would be set up as:

```
PATTERN     DC      X'20202020'
```

The high-order byte of each pattern is assumed to contain the *fill character*. During editing, all zeroes and punctuations to the left of the first non-zero digit are replaced by the fill character. Thus, the fill character position of a pattern should contain the character which is to be used to replace the leading zeros and punctuation characters. Although any valid character may be used, the most common fill character is a blank (Hex 40). Thus, a pattern containing 4 digit select characters and a blank as the fill character would be established as follows:

```
PATTERN     DC      X'4020202020'
```

The coding and the edit examples below show a series of edit results. Consider each instruction independently.

```
        MVC     TEMP,PATTERN
        ED      TEMP,AMOUNT
```

[3]Some authors use the notations on the left.

Example:
   The edit pattern contains: X'4020202020202020'

AMOUNT	Edited result in TEMP
1234567	b1234567
0234000	bb234000
0013401	bbb13401
0000703	bbbbb703
0000000	bbbbbbbb

Example:
   The edit pattern contains: X'5C20202020202020'

AMOUNT	Edited result in TEMP
1234561	*1234561
0234000	**234000
0013400	***13400
000700	*****700
0000000	*******

Note: 5C is the hex representation for an asterisk.

From the examples given above it is seen that for every digit position in the source field, the edit pattern must have a digit select character. During the course of editing, depending on whether or not a non-zero digit has been inserted in the edit pattern, one of the following two actions will be taken:

1. If a significant digit has not been encountered and the source digit is a zero, the fill character will be stored in the digit select position of the edit pattern.
2. If a significant digit has been encountered, the source digit, zero or non-zero, will be stored in the digit select position of the edit pattern. The digit being stored is supplied with the zone coding of 1111 or Hex F, i.e., unpacking takes place automatically.

Note: Any zero digit to the right of the first significant character will not be suppressed.

Only the digit select character and one other character (significant start character, to be discussed shortly) can receive a digit from the source field. All other characters constituting a pattern are either replaced by the fill character or are left unchanged. For example, consider an edit pattern consisting of:

   PATTERN   DC   X'40202020206B202020'

6B, is hexadecimal coding for a comma (,). The edited results shown in the chart below illustrate the rule stated above. Consider each example individually.

```
MVC        TEMP,PATTERN
ED         TEMP,AMOUNT
```

AMOUNT	Edited result in TEMP
1123456	b1123,456
0023400	bbb23,400
0001400	bbbb1,400
0000400	bbbbbb400
0000040	bbbbbbb40
0000000	bbbbbbbbb

From this example, it is clear that the comma in the edit pattern is replaced by the fill character if it appears to the left of the first significant digit, otherwise it is left in place.

Zero suppression of the leading zeros and punctuation characters is actually controlled by a special indicator of System 360, known as *S-trigger*. At the beginning of each edit instruction this trigger is set to zero or turned OFF. As the execution of the edit instruction begins, the CPU examines the status of the S-trigger. If the trigger is OFF any non-significant digit from the source field or the punctuation character in the edit pattern will be replaced by the fill character. The S-trigger is turned ON when a significant digit from the source field is stored into the edit pattern[4]. Once the S-trigger is turned ON, any punctuation in the edit pattern stays undisturbed and even a zero digit from the source field will get stored in the edit pattern. Once ON, the S-trigger can be turned OFF by either a field-separator character or a plus sign in the source field. Let us take a look at another set of edit results. The edit pattern in this case is:

```
PATTERN    DC        X'4020206B2020204B2020'
```

Note: 4B is the hex representation of a decimal point (.)

AMOUNT	Edited Result
0123456	bb1,234.56
0023400	bbbb234.00
0000700	bbbbbb7.00
0000070	bbbbbbb70
0000000	bbbbbbbbb

---

[4]The S-trigger can also be turned ON by a significant start digit. This special character will be discussed shortly.

The last two examples tell us that this type of pattern field is not very desirable, as even the decimal point has been replaced by the fill character and when printing dollar and cent amounts, the practice is to leave the decimal point in place. The reason for the suppression of the decimal point can be best understood by taking a look at the functioning of the S-trigger.

From what we have learned, we know that the S-trigger is turned ON only when a significant digit from the source field is inserted into the edit pattern. In case of the last two AMOUNT fields (in the example above) it is seen that by the time S-trigger is turned ON it is too late as the decimal points have already been suppressed. We very well know that if the S-trigger was turned ON before the editing process encountered the decimal point, it would have been left undisturbed. This can be accomplished by the use of the special character known as the *significant-start digit*. This character, in addition to functioning like a digit select character, has a special meaning to the CPU. During editing, when a significant-start digit is encountered, the S-trigger is turned ON even though a significant digit has not been inserted into the edit pattern and editing continues. We could say that the significant-start digit *forces* the S-trigger to be turned ON. Let us look at an example of editing using the significant-start digit.

Example:

PATTERN   DC   X'40206B2020214B202020'

AMOUNT	Edited Result
1234563-	b1,234.563 ††
0003244	bbbbb3.244
0000442	bbbbbb.442
0000000	bbbbbb.000

Note: 1. The significant-start digit, Hex 21, receives either a digit from the source field or is replaced by the fill character.

2. The significant-start digit indicates the *rightmost limit* of zero suppression. Any zeros or punctuations to the right of it are not suppressed. Of course, if the S-trigger has already been turned ON, the significant-start digit has no effect on the editing operation.

†† 3. In the case of the first example where the source field is a negative number we see that the edited result is 1,234.563 (a positive amount). The reason for this is the fact that during editing each source field digit being edited is supplied with a zone coding of $(1111)_2$ or Hex F.

Sign control

In case of negative numbers it is necessary to print some sign indicator to identify the status of the source field. Most commonly used sign indicators are CR, DB, -, etc.

The sign indicator insertion is indirectly controlled by the S-trigger. The process is as follows:

During each edit operation the rightmost 4 bits of the source field, the sign bits, are examined and used to set the S-trigger according to the rules stated below:

1. If the sign of the source field is negative, the S-trigger is turned ON.
2. If the sign of the source field is positive, the S-trigger is turned OFF.

This checking of the sign of the source field and setting of the S-trigger is done every time an edit instruction is executed. In the case of the examples discussed so far this happened after completion of the scan of the edit pattern and, as such, had no effect on the edited output. To add extra characters, for example the sign indicators, to the right of the rightmost digit select character in the edited pattern, the above stated characteristics (rules 1 and 2) would enable the programmer to include the sign indicators. The next step, then, is to include in the edit pattern the characters we wish to print if the sign of the source field is negative. For example:

```
PATTERN        DC         X'4020206B2020214B2020C3D9'
```

Note: C3 is the Hex representation for character C and D9 is the Hex representation for character R.

In case of the PATTERN above, the characters C3 and D9 do not have any special meaning to the CPU and in fact have no bearing on the editing process itself. Actually it is the S-trigger's setting that determines whether these characters will stay undisturbed or be replaced by the fill character. So, if the source field is positive, the S-trigger will be turned OFF upon encountering the sign bits and any characters to the right of the sign position will be replaced by the fill character. On the other hand, if the source field has a negative value the S-trigger will be turned ON and any characters to the right of the sign position will stay undisturbed. Further examples follow.

```
PATTERN        DC         X'4020206B2020214B2020C3D9'
```

AMOUNT	Edited Result
1234567	b12,345.67bb
0234567	bb2,345.67bb
0004567-	bbbbb45.67CR
0000030-	bbbbbbb.30CR
0000000	bbbbbbb.00bb
0000000-	bbbbbbb.00CR

```
PATTERN        DC         X'5C20206B2020214B202040C3D9'
```

AMOUNT	Edited Result
1234567	*12,345.67***
0021200	****212.00***
0021200-	****212.00 CR
0000000	*******.00***

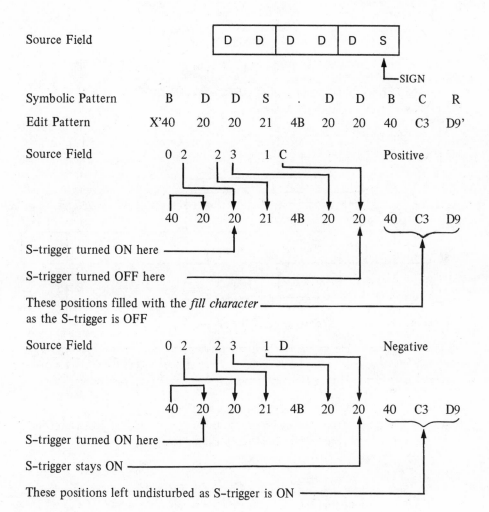

Source Field

Symbolic Pattern

Edit Pattern

Source Field

S–trigger turned ON here

S–trigger turned OFF here

These positions filled with the *fill character*
as the S–trigger is OFF

Source Field

S–trigger turned ON here

S–trigger stays ON

These positions left undisturbed as S–trigger is ON

Example:

   Given an amount field in the card area, columns 1 − 5, we are required to edit this field and place the edited result in print positions 10 − 18. The edited result's format is:

$$xx\emptyset.xxCR$$

   The first step is to pack the source field and this would require 3 bytes. The next step is to position the edit pattern in the output area and then to issue the edit instruction.

```
       PACK      TEMP,IN(5)
```

(continued)

```
              MVC      OUT+9(9),PATTERN
              ED       OUT+9(9),TEMP
                 .
                 .
   PATTERN    DC       X'402020214B2020C3D9'
   TEMP       DC       CL3
```

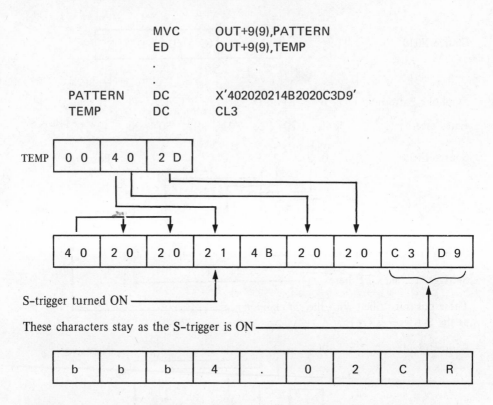

Example:

Given an amount field in card columns 1 − 6, edit this field and place the edited result in an area named TEMP. The edited result should look like:

x,xxØ.xx

The first step as always is to pack the source field. This field would require 4 bytes to pack the data. Assume that the card columns 1 − 6 contain 234050.

0	2	3	4	0	5	0	F

From the figure above you can see that we have ended with 7 digits instead of the 6 digits from the card columns. The packing operation has supplied us with a padded zero thus increasing the size of the field by 1 digit position. As editing is executed from left to right, it is necessary that we provide for this extra digit in our edit pattern.

```
              PACK     AREA,IN(6)
              MVC      TEMP,PATTERN
```

(continued)

```
              ED        TEMP,AREA
                .
                .
     AREA       DS       CL4
     TEMP       DS       CL10
     PATTERN    DC       X'4020206B2020214B2020'
                .
```

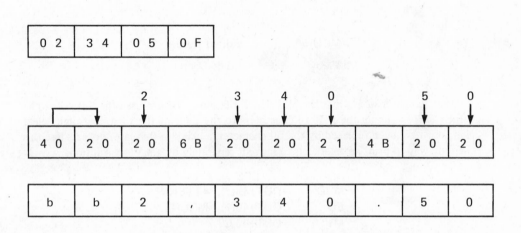

When printing group indicated reports it is a common practice to identify the group totals by placing an asterisk or asterisks to the right of the edited result. For example:

DEPT. NO.	SALESMAN NO.	AMOUNT
2342	4721	400.00
	4722	200.00
	5671	40.00
	5678	200.00
		840.00 *

Position for fill character ⟶

OUT+49 ⟶

This type of asterisk indication is not possible with the edit instruction.

```
            MVC       OUT+48(9),PATTERN
            ED        OUT+48(9),AMOUNT
            .
            .
PATTERN     DC        X'402020214B2020405C'
AMOUNT      DS        CL3
            .
```

```
AMOUNT            Edited Result

84 00 0+            b84.00bb
```

What has happened is that the plus sign in the source field caused the S-trigger to be turned OFF, thus all the pattern characters to the right of the rightmost digit select character have been replaced by the fill character, a blank in this case. In cases like this the only way to print an asterisk is to move it separately by a MVI instruction.

```
            MVC       OUT+48(7),PATTERN
            ED        OUT+48(7),AMOUNT
            MVI       OUT+56,C'*'
            .
PATTERN     DC        X'402020214B2020'
AMOUNT      DS        CL3
            .
```

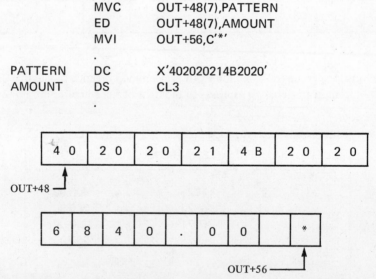

Resulting Condition Code. The EDIT instruction sets the condition code in the following manner:

Resulting Condition Code	Meaning
0	Result field is zero
1	Result field is less than zero
2	Result field is greater than zero
3	Not used

The condition code setting can be used to distinguish between or test for positive, negative or zero quantities when it is necessary to indicate the sign of the source field in a manner not provided by the edit instruction. For example, we may be required to place a + or - sign to the left of the edited result instead of the more commonly used sign indicators, such as CR, etc.

```
READ          GET        INFILE
              .
              MVC        OUT+10(7),PATTERN
              ED         OUT+10(7),AMOUNT
              BC         4,MOVENEG
              BC         2,MOVEPOS
BACK          .

              .
              BC         15,READ
MOVEPOS       MVI '      OUT+10,C'+'
              BC         15,BACK
MOVENEG       MVI        OUT+10,C'-'
              BC         15,BACK
              .

              .
PATTERN       DC         X'402020214B2020'
AMOUNT        DS         CL3
IN            DS         CL80
OUT           DS         CL132
              .

              .
```

AMOUNT	Edited Result
12 34 5–	–123.45
12 34 5+	+123.45

Multiple field editing

The edit feature allows a programmer to edit a series of adjacent source fields with a single edit instruction. This is made possible by a special character called the *field separator character* whose hexadecimal notation is X'22'. This character indicates to the CPU the beginning of each new edit pattern after the first (leftmost) pattern. The field separator character itself is replaced by the fill character.

Example:

Given three source fields consecutively located in storage as follows:

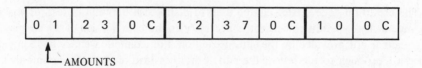

AMOUNTS

The edit pattern required would be:

D D S . D D F D D S . D D F S . D D

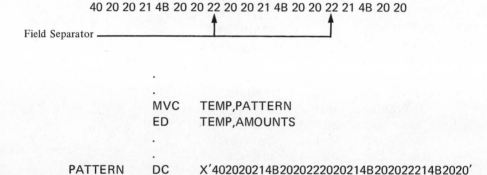

Field Separator

```
              MVC    TEMP,PATTERN
              ED     TEMP,AMOUNTS

   PATTERN    DC     X'402020214B2020222020214B202022214B2020'
```

Result   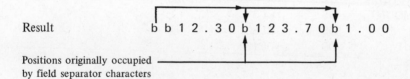

Positions originally occupied
by field separator characters

Note: 1. The source fields must be adjacent to each other.

    2. The resulting condition code setting reflects the status of the *last* field edited.

In the chart below are given the various edit pattern characters along with their hex and substitute characters.

Pattern Character	Hex Notation	Substitute Character
Digit Select	20	d or D
Significant Start	21	(or S
Field Separator	22	) or F
Blank	40	b
Decimal point	4B	.
Comma	6B	,
Asterisk	5C	*
Dollar sign	5B	$

At times it may be desirable to insert a dollar, $, sign to the left of the first significant digit in the edited result. This is generally done as a protection feature. For example:

$12,300.00
$3,298.07
$100.00
$78.87
$1.00
$.65

This is also known as the *floating dollar sign feature*. It is not possible to obtain this type of editing with the EDIT instruction, as shown below.

PATTERN   DC   X'5B20206B2020214B2020'

AMOUNT	Edited Result
1230000	$12,300.00
0329807	$$3,298.07
0010000	$$$$100.00
0007887	$$$$$78.87
0000100	$$$$$$1.00
0000065	$$$$$$.65

From the edited results you can see that the dollar sign protection feature is giving us too much protection. It does not look as good with all these dollar signs.

The next instruction, Edit and Mark, gives us the capability of inserting a single floating dollar sign in the edited result.

Edit and Mark Instruction

Instruction Name	Edit and Mark
Mnemonic OP Code	EDMK
Machine OP Code	DF
Type	SS
Program Interruptions	Operation, Protection, Addressing, Data
Condition Code	is affected
Assembler Format	EDMK D1(L,B1),D2(B2)

This instruction works identically to the EDIT instruction except for one very unique feature. During execution of a EDMK instruction, when a significant digit is encountered and stored into the edit pattern, the address of that particular pattern position is placed in general register 1 by the IOCS. This particular feature of the EDMK instruction makes it possible for us to insert floating currency symbol in the edited result.

Example:

We are to edit a 3 byte long packed decimal field and place the result into an area named TEMP. The format of the edited result is xxx.xx and floating currency feature is required.

```
            .
        MVC     TEMP,PATTERN     POSITION PATTERN
        EDMK    TEMP,AMOUNT      EDIT SOURCE FIELD
        SH      1,ONE
        MVI     0(1),C'$'        MOVE $ SIGN
            .
PATTERN DC      X'402020204B2020'
ONE     DC      H'1'
```

Assume that the field named AMOUNT contains 00 12 2+. The result of the EDMK instruction (see coding above) is illustrated below:

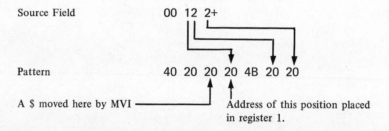

The instruction following the EDMK instruction subtracts 1 from the contents of general register 1, thereby pointing register 1 to the address of the location where the currency symbol is to be inserted. The next instruction, the MVI, moves a dollar sign to the address indicated by register 1. The result of this routine will be:

bb$1.22

Consider another example with the same routine, but in this case the field named AMOUNT contains 02 12 2+. The result of the editing routine is shown below.

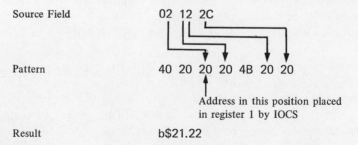

However, there is one complication with the EDMK instruction. This is, if a significant-start digit is used to force significance, *nothing is done with register 1*. In such cases, this method of inserting floating dollar sign is of no avail. An alternative way to insert dollar signs, in such cases, is to place into register 1 the address of the position to the right of the significant-start digit, i.e., the address of the significant-start digit plus one, and then to execute the EDMK instruction. Hence, if nothing happens to register 1, we still get the floating currency sign in the desired position. This technique is illustrated by the coding and the examples that follow.

```
          .
          MVC      TEMP,PATTERN
          LA       1,TEMP+4    SEE NOTE FOLLOWING CASE 2
          EDMK     TEMP,AMOUNT
          SH       1,ONE       SUBTRACT 1 FROM REG 1
          MVI      0(1),C'$'    MOVE $ SIGN
          .
PATTERN   DC       X'402020214B2020'
ONE       DC       H'1'
TEMP      DS       CL7
          .
```

Case 1:   AMOUNT contains 01 20 2+

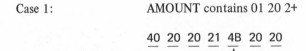

Address of this position placed ─────┘
in register 1 by problem program

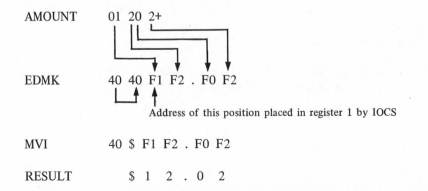

RESULT $ 1 2 . 0 2

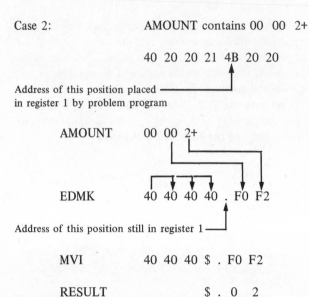

Case 2:   AMOUNT contains 00 00 2+

                                40 20 20 21 4B 20 20

Address of this position placed
in register 1 by problem program

                AMOUNT   00 00 2+

                EDMK   40 40 40 40 . F0 F2

Address of this position still in register 1

                MVI   40 40 40 $. F0 F2

                RESULT $. 0 2

Note: The LA (Load Address) instruction is covered in Section 12.1. This instruction is used to load into the register specified as the first operand the *address* of the second operand.

When a single EDMK instruction is used to edit several fields and a significant-start digit is not used to force significance, the address in register 1 at the end of instruction execution points to the last field edited.

EXERCISE:

Write programming steps necessary to have the computer perform editing with a floating dollar sign on the packed decimal fields –8734232, and +3247329. Use the same edit pattern for both fields and use CR to the right of the edited amount field for negative indication. Use blank as the 0-suppression character.

Example:

We are given a card file containing two types of records. The identifying code is punched in c.c. 80 and it could be either a 1 punch or the alpha character A. Write a program to separate these two types of cards, code 1 cards into stacker 1 and code A cards into stacker 2, and to list all of the A type records. Any other code in c.c. 80 is an error, and such records are to be selected in stacker 3. The formats of the input card record and the output listing are as follows:

Card Record Format

        c.c.   1 – 6   Account Number
                                      1 – 3 Prefix

                        (continued)

	4 – 6 Suffix
10 – 25	Account Name
70 – 74	Amount xxx.xx
	Negative amounts contain an 11
	punch in c.c. 74
80 – 80	Type Code

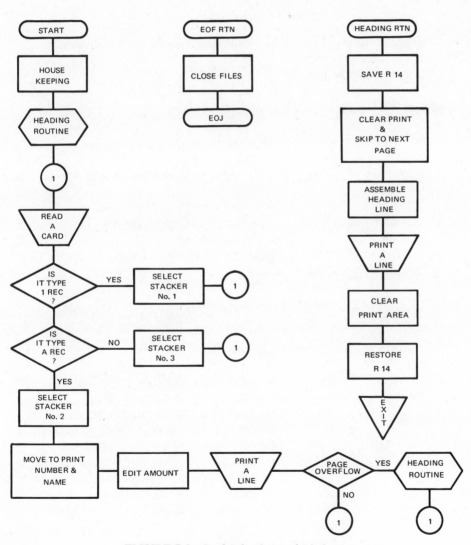

FIGURE 7.8. Card Selection and Listing.

Output Record Format (Listing)

p.p.	11 – 13	Account Number Prefix	
	14 – 14	—	
	15 – 17	Account Number Suffix	
	27 – 42	Account Name	
	47 – 55	Amount	xx0.xx CR

The report heading is:

LISTING OF TYPE A RECORDS

The heading goes into p.p. 15 – 39 and should appear on the top of each page.
Note: c.c. stands for card column.

p.p. stands for print position.

Figure 7.8 illustrates the flow chart and Figure 7.9 contains the coding for this problem.

```
Name        Oper     Operand
            START    0
CARDIN      DTFCD    DEVADDR=SYS008,IOAREA1=CARD,          X
                     CONTROL=YES,                          X
                     EOFADDR=NOCARD
REPORTS     DTFPR    DEVADDR=SYS010,IOAREA1=LINE1,         X
                     WORKA=YES,                            X
                     BLKSIZE=55,PRINTOV=YES,CONTROL=YES
BEGIN       BALR     R2,0
            USING    *,R2
            OPEN     CARDIN,REPORTS
*                                   OPEN FILES
*
*BRANCH TO HEADING ROUTINE VIA REG 14
*
            BAL      14,HEADING    BRANCH TO HEADING ROUTINE
F1          GET      CARDIN        READ A CARD
            CLI      CARD+79,C'1'  BRANCH TO FOUND1
            BC       8,FOUND1       IF IT IS TYPE 1 RECORD
            CLI      CARD+79,C'A'  BRANCH TO FOUNDA
            BC       8,FOUNDA       IF IT IS TYPE A RECORD
            CNTRL    CARDIN,PS,3   SELECT ERROR CARD IN STKR 3
            BC       15,F1         UNCONDITIONAL BRANCH
FOUND1      CNTRL    CARDIN,PS,1   SELECT TYPE 1 IN STKR 1
            BC       15,F1
```

(continued)

```
FOUNDA      CNTRL      CARDIN,PS,2   SELECT TYPE A IN STKR 2
*
*ASSEMBLE PRINT LINE
*
            MVC        LINE+10(3),CARD
*                                    MOVE ACCOUNT PREFIX
            MVI        LINE+13,C'-'   MOVE -
            MVC        LINE+14(3),CARD+3
*                                    MOVE ACCOUNT SUFFIX
            MVC        LINE+26(16),CARD+9
*                                    MOVE NAME
            PACK       CARD+71(3),CARD+69(5)
*                                    PACK AMOUNT
            MVC        LINE+45(10),PATTERN
*                                    MOVE EDIT PATTERN
            ED´        LINE+45(10),CARD+71
*                                    EDIT AMOUNT
            PUT        REPORTS,LINE
*                                    PRINT A LINE
            PRTOV      REPORTS,12,HEADING
*                                    CHECK FOR PAGE END
            BC         15,F1
*
*HEADING ROUTINE
*
HEADING     ST         R14,SAVE       SAVE REG 14
            CNTRL      REPORTS,SK,1
*                                    SKIP TO NEW PAGE
            MVC        LINE+1(54),LINE
*                                    CLEAR PRINT AREA
            MVC        LINE+14(25),HDG
*                                    MOVE PAGE HEADING
            PUT        REPORTS,LINE
*                                    PRINT PAGE HEADING
            MVC        LINE+1(54),LINE
*                                    CLEAR PRINT AREA
            L          R14,SAVE       RESTORE REG 14
            BCR        15,R14         RETURN
*
*END OF FILE ROUTINE
*
NOCARD      CLOSE      CARDIN,REPORTS
```

(continued)

```
                EOJ
        *
        *       DECLARATIVES
        *
        CARD    DS      CL80          IOAREA FOR CARD FILE
        LINE    DC      CL55' '       WORK AREA FOR PRINTER
        LINE1   DS      CL55          IOAREA FOR PRINTER
        SAVE    DS      F
        HDG     DC      C'LISTING OF TYPE A RECORDS'
        PATTERN DC      X'4020214B202040C3D9'
        R2      EQU     2
        R14     EQU     14
                END     BEGIN
```

FIGURE 7.9. Suggested Solution.

[8]

Bit Manipulation and Program Switches

8.1 Bit Manipulation

As you know, the smallest addressable unit in the System 360 is the byte. However, it is possible to test, set, or manipulate on the individual bits of a byte. Often it is useful to utilize single bits to store discrete items of information. This becomes very useful when each item of the information has only two possible values. However, symbolic labeling of individual bits is not possible and the programming effort required to test and set individual bits may become very extensive. Thus, the decision to use individual bits over full bytes should be weighed very carefully. The instructions discussed in this section are directly involved with bit manipulation. Various instructions that fall under this category are:

1. Logical AND.
2. Logical OR.
3. Exclusive OR.
4. Test Under Mask.
5. Shifts.
6. Execute.

The first 4 bytes of bit manipulation instructions will be discussed in this section. Shifts are discussed in Section 9.3 and the Execute instruction is discussed in Section 11.2.

Logical AND Instruction

Logical AND instructions permit four types of operations. These are as follows:

Instruction Name	AND Register to Register
Mnemonic OP Code	NR
Machine OP Code	14
Type	RR
Condition Code	is affected
Assembler Format	NR R1,R2

Instruction Name	AND Fullword to Register
Mnemonic OP Code	N
Machine OP Code	54
Type	RX
Condition Code	is affected
Assembler Format	N R1,D2(X2,B2)

Instruction Name	AND Immediate
Mnemonic OP Code	NI
Machine OP Code	94
Type	SI
Condition Code	is affected
Assembler Format	NI D1(B1),I2

Instruction Name	AND Storage to Storage
Mnemonic OP Code	NC
Machine OP Code	D4
Type	SS
Condition Code	is affected
Assembler Format	NC D1(L,B1),D2(B2)

Program Interruptions	Protection	(N, NC, NI)
	Specification	(N, NC, NI)
	Addressing	(N)

Resulting Condition Code	Meaning
0	Result is zero
1	Result is not zero
2	———
3	———

Both operands are treated as unstructured logical quantities. Each bit of the second operand is compared (or AND'd) with the corresponding bit of the first operand the resulting, i.e., the first operand bits, are set as follows:

If the receiving field, the first operand, and the corresponding second operand bits contain a 1 bit, the bit position in the first operand is set to 1. Otherwise, the first operand bit(s) is set to zero. The second operand is not altered in any way. The bit position settings are done in accordance with the rules shown below.

Second Operand Bit	First Operand Bit	Result Bit First Operand
1	1	1
1	0	0
0	1	0
0	0	0

Note: The result bit is stored in the first operand.

Application: The AND instruction can be used to set a bit(s) to 0.

EXERCISE:

Consider the coding below:

```
          LH        2,HALF
          N         2,FULL
          .
          .
HALF      DC        X'FFFF'
FULL      DC        F'65535'
          .
```

Show the contents of register 2, in hexadecimal code, after the above coded instructions have been executed.

Application of the AND instruction

This instruction can be used to set first operand bit(s) to zero(s).

Example:

```
          NR        2,4
```

Register 2 before	0 0 1 1 0 0 1 1
Register 4 before	0 1 0 1 0 1 0 0
Register 2 after	0 0 0 1 0 0 0 0
Register 4 remains unaltered.	

Example:

```
          NC        FLDA,FLDB
```

FLDA before	1 1 0 1 0 0 0 0
FLDB before	1 0 1 0 1 0 1 1
FLDA after	1 0 0 0 0 0 0 0

FLDB remains unaltered.

Example:

NI   IN+79,B'11110000'

IN+79 before	0 0 0 0 1 1 1 1
Immediate data	1 1 1 1 0 0 0 0
IN+79 after	0 0 0 0 0 0 0 0

Example:

NI   SWITCH+1,X'0F'
.
.

SWITCH   BC   15,0(3,5)
.

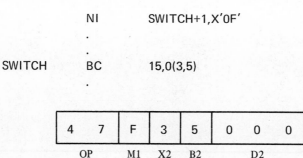

In this example, we are ANDing the second byte of an unconditional branch instruction. The result of this AND instruction is illustrated below.

Branch Instruction before	47 F3 50 00
AND	0F
Branch Instruction after	47 03 50 00

If the resulting branch instruction is represented in assembler format, it would appear as:

SWITCH   BC   0,0(3,5)

It is clear that we have changed an unconditional branch instruction to a No-operation instruction. This is one of the important applications of the AND instruction.

Logical OR Instructions

Four different formats of this instruction are available. These are:

Instruction Name	OR Register to Register
Mnemonic OP Code	OR

Machine OP Code	16
Type	RR
Condition Code	is affected
Assembler Format	OR R1,R2

Instruction Name	OR Fullword to Register
Mnemonic OP Code	O
Machine OP Code	56
Type	RX
Condition Code	is affected
Assembler Format	O R1,D2(X2,B2)

Instruction Name	OR Immediate
Mnemonic OP Code	OI
Machine OP Code	96
Type	SI
Condition Code	is affected
Assembler Format	OI D1(B2),I2

Instruction Name	OR Storage to Storage
Mnemonic OP Code	OC
Machine OP Code	D6
Type	SS
Condition Code	is affected
Assembler Format	OC D1(L,B1),D2(B2)

Program Interruptions	Protection	(O, OI, OC)
	Addressing	(O, OI, OC)
	Specification	(O)

Resulting Condition Code	Meaning
0	Result is zero
1	Result is not zero
2	— — —
3	— — —

Each bit position of the first operand is compared or OR'd with the corresponding bit of the second operand. The resulting bit(s), i.e., the first operand bits, are set according to the following rule:

The first operand's bit is set to 1 when either or both corresponding bits contain a 1, otherwise the first operand's bit is set to 0. This rule is further illustrated by the chart below.

Second Operand Bit	First Operand Bit	Result Bit First Operand
1	0	1
1	1	1
0	1	1
0	0	0

Note: The result bit is stored in the first operand bit position.

Application: The OR instruction can be used to set a bit(s) to 1.

Example:

Assume that we need to set bit positions 1, 3, 4 and 6 of a byte named DATA to ones. This byte originally contains X'00'. The instruction will be:

<pre>
         OI   DATA,X'5A'
</pre>

DATA before	0 0 0 0 0 0 0 0
Immediate data	0 1 0 1 1 0 1 0
DATA after	0 1 0 1 1 0 1 0

Example:

<pre>
         OR   3,4
</pre>

Register 3 before	0 1 1 0 1 1 1 0
Register 4 before	0 1 0 1 0 1 1 0
Register 3 after	0 1 1 1 1 1 1 0

Example:

The OR instruction can be used to convert a No-operation instruction into an unconditional branch. Consider the coding below.

<pre>
         OI   SWITCH+1,X'F0'
         .
         .
         .
SWITCH   BC   0,0(3,5)
         .
</pre>

Branch Instruction before	47 03 50 00
Immediate data	F0

Branch Instruction after   47 F3 50 00

The resulting branch instruction if written in assembler format would appear as:

SWITCH   BC   15,0(3,5)

It is important to note that only the high-order 4 bits of the second byte of the branch instruction is affected by this OI instruction. In fact, that is exactly what we want to do. The low-order 4 bits of this byte contains the index register and we should not change this register number.

Exclusive OR Instructions

Instruction Name	Exclusive OR Register to Register
Mnemonic OP Code	XR
Machine OP Code	17
Type	RR
Condition Code	is affected
Assembler Format	XR R1,R2

Instruction Name	Exclusive OR Fullword to Register
Mnemonic OP Code	X
Machine OP Code	57
Type	RX
Condition Code	is affected
Assembler Format	X R1,D2(X2,B2)

Instruction Name	Exclusive OR Immediate
Mnemonic OP Codw	XI
Machine OP Code	97
Type	SI
Condition Code	is affected
Assembler Format	XI D1,(B1),I2

Instruction Name	Exclusive OR Storage to Storage
Mnemonic OP Code	XC
Machine OP Code	D7
Type	SS
Condition Code	is affected
Assembler Format	XC D1(L,B1),D2(B2)

Program Interruptions	Protection	(X, XI, XC)
	Addressing	(X, XI, XC)
	Specification	(X)

Resulting Condition Code	Meaning
0	Result is zero
1	Result is not zero
2	---
3	---

The bit positions of the first operand are compared to the corresponding bit positions of the second operand and the first operand's bits are set as follows:

> If the bit in the second operand matches the bit in the first operand, a 0 bit is stored in the first operand bit position. If the bits do not match, a 1 bit is stored in the first operand. Another way of stating this rule is that, unlike corresponding bits result in a 1 bit in the first operand, otherwise, the result bit is set to 0.

First Operand Bit	Second Operand Bit	Result Bit First Operand
1	0	1
0	1	1
1	1	0
0	0	0

The following are some applications of the exclusive OR instruction.
1. This instruction can be used to invert a bit, an operation very useful in setting and testing of binary switches.
2. If a field is exclusive OR'd with itself, it will be set to zeros — a good way to clear a field.
3. Exclusive OR instruction can be used to exchange the contents of two areas without the use of a temporary hold area. This is illustrated by the example below.

Assume that FLD1 contains X'AB' and FLD2 contains S'BA'. Consider the following coding:

		Resulting FLD1	Resulting FLD2
XC	FLD1,FLD2	0 0 0 1 0 0 0 1	1 0 1 1 1 0 1 0
XC	FLD2,FLD1	0 0 0 1 0 0 0 1	1 0 1 0 1 0 1 1
XC	FLD1,FLD2	1 0 1 1 1 0 1 0	1 0 1 0 1 0 1 1

After the last instruction, FLD1 contains X'BA' and FLD2 contains X'AB'. Interesting, isn't it? The exclusive OR instruction can also be used to alter the mask bits of a branch instruction. Consider the coding below.

```
                XI        SWITCH+1,X'F0'
                .
SWITCH      BC        0,LOOP
                .
```

The XI instruction will set the mask bits of the branch instruction to $(1111)_2$, thus making the branch an unconditional branch instruction.

Instruction Name	Test Under Mask
Mnemonic OP Code	TM
Machine OP Code	91
Type	SI
Program Interruptions	Protection, Addressing
Condition Code	is affected
Assembler Format	TM D1(B2),I2

While the OR, AND and Exclusive OR instructions may be used to set the individual bits in a byte, the *Test Under Mask* instruction is used to test the setting of various bits of a byte. With the help of this instruction, a programmer can find out if selected bits in a particular byte are all zeros, all ones or a mixture of ones and zeros. As this is a SI type of instruction only a maximum of 8 bits can be tested with one instruction.

Note: The test is made without altering the bit settings of either operand.

The byte of immediate data, the I2 field, is used as a 8-bit mask. Only those bits in the first operand are tested which have a corresponding 1 bit in the mask, all other bits are ignored. If all the selected bits are zeros the condition code is set to 0. If the selected bits are all one, the condition code is set to 3. In case the selected bits are a mixture of ones and zeros, the condition code is set to 1.

Resulting Condition Code	Meaning
0	Selected bits or mask bits all zeros
1	Selected bits mixture of ones and zeros
2	———
3	Selected bits all ones

Note: It is important to note that a mask bit of one indicates that the corresponding storage bit is to be tested.

EXERCISE:

What is the maximum number of bits that can be tested with one TM instruction? Explain your answer briefly.

Example:

We are required to branch to RTN1 if the bits 0, 1, 3 and 4 of a byte named

SWITCH are all ones and to RTN2 if these bits are all zeros.

```
        TM      SWITCH,X'D8'
        BC      1,RTN1
        BC      8,RTN2
        .
        .
```

EXERCISE:
Write program steps to test the high-order bit of a byte of data named SWITCH. If the tested bit is 0, set the whole byte to zeros else set the byte to ones.

Use of bit manipulation instructions

Any part of an instruction may be modified by the use of the AND, OR, and Exclusive OR instructions. The most frequently altered part of an instruction is the first or the second byte. The least altered part of an instruction is its address operands[2].

Example:
Altering the operation code of an instruction.

```
                    .
SWITCH      A       7,FOUR
            XI      *-4,X'01'
                    .
                    .
FOUR        DC      F'4'
                    .
```

A switch that will alternately add and subtract 4 from general register 7.

Explanation: The OP Code for Add Fullword is X'5A' and for Subtract Fullword is X'5B'. The exclusive OR instruction above will change the OP code of the instruction named SWITCH to 5B thus making it a subtract instruction.

```
            0 1 0 1 1 0 1 0         X'5A'
            0 0 0 0 0 0 0 1         X'01'
Result      0 1 0 1 1 0 1 1         X'5B'
```

An alternate way of writing this exclusive instruction is:

```
                    .
SWITCH      A       7,FOUR
            XI      SWITCH,X'01'
                    .
```

(continued)

[2]Indexing technique is most commonly used to alter the address specification of an instruction. This is discussed in Chapter 12.

```
FOUR        DC       F'4'
             .
```

Example:

A switch that alters between No-op and Branch instruction is:

```
             .
XI           *+5,X'F0'
BC           0,OUT
             .
```

The exclusive OR instruction above alters the mask (M1) field of the branch instruction from 0000 to 1111 and next time through from 1111 to 0000. The same set of instructions could be written as:

```
             .
             .
BC           0,OUT
XI           *-3,X'F0'
             .
```

Example:

We need to go to two different routines, alternately, from one point in a program. The two routines are named RTN1 and RTN2.

```
                 .
                 .
BEGIN            .
                 .
SW1      BC      15,RTN1
         BC      15,RTN2
                 .
                 .
RTN1     NI      SW1+1,X'0F'        TURN SW1 OFF
                 .
                 .
         BC      15,BEGIN
RTN2     OI      SW1+1,X'F0'        TURN SW1 ON
                 .
                 .
         BC      15,BEGIN
                 .
                 .
```

The same result could be obtained by writing the coding as follows:

```
              .
              .
BEGIN         .
              .
SW1      BC        15,RTN1
RTN2     OI        SW1+1,X'F0'              TURN SW1 ON
              .
              .
         BC        15,BEGIN
RTN1     NI        SW1+1,X'0F'              TURN SW1 OFF
              .
              .
         BC        15,BEGIN
```

Yet, another approach would be:

```
              .
              .
BEGIN         .
              .
SW1      BC        0,RTN2
RTN1     OI        SW1+1,X'F0'              TURN SW1 ON
              .
         BC        15,BEGIN
RTN2     NI        SW1+1,X'0F'              TURN SW1 OFF
              .
         BC        15,BEGIN
```

Altering the mask bits of a conditional branch instruction is not the only way to alter the path of a program. There are other methods of accomplishing this. Consider the coding below.

```
              .
              .
BEGIN         .
              .
         CLI       SW,C'0'
         BC        8,RTN1
         BC        15,RTN2
RTN1     MVI       SW,C'1'                  TURN SW ON
              .
         BC        15,BEGIN
```

(continued)

```
RTN2        MVI       SW,C'0'                TURN SW OFF
             .
             .
            BC        15,BEGIN
             .
SW          DC        C'0'
             .
```

Still another way to do the same is to use the individual bits of a byte as indicators for taking different paths through a program.

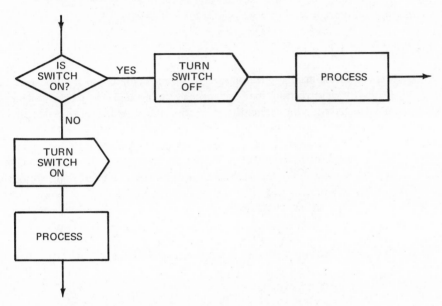

FIGURE 8.1. Graphic Representation of a Program Switch.

```
 SW          DC        X'00'
             .
BEGIN        .
             .
            TM        SW,X'80'
            BC        8,RTN1    IF SELECTED BIT IS ZERO BRANCH
            BC        15,RTN2
RTN1        XI        SW,X'80'  TURN SW ON
             .
             .
```

(continued)

```
                    BC      15,BEGIN
          RTN2      XI      SW,X'80'  TURN SW OFF
                    .
                    .
                    BC      15,BEGIN
```

It is clear, therefore, that there are many ways of setting up logic for alternating the path of a program at a given point in the program. The point where a program takes an alternative path is generally referred to as a *Program Switch*. Graphically represented, a program switch and the modifying instructions look somewhat like Figure 8.1.

In the next section, we will discuss the application of the program switches in real programming situations.

8.2 Program Switches

In this section one of the main applications of the bit manipulation instructions will be discussed. In the previous section, the basic mechanism of these instructions and some of the examples illustrating the technique of altering the mask bits of the conditional branch instructions were introduced. This particular application of the bit manipulation instruction becomes very helpful in those programming applications where we need to take different paths from the same point during program execution time. Rather than going into lengthy explanations of program switches and their workings, we will introduce a problem and then develop two solutions for it, one without and then one with program switches.

Example:

Read three cards and store these into three different areas named CARD1, CARD2, and CARD3. Figure 8.2 (shown on the next page) is a flow chart for this problem, which does not use program switches.

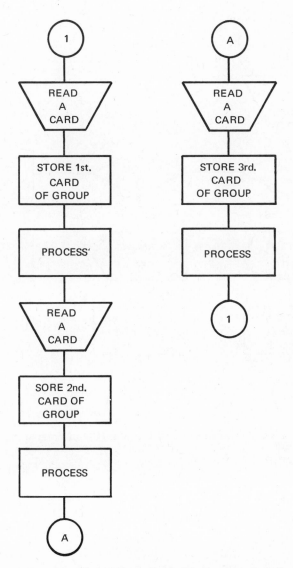

FIGURE 8.2. Reading of Three Cards (No Program Switches).

In the approach outlined in Figure 8.2, we have to issue a GET command for each of the three cards. It is possible to use only one GET command in the routine; however, two program switches are needed. The flow chart in Figure 8.3 illustrates this approach.

Note: In this problem all switches are assumed to be ON, i.e., the branch instructions have a mask of $(1111)_2$.

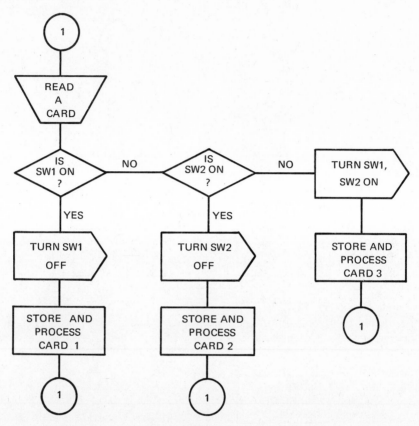

FIGURE 8.3. Reading of Three Cards (Use of Program Switches).

Figure 8.4 illustrates the coding for the flow chart shown in Figure 8.3.

```
              START    0
                 .
                 .
F1               GET     CARDIN,TEMP
SW1              BC      15,PROCESS1
SW2              BC      15,PROCESS2
                 BC      15,PROCESS3
PROCESS1         NI      SW1+1,X'0F'          TURN SW1 OFF
                 .
                 .
                 BC      15,F1
```

(continued)

```
PROCESS2    NI      SW2+1,X'0F'              TURN SW2 OFF
            .
            .
            .
            BC      15,F1
PROCESS3    OI      SW1+1,X'F0'              TURN SW1 ON
            OI      SW2+1,X'F0'              TURN SW2 ON
            .
            .
            BC      15,F1
            .
```

FIGURE 8.4. Coding for Figure 8.3.

Example:

Compare the two methods of solving a given problem, i.e., no switches against the use of switches in more detail. This will be done by solving a problem with both of these approaches. We are to write a program to print address labels. The labels are to be printed three up.

At first glance this problem seems rather simple. The main logic for the program could be stated as: read three cards into the main storage, print a row of labels and proceed to read and print the next group of address labels, and so forth. The flow chart for the problem may look somewhat like the one in Figure 8.5 below. But *there is a bug* in this flow chart.

Process a file containing a total of five records as the computer would. To process such a file, first read three cards into the main storage and then print a row of (three) labels and branch back to the first read command to read the next group of cards. Now, read and store the fourth and the fifth card and execute the third read command. At this time, the IOCS senses the end-of-file condition, and causes a branch to the end-of-file routine.

This routine simply closes the files and issues the EOJ macro to the system. So the result is three address labels instead of five. (This type of programming may be the reason for the magazines you miss occasionally.

To solve this bug in the problem, some extra processing needs to be done at end-of-file condition. Figure 8.6 illustrates the solution to this problem.

One solution to this is to maintain a card counter and to increment this counter by one, for both the first and second card (each). After reading the third card the counter is set to zero. Thus, the counter can attain only three values, i.e., 1, 2 or 0. When the program branches to the end-of-file routine, check the value of this counter. If its value is equal to zero, simply close the files and end the job, as there are no unprocessed card records. On the other hand, if the counter equals one, we know that there is one unprocessed card record, the first record of the group. However, if the counter is not equal to one, it must be equal to two, indicating that two records need to be processed. Therefore, the end-of-file routine will be as follows:

1. If the counter is equal to one, write a completely new routine to process the last

label. The data is retrieved from the area reserved for the first card of the group.

2. If the counter is not equal to one, write a routine to process the last two labels. Data in this case is retrieved from the areas reserved for the first and the second card of each group.

3. If the counter is equal to zero, close files.

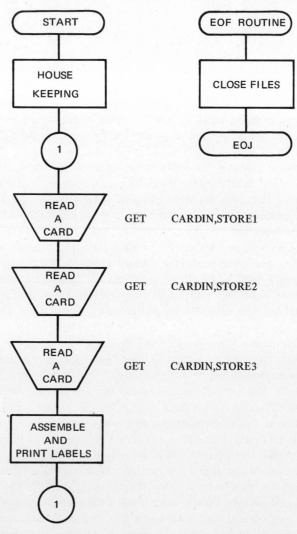

FIGURE 8.5. Printing Three-Up Labels (Program With a Bug).

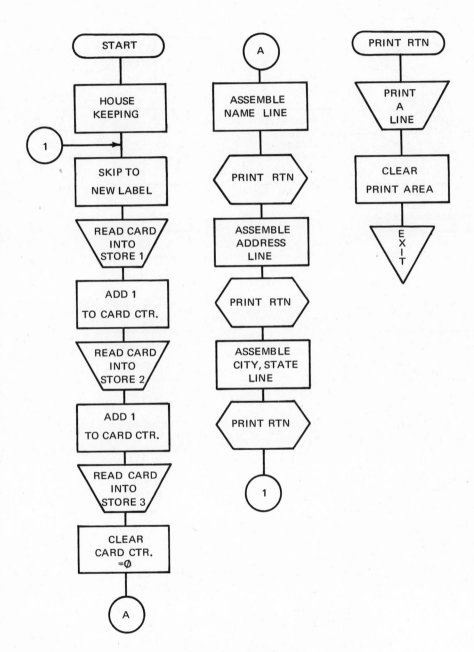

(continued)

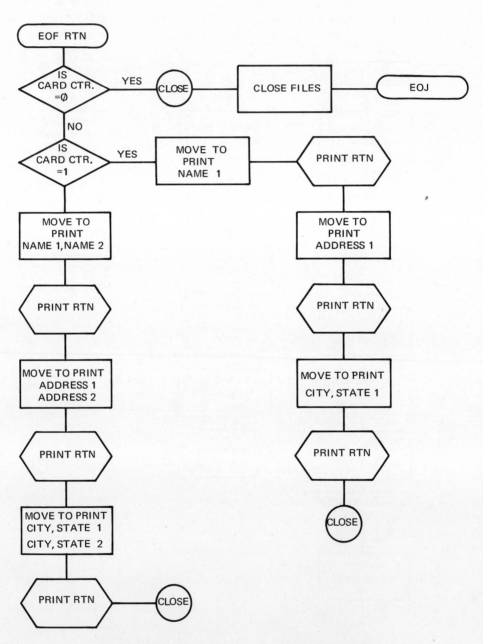

FIGURE 8.6. Printing Three-Up Labels (No Switches).

Next, the same problem is solved by the use of a program switch. Figure 8.7 is the flow chart for this new approach. You can certainly see the amount of flow charting and coding time that can be saved when this approach is used.

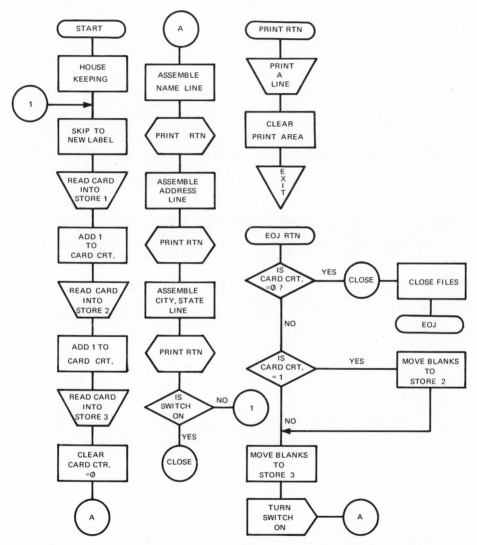

FIGURE 8.7. Printing Address Labels Three-Up (to begin with the switch is off).

The main difference is in the use of the switch and the end-of-job routine. The action taken at the end-of-file condition can be outlined as follows:

1. *Counter equal to one.* Move blanks to the areas reserved for the second and third card, turn the switch ON and branch to the main line print routine. Important point to note is that the program still goes through the instructions which move the different fields for label-2 and label-3 but only blanks are moved.

2. *Counter not equal to one.* This condition indicates that two cards need to be processed, thus we move blanks to the storage area for third card, turn the switch ON and branch to the print routine.

After printing the appropriate labels when the computer encounters the instruction labeled SWITCH, a branch is taken to the symbol CLOSE. At this point, we close the files and issue the EOJ macro. The difference in the amount of coding required by these two approaches is certainly clear.

Note: A word of caution. Programmers, beginners and otherwise, sometimes tend to get in the undesirable habit of using too many switches in a program. This becomes very troublesome when someone else or even the programmer himself needs to do some modifications to the program. The task of finding the status of the various switches at a given point becomes very time consuming. Therefore, such a habit will obviously bring about more mistakes and bugs in a program.

Self Evaluation Quiz

1. Write coding for the flow chart illustrated in Figure 8.6. Design your own input and output record formats.

2. Write coding for the flow chart illustrated in Figure 8.7. Assume the same input and output formats as in problem 1 above.

[9]

Binary Compares, Binary Multiplication and Division

9.1 Binary Compares

In Section 5.3 we discussed the uses and programming applications of compare instructions. In that section, the decision-making instructions dealt with data in EBCDIC format and the operands being compared were treated as pure binary numbers. There are times when it becomes necessary to compare data that exists in signed binary (fixed-point) form. For example, after calculating gross salary of an employee (in a general register), it may be necessary to compare it to some given constant. This type of comparison falls under binary compares. Three binary compare instructions are provided for comparing binary numbers.

Instruction Name	Binary Compare Register to Register
Mnemonic OP Code	CR
Machine OP Code	19
Program Interruptions	None
Condition Code	is affected
Type	RR
Assembler Format	CR R1,R1

Instruction Name	Binary Compare Register to Fullword
Mnemonic OP Code	C
Machine OP Code	59
Program Interruptions	Protection, Addressing, Specification
Condition Code	is affected
Type	RX

Assembler Format	C R1,D2(X2,B2)

Instruction Name	Binary Compare Register to Halfword
Mnemonic OP Code	CH
Machine OP Code	49
Program Interruptions	Protection, Addressing, Specification
Condition Code	is affected
Type	RX
Assembler Format	CH R1,D2(X2,B2)

Resulting Condition Code	Meaning
0	Both operands equal
1	First operand is low
2	First operand is high
3	———

Note: The resulting condition code setting always reflects the status of the first operand.

All three instructions perform an algebraic comparison of the first and second operand. In case of the CR and C instructions, both operands are treated as 32 bits signed integers, i.e., 31 data bits and 1 sign bit. All 32 bits are compared before the condition code is *set to* one of its settings. The contents of either of the operands are not altered.

By algebraic comparison we mean that comparison is done based on absolute values of the operands, i.e., the negative number will be considered to have a lesser value than the positive numbers.

Example:

	CR	R1,R2
	s	
R1	0 000	0001 +1
	s	
R2	1 111	1111 −1

As a result of the compare instruction above, the condition code of the PSW will be set to 2, i.e., the first operand is higher than the second.

The third of the binary compare instructions, CH, is used to compare a halfword, i.e., 16-bit signed integer, to a register. Before the comparison is done the halfword second operand is expanded to a fullword by propagating the sign bit through the extra 16 high-order bits. The expansion is done after the halfword operand has been fetched and actually takes place in the control unit. After the expansion, the compare halfword instruction works identically to the compare fullword.

EXERCISE:

Positions 11–14 of each record contain the hours worked (in EBCDIC) by each employee of a firm. Write program steps to branch to REGPAY if the number of hours worked is equal to, or less than, 40.00; otherwise, branch to OVERTM.

9.2 Binary Multiplication Instructions

Before discussing the instructions which are used to multiply fixed-point numbers, it will be wise to review some of the basic principles of multiplication.

1. Product of two numbers is never larger than the sum of the digits in the multiplier and the multiplicand. The same rule can be applied to fixed-point numbers as follows: the number of significant bits in the product will not be larger than the sum of the number of significant bits in the multiplier and the multiplicand.
2. The sign of the product is always governed by the following rules:
   a. Like signs produce positive result.
   b. Unlike signs produce negative result, *except* when the result is zero.

Instruction Name	Multiply Binary Register to Register
Mnemonic OP Code	MR
Machine OP Code	1C
Program Interruptions	None
Condition Code	is not affected
Assembler Format	MR R1,R2

Instruction Name	Multiply Binary Fullword to Register
Mnemonic OP Code	M
Machine OP Code	5C
Program Interruptions	Protection, Addressing, Specification
Condition Code	is not affected
Assembler Format	M R1,D2(X2,B2)

Instruction Name	Multiply Binary Halfword to Register
Mnemonic OP Code	MH
Machine OP Code	4C
Program Interruptions	Protection, Addressing, Specification
Condition Code	is not affected
Assembler Format	MH R1,D2(X2,B2)

In all three binary multiplication instructions, the first operand must always be a register. The second operand may be another general register or a fullword or a halfword in main storage. In case of the latter two, the data in storage must be located on integral boundary and be a fixed-point quantity. First, we will discuss the MR and

M instructions.

The product of the multiplier (the second operand) and the multiplicand (the first operand) replaces the multiplicand. Both the multiplier and the multiplicand are 32-bit signed integers. The product, which is always a 64-bit signed integer, replaces the multiplicand. In the multiply instruction itself the second operand addresses either a fullword or a general register (the multiplier) and the first operand addresses a register (the multiplicand).

In binary multiplication the first operand must be a pair of even—odd registers where the multiplicand must be positioned in the odd-numbered register. These registers must be adjacent to each other and the even-numbered register must be one less than the odd-numbered register. An example of this would be 2—3, 4—5, 6—7, etc. A *common mistake* made by beginner programmers is to choose a pair of registers where the even-numbered register is greater than the odd register, for example, 3—4, 5—6, etc.

Note: Positioning of the multiplicand into the odd-numbered register is not a part of the multiplication instruction. The positioning, which can be done by numerous instructions, e.g., CBV, Load, etc., is a preliminary step to multiplication,

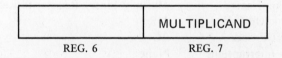

REG. 6   REG. 7

In the multiply instruction, the first operand must address the even-numbered register of the even—odd pair of registers. Violation of this rule will cause specification exception. The product, always a 64-bit signed number, replaces the contents of the even—odd pair, thus destroying the multiplicand. An overflow cannot occur in binary multiplication. The original contents of the even-numbered register of the even—odd pair are *ignored,* unless the register contains the multiplier.

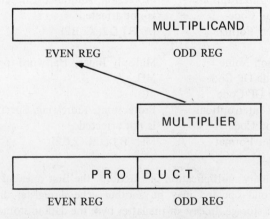

FIGURE 9.1. Use of Registers in Multiplication.

Note: The significant part of the product usually occupies 62 bits or fewer. When two maximum negative numbers are multiplied, the product formed has 63 significant bits. For conversion of 63 bit binary number to packed decimal and EBCDIC see page 533.

Example:

Input record contains two fields: number of cases sold in c.c. 1—3; and, number of units per case in c.c. 5—6. Calculate the total number of units and store the result in a 5 byte long area named RESULT.

```
        PACK      DOUB,IN(3)
        CVB       7,DOUB
        PACK      DOUB,IN+4(2)
        CVB       5,DOUB
        MR        6,5
        CVD       7,DOUB
        UNPK      RESULT,DOUB
          .
DOUB    DS        D
RESULT  DS        CL5
          .
```

EXERCISE:

Register 5 contains +128 and a fullword named UNITS contains the binary equivalent of +12; is the following instruction valid?

```
        M         5,UNITS
```

EXERCISE:

Register 9 contains the binary equivalent of +7000. Will the following set of instructions multiply this number by 4? If not, why?

```
        LH        8,H4
        MR        8,8
          .
H4      DC        H'4'
          .
```

Example:

Take the contents of a fullword (TEMP), square the number and place the result in another fullword (SQUARE).

```
          .
          .
        L         3,TEMP
        M         2,TEMP
```

(continued)

	ST	3,SQUARE
	.	
TEMP	DS	F
SQUARE	DS	F
	.	

Multiply halfword

The product of the halfword multiplier (second operand) and the multiplicand (first operand) replaces the multiplicand.

The halfword second operand, which must be located on integral boundary, is expanded to a fullword after it has been fetched from its core locations. The multiplicand may be in any general register, but must be the same register as specified by the R1 operand of the multiply instruction. The low-order 32 bits of the product formed as a result of multiplication are stored in the first operand location. The bits to the left of 32 low-order bits are not tested for significance, and no overflow indication is given.

Note: A programmer has to be very careful when deciding to use this multiply instruction. Very undesirable results may develop if the multiplier and the multiplicand occupy more than 32 significant digits. This can happen as the significant part of the product may occupy 46 bits or 47 bits when two maximum negative numbers are multiplied.

9.3 Shifting of Registers

There are two main categories of shift instructions: Algebraic shifts, and logical shifts. All shift instructions deal with data in general registers only and the shifting is always specified by number of bits. All of the shift instructions are of RS type. Algebraic shifts depart from the RS format in two ways:

1. R3 field is not used, and during instruction execution this operand is ignored.

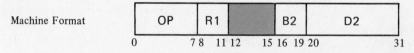

Machine Format	OP	R1		B2	D2
	0	7 8 11	12 15	16 19 20	31

2. The second operand D2+B2 is not used to address core location positions. On the contrary, the low-order 6 bits of the second operand address (formed by D2 plus the contents of the general register B2) indicate the number of bits to be shifted.

Algebraic Shift Instructions

Instruction Name	Shift Left Single Algebraic
Mnemonic OP Code	SLA
Machine OP Code	8B

Program Interruptions   Fixed-Point Overflow
Condition Code   is affected
Assembler Format   SLA R1,D2(B2)

The first operand of the shift instruction may refer to any one of the general purpose registers. The integer part of the register specified by the first operand is shifted left. The number of bits to be shifted is indicated by the second operand (B2+D2). All of the 31 integer bits of the first operand register participate in the shift except for the sign bit, which is not shifted. If a bit different from the sign bit is shifted out, a fixed-point overflow occurs which causes a program interruption. Vacated low-order register positions are filled with zeros.

Resulting Condition Code	Meaning
0	Result is zero
1	Result is less than zero
2	Result is greater than zero
3	Fixed-point overflow

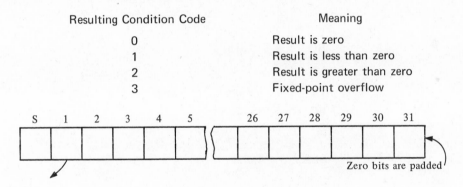

Note: 1. A left shift of zero does not result in any shifting; however, the condition code is set according to the magnitude of the register specified as R1.

2. Shift amount of 31 bits will cause the entire integer portion of the R1 register to be shifted out (the sign bit is not shifted out).

3. The low-order 6 bits of the address formed by B2+D2 indicate the number of bit positions to be shifted. The remainder of the address is ignored. This applies to all the shift instructions.

Example:

SLA   4,3   SHIFT REG 4 LEFT 3 BITS

In this case the second operand specifies only the D2 and the assembler assumes that B2 operand is zero. The instruction above specifies that register 4 is to be shifted left 3 bit positions.

Register 4 before | 0 0 0 0 1 1 1 1 |

Register 4 after | 0 1 1 1 1 0 0 0 |

SLA   4,0(2)

Machine Format of the above instruction is:

8	B	4	0	2	0	0	0
OP		R1	R3	B2		D2	

Upon execution of this instruction the integer bits of register 4 will be shifted left. The number of bit positions shifted will be equal to the number contained in general register 2.

Note: When a general register is used to specify the shift amount, a programmer can use the same shift instruction to specify different shift amounts. For example:

```
        .
    L       2,FOUR
    BC      15,SHIFT
        .
        .
        .
    L       2,TWO
    BC      15,SHIFT
        .
        .
SHIFT   SLA     4,0(2)
        .
```

Instruction Name	Shift Right Single Algebraic
Mnemonic OP Code	SRA
Machine OP Code	8A
Program Interruptions	None
Condition Code	is affected
Assembler Format	SRA R1,D2(B2)

The first operand specifies one of the general purpose registers. The integer part of the R1 register is shifted right. The number of bit positions shifted is specified by the low-order 6 bits of the address formed by the second operand, i.e., B2+D2. All 31 integer bits of the R1 register participate in the shift except for the sign bit, which is not changed. The low-order bits being shifted out are lost and the sign bit is propagated through the high-order vacated bit position.

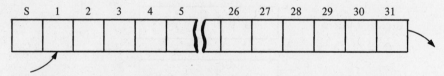

Bits supplied are the same configuration as the sign bit.

Resulting Condition Code	Meaning
0	Register is zero
1	Result is less than zero
2	Result is greater than zero
3	———

Note: 1. A shift amount of zero does not cause any shifting; however, the condition code is set according to the magnitude of the R1 register.

2. Only the low-order 6 bits of the address formed by D2+B2 are used to specify the shift amount. The remainder of the address is ignored. This applies to all the shift instructions.

Example:

Assume register 5 contains 3 and the contents of register 7 are:

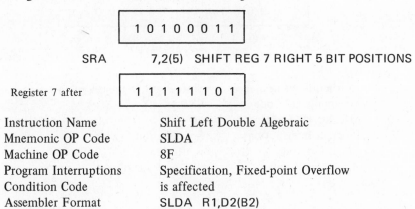

1 0 1 0 0 0 1 1

SRA 7,2(5) SHIFT REG 7 RIGHT 5 BIT POSITIONS

Register 7 after 1 1 1 1 1 1 0 1

Instruction Name	Shift Left Double Algebraic
Mnemonic OP Code	SLDA
Machine OP Code	8F
Program Interruptions	Specification, Fixed-point Overflow
Condition Code	is affected
Assembler Format	SLDA R1,D2(B2)

This instruction is used to shift left the contents of a doubleword located in two adjacent general registers. The registers *must* be a pair of even–odd registers where the even-numbered register is always one number lower than the odd-numbered register. For example, 2–3, 4–5, 6–7, etc. All double shift instructions treat the even–odd pair of registers as a 64-bit signed binary number, i.e., 63 integer bits and 1 sign bit. The first operand of the shift instruction *must* refer to the even-numbered register of the even–odd pair, otherwise a specification exception is recognized. All 63 integer bits participate in the shift; however, the sign bit is not shifted. The low-order vacated bit positions are filled with zeros. In case a bit different than the sign bit is shifted out, a fixed-point overflow is recognized.

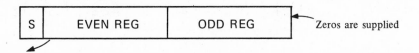

| S | EVEN REG | ODD REG | | Zeros are supplied |

Resulting Condition Code	Meaning
0	Result is zero
1	Result is less than zero
2	Result is greater than zero
3	Fixed-point overflow

Example:

Assume a doubleword located into a pair of even—odd registers:

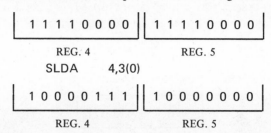

1 1 1 1 0 0 0 0	1 1 1 1 0 0 0 0
REG. 4	REG. 5

SLDA   4,3(0)

1 0 0 0 0 1 1 1	1 0 0 0 0 0 0 0
REG. 4	REG. 5

Note: A shift amount of zero results in condition code setting without affecting the registers.

Instruction Name	Shift Right Double Algebraic
Mnemonic OP Code	SRDA
Machine OP Code	8E
Program Interruptions	Specification
Condition Code	is affected
Assembler Format	SRDA R1,D2(B2)

The rules about register specification are the same as specified in Shift Left Double. All 63 integer bits participate in the shift. The low-order bits shifted out of the odd-numbered register are lost and the sign bit is propagated through the high-order vacated positions. The sign bit is not altered.

Resulting Condition Code	Meaning
0	Result is zero
1	Result is less than zero
2	Result is greater than zero
3	———

Sign bit is propagated | S | Bits shifted are lost

Note: A shift amount of zero results in condition code setting without affecting the registers.

Logical Shift Instructions

Instruction Name	Shift Left Single Logical
Mnemonic OP Code	SLL
Machine OP Code	89
Program Interruptions	None
Condition Code	is not affected
Assembler Format	SLL R1,D2(B2)

The first operand register is shifted left. The number of bits to be shifted is specified by the second operand. Only the low-order 6 bits of the address formed by the second operand address are used to specify the shift amount. The remainder of the address bits are ignored. All 32 bits of the register specified as R1 participate in the shift[1].

The high-order bits being shifted out are lost and zeros are supplied to the vacated low-order bit positions.

Example:

SLL   6,4   SHIFT LEFT REG 6 BY 4 BITS

The instruction above specifies a left shift of 4 bits for general register 6.

Machine Format

89	6	0	8	0	0	4
OP	R1	R3	B2		D2	

Example:

Assume that register 8 contains a four, the following instruction will shift the contents of register 6 by 4 bits.

SLL   6,0(8)

Machine Format

89	6	9	8	0	0	0
OP	R1	R3	B2		D2	

Instruction Name	Shift Right Single Logical
Mnemonic OP Code	SRL
Machine OP Code	88
Program Interruptions	None
Condition Code	is not affected
Assembler Format	SRL R1,D2(B2)

[1] In logical shifts all 32 bits participate in shifting as opposed to algebraic shifts where the sign bit does not participate in the shift.

The 32 bits of the register specified as R1 are shifted right the number of bits specified by the second operand address. Only 6 low-order bits of the address formed by B2+D2 are used to specify the shift amount. The low-order bits shifted out of the register are lost and zeros are supplied into the vacated high-order register bits.

Instruction Name	Shift Left Double Logical
Mnemonic OP Code	SLDL
Machine OP Code	8D
Program Interruptions	Specification
Condition Code	is not affected
Assembler Format	SLDL R1,D2(B2)

The register specified as R1 *must* be the even-numbered register of an even—odd pair of registers. Violation of this rule causes a specification exception. The shift instruction treats the pair of registers as 64 signed binary number. All 64 bits participate in the shift. The high-order bits being shifted out of the even-numbered register are lost and the low-order vacated bit position are supplied with zeros.

Instruction Name	Shift Right Double Logical
Mnemonic OP Code	SRDL
Machine OP Code	8C
Program Interruptions	Specification
Condition Code	is not affected
Assembler Format	SRDL R1,D2(B2)

This instruction works exactly like the shift left double except for the fact that shifting is to the right. The vacated high-order positions are filled with zeros.

Note: The logical shift instructions differ from the algebraic shifts in that the sign bit participates in the shift and is not propagated; instead zeros are supplied to the vacated bit positions. Condition code is not changed and overflow does not occur.

EXERCISE:
What will be the contents of register 8 and 9 when the program reaches EOJ?

	L	8,CONST
	LR	9,8
	AR	8,8
	AR	9,9
	SR	8,9
	BC	4,EOJ
	A	8,DATA
	AR	9,8
	SRA	9,2
	SLDA	8,1
	M	8,F2
	MH	8,H2
EOJ	EOJ	
CONST	DC	F'+128'
DATA	DC	F'−32'
F2	DC	F'2'
H2	DC	H'2'

Multiplication and division by shifting

Shift instructions can be used to multiply or divide fixed-point data that exists in general registers. However, the multiplier or the divisor must be a power of two.

Multiplication. For numbers with an absolute value of less than 2^{30}, a left shift of 1 bit position is the same as multiplication by 2. To multiply a fixed-point quantity contained in a general register, the first step is to express the multiplier in terms of power of two, i.e., 2^n. Then a shift left instruction can be used where the number of bits shifted must be equal to n.

Example:

Multiply the contents of general register 3 by 16. Assume register 3 contains a one.

$$2^4 = 16$$

Therefore the instruction will be:

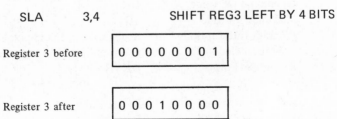

| SLA | 3,4 | SHIFT REG3 LEFT BY 4 BITS |

Register 3 before   0 0 0 0 0 0 0 1

Register 3 after   0 0 0 1 0 0 0 0

Note: A shift amount of 31 will cause the entire integer portion of the register to be shifted out.

Division. A right shift of 1 bit position is equivalent to division by 2 with *rounding downward*. When an .even number is shifted right 1 bit position, the value of the result is equal to the number divided by two. However, when an odd number is shifted right one position, the value of the quotient is that obtained by dividing the next lower number by 2. For example, +7 shifted right 1 bit position will yield +3, whereas −7 will yield −4.

Example:

Register 7 contains +16. Divide the number by 16.

$$2^4 = 16$$

SRA   7,4

Register 7 before $0\ 0\ 0\ 1\ 0\ 0\ 0\ 0 \equiv (16)_{10}$

Register 7 after $0\ 0\ 0\ 0\ 0\ 0\ 0\ 1 \equiv (1)_{10}$

Example:

Register 9 contains +13. Divide by 4.

SRA   9,2

Register 9 before $0\ 0\ 0\ 0\ 1\ 1\ 0\ 1$

Register 9 after $0\ 0\ 0\ 0\ 0\ 0\ 1\ 1 \equiv (3)_{10}$

Example:

Register 9 contains −13. Divide by 4.

SRA   9,2

Register 9 before $1\ 1\ 1\ 1\ 0\ 0\ 1\ 1$

Register 9 after $1\ 1\ 1\ 1\ 1\ 1\ 0\ 0 \equiv (4)_{10}$

9.4 Binary Divide Instructions

Instruction Name	Divide Register into Register
Mnemonic OP Code	DR
Machine OP Code	1D
Program Interruptions	Specification, Fixed-point divide
Condition Code	is not affected
Assembler Format	DR R1,R1

Instruction Name	Divide Fullword into Register
Mnemonic OP Code	D
Machine OP Code	5D
Program Interruptions	Protection, Addressing,

	Specification, Fixed-point divide
Condition Code	Is not affected
Assembler Format	D R1,D2(X2,B2)

The dividend is a 64-bit signed integer and occupies a pair of even—odd registers.

EVEN REG   ODD REG

The divisor, a 32-bit signed number, may be located in another general purpose register or in a fullword. In the latter case, the fullword must be located on integral boundary. The first operand, R1, of the divide instruction must reference the even-numbered register of the even—odd pair of registers containing the dividend. A specification exception occurs when the R1 register of the divide instruction does not reference an even-numbered register. As a result of the divide instruction, the remainder and the quotient, each a 32-bit signed number, replace the dividend in the even—odd registers respectively.

REMAINDER	QUOTIENT

EVEN REG   ODD REG

The signs of the quotient and the remainder are determined by the rules of the algebra, i.e., the quotient will be positive if both the dividend and the divisor have the same sign. Otherwise, the quotient will be a negative quantity; the remainder always carries the same sign as the dividend. Exception to this is noted in the rule below.

Note: A zero quotient or zero remainder is always positive.

It is important to note that the dividend is a 64-bit signed integer; as such, the contents of the even-numbered register are not ignored during division. If the dividend is of such a magnitude that it can be contained in one register, it must be positioned in the low-order register of the even—odd pair, i.e., the odd-numbered register. The even-numbered register must be set to zeros for a positive number and to ones for a negative number.

Example:

Dividend = −16, registers to be used to contain the dividend are registers 6 and 7.

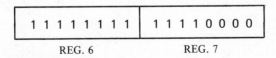

REG. 6   REG. 7

Positioning of dividend

In case of positive quantity, the simplest method of positioning the dividend is as follows:

```
PACK    DOUB,DIVD    PACK DIVIDEND
CVB     7,DOUB       POSITION DIVIDEND
SR      6,6          SET REG 6 TO ZEROS
.
```

The PACK and CVB instructions place the dividend in register 7 and the SR instruction is used to set the even-numbered register to zeros, the sign of a positive fixed-point quantity.

There are times when a programmer may not know the sign of the dividend and there may be the possibility of both negative and positive quantities. In cases like this, one of the methods of positioning the dividend is explained in the example below.

Example:

Even—odd pair of registers is 4 and 5.

```
.
.
PACK    DOUB,DIVD
CVB     4,DOUB
SRDA    4,32
.
.
```

In this case, we first place the dividend in the even-numbered register and then issue a shift right double algebraic instruction with a shift amount of 32. The shift instruction will cause the contents of register 4 to be shifted to register 5 and the sign bit (0 or 1) will be propagated through the even-numbered register, i.e., register 4 in this case.

In case of binary division if the magnitude of the dividend and the divisor is such that the resulting quotient can not be expressed by a 32-bit signed integer, fixed-point divide exception is recognized and a program interruption occurs. In such a case, division will not be attempted and the dividend remains unchanged.

Example:

Compute the average number of remote runs per programmer and place the result in REMOTES. Total number of remotes is given in c.c. 1 − 5 and the total number of programmers is contained in c.c. 6 − 7.

```
.
.
PACK    DOUB,IN(5)
CVB     6,DOUB        PLACE DIVIDEND
SRDA    6,32          POSITION DIVIDEND
PACK    DOUB,IN+5(2)
CVB     3,DOUB        POSITION DIVISOR
        (continued)
```

```
                DR        6,3              DIVIDE
                CVD       7,DOUB
                UNPK      REMOTES,DOUB
                  .
REMOTES         DS        CL5
IN              DS        CL80
                  .
```

Note: If in a programming application there is ever a chance of a zero divisor, the programmer must check for such a possibility and by-pass the divide instruction if a zero divisor exists before issuing the divide instruction.

There are a number of ways to check for this possibility. One of the easier methods is to use the Load and Test Register instruction. Assume the same data as in the previous example.

```
                  .
                PACK      DOUB,IN(5)       PACK DIVIDEND
                CVB       6,DOUB           PLACE DIVIDEND
                SRDA      6,32             POSITION DIVIDEND
                PACK      DOUB,IN+5(2)     PACK DIVISOR
                CVB       3,DOUB           POSITION DIVISOR
                LTR       3,3              LOAD AND TEST R3
                BC        8,BYPASS         BYPASS IF R3 = 0
                DR        6,3              DIVIDE
                CVD       7,DOUB
                UNPK      REMOTES,DOUB     POSITION RESULTS
BACK              .
                  .
BYPASS          MVC       REMOTES,ZEROS
                BC        15,BACK
                  .
REMOTES         DS        CL5
ZEROS           DC        CL5'00000'
                  .
```

The example that follows illustrates the use of binary arithmetic instructions.

Example:

Given AMT1 and AMT2, compute PROD = AMT1 * AMT2. The formats of these fields are as follows:

```
AMT1        xx.xx
AMT2        x.xx
```

RESULT is to have two decimal places only.

```
         .
RESULT   DS      F
AMT1     DC      F'4550'
AMT2     DC      F'175'
ROUND    DC      F'50'
HUNDRD   DC      F'100'

         .
L        7,AMT1
SR       6,6
M        6,AMT2
A        7,ROUND
SR       6,6
D        6,HUNDRD
ST       7,RESULT
         .
         .
```

EXERCISE:

Given three fullword binary constants named A1, A2 and A3, compute:

$$\frac{A1 \ * \ A3}{A2} - 600$$

If the result is negative, branch to NEGRES. If the result is zero, branch to ZERORES. Otherwise, branch to POSRES.

EXERCISE:

Given twelve consecutive words, each containing binary data, compute:

$$\frac{word1+word2+\ldots\ldots\ldots\ldots word12}{12}$$

Place the result in register 7.

Self Evaluation Quiz

1. Register 3 contains −17. What will be the contents of this register after the following instructions have been executed?

```
         .
AR       3,3
SRA      3,1
LTR      3,3
SLA      3,31
         .
```

2. Register 4 contains a value of −4. What will be its contents after the execution of the following instruction?

$$\text{SRA} \qquad 4,31$$

3. In case of the binary divide instructions, the resulting quotient is placed in the:
   a. Even-numbered register
   b. Odd-numbered register

4. Given the following two fixed-point quantities

DIVIDND	DS	F
DIVISOR	DS	F

   (DIVIDND may assume negative or positive value)

write instructions necessary to compute the following:

$$\text{RESULT (in register 2)} = \text{DIVIDND/DIVISOR}$$

5. Register 3 contains +16. Will the branch instruction coded below cause a successful branch to LOOP?

```
          .
      AR      3,3
      SRA     3,6
      BC      7,LOOP
          .
          .
LOOP      .
          .
```

6. Under what conditions can a specification exception occur in case of MR and DR instructions?

7. What is the maximum size of the multiplicand (in terms of bits) that can be used in binary multiplication instructions?

8. Given four fixed-point quantities in storage:

X	DS	F
Y	DS	F
Z	DS	F
ANSWER	DS	F

write the instructions necessary to compute:

$$\text{ANSWER} = \frac{X + Y - Z}{5} * 7$$

9. Given the same fixed-point quantities as in the problem above, compute:

$$ANSWER = ((X + Y + Z) * 14)$$

10. Given three fixed-point quantities which represent total cases, units/case and price/unit, compute:

$$VALUE = (Total\ cases * Units/case) * Price/unit$$

CASES	DS	F
UNITS	DS	F
PRICE	DS	H
VALUE	DS	F

11. Given three fixed-point quantities as follows:

AVERAGE	DS	F
GAMES	DS	F
SCORE	DS	F

where GAMES stands for the total number of games played by a player, and SCORE stands for the total score for the player for *all* games played; compute AVERAGE = Total score/Number of games played. If the number of games played is zero, bypass the calculation steps and branch to a symbol NOSCORE.

12. What will be the values of the variables X, Y and A when the program reaches FINISH?

X	DC	H'20'
Y	DC	H'−10'
A	DC	H'−5'
	LH	2,X
COMP	CH	2,Y
	BC	6,ADD
	BC	8,FINISH
ADD	AH	2,A
	BC	15,COMP
FINISH	.	
	.	

13. What will be the values of the variables X, Y and Z when the program reaches FINISH?

X	DC	H'10'
Y	DC	H'−5'
Z	DC	H'−25'
	LH	3,Y
BACK	CH	3,Z
		(continued)

```
          BC      2,ADD
          AH      3,Y
          STH     2,Z
          BC      15,FINISH
ADD       LH      4,Z
          AH      4,Y
          STH     4,Z
          BC      15,BACK
```

[10]

Decimal Instructions

10.1 Add Decimal, Subtract Decimal, and Zero and Add Instructions

Decimal instructions operate on data that are in packed decimal format. In this format, each byte of the field contains 2 digits except the rightmost byte. The low-order 4 bits of the rightmost byte contain the sign code while the high-order 4 bits contain a digit code.

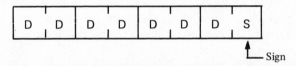

During execution of the decimal instructions, related data fields *are checked* for validity, i.e., the fields must contain valid digit and sign codes in the appropriate locations. Invalid fields will cause a data exception and program interruption results. Valid digit and sign codes are:

Digit codes	0000 to 1001	
Sign codes	1010, 1100, 1110 and 1111	(positive)
	1011 and 1101	(negative)

Decimal instructions deal with variable length data as opposed to the fixed-point instructions which deal with fixed-length data only.

Instruction Name	Add Decimal
Mnemonic OP Code	AP

Machine OP Code	FA
Type	SS
Program Interruptions	Operation, Protection, Addressing Data, Decimal Overflow
Condition Code	is affected
Assembler Format	AP D1,(L1,B1),D2(L2,B2)

Resulting Condition Code	Meaning
0	Result is Zero
1	Result is less than zero
2	Result is greater than zero
3	Decimal overflow

The contents of the second operand are added to the contents of the first operand and the resulting sum is placed in the first operand location. The sign of the result is determined by the rules of algebra. Add decimal is a SS type of instruction with two length codes (L1 and L2).

Variable length fields are allowed; however, the length of either operand can not exceed 16 bytes. Sixteen bytes of packed data allows us to operate upon fields that are capable of containing 31 digits and a sign. Both operands are checked for valid digit and sign codes and, if needed, high-order packed zeros are supplied to either operand.

A decimal overflow can occur due to two possible causes. The first is the loss of a carry out of the high-order digit position of the result field. The second cause is an over-sized result, which occurs when the first operand location, the receiving field, is too short to contain all the significant digits of the resulting sum. Please note that the field sizes, per se, have no bearing on the overflow condition.

If the operation is completed without an overflow, a zero sum is always positive, but on the other hand if the high-order digits are truncated due to an overflow condition, a zero sum may assume a positive or a negative sign.

Note: Both operands are referenced by their high-order byte address; however, the execution of the instruction proceeds from right to left.

Example:
Given three packed decimal quantities as established by the constants below:

FLDA	DC	PL3'125'		0	0	1	2	5	C

FLDB	DC	PL2'+75'					0	7	5	C

FLDC	DC	PL2'+325'					3	2	5	C

Add all three quantities and place the resulting sum in FLDB.

AP   FLDB,FLDA | 2 | 0 | 0 | C |

AP   FLDB,FLDC | 5 | 2 | 5 | C |

Example:

Given three quantities in a card record as follows:

FLDA	c.c 1 − 5
FLDB	c.c. 7 − 9
FLDC	c.c. 12 − 13

Add all three quantities and place the result in a 3 byte long area named SUM. Assume that the IOAREA is IN.

```
          PACK      IN+2(3),IN(5)
          AP        SUM,IN+2(3)
          PACK      IN+7(2),IN+6(3)
          AP        SUM,IN+7(2)
          PACK      IN+11(2),IN+11(2)
          AP        SUM,IN+11(2)
                      .
SUM       DC        PL3'0'
```

Note: In the example above please note that the area named SUM was set aside as packed constant. This is very important as both the receiving and sending fields must be in packed format. This constant could have been set as X' 00 00 0C'.

Overlapping of fields

The first and second operand fields may overlap as long as their low-order bytes coincide.

Example:

```
FLDA      DC        PL3'+42137'
          AP        FLDA,FLDA+1(2)
```

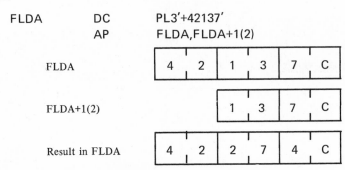

FLDA | 4 | 2 | 1 | 3 | 7 | C |

FLDA+1(2) | 1 | 3 | 7 | C |

Result in FLDA | 4 | 2 | 2 | 7 | 4 | C |

Example:

AP   FLDA,FLDA

In this case both operands specify the same operand location and the result of this instruction will double the contents of FLDA, i.e., FLDA will be added to itself. This is one simple way to multiply a field by 2.

Instruction Name	Subtract Decimal
Mnemonic OP Code	SP
Machine OP Code	FB
Type	SS
Program Interruptions	Operation, Protection, Addressing Data, Decimal Overflow
Condition Code	is affected
Assembler Format	SP D1(L1,B1),D2(L2,B2)

The contents of the second operand are subtracted from that of the first operand and the resulting difference is placed in the first operand location. The subtract instruction works very much like the add instruction and the rules for decimal overflow, field sizes, sign control and operand overlapping are all the same as discussed for the add decimal instruction.

Note: Subtracting a field from itself will set the field to packed zeros.

Example:

Assume that FLDA contains	34 72 4C
SP	FLDA,FLDA
Resulting FLDA	00 00 0C

Example:

Assume that FLDA contains	12 72 3C
SP	FLDA,FLDA+1(2)

	1	2	7	2	3	C
FLDA originally	1	2	7	2	3	C
FLDA+1(2)			7	2	3	C
Resulting FLDA	1	2	0	0	0	C

This example illustrates how we can set low-order bytes of a field to zeros.

Resulting Condition Code	Meaning
0	Difference is zero
1	Difference is less than zero
2	Difference is greater than zero
3	Decimal overflow

Instruction Name	Zero and Add
Mnemonic OP Code	ZAP
Machine OP Code	F8
Type	SS
Program Interruptions	Operation, Protection, Data, Addressing, Decimal Overflow
Condition Code	is affected
Assembler Format	ZAP D1(L1,B1),D2(L2,B2)

Resulting Condition Code	Meaning
0	Result is zero
1	Result is less than zero
2	Result is greater than zero
3	Decimal overflow

The zero and add instruction *places* the second operand's contents into the first operand location. This instruction is equivalent to an addition to a zero field. The second operand, the sending field, must be in packed decimal format. The contents of the first operand are not checked for valid digit or sign codes.

The instruction is executed from right to left, if the receiving field is longer than the sending field, the extra high-order positions are supplied with packed zeros. On the other hand, if the receiving field is not long enough to contain all the significant digits from the sending field, a decimal overflow occurs and results in a program interruption. When high-order digits are lost due to an overflow condition, a zero result assumes the sign of the sending field.

Example:

```
FLDA        DC        C'123'
FLDB        DC        PL4'+7273'
```

FLDA before	F	1	F	2	F	3

FLDB before	0	0	0	7	2	7	3	C

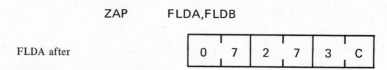

ZAP   FLDA,FLDB

FLDA after

| 0 | 7 | 2 | 7 | 3 | C |

Note: Sending field is not altered in any way.

Example:

```
FLDA       DC       C'1234'
FLDB       DC       PL2'+172'
           ZAP      FLDA,FLDB
```

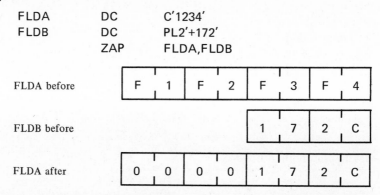

FLDA before

| F | 1 | F | 2 | F | 3 | F | 4 |

FLDB before

| 1 | 7 | 2 | C |

FLDA after

| 0 | 0 | 0 | 0 | 1 | 7 | 2 | C |

Example:

```
FLDC       DS       CL4
FLDA       DS       CL6
ZERO       DC       P'0'
           ZAP      FLDA,ZERO
           ZAP      FLDC,ZERO
```

The result of the ZAP instruction would be:

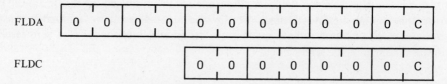

FLDA

| 0 | 0 | 0 | 0 | 0 | 0 | 0 | 0 | 0 | 0 | 0 | C |

FLDC

| 0 | 0 | 0 | 0 | 0 | 0 | 0 | C |

Note: When both operands of a ZAP instruction reference the same data field the net result is the setting of the condition code without affecting the data. This is a neat method to check a packed field for zeros.

Overlapping

The first and the second operand fields may overlap as long as the low-order byte of the first operand coincides or is to the right of the low-order byte of the second operand. This aspect of the ZAP instruction can be used to shift a field to the right.

Decimal point alignment

When dealing with numbers containing decimal points it is often necessary to align the decimal points in various data fields to obtain the correct answer. For example, consider two fields whose formats are XX.XX and X.X. To add these quantities together we need to manipulate these fields to align the decimal points correctly. These two data fields have to take the following format:

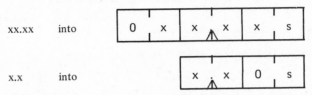

There is no one instruction or a set method available to achieve this objective. We can perform decimal point alignment with the help of a number of instructions and in a number of different ways. Some of these instructions we have already discussed, for example, MVZ and Bit Manipulation Instructions. In this section, we will discuss two more instructions and then see some examples of decimal point alignment.

Instruction Name	Move Numerics
Mnemonic OP Code	MVN
Machine OP Code	D1
Type	SS
Program Interruptions	Protection, Addressing
Condition Code	is not affected
Assembler Format	MVN D1(L,B1),D2(B2)

The MVN instruction moves the low-order 4 bits of each byte in the second operand to the low-order 4 bits of the corresponding byte of the first operand field.

This is a storage-to-storage type of instruction with one length code thus a maximum of 256 bytes can be specified with one move-numeric instruction. The movement is left to right through each field 1 byte at a time. The two operands may overlap in any way desired.

It is important to note that the numerics being moved are *not* checked for valid numeric codes. For all practical purposes, this portion of the byte being moved may contain a zone code or any other valid System 360 code.

Note: It is not valid to specify explicit length code for the second operand for this instruction. The second operand is assumed to be the same length as the first.

Example:

    FLDA   DC   C'1234'

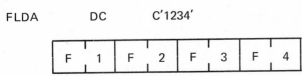

MVN   FLDA+2(2),FLDA

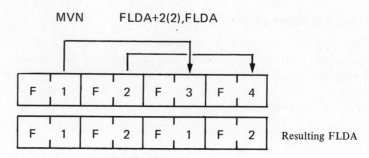

Resulting FLDA

Note: The zone bits of each byte affected remain unchanged.

EXERCISE:

What will be the contents of FLDA and FLDB after the following instructions have been executed?

```
FLDA        DC          X'12345C'
FLDB        DS          CL5
            .
            ZAP         FLDB+3(2),ZERO
            ZAP         FLDB(3),FLDA
            MVN         FLDB+4(1),FLDB+2
            MVN         FLDB+2(1),FLDB+3
            .
ZERO        DC          P'0'
```

Instruction Name	Move with Offset
Mnemonic OP Code	MVO
Machine OP Code	F1
Type	SS
Program Interruptions	Protection, Addressing
Assembler Format	MVO D1(L1,B1),D2(L2,B2)

This instruction basically is a move instruction with one significant difference. The MVO instruction moves the contents of the second operand to the first operand location; however, during the move the receiving field is offset by 4 bits to the left. The result is that the data from the numeric bits of the sending byte is moved to the zone bits of the receiving byte.

The fields are processed from right to left. If the receiving field is larger than the sending field the extra high-order positions are filled with zeros. On the other hand, if the sending field is larger than the receiving field, the extra high-order positions of the sending field are ignored. None of the fields is checked for valid codes. The two operands may overlap in any manner and are processed by storing a result byte as soon as the necessary operand bytes are fetched.

Example:

```
FLDA        DC        PL3'+12347'
FLDB        DS        CL4
            MVO       FLDB,FLDA
```

FIGURE 10.1. Use of MVO Instruction.

Example:

```
FLDA        DC        X'7234721C'
            MVO       FLDA,FLDA(3) EXAMPLE OF OVERLAPPING
```

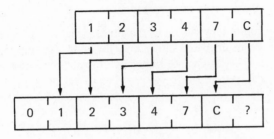

The execution of this MVO instruction can best be explained by the illustration below.

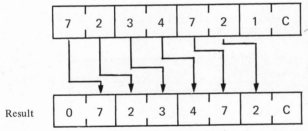

Note: MVO instruction with overlapping operand addresses lends itself very well for truncating excess decimal digits. This is discussed later in this section.

Example:

We are given two quantities in a card record. Their format is as follows:

c.c.	1 − 5	xx.xxx	contents	34721
c.c.	6 − 8	x.xx	contents	124

We are to add these quantities together. Before issuing the Add Decimal instruction, data in the two fields must be converted to packed decimal format and the decimal points have to be aligned to obtain the correct answers. These two fields *must* be transformed into the following format:

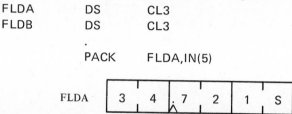

| 3 | 4 | ‸7 | 2 | 1 | S |

Data from c.c. 1 − 5

| 0 | 1 | ‸2 | 4 | 0 | S |

Data from c.c. 6 − 8

Note: The decimal points (∧) shown in the illustrations above do not exist in the input data, these are assumed and shown only for illustration purposes.

Data contained in c.c. 1 − 5 can be positioned by a simple PACK instruction:

```
FLDA        DS      CL3
FLDB        DS      CL3
            .
       PACK      FLDA,IN(5)
```

FLDA

| 3 | 4 | ‸7 | 2 | 1 | S |

Data from c.c. 6 − 8 will require some manipulation before the desired format is obtained.

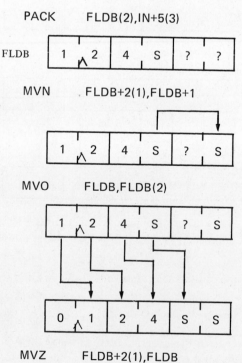

```
       PACK      FLDB(2),IN+5(3)
```

FLDB

| 1 | ‸2 | 4 | S | ? | ? |

```
       MVN      FLDB+2(1),FLDB+1
```

| 1 | ‸2 | 4 | S | ? | S |

```
       MVO      FLDB,FLDB(2)
```

| 1 | ‸2 | 4 | S | ? | S |

| 0 | ‸1 | 2 | 4 | S | S |

```
       MVZ      FLDB+2(1),FLDB
```

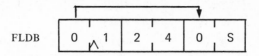

Write all these instructions together.

```
FLDA        DS      CL3
FLDB        DS      CL3
            .
            PACK    FLDA,IN(5)
            PACK    FLDB(2),IN+5(3)    PACK
            MVN     FLDB+2(1),FLDB+1   AND
            MVO     FLDB,FLDB(2)       ALIGN
            MVZ     FLDB+2(1),FLDB        FLDB
            AP      FLDA,FLDB          ADD FLDB TO FLDA
```

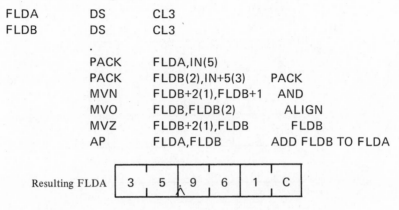

Example:

Given the following data, write a routine to accumulate the contents of all three fields and place the result, packed format, into ACCUM.

c.c.	1 − 5	xxx.xx
c.c.	7 − 10	x.xxx
c.c.	12 − 14	xx.x

Probably the first step in solving this type of problem is to establish the final format we need to get the data into. Then we can proceed with writing the actual instructions.

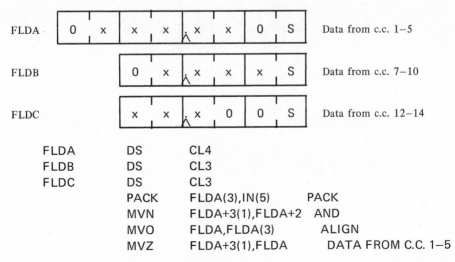

```
FLDA        DS      CL4
FLDB        DS      CL3
FLDC        DS      CL3
            PACK    FLDA(3),IN(5)      PACK
            MVN     FLDA+3(1),FLDA+2   AND
            MVO     FLDA,FLDA(3)       ALIGN
            MVZ     FLDA+3(1),FLDA        DATA FROM C.C. 1−5
```

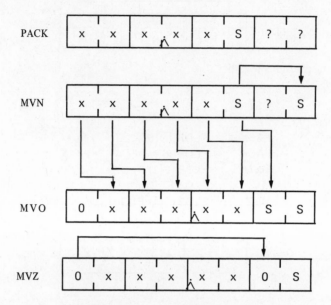

Data from c.c. 7 − 10 can be aligned by a single **PACK** instruction.

```
PACK        FLDB,IN+6(4)
```

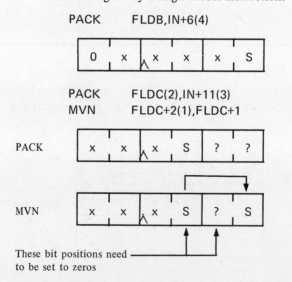

```
PACK        FLDC(2),IN+11(3)
MVN         FLDC+2(1),FLDC+1
```

We can use the AND instruction to set the above mentioned bits to zeros. It is important, at this point, to review the mechanics of the AND instruction.

A bit position in the first operand is set to one if the corresponding bit position in both operands contain a one; otherwise the first operand bit is set to zero. So our instructions would be:

```
          NI        FLDC+1,X'F0'
          NI        FLDC+2,X'0F'
```

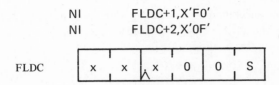

FLDC

Now we can add all these fields together.

```
          AP        ACCUM,FLDA
          AP        ACCUM,FLDB
          AP        ACCUM,FLDC
                 .
ACCUM     DC        PL4'0'
```

It is important to point out that ACCUM must contain packed zero.

Rounding off

Rounding is used when the number of decimal positions in a number field are more than required. Assume that we were dealing with dollars and cents and the result obtained after some arithmetic operations was:

0	1	6	1	3	6	8	C

In this case, it is necessary to round off the cents positions as well as truncate the excess low-order digit, 8, so that the end result is:

0	0	1	6	1	3	7	C

On the other hand, if the contents of the field were:

0	1	6	1	3	6	4	C

the rounded result would be:

0	0	1	6	1	3	6	C

From these two examples we can say that to round off a number we need to examine the leftmost digit to be eliminated. If this digit's value is equal to, or greater than, 5, we add 1 to the next high-order digit and then truncate the excess digit(s); if the digit position being examined has a value less than 5 we simply truncate the excess digit(s). This method seems rather easy, but in a program it would become very involved to do all this checking and calculating. An easier way to achieve the same result is to add a 5 to the leftmost digit that needs to be truncated. Consider the same two numbers again, using this method.

Example:

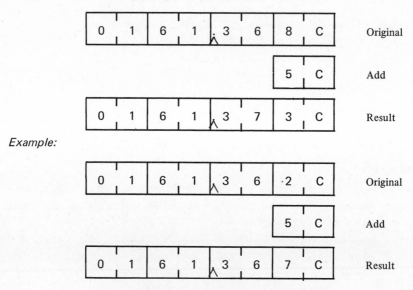

Example:

FIGURE 10.2. Example of Rounding-Off.

Note: It is important to point out that the signs of the two numbers being added must be identical. This can be done by moving the sign of the original field to the constant.

Another method of rounding off is to add a part of the number back to itself. This works only if the number of digits to be rounded is odd. In case an even number of digits need to be rounded, we first have to shift 1 low-order digit off before issuing the add decimal instruction. Please note that we need to shift an extra low-order digit and not the sign of the field.

Example:

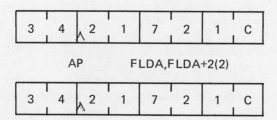

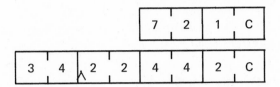

Example:

3 ᴧ 4	2	1	7	2	1 ¦ C

In this case, the number of digits to be truncated is even. Therefore, our instructions would be:

```
MVO     FLDA,FLDA(3)
AP      FLDA,FLDA+2(2)
```

	3 ᴧ 4	2	1	7	2	1 ¦ C

MVO	0 ¦ 3	ᴧ 4	2	1	7	2 ¦ C

AP				1	7	2 ¦ C

Result	0 ¦ 3	ᴧ 4	2	3	4	4 ¦ C

The next and the final step in rounding off is the truncation of the excess low-order digits. This can very easily be done with the help of MVO instruction. For example, to truncate the 3 low-order digits from the result obtained in the example above we would give the following instruction.

```
MVO     FLDA,FLDA(2)
```

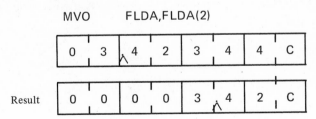

EXERCISE:
Write two P-type DC statements to store −13.4272 and +3.271 and name these A1

and A2 respectively. Add these constants and round off the result to two decimal places. Unpack the result of this addition and place it into a 5 byte long area named RESULT. Show the contents of result.

10.2 Decimal Multiplication and Division

Instruction Name	Multiply Decimal
Mnemonic OP Code	MP
Machine OP Code	FC
Type	SS
Program Interruptions	Operation, Protection, Addressing, Data
Condition Code	is not affected
Assembler Format	MP D1(L1,B1),D2(L2,B2)

The first operand (multiplicand) is multiplied by the second operand (multiplier) and the product replaces the first operand (multiplicand). Various rules to be followed are outlined below.

1. Both operands must contain packed decimal data. Violation of this rule will cause a program interruption.
2. The multiplier size is limited to 8 bytes, i.e., 15 digits and a sign.
3. The multiplier length must be less than the length of the multiplicand, the first operand.
4. Since the number of digits in the product is equal to the sum of the number of digits in the multiplicand and the multiplier, the first operand must have high-order zero digits for at least a field size that equals the multiplier field size.

Violation of rules 2 and 3 is recognized as specification exception. The operation is suppressed and a program interruption occurs. Violation of rule 4 is recognized as data exception and a program interruption occurs. Rule 4, regarding the size of the first operand, insures that no product overflow can occur. The maximum possible size of the product is 31 digits and a sign and at least 1 high-order digit of the product is always zero. The sign of the product is determined by the rules of algebra from the multiplicand and multiplier signs. The multiplier and the product fields may overlap if their low-order bytes coincide.

Example:

Assume that we are given two quantities in a card record with formats as follows:

c.c.	$1-5$	xxxxx
c.c.	$7-9$	xxx

Before issuing the multiply instruction we need to pack this data and position it in appropriate fields. Data from c.c. 1–5 will require 3 bytes to pack and data from c.c. 7–9 will need at least 2 bytes. The correct size of the field to hold the multiplicand is therefore at least 5 bytes.

```
            PACK      PROD,IN(5)
            PACK      MPLR,IN+6(3)
            MP        PROD,MPLR
              .
              .
              .
PROD        DS        CL5
MPLR        DS        CL2
```

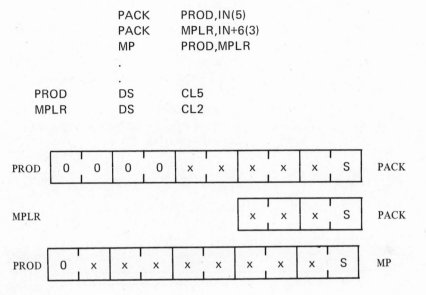

Example:

Given two data fields which have been defined as follows:

```
    FLDA      DC        PL3'12345'
    FLDB      DC        PL2'678'
```

In this case the data to be multiplied is already in packed format. We can use a ZAP instruction to position the multiplicand, FLDA, into a larger field which will contain the product. This field must be at least 5 bytes in length.

```
            ZAP       PROD,FLDA
            MP        PROD,FLDB
              .
PROD        DS        CL5
```

Example:

Given two data fields as shown below

	c.c.	1 − 4	Hours worked	xx.xx
	c.c.	7 − 9	Rate/hour	x.xx

calculate the salary, which is:

$$\text{Salary} = \text{Hours worked} * \text{Rate/hour}$$

Format for salary field is XXX.XX. The coding below would compute the salary.

Name	Oper	Operand	
	PACK	PROD,IN(4)	PACK HOURS WORKED
	PACK	RATE,IN+6(3)	PACK RATE
	MP	PROD,RATE	MULTIPLY HOURS * RATE
	MVO	PROD,PROD(4)	SHIFT 1 DIGIT
	AP	PROD,PROD+4(1)	ROUND SALARY
	MVO	PROD,PROD(4)	TRUNCATE 1 DIGIT
	UNPK	SALARY,PROD	UNPACK SALARY
	MVZ	SALARY+4(1), SALARY	
*			REMOVE ZONE
PROD	DS	CL5	
SALARY	DS	CL5	
RATE	DS	CL2	

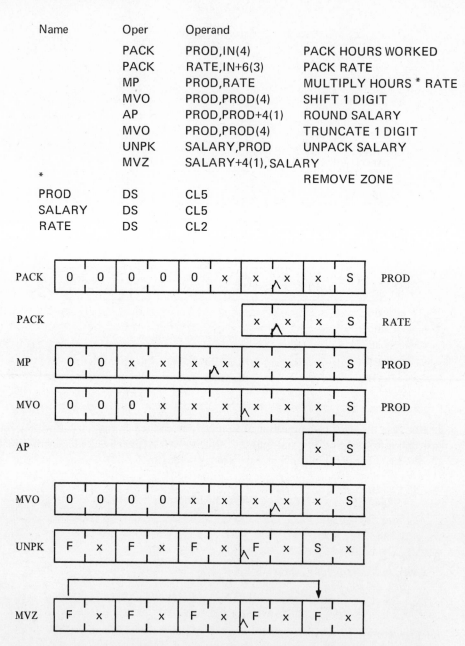

Note: 1. In the above examples S stands for the sign of the field, F stands for the no zone coding of 1111, and x stands for a digit position in the data field.

2. The number of decimal places in the resulting product is always equal to the sum of the decimal places in the multiplicand and the multiplier.

Instruction Name   Divide Decimal
Mnemonic OP Code   DP
Machine OP Code   FD
Type   SS
Program Interruptions   Operation, Protection, Data,
                                  Addressing, Specification,
                                  Decimal Divide
Condition Code   is not affected
Assembler Format   DP   D1(L1,B1),D2(L2,B2)

Both operands, the dividend and the divisor, must contain packed decimal data. The first operand contains the dividend and the divisor is contained in the second operand location.

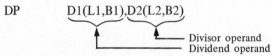

The dividend is divided by the divisor and is replaced by the resulting quotient and the remainder. The quotient field is placed leftmost and the remainder is placed rightmost in the first operand location. Therefore, the dividend operand must be large enough to contain both the resulting quotient and the remainder. The length of the remainder is always the same as that of the divisor. If a quotient larger than what has been allowed is developed, the system recognizes this as a decimal divide exception and an interruption follows. The easy way to calculate the length of the first operand field is as follows:

1. Calculate the number of bytes required to contain the dividend in packed format, identified as L1.
2. Calculate the number of bytes required to contain the divisor in packed format, identified as L2.
3. The length of the first operand field in bytes is L1 + L2.

There are two more rules that must be followed when using decimal divide instruction. These are:

1. The divisor must not exceed 8 bytes, i.e., 15 digits and a sign.
2. The length of the divisor must not be equal to or greater than the dividend field.

If either of these two rules is violated, a specification exception is recognized and a program interruption follows. The dividend, divisor, quotient and the remainder are all signed integers, right-aligned in their fields. The sign of the quotient is determined by the rules of algebra from the signs of the dividend and the divisor. The sign of the remainder is always the same as that of the dividend.

Example:

Write program steps to divide +7328 by +33. These two quantities have been defined as follows:

```
DIVIDND      DC        PL3'+7328'
DIVISOR      DC        PL2'+33'
             .
             ZAP       WORK,DIVIDND      00 00 07 32 8C
             DP        WORK,DIVISOR      00 22 2C 00 2C
             .
WORK         DS        CL5
```

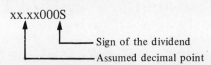

Quotient ———
Remainder ———

Note: The size of the quotient in 8 bit bytes is L1 − L2, in this case 5 − 2 = 3 bytes. To retrieve the quotient from the first operand field we need to specify an explicit length code of L1 − L2 bytes.

```
             UNPK      RESULT,WORK(3)    F0 F0 F2 F2 C2
             MVZ       RESULT+4(1),RESULT  F0 F0 F2 F2 F2

RESULT       DS        CL5
```

Division with decimal points

In case a resulting quotient needs to be carried to extra decimal places, we have to extend the dividend by adding low-order zeros before issuing the divide instruction. For example, to divide a number with a format of xx.xx by another number of the same format, the resulting quotient would not be carried to any decimal places, the reason being that the decimal places in the divisor will cancel the dividend's decimal places. To carry this division to 3 extra fraction points, we need to add 3 low-order zeros to the dividend so that it takes a format of:

$$xx.xx000S$$

——— Sign of the dividend
——— Assumed decimal point

Example:

Divide CONST1 by CONST2 and carry the division to 3 fractional places. These two constants have been defined as follows:

```
CONST1       DC        P'+7328'          format xx.xx
CONST2       DC        P'3333'           format xx.xx
```

In its new format, the dividend would require 4 bytes as we need to add 3 low-order zero digits. Dividend would have the following format:

$$73.28000C$$

———Padding

Therefore, the length of the first operand field of the divide instruction is 4 + 3 = 7 bytes.

```
WORK        DS      CL7
            ZAP     WORK(5),CONST1      00 00 07 3.2 8C ?? ??
            MVN     ZERO,WORK+4                            0C
            MVO     WORK(6),WORK(5)     00 00 00 73.28 C? ??
            ZAP     WORK+5(2),ZERO      00 00 00 73.28 00 0C
            DP      WORK,CONST2         00 02.10 8C 01 03 6C

ZERO        DC      P'0'
```

Quotient ————
Remainder ————

Note: The decimal positions shown are assumed. These are not assembled in the constants.

EXERCISE:

Write two P-type constants to store −472 and +19 and name these constants CONST1 and CONST2 respectively. Divide CONST1 by CONST2 to produce a quotient with three decimal points. Round the resulting quotient to two decimal places.

Division and multiplication by shifting

Division. Assume that ACCUM contains Hex 2343422C and we wish to divide this number by 100 (decimal). This can be accomplished with the help of a MVN instruction.

```
            MVN     ACCUM+2(1),ACCUM+3
```

The result would be:

```
            23  43  4C  2C
```

Of course, from this point on the instructions referencing ACCUM should use a length of 3. An alternate method would be:

```
            MVO     ACCUM,ACCUM(3)
            MVO     ACCUM,ACCUM(3)
```

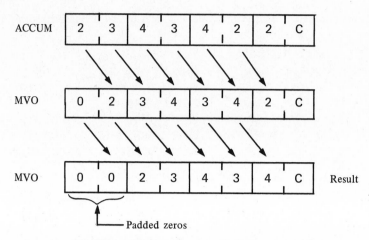

FIGURE 10.3. Division By Shifting.

Multiplication. Assume that FLDA contains 11 34 2C. Multiply this number by 100 (decimal). The product will require 4 bytes.

```
PROD            DS       CL4
                .
                .
                MVC      PROD(3),FLDA
                MVN      PROD+3(1),PROD+2
                NI       PROD+2,X'F0'
                NI       PROD+3,X'0'
```

1	1	3	4	2	0	0	C

FIGURE 10.4. Multiplication By Shifting.

Packed decimal vs fixed-point arithmetic

One of the most frequently asked questions by the average programmer is, "which arithmetic operation shall I use . . . packed decimal or fixed-point?" There is no clear-cut answer to this question, as both types of arithmetic operations have offsetting values over the other. One has to evaluate the overall conditions and processing requirements of a program before a decision can be made in favor of one type or the other. It is not uncommon practice to use both types of arithmetic operations in the same program.

Fixed-point arithmetic operations perform their functions more rapidly than the packed decimal operations. However, when using fixed-point instructions the data has to be converted to binary format and in most cases back into packed decimal. The CVB and CVD instructions use considerable time and may offset any time saved by the use of the fixed-point instructions. Thus, if the data entering the core is in fixed-point format or will be stored in fixed-point format or will be repetitiously used in fixed-point format, it will be wise to use binary operations. On the other hand, if the data entering the core is in character or packed decimal format and would be written or stored in character or packed decimal format, without much arithmetic operations, it will be wise to use the decimal operations. Another important factor to consider is the size of the data fields involved. Packed decimal instructions allow us to work with numbers as large as 31 digits, whereas fixed-point operations can handle only fullwords of fixed-point data. Another factor involved is the availability of general registers. Fixed-point instructions need at least one general register, and at times a programmer may have to go through many instructions to make a register available for arithmetic operations.

General experience has indicated that if the data resulting from arithmetic operations is to be stored, printed or displayed in packed decimal/character format, much time and effort can be spared by the use of packed decimal operations.

Self Evaluation Quiz

1. Given three packed decimal constants, as coded below, write a routine to add these together and place the result in EBCDIC form in a 6 byte long field named RESULT.

FLDA	DC	P'1234.123'
FLDB	DC	P'1234'
FLDC	DC	P'12.34'
RESULT	DS	CL6

Note: The resulting field should have only two decimal positions.

2. Given six packed decimal constants, write a routine to find the largest and the smallest values and place these in two fields named LARGE and SMALL respectively.

| DATA | DS | 6PL4 |

3. FLDA contains 01 03 45 6D; indicate the contents of this field after each of the following instructions. Consider each instruction independently.

MVO	FLDA,FLDA(3)
MVO	FLDA+1,FLDA+2(2)
MVO	FLDA,FLDA+1(3)
MVO	FLDA,FLDA

4. Given the following data fields,

Hours worked	c.c. 1 — 4
Rate per hour	c.c. 5 — 7
Deductions	c.c. 8 — 12

write program steps to compute:

Salary = (Hours worked * Rate per hour) — Deductions

5. Given six packed decimal fields named F1, F2, F3, F4, F5 and F6, each 3 bytes in length, compute:

$$RESULT = 3(F1 + F2 - F3) + (F4 + F5)$$

6. Using the same data fields as in the previous problem, compute:

$$RESULT = (F4 - F1) + (F2 - F1) + (F3 - F1)$$

If the RESULT has a negative value, branch to NEGVAL.

7. FIELDA contains 87 56 9C, FIELDB contains 00 00 01 35 4C, would the instruction AP   FIELDA,FIELDB cause an overflow?

8. What will be the resulting values in FIELDA and FIELDB after execution of the following instructions?

```
FIELDA      DC      P'-01458'
FIELDB      DC      P'+03237'
            .
            SP      FIELDB,FIELDA
            ZAP     FIELDA,FIELDB
            AP      FIELDB+2(2),FIELDB+2(2)
            MVO     FIELDB+1(1),FIELDB+2(1)
```

9. Will the following instruction be executed successfully?

```
FIELDA      DC      CL10' '
FIELDB      DC      X'423C'
            .
            ZAP     FIELDA,FIELDB
```

10. Given the following data

FIELDA	c.c.	1 − 5	format xx.xxx
FIELDB	c.c.	6 − 10	format x.xxxx

write program steps to compute:

$$PRODUCT = FIELDA * FIELDB$$

PRODUCT has been defined as a 5 byte long area and its format is to be xxx.xx. Please round the result before placing it into PRODUCT.

[11]

Literals, Extended Mnemonics and Address Constants

11.1 Literals and Literal Assignments

Until now any constants needed in a program were entered with the help of DC instructions and to refer to these constants we assigned symbols. A constant could be accessed any time by entering its symbolic name in the operand of an instruction. Literals, on the other hand, provide means of entering constants into a program by specifying the constant in the operand of the instruction in which it is used. However, there are certain rules to be followed when writing literals. These are:

1. A literal is written like a constant preceded by an equal sign (=). For example,

       MVC   OUT+30(3),=C'ABC'

   The MVC instruction above would move ABC to the first operand location.
2. Only one reference to a literal is allowed in a machine instruction statement.
3. A literal may not be used as the receiving field of an instruction that modifies storage.
4. A literal may not be specified in an address constant, shift instruction and any assembler instruction.

Some examples of literals are given below.

```
LOAD        L         3,=F'173'
*                              LOAD INTO REG3 BINARY VALUE OF 173
MOVE        MVC       OUT+20(5),=C'ERROR'
SUBTR       SH        4,=H'1'
*                              SUBTRACT 1 FROM REG4
```

The statement LOAD is a load instruction which used a literal as the second operand. The statement MOVE above will move ERROR to the first operand location and the last instruction will subtract 1 from the contents of register 4.

```
SOURCE  STATEMENT

         MVC     LINE(5),=C'ABCDE'
         MVC     LINE+10(3),=C'FGH'
         MVC     LINE+20(2),=C'12'
         LTORG
                 =C'12'
                 =C'ABCDE'
                 =C'FGH'
         MVC     LINE+25(5),=C'IJKLM'
         MVC     LINE+35(3),=C'345'
         LTORG
                 =C'IJKLM'
                 =C'345'
LINE     DC      CL132' '
         END
```

FIGURE 11.1(a). Literals and Literal Pool.

```
SOURCE  STATEMENT

         MVC     LINE(5),=C'ABCDE'
         MVC     LINE+10(3),=C'FGH'
         MVC     LINE+20(2),=C'12'
         LTORG
                 =C'12'
                 =C'ABCDE'
                 =C'FGH'
         MVC     LINE+25(5),=C'IJKLM'
         MVC     LINE+35(3),=C'345'
LINE     DC      CL132' '
         END
                 =C'IJKLM'
                 =C'345'
```

FIGURE 11.1(b). Literals and Literal Pool.

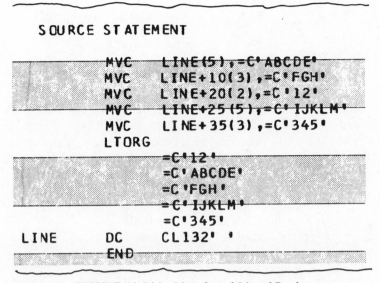

```
        SOURCE STATEMENT

             MVC     LINE(5),=C'ABCDE'
             MVC     LINE+10(3),=C'FGH'
             MVC     LINE+20(2),=C'12'
             MVC     LINE+25(5),=C'IJKLM'
             MVC     LINE+35(3),=C'345'
             LTORG
                     =C'12'
                     =C'ABCDE'
                     =C'FGH'
                     =C'IJKLM'
                     =C'345'
   LINE      DC      CL132' '
             END
```

FIGURE 11.1(c). Literals and Literal Pool

During assembly time the assembler generates the literals, collects them, and places them in a specific area of storage known as the Literal Pool.

From the Figure 11.1 it can be seen that in the statements specifying a literal, the address of the literal, rather than the literal itself, will be assembled. This address is obtained from the literal pool. A literal should not be confused with the immediate data in the SI type instructions. Immediate data are assembled into the instruction itself.

The manners in which literals are assigned are very similar to the methods for specifying constants. The main difference is that a literal must always be preceded by an equal sign (=). Some additional examples of literals are given below.

```
        =F'1734'
        =H'-1'
        =C'OUT OF SEQUENCE'
        =X'F0'
        =B'11000001'
```

Duplicate literals

If duplicate literals occur within one literal pool, only one literal is stored. To be recognized as duplicate, a literal must have identical specification as another literal.

Example:
```
        =X'F4'
                   BOTH ARE STORED
        =C'4'
```

=X'F1'

ONLY ONE OF THESE IS STORED

=X'F1'

The literal pool

During assembly time the literals are generated, collected, and placed in a special area called the *literal pool*. In the instructions specifying literals, the location of the literal, rather than the literal itself, is assembled. The positioning of a literal pool may be controlled by a programmer and through the use of the assembler instruction LTORG he can also direct the assembler to create multiple literal pools. However, the sequence in which the literals are arranged within the pool is controlled by the assembler.

Instruction Name	Begin Literal Pool
Mnemonic OP Code	LTORG
Machine OP Code	None
Type	Assembler

The LTORG instruction causes all literals, since the previous LTORG or the beginning of the program, to be assembled starting at the first doubleword boundary following the LTORG instruction. (The literals are assembled at appropriate boundaries.) In case no literals follow the LTORG instruction, alignment will be performed for the next instruction. Bytes skipped to obtain alignment are not zeroed.

Name	Operation	Operand
Any symbol or not used	LTORG	Not used

If a symbol is assigned, its length attribute is always one.

Note: If there are no LTORG instructions in a program, all literals used are placed at the end of the first control section.

Extended mnemonics

For the convenience of the programmers, the Assembler Language provides extended mnemonic operation codes for branch on condition instructions. The extended mnemonic codes specify not only the machine branch instruction but also the condition on which the branch is to occur, thus allowing a programmer to omit the mask from the symbolic instruction. During assembly time the extended mnemonic operation codes are *translated* into the corresponding machine operation codes and appropriate condition code (mask) combination. Various extended mnemonic codes together with their machine instruction equivalents are listed below.

Extended Code		Meaning	Machine-Instruction
B	D2(X2,B2)	Branch Unconditional	BC 15,D2(X2,B2)
BR	R2	Branch Unconditional (RR format)	BCR 15,R2
NOP	D2(X2,B2)	No Operation	BC 0,D2(X2,B2)
NOPR	R2	No Operation (RR format)	BCR 0,R2
		Used After Compare Instructions	
BH	D2(X2,B2)	Branch on High	BC 2,D2(X2,B2)
BL	D2(X2,B2)	Branch on Low	BC 4,D2(X2,B2)
BE	D2(X2,B2)	Branch on Equal	BC 8,D2(X2,B2)
BNH	D2(X2,B2)	Branch on Not High	BC 13,D2(X2,B2)
BNL	D2(X2,B2)	Branch on Not Low	BC 11,D2(X2,B2)
BNE	D2(X2,B2)	Branch on Not Equal	BC 7,D2(X2,B2)
		Used After Arithmetic Instructions	
BO	D2(X2,B2)	Branch on Overflow	BC 1,D2(X2,B2)
BP	D2(X2,B2)	Branch on Plus	BC 2,D2(X2,B2)
BM	D2(X2,B2)	Branch on Minus	BC 4,D2(X2,B2)
BZ	D2(X2,B2)	Branch on Zero	BC 8,D2(X2,B2)
BNP	D2(X2,B2)	Branch on Not Plus	BC 13,D2(X2,B2)
BNM	D2(X2,B2)	Branch on Not Minus	BC 11,D2(X2,B2)
BNZ	D2(X2,B2)	Branch on Not Zero	BC 7,D2(X2,B2)
		Used After Test Under Mask Instructions	
BO	D2(X2,B2)	Branch if Ones	BC 1,D2(X2,B2)
BM	D2(X2,B2)	Branch if Mixed	BC 4,D2(X2,B2)
BZ	D2(X2,B2)	Branch if Zeros	BC 8,D2(X2,B2)
BNO	D2(X2,B2)	Branch if Not Ones	BC 14,D2(X2,B2)

FIGURE 11.2. Extended Mnemonic Codes.

Note: Except for BR and NOPR, all other extended mnemonics shown are for RX type of instructions. The branch address can be specified in either explicit format or can be implied by the use of symbols.

```
B           30(2,3)   SAME AS   BC    15,30(2,3)
B           LOOP                BC    15,LOOP
NOP         SWITCH              BC    0,SWITCH
BL          LOWCOMP             BC    4,LOWCOMP
BR          4                   BCR   15,4
```

FIGURE 11.3. Example of Extended Mnemonics.

The use of extended mnemonics not only saves coding time but also makes a program more readable. For instance, look at the two examples given below:

```
CLC         IN+70(4),SEQKEY
BC          8,EQUCOMP
BC          4,LOWCOMP
BC          15,ERRORS
```

FIGURE 11.4. Coding Without Extended Mnemonics.

```
CLC         IN+70(4),SEQKEY
BE          EQUCOMP
BL          LOWCOMP
B           ERRORS
```

FIGURE 11.5. Coding With Extended Mnemonics.

Note: The extended mnemonics are not part of the universal set of machine instructions, but are translated by the assembler into the corresponding operation and mask combinations.

Example:

```
READ        GET     INFILE
SW1         NOP     COMPARE
            OI      SW1+1,X'F0'
            .
            .
            B       READ
COMPARE     .
```

At assembly time the NOP instruction above will be assembled as a branch instruction with the mask field set to zero. At program execution time the OI instruction, when executed, will change the mask to Hex F, thus making it an unconditional branch instruction.

Address constants

An address constant is a storage address that is translated into a constant. An address constant is established with a DC and follows the same general format and rules as we have outlined for the regular DC instruction; however, the operand part of an address constant specifies a storage address. This address is translated into an absolute form and is stored as a fullword or halfword depending on the type of constant specified.

The four types of address constants are: A; Y; S; and V. In this section we will discuss the first three in detail.

Address constants can be used for initializing base registers and for establishing communication between different control sections of a multi-section program. Also, in case of V type address constants a programmer can set up communication between different programs.

Before we discuss these various types of address constants, two terms need to be defined.

Absolute expression: an expression is called absolute if its value is unaffected by program relocation.

Relocatable expression: a relocatable expression is one whose value would change by N if the program in which it appears is relocated N bytes away from its originally assigned area of storage.

A—Type Address Constant. An A-type address constant is specified as an absolute or relocatable expression. The address must be enclosed in parenthesis and not single quotation marks. For example:

DC   A(*+30)

The address specified by the operand portion of the constant, i.e., present setting of location counter plus 30, is stored in absolute form in a fullword aligned on integral boundary. The implied length of the constant is 4 bytes unless a length code is specified in which case boundary alignment is not performed. Some additional examples of A-type address constants are given below.

ADCON1   DC   A(START+4096)
ADCON2   DC   A(START)

ADCON1 will establish a word constant which will contain the binary equivalent of the address developed by adding 4096 to the address symbol START.

ADCON2 will establish a constant which will contain the address of the symbol START.

Note: Each of the address constants will be established in a fullword, aligned on integral boundaries.

A-type address constants can be written as literals.

L   7,=A(START+4096)
L   6,=A(START)
L   3,=A(*+4)

Example:

```
ADCON        DC           A(BASE+4096,BASE+8192,BASE+1288)
```

DC above specified multiple address constants. Each of these will be set up as a fullword constant aligned on word boundary. A total of 12 bytes will be required.

Multiple base registers. A-type address constants are generally used to load multiple base registers. However, a USING instruction assigning multiple base registers is also required.

Example:

```
             START   0
BEGIN        BALR    3,0
             USING   LOAD,3,4
LOAD         L       4,ADCON
             B       OUT
ADCON        DC      A(LOAD+4096)
OUT          .
             .
             .
```

The coding below illustrates the use of multiple address constant for loading base registers.

```
             START   0
BEGIN        BALR    2,0
             USING   BASE,2,3,4,5
BASE         LM      3,5,ADCON
             B       OUT
ADCON        DC      A(BASE+4096,BASE+8192,BASE+12288)
OUT          .
             .
             .
```

Y—Type Address Constant. Y-type address constants are very much like the A-type except that these have an implied length of 2 bytes and are aligned on halfword integral boundary. If a length code is specified for Y-type address constants the alignment is not performed.

Note: Since the addressing capability of a halfword is only 32,767 bytes of storage, the Y-type address constants should be avoided in programs destined to be executed on computers with storage over 32K.

Some examples of Y-type address constants are given below.

```
    ADCON1       DC           Y(START)
    ADCON2       DC           Y(*+4096)
```

These can also be written as literals.

```
LH        3,=Y(START)
LH        7,=Y(*+4096)
```

S—Type Address Constants. This type of constant stores the address in base and displacement form. If length code is not specified the constant is established as a halfword aligned on integral boundary. The constant may be specified in two different ways:

1. An absolute or relocatable expression, for example:

```
CONST     DC        S(ALPHA)
```

The assembler will break down the address of the symbol into proper base register and displacement value.

2. As two absolute expressions, the first of which represents the displacement value and the second, the base register

```
ADCON     DC        S(600(9))
```

The leftmost 4 bits of the assembled constant represent the base register and the remaining 12 bits the displacement value. S-type address constants *can not* be written as a literal.

Note: V-type address constants are discussed in Chapter 13.

11.2 LCR, LPR, LNR, IC, STC, EX and TR Instructions

In this section we will discuss some of the less commonly used instructions of System 360 Assembler Language.

```
     Load Complement                    RR Type


           LCR       R1,R2
```

This instruction places into the R1 operand register the two's complement of the second operand register.

Example:
R6 contains −16, R5 contains +128

```
           LCR       5,6
```

After execution of this instruction register 5 will contain the binary equivalent of +16.

Example:
R3 contains +16, R4 contains +4

```
           LCR       4,3
```

After execution of this instruction register 4 will contain the binary equivalent of −16.

Resulting Condition Code	Meaning
0	Result is zero
1	Result is less than zero
2	Result is greater than zero
3	Overflow

Program Interruptions	Fixed-Point overflow
Load Positive	RR Type

LPR   R1,R2

The absolute value of the second operand is placed in the first operand location. If the number contained in the second operand register is positive, it is moved to the first operand without any alteration. On the other hand, if the second location contains a negative number, it is first made positive and then placed into the first operand location.

Note: The resulting number in R1 operand register is always positive.

Resulting Condition Code	Meaning
0	Result is zero
1	———
2	Result is greater than zero
3	Overflow

Program Interruptions	Fixed-point overflow
Load Negative	RR Type

LNR   R1,R2

The contents of the register specified by the second operand are placed in the first operand with the following stipulations:

1. If the second operand register contains a negative number, it is moved to the first operand without any alterations.
2. If the second operand contains a positive number, its two's complement is placed in the first operand location.

Note: The resulting number in the first operand is always negative.

Resulting Condition Code	Meaning
0	Result is zero
1	Result is less than zero
2	———
3	———

Program Interruptions   None

Insert Character   RX Type

       IC   R1,D2(X2,B2)

The 8-bit byte at the second operand location is placed into bits 24–31 (low-order 8 bits) of the register specified by R1 operand. The bits being moved are not inspected or tested. The remaining high-order bits, 0–23, of the register are not altered. This instruction does not affect the condition code.

Program Interruptions   Addressing, Protection

Example:
Register 4 contains 00 00 00 00

       IC   4,CONST
       .
       .
CONST   DC   X'FF'

After execution of this instruction, register 4 will contain 00 00 00 FF.
Note: Please note that most of the RX type of instructions require that the second operand be a fixed-point quantity located on some type of integral boundary. Insert-Character instruction, RX type, does not have this requirement.

Store Character   RX Type

       STC   R1,D2(X2,B2)

Bits 24–31, the low-order 8 bits, of the register specified by the first operand are stored at the storage location specified by the second operand. The bits being transferred are not tested. This instruction does not affect the condition code.

Program Interruptions   Protection, Addressing

Example:
Register 4 contains 00 00 00 FF

```
              STC       4,CONST
              .
              .
CONST         DC        X'00'
```

After execution of this instruction CONST will contain FF.

Example:

Register 4 contains 00 00 00 FF

```
              STC       4,MOVE+1
              .
              .
              .
MOVE          MVI       0(6),X'00'
```

Before the STC instruction is executed, the instruction at MOVE is:

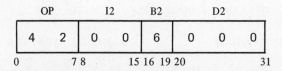

After execution of the STC instruction, the MVI instruction would be:

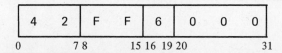

Symbolically represented, this instruction would be:

```
              MVI       0(6),X'FF'
```

Example:

```
              IC        4,=X'FF'
              STC       4,MOVE+1
              .
              .
MOVE          MVC       0(3,2),0(5)
```

Originally, the MVC instruction when assembled would be:

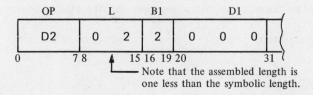

After execution of the STC instruction, the MVC instruction would be:

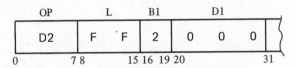

OP		L	B1	D1			
D2		F F	2	0	0	0	

0   7 8   15 16 19 20   31

This instruction, when executed, will move a total of 256 bytes.

Execute Instruction   RX Type

EX   R1,D2(X2,B2)

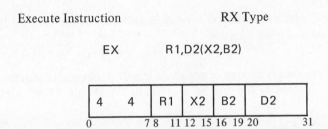

4	4	R1	X2	B2	D2	

0   7 8   11 12 15 16 19 20   31

This is a very versatile instruction and operates in the following manner:

1. The instruction addressed by the second operand is first modified as follows: The bit positions 8–15, the second byte of the instruction addressed, is OR'd with the low-order 8 bits (bits 24–31) of the register specified as R1 operand of the execute instruction. This modification occurs in the CPU after the instruction has been fetched from its location in the core. If the R1 operand of the execute instruction specifies register 0, the instruction addressed by the second operand is executed without modification.
2. The Modified (or unmodified) instruction is then executed.
3. The control then flows back to the instruction following the execute instruction.

Application of execute instruction

The execute instruction is generally used to modify (temporarily) the length, index, mask, immediate data, and arithmetic register specification.

Example:

```
          IC        1,=X'F3'
          EX        1,ADD
                    .
                    .
                    .
ADD       AR        3,4
```

The AR instruction as executed by the Execute instruction will be:

```
          AR        15,3
```

However, the AR 3,4 instruction as located in the core will not be altered in any way.

```
              IC        1,=X'FF'
              EX        1,MOVE
                        .
                        .
   MOVE       MVC       0(4,2),10(6)
```

The Move Character instruction actually executed by the Execute instruction will move a total of 256 bytes.

Note: As the Move Character instruction is being modified at object time the length code being inserted is one less than 256.

Example:

Write program steps to set an area of unknown length to hexadecimal zeros. The starting and ending addresses of the area are supplied in 2 fullwords: TBLSTART and TBLEND respectively.

```
   Name         Oper    Operand
                        .

   *

   *COMPUTE LENGTH OF AREA = (TBLEND – TBLSTART) + 1
   *
                LA      3,TBLSTART
   *                              LOAD STARTING ADDRESS
                LA      4,TBLEND  LOAD ENDING ADDRESS
                SR      4,3       SUBTRACT STARTING FROM ENDING
                LA      4,1(4)    ADD 1
   *
   *
   ZEROMOVE     MVI     0(3),X'00'   MOVE HEX 00 TO FIRST BYTE
                BCTR    4,0       REDUCE LENGTH BY 1
   AGAIN        CH      4,=H'0'   IS AREA SET TO ZEROS
                BE      EXIT      IF SO GO TO EXIT
                CH      4,=H'256' IS REMAINING LENGTH   256
                BL      LASTZERO  IF SO GO TO LASTZERO
                IC      7,=X'FF'  MOVE HEX FF = 255 TO REG 7
                EX      7,SETZERO EXECUTE SETZERO INSTRUCTION
                SH      4,=H'256' REDUCE LENGTH BY 256
                LA      3,256(3)  INCREMENT REG 3 BY 256
                B       AGAIN
   LASTZERO     BCTR    4,0       SET REG 4 TO MACHINE L CODE
                EX      4,SETZERO EXECUTE MOVE INSTRUCTION
   EXIT                 .
```

(continued)

```
SETZERO      MVC    1(0,3),0(3)   MOVE ZEROS
*
*            DECLARATIVES
*
TBLSTART     DS     F
TBLEND       DS     F
              .
              .
```

Translate Instruction   SS Type

TR   D1(L,B1),D2(B2)

Condition Code   Not affected
Program Interruptions   Protection and Addressing

This is one of the most versatile instructions of System 360 Assembler Language and is used to convert from one coding system of 8 or fewer bits to another coding system. The operation of this instruction is as follows:

A byte is obtained from the first operand location and the 8-bit byte, interpreted as binary number, is added to the address developed by the second operand, thereby giving a new address. Then the CPU retrieves the data located in the byte addressed by this new address and places this into the position occupied by the first operand byte. The bytes of the first operand are selected one by one for translation, proceeding from left to right. The operation, translation of the first operand bytes, proceeds until the first operand is exhausted.

Example:

Assume that register 9 contains 00 00 21 00 and register 12 contains 00 00 10 00, and the translate instruction is as follows:

TR   0(1,12),0(9)

When this instruction is executed, the binary value of the byte addressed by the first operand is first added to the address developed by the second operand, and the byte at the resulting address is fetched and placed into the first operand location.

Address developed by the second operand: 0 + 2100 = 2100
Byte at the first operand location (02):   02 + 2100 = 2102

Result:

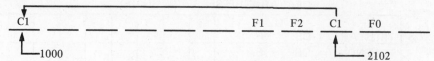

To translate one set of codes to any other desired code, provided that each coded character consists of 8 or fewer bits, we need to arrange a table so that we will find at each table function byte, the replacement character for the argument byte.

Note: The translate table should contain the characters of the code into which you are translating. This table must be in order by the binary sequence of the characters of the original code.

Consider an example of translate instruction that is used to translate one 8-bit code into another such code.

Example:

Assume that you are working for a highly secret organization named GOOD GUYS and have just captured an agent of BAD GUYS with a secret message along with the decoding book. Your job is to write a program to translate the coded message into EBCDIC code. The secret code is as follows:

Code:	A	B	C	D	E	F	G	H	I
Meaning:	K	L	M	N	O	P	Q	R	S
Code:	J	K							
Meaning:	T	.							
Code:	S	T	U	V	W	X	Y		
Meaning:	U	V	W	X	Y	Z	b	(b indicates a blank)	
Code:	0	1	2	3	4	5	6	7	8	9
Meaning:	A	B	C	D	E	F	G	H	I	J

The coded message is as follows:

J74YI703EUYADEUIK

When creating a translate table, the primary consideration is to make sure that the table is in order, not by the binary value of the characters it contains, but by the *binary sequence* of characters of the original code. The various entries in the translate table consist of the characters of the code into which you are translating. Therefore, this translate table should contain the characters of the EBCDIC code, but must be in sequence by the binary value of the coded code characters. Assume that the table starts at Hex 2000, according to the coded code characters, in position 2000+X'C1' we should place the EBCDIC character K, in position 2000+X'C2' the EBCDIC character L, and so forth.

Note: X'C1' is the same as EBCDIC A.

Figure 11.6 below illustrates a conceptual table and various entries required for our program.

ADDRESSES SHOWN IN HEX

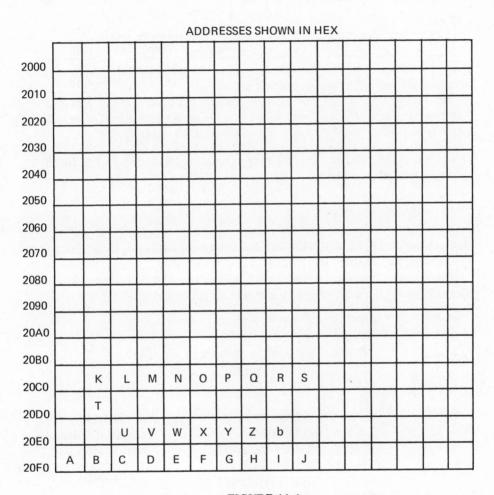

FIGURE 11.6.

Now assume that the coded message is located in core starting at Hex 3000. Assume also that Register 2 contains 00 00 30 00, and, Register 3 contains 00 00 20 00. To translate the coded message into EBCDIC, we issue a Translate command:

TR   0(17,2),0(3)

As the length code specifies a value of 17, in all 17 bytes will be translated into EBCDIC. First time through, the action taken will be as follows:

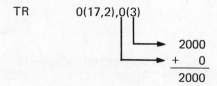

$$
\begin{array}{r}
2000 \\
+\quad 0 \\
\hline
2000
\end{array}
$$

First byte addressed by the first operand contains $J = (D1)_{16}$. Therefore, the resulting address developed by the second operand will be:

$$
\begin{array}{r}
2000 \\
+\quad D1 \\
\hline
20D1
\end{array}
$$

If we look at the translate table, the byte at location 20D1 contains EBCDIC T, the next byte fetched would be at:

$$
\begin{array}{r}
2000 \\
+\quad F7 \\
\hline
20F7
\end{array}
$$

Byte at location 20F7 contains EBCDIC H, and so forth until all of the 17 bytes of the first operand are translated into EBCDIC.

Among many ways of setting up of a translate table is coding below which illustrates one of the quickest and easiest methods of doing this.

Name	Oper	Operand	
	START	0	
REPORTS	DTFPR	DEVADDR=SYS010,BLKSIZE=17,	X
		IOAREA1=LINE1	
BEGIN	BALR	9,0	
	USING	*,9	
	OPEN	REPORTS	OPEN FILES
	LA	3,TABLE	LOAD ADDRESS
	MVC	LINE1,MESSAGE	MOVE MESSAGE
	TR	LINE1,0(3)	TRANSLATE MESSAGE
	PUT	REPORTS,LINE1	PRINT TRANSLATION
	CLOSE	REPORTS	CLOSE FILES
	EOJ		
LINE1	DS	CL17	
MESSAGE	DC	C'J74YI703EUYADEUIK'	
TABLE	DC	XL256'00'	
	ORG	TABLE+X'C1'	
	DC	X'D2D3D4D5D6D7D8D9E2'	KLMNOPQRS
	ORG	TABLE+X'D1'	
	DC	X'E34B'	T.

(continued)

```
ORG     TABLE+X'E2'
DC      X'E4E5E6E7E8E940'           UVWXYZb
ORG     TABLE+X'F0'
DC      X'C1C2C3C4C5C6C7C8C9D1' ABCDEFGHIJ
ORG     TABLE+X'100'
END     BEGIN
```

FIGURE 11.7. Suggested Coding.

Note: This message will print as follows:

THE SHADOW KNOWS.

[12]

Looping, Indexing and Table Look-Ups

12.1 Looping

Often it becomes necessary to execute a given routine (a sequence of instructions) a specific number of times. This is termed as *looping*. The coding shown in Figure 12.1 illustrates one of the techniques of looping.

```
              .
              L      R2,=F'30'    INITIATE COUNT REG
START         .
              .
              .
              S      R2,=F'1'     SUBTRACT 1 FROM COUNT REG
              BZ     OUT          BRANCH IF R2 = 0
              B      START        OTHERWISE BRANCH TO START
OUT           .
              .
```

FIGURE 12.1. A Routine Executed 30 Times.

The subtract-one-and-test sequence of instructions to make an exit loop occurs so frequently that a single instruction has been provided to accomplish the same results.

Instruction Name	Branch On Count Register
Mnemonic OP Code	BCTR
Machine OP Code	06
Type	RR

327

Program Interruptions	None
Condition Code	is not affected
Assembler Format	BCTR R1,R2
Instruction Name	Branch On Count
Mnemonic OP Code	BCT
Machine OP Code	46
Type	RX
Program Interruptions	None
Condition Code	is not affected
Assembler Format	BCT R1,D2(X2,B2)

The contents of the general register specified as R1 is algebraically reduced by 1 and a test is made to see if the result is zero. If the result is not zero, a branch is taken to the address specified by the second operand. (In case of RX format the branch address is in the form of base, displacement and index register, and for the RR format the branch address is specified by the R2 register.) In case the contents of R1 register are not equal to zero, normal sequential instruction execution proceeds and the control flows to the next sequential instruction.

Note: The branch address is determined prior to counting operation. Overflow occurring due to maximum positive number is ignored.

The coding in Figure 12.2 will cause the routine starting with FIRST and ending with LAST to be executed 30 times.

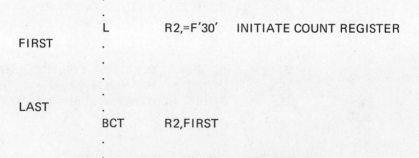

```
               .
               .
               .
               L        R2,=F'30'    INITIATE COUNT REGISTER
    FIRST      .
               .
               .
               .
               .
    LAST       .
               BCT      R2,FIRST
               .
               .
```

FIGURE 12.2. Use of BCT Instruction.

If you wanted to speed it up, the same routine could be written as follows:

```
               .
               L        R2,=F'30'    INITIATE COUNT REG
```

(continued)

```
                    L          R3,=A(FIRST)      LOAD ADDRESS OF FIRST
        FIRST       .

                    .
        LAST        .
                    BCTR       R2,R3

                    .
```

In case of the RR format of the Branch on Count instruction, if the R2 operand specifies 0, the counting is performed without branching. Thus, a BCTR instruction with R2 operand as 0 can be used to subtract one from a general register.

```
                    BCTR       4,0
```

This instruction will cause a one to be subtracted from the contents of register 4 and the sequential instruction execution will continue. This instruction is equivalent to S 4,=F'1' except that it does not require any constant (literal in this case), is compact and faster.

EXERCISE:
    What will be the net effect of the instruction coded below? Assume register 4 contains a positive quantity.

```
                    BCTR       4,*
```

EXERCISE:
    Consider the coding below:

```
        LOOP        LA         2,4               ENTRY POINT
        START       LA         3,6
        START1      .

                    .
        ADD         AH         4,H1
                    BCT        3,START1
                    BCT        2,START
                    BC         15,OUT            EXIT POINT

                    .

                    .
        H1          DC         H'2'

                    .
```

    How many times will the instruction named ADD be executed before an exit is made from this routine?

EXERCISE:

    How many times will the loop coded below be executed?

```
LOOP          L           R0,=F'4'                  INITIATE COUNT REGISTER
              .
              .
              BCT         R0,LOOP
```

Your answer should be — indefinitely. The instruction named LOOP initiates register 0 to 4. The BCT instruction, first time through, will reduce the content of register 0 to 3 and a branch will be taken to LOOP — and at this time register 0 will again be set to 4. We have a closed loop.

The example coded above points out one of the pitfalls of a beginning student. It is important to note the instruction that *initializes* the count register should be *outside* the loop.

Instruction Name	Load Address
Mnemonic OP Code	LA
Machine OP Code	41
Type	RX
Program Interruptions	None
Condition Code	is not affected
Assembler Format	LA R1,D2(X2,B2)

The address of the second operand is inserted in the low-order 24 bits of the general register specified by R1. The remaining 8 bits of the general register are made zero. The address is computed by the rules of address arithmetic, i.e., displacement value + contents of base register + contents of index register.

Note: If general register 0 is specified as either the base or index register it means that this element of the instruction is to be *ignored*.

Example:

```
              LA          2, 10(0,0)
```

The instruction coded above will load into register 2 the address of core position 10, which of course is 10. As a result of this instruction, general register 2 will contain a binary equivalent of 10.

```
              LA          3,0(0,0)
```

This instruction will set general register 3 to zeros.

Note: Whenever the index register or the base register is register 0, we can omit the register specification and the assembler assumes and inserts register 0 in the assembled instruction. For example, we could have written the LA instruction coded above as:

```
              LA          3,0
```

If only one of the registers (the base or index) is to be omitted, the instruction can be written as:

        LA   3,10(4)

This instruction will load into general register 3 the address value which will be obtained by adding the contents of register 4 plus the displacement value of 10.

    The example that follows illustrates one of the many applications of Load Address instruction.

```
            .
            LA      2,20       INITIALIZE COUNT REGISTER
            LA      3,FIRST    LOAD ADDRESS OF FIRST
   FIRST    .

   LAST     .
            BCTR    2,3        BRANCH IS VIA REG 3
```

The sequence of instructions between the symbolic names FIRST and LAST will be executed 20 times.

    It is possible to increment any general register (except 0) by the contents of D2 field of the instruction. The register to be incremented should be specified by R1 and by either X2 (with B2 set to zero) or B2 (with X2 to zero).

        LA   3,20(3)

This instruction will increment the contents of register 3 by 20.

Example:

```
            .
            LA      R3,0       SET REGISTER 3 TO ZEROS
            GET     INFILE     READ A CARD
            LA      R3,1(R3)   ADD 1 TO REGISTER 3
            .

            .
```

This example shows how LA instruction can be used to count the number of cards read from a card file.

Example:

    Given 10 consecutive fullwords of data in storage, we are required to add all these and place the resulting sum in general register 7.

```
   DATA     DS      10F
            .
            LA      2,DATA     LOAD ADDRESS OF DATA
            LA      3,10       INITIALIZE COUNT REG
```

(continued)

```
                  LA        7,0           SET REGISTER 7 TO ZEROS
       ADD        A         7,0(2)        ADD ONE FULLWORD TO REG 7
       MODIFY     LA        2,4(2)        INCREMENT REG2 BY 4
                  BCT       3,ADD
```

FIGURE 12.3. Application of Load Address Instruction.

The sequence of instructions would remain the same even if the number of words were increased many folds. The only difference would be in the initializing value of the count register.

Note: It is important to note that the approach coded above will require more computer time as simply coding ten successive add instructions. The extra time is taken up by the instruction to increment the general register 2 and the BCT instruction. However, the approach illustrated above does save some storage.

EXERCISE: Use of LA, BCT, BCTR

A card file needs to be listed on the console typewriter. A simple way to do this would be to define the record size for the console file as 80 bytes long and list all records. This, however, is an extremely slow process. The reason for lack of speed is that for each PUT instruction issued the type ball will travel through 80 print positions. For cards which have only a few of the high-order columns punched, this is a great waste of computer time. To avoid this, the console records are treated as undefined and before every PUT instruction the program calculates and supplies to the IOCS the length of each record.

Indexing

The term indexing, as used in programming, can be defined as the technique of address modification. This technique becomes very valuable when a programmer has to deal with tabular data, especially when the table elements are of identical length.

One example of indexing was given in Figure 12.3. The LA instruction, with the symbolic name MODIFY, increments the contents of register 2 by a value of 4. There are two other ways to achieve indexing and these are: use of Index Register; and, Storage-to-Storage Indexing.

Use of Index Register. By the use of index register and its manipulation, the programmer can modify the operand address of instruction while a program is being executed. Until now the index register specification has been omitted and the assembler inserted register 0 for the index register in the assembled instruction. As previously mentioned, the use of register 0 implies no indexing.

Assume that 5 fullwords of data are located consecutively in storage. Add these together and place the sum in register 7. This could be accomplished with conventional method of coding as illustrated below:

```
          .
          LA        7,0        CLEAR REGISTER 7
          A         7,DATA     ADD FIRST WORD
          A         7,DATA+4   ADD SECOND WORD
          A         7,DATA+8      THIRD WORD
          A         7,DATA+12     FOURTH WORD
          A         7,DATA+16     FIFTH WORD
          .

DATA      DS        5F
          .
```

The coding above uses 5 add instructions. With the use of the indexing technique, the number of add instructions can be reduced to one. Consider the coding below.

```
          .
          LA        7,0
          LA        3,0
          LA        4,0
          LA        6,DATA
ADD       A         7,0(3,6)
          LA        3,4(3)
          BCT       4,ADD
          .
DATA      DS        5F
          .
```

The number of instructions in this routine will not vary even if we were to increase the size of the field named DATA. For example:

```
          .
          LA        7,0
          LA        3,0
          LA        4,100
          LA        6,DATA
ADD       A         7,0(3,6)
          LA        3,4(3)
          BCT       4,ADD
          .
DATA      DS        100F
          .
```

If the second operand of an RX type of instruction specifies a symbolic address and indexing is desired, the index register is written in parentheses immediately following the symbolic name. The example illustrates this.

```
                LA      7,0            CLEAR REG 7
                LA      3,0            CLEAR INDEX REG
                LA      4,5            INITIALIZE COUNT REG
ADD             A       7,DATA(3)      ADD A FULLWORD
                LA      3,4(3)         INCREMENT INDEX REG
                BCT     4,ADD
                .
                .
DATA            DS      5F
                .
```

FIGURE 12.4. Use of Index Register.

To understand how indexing works, we must look into the structure and mechanism of RX type of instruction. The format of RX type is:

$$OP \qquad R1,D2(X2,B2)$$

where X2 is the index register. Assume that the value of D2=1002, X2 specifies register 3 and B2 specifies register 4. Further, assume that register 3 contains 0 and register 4 contains 4002.

Add fullword instruction could be written as:

$$A \qquad 7,1002(3,4)$$

Figure 12.5 explains the address arithmetic calculations.

If the contents of the index register were incremented by a value of 4, the address developed by the second operand of the add instruction would be:

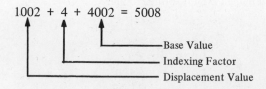

$$1002 + 4 + 4002 = 5008$$

Base Value
Indexing Factor
Displacement Value

Note: When indexing is used, an additional register comes into play. The contents of the index register, which can be any one of the general purpose registers except register 0, are added to the sum of base plus displacement.

Returning to Figure 12.4, on the first pass through the loop, the index register 3=0; therefore, the first of the 5 words will be added to register 7. On the second iteration, index register = 4 and the add instruction will add the contents of the second word, i.e., DATA +4 to register 7. While register 3 is being incremented the count register (register 4) is being stepped down. During the fifth pass through the loop the index register 3=16 and the last word will be added to register 7. At this time BCT instruction will make the contents of register 4=0 and an exit will be made from the loop.

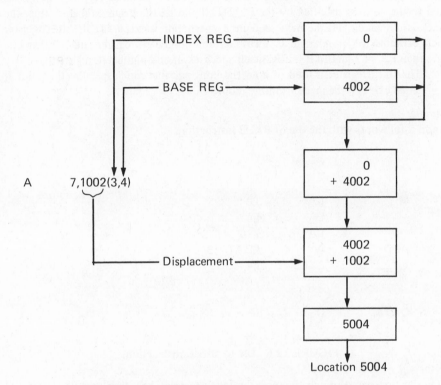

A   7,1002(3,4)

FIGURE 12.5. Address Arithmetic Schematic (Indexing).

In the indexing example discussed above it is necessary to use BCT instruction to terminate the loop, and another instruction to increment the index register. The BCT instruction allows us to make an exit from a loop on the count of zero and at times program logic may require us to terminate a loop on a count other than zero.

System 360 has two instructions which give us the capability of doing this. These instructions are Branch on Index Low or Equal and Branch on Index High.

Instruction Name	Branch on Index Low or Equal
Mnemonic OP Code	BXLE
Machine OP Code	87
Type	RS
Program Interruptions	None
Condition Code	is not affected
Assembler Format	BXLE R1,R3,D2(B2)

The contents of the register specified by R3 are added to the contents of the register specified as R1 and the sum is algebraically compared to a third register. If the sum in register R1 is lower or equal to the contents of the third register a branch is taken to the address specified by the B2+D2. If the resulting sum is higher, then the branch is not taken and the next sequential instruction is executed. The third register which contains the comparand is always an odd-numbered register and is either one larger than R3, or equal to R3, if R3 itself specifies an odd-numbered register.

Note: The third register is used to hold the limiting value which specifies the point at which an exit is to be made from the loop.

Example:
Add 5 fullwords with the use of BXLE instruction.

```
              .
              .
              .
              LA        3,0
              LA        4,4
              LA        5,16
ADD           A         7,DATA(3)
              BXLE      3,4,ADD
              .
              .
DATA          DS        5F
              .
```

FIGURE 12.6. Use of BXLE Instruction.

On the first pass through the loop the index register 3=0, thus, the first word will be added to register 7. At this time the BXLE instruction will add the contents of register 4 to that of register 3 and a branch will be taken to the symbol ADD. On the second iteration through the loop the next word, i.e., DATA+4, will be added to register 7. During the fifth pass through the loop the index register 3=16, thus, the last word (DATA+16) will be added to register 7 and at this point the BXLE instruction will increment the contents of register 3 to 20. The index is no longer less than or equal to the comparand contained in register 5 and the branch to symbol ADD will *not* take place and the control will pass to the next sequential instruction.

Note: The indexing approach, while helping to reduce coding, will require approximately twice as much CPU time that five add instructions will require. The extra time is used by the BXLE and the use of indexing in the add instruction.

We can develop a simple notation for the indexing parameters, i.e., the initial index value, the increment value and the final limiting value. For example, in the coding discussed above these parameters would be 0, 4, 16. These three parameters could be set up by three consecutive DC instructions and then only one LM instruction could be used to initialize the appropriate registers:

```
            LM        3,5,NDXFACTR
            .
            .
NDXFACTR    DC        F'0'
            DC        F'4'
            DC        F'16'
DATA        DS        5F
```

Example:

Given a 200-word array, the contents of these words are to be summed and the result is to be placed in register 6.

```
            .
            LA        6,0              CLEAR REGISTER 6
            LM        1,3,NDXFACTR     LOAD PARAMETERS
ADD         A         7,ARRAY(1)
            BXLE      1,2,ADD
            .
NDXFACTR    DC        F'0'
            DC        F'4'             INDEXING FACTOR
            DC        F'796'           LIMITING VALUE
ARRAY       DS        200F
            .
```

EXERCISE:

Register 3 contains the binary equivalent of +16.

Register 4 contains the binary equivalent of +2.

Register 5 contains the binary equivalent of +26.

Show the contents of register 3 on each iteration of the following instruction.

```
            BXLE      3,4,LOOP
```

Example:

Given a 200-word array, count the number of zero words in this array and place the count in a fullword — COUNT.

```
            SR        5,5
            LA        2,200
            LA        3,TABLE
            SR        4,4
SEARCH      C         4,0(3)
            BE        ADD1
INCR        LA        3,4(3)
            BCT       2,SEARCH
```

(continued)

```
                    B          ENDRTN
        ADD1        AH         5,=H'1'
                    B          INCR
        ENDRTN      ST         5,COUNT
                    .
        TABLE       DS         200F
        COUNT       DS         F
                    .
```

Instruction Name	Branch on Index High
Mnemonic OP Code	BXH
Machine OP Code	86
Type	RS
Program Interruptions	None
Condition Code	is not affected
Assembler Format	BXH R1,R3,D2(B2)

The contents of the register specified by R3 are added to the contents of the register specified by R1; the resulting sum is compared to a comparand contained in a third register. If the resulting sum in register R1 is greater than the comparand, a branch is taken to the address specified by D2+B2; on the other hand if the contents of R1 are equal to or lower than the comparand an exit is made from the loop. The comparand is always contained in an odd-numbered register whose number is implied by R3 register. This third register is either one larger than R3, or equal to R3 if R3 itself specifies an odd-numbered register.

This discussion of the BXH instruction clearly indicates that it works very much like the BXLE instruction, except for the fact that BXH is used for counting down while BXLE is used for counting up.

Example:

Given 5 words of data located consecutively in storage, add these together and place the result in register 7.

```
                    .
                    LM         2,3,NDXFACTR
        ADD         A          7,DATA(2)
                    BXH        2,3,ADD
                    .
        NDXFACTR    DC         F'16'
                    DC         F'-4'
        DATA        DS         5F
                    .
```

On the first pass through the loop the general register 2, the index register, contains

16, thus the effective address developed by the second operand of the ADD instruction will be DATA+16, which is the address of the last word. Next, the BXH instruction will cause −4 to be added to general register 2 giving a result of +12 and a branch will be taken to the symbol ADD.

During the second iteration, the fourth word whose address is DATA+12 will be added to register 7. During the fourth pass through the loop, the BXH instruction will reduce the contents of register 2 to zero and will also cause a branch to the symbol ADD. During the fifth pass through the loop, the first word will be added to general register 7 as DATA+0 = DATA. At this time, the BXH instruction will cause −4 to be added to register 2, and the resulting sum in register 2 will become −4. As this number is greater than the comparand an exit will be made from the loop and sequential instruction execution will continue.

Note: In case of BXH instruction, if the register specified by R3 is odd numbered, the additional register to contain the comparand is not needed. The assembler would assume the R3 register to be the third register also.

EXERCISE:

Register 5 contains +17.

Register 6 contains −3.

Register contains −3.

Show the contents of register 5 on each iteration of the following instruction.

         BXH   5,6,LOOP

Storage-to-Storage Indexing. Indexing is not restricted to instructions of RX type only. It is possible to modify the operand addresses of SS type instructions. However, the conventional method of indexing can not be used, as the SS type instructions do not have index-register fields. The approach we will take is to write explicit addresses for the operand and to use the base register for indexing purposes also.

Note: Since we alter the contents of an index register, it is important to point out that the register being used as both the index and base register in a storage-to-storage indexing routine must not be the same register that is being used as base register by other instructions outside the loop.

Example:

Given 5 packed decimal fields in storage located consecutively, each field being 3 bytes in length, we are to add these together and place the sum in ACCUM.

```
START   0
BALR    9,0
USING   *,9
  .
LA      3,5          LOAD COUNT IN REG 3
LA      2,DATA       LOAD ADDRESS OF DATA
```

(continued)

```
ADD          AP      ACCUM,0(3,2)    ADD
             LA      2,3(2)          INCREMENT REG 2
             BCT     3,ADD
              .
DATA         DC      5PL3'0'
ACCUM        DC      PL3'0'
              .
```

Examine the AP instruction used in the coding example above.

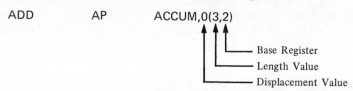

```
ADD          AP      ACCUM,0(3,2)
```
— Base Register
— Length Value
— Displacement Value

Note: The base register being used in this instruction is not the same as the one being used for the other instruction in the program. We temporarily use register 2 as the base and in it load the address of the area named DATA.

In the example above, during each pass through the loop the contents of register 2 will be incremented by a value of three, so that during each successive pass the AP instruction will add the next 3 bytes long area to ACCUM. The BCT instruction will terminate the loop after five iterations.

Example of Indexing. A department store maintains a punched card file of all delinquent accounts. Each card in the file contains in columns 1 – 4 the customer's account number. Our job is to write a routine to validate each incoming transaction against this file, i.e., if the account number on any one of the transactions matches a number on this file, a special message is to be printed.

The delinquent accounts file is read by a separate routine which stores the account numbers in a table in the main storage (each entry in the table is 4 bytes in length). This program stores the address of this table and the total number of entries in fullwords TABLE and ENTRIES respectively. A suggested solution is given below.

```
Name        Oper     Operand
             .
READ        GET      TRANSFL, RECORD
  *                           READ TRANSACTION FILE
            L        2,TABLE    LOAD ADDRESS OF TABLE
            L        3,ENTRIES  LOAD NO. OF TABLE ENTRIES
COMPARE     CLC      0(4,2),RECORD
  *                           TABLE REC:TRANS REC
            BE       DELIQNT    IF EQUAL GO TO DELIONT
            LA       2,4(2)
                     (continued)
```

```
            BCT      3,COMPARE        IS SEARCH COMPLETE
            B        READ
DELIQNT     MVC      . . .            MOVE AND
                                         PRINT MESSAGE
            .
            B        READ
            .
            .
```

Note: This type of search is very time-consuming. For example, if the total number of entries in the table above was 1000, on the average 500 compares would be needed for each search. There are programming techniques by which we can reduce the number of unsuccessful compares considerably. Some of these are discussed in the next section.

12.2 Table and Table Look-Ups

Many programming situations require a search through a table of values. One example of this was given in the previous section. This searching through a table of values is known as *table look-ups*. Table look-up is primarily the technique of locating a corresponding function for a given search argument. There are two points to keep in mind. These are:

1. If there is a corresponding table entry for a given search argument, one must be able to locate and retrieve this information.
2. In case a corresponding table entry does not exist, one must program for terminating the search when the end of the table is reached and in some cases even before.

In System 360 Assembler Language there is no single instruction that allows us to do table look-ups. However, various programming techniques have been developed to achieve this objective. In this section we will concern ourselves with exploring some of these techniques.

Nature of tables and table entries

A table's basic element is a *table entry* which is usually made of a table argument and a function. Several different combinations of arguments and functions are possible. The simplest and the most common is a single argument and a single function. However, it is possible to have other combinations, such as: single argument, multiple functions; multiple arguments, single functions; and, multiple arguments, multiple functions.

In this text we will restrict our discussion to single arguments, single function tables.

Note: The table argument should be the same size and format (bit configuration) as the search argument. (It is possible to have these elements existing in different formats, but extra programming steps will be required to make the data ready for comparison.)

An example of these various table elements is:

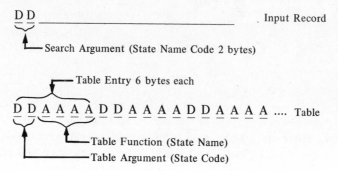

Another format of a table could be:

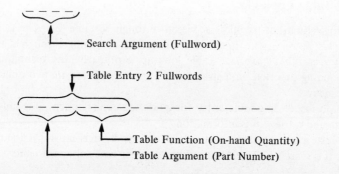

Tabular Data. The arrangement of arguments within a table is of great significance as it is this characteristic that guides the method of table look-up that is to be employed. One of the arrangements is to place the table arguments at random. This type of organization makes it necessary for us to examine table arguments until a match is made with the search argument or the end of the table is reached. Another method of arranging a table is to sort the table arguments in a given order, ascending or descending, the former being the usual practice. This type of organization still requires that the search be started at the beginning of the table and proceed sequentially until a match is made or the end of the table is reached. However, in this type of table arrangement we can terminate an unsuccessful search when a table argument is found to be higher than the search argument. In case of tables arranged in descending order, the search will be terminated when a table argument that is lower than the search argument is found. For sequentially arranged tables, probably the most efficient search method is binary search.

Sequential Search. The most simple and hence common method of table look-up is sequential search. This method involves investigating each table argument starting from the beginning and proceeding sequentially one by one until a match is made or the end of the table is reached. The figure below illustrates the basic logic.

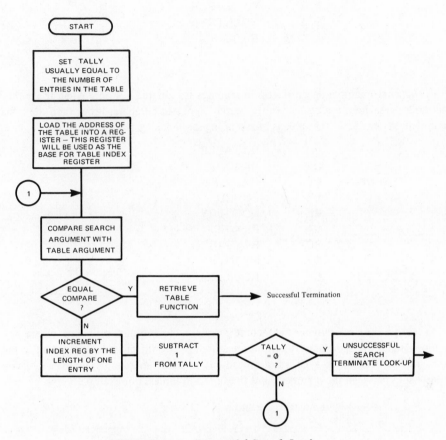

FIGURE 12.7. Sequential Search Logic.

The following example illustrates the coding for this type of table look-up.

Example:

A table of 100 elements, where each element is made up of a fullword argument followed by a fullword function is given. Register 2 contains the search argument and the table has been labeled TABLE. Locate the corresponding function, if any, and place it in register 6. In case of an unsuccessful search, branch to a routine named NOENTRY.

```
            LA       R3,TABLE
            LA       R4,100
SEARCH      C        R2,0(0,R3)
                     (continued)
```

```
              BE        FOUND
              LA        R3,4(R3)
              BCT       R4,SEARCH
              B         NOENTRY
FOUND         L         R6,0(0,R3)
              .
              .
              .
```

In the next example an unsuccessful search is terminated not only when the end of the table is reached, but also when the search argument compares lower than the table argument. Assume that the table is in ascending sequence by table arguments.

```
              LA        R3,TABLE
              LA        R4,100
SEARCH        CL        R2,0(0,R3)
              BE        FOUND
              BL        NOENTRY
              LA        R3,4(R3)
              BCT       R4,SEARCH
              B         NOENTRY
FOUND         L         R6,0(0,R3)
              .
              .
              .
```

At times the programmer will come across table look-up problems where the arguments and the associated functions are stored in two different tables instead of the same table. When this type of arrangement is used, there must exist a definite relationship between the argument and the function tables. For example:

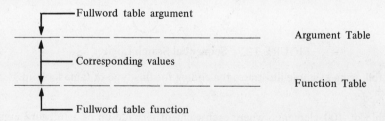

Example:

Consider two tables each 1000 elements long. One of the tables, named PARTNO, consists of 1000 fullword entries, each containing the code number of a part. Another table, named ONHAND, contains the number of parts on hand. Both of these tables have been sorted in ascending order and there is *one-to-one* relationship between these two tables.

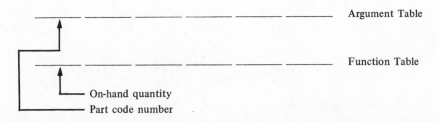

During inventory update we read in a part number and need to find the corresponding on-hand value. The search argument, input part code number, has been placed in register 5 and the on-hand quantity searched from the table is to be placed in register 6.

```
            LA      R4,1000
            LA      R3,0
COMP        C       R5,PARTNO(R3)
            BE      FOUND
            BL      ERROR
            LA      R3,4(R3)
            BCT     R4,COMP
FOUND       L       R6,ONHAND(R3)
            .
            .
```

Note: Another method for reducing the search time for tables is to place toward the beginning of the table those entries which are most likely to occur. This method, though helpful in cutting down search time, is not always applicable.

Binary Search. In the previous examples, we discussed the technique of sequential search. This method, though easy to program, requires a great number of compares. Consider a table containing 3000 entries. On the average 1500 compares are required to find a given function. To improve on the time element, other search methods can be employed to reduce the number of comparisons significantly. In this section, we will discuss one such method — *binary search.*

The basic principle of binary search is to divide the table in half, determining which part contains the desired table argument, dividing this half and so forth until a match is made. The most *important* point is the selection of the point *where* our search is to begin.

There are several ways to calculate this and some are rather elaborate. The simplest of all is to make the first division at a point which is greater than half the table size and at the same time a power of two. This point should be nearest to the middle point of the table. For example:

Table Size*	Starting Point
500	$256 = 2^8$
1000	$512 = 2^9$
1500	$1024 = 2^{10}$
2000	$1024 = 2^{10}$

* Number of entries in the table

Example:

Consider two tables, both sorted in ascending sequence. The first is a table of 1000 arguments each 4 bytes in length containing a 4-digit part number. The second is a table of corresponding functions containing the quantity on hand for each part. This table is the same size as the part number table. We are given a part number (search argument) in columns 1 — 4 of a record named IN and need to find the corresponding on-hand value.

As an example of a binary search through this table, assume that the desired value is located in entry 837. First we divide the table at 512 and start comparison at this point in the table.

PARTNO(837) compares high; second try is 512+256=768, part number still high; third, 768+128=896, now the part number compares low; so we fall back to the next lower half-way point; fourth, 896−64=832, the part number is high; fifth, 832+32=864, part number low; sixth, 864−16=848, part number still low; seventh, 848−8=840, part number low; eighth, 840−4=836, part number higher; ninth, 836+2=838, part number low; tenth, 838−1=837, a match. Thus, only ten compares are needed as opposed to 837 compares which would be required for sequential search. The extra programming time needed to write binary search routine can be well compensated by the computer time saved.

Example:

Two tables, each sorted in ascending order, are given. The first table, named PARTTBLE, contains a string of 100 part numbers, each a fullword binary value. The second table, STOCKTBL, consists of 100 entries containing on-hand quantity for each part; each entry in this table is also a fullword numeric value. The search argument, PARTNUM, is given in a fullword and we desire to locate the corresponding on-hand quantity. This on-hand quantity obtained from the table is to be stored in a fullword — ONHAND. Solution to this problem follows.

Name	Oper	Operand	
	L	1,PARTNUM	LOAD SEARCH ARGUMENT
	LH	2,=H'256'	SEARCH POINT = 64 * 4 INDEX
	LH	3,=H'128'	HALF = 32 * 4

(continued)

```
            LH      0,=H'400'          LOAD LIMIT = 100 * 4
SEARCH      CR      2,0                COMPARE INDEX TO LIMIT
            BNH     COMPARE            BRANCH IF INDEX = OR < 400
            B       LOWRANGE           BRANCH IF INDEX > 400
COMPARE     C       1, PARTTBLE−4(2)
*                                      PARTNUM:PARTTBLE
            BH      HIGHRANG           BRANCH IF PARTNUM IS HIGH
            BE      FOUND              BRANCH IF A MATCH IS MADE
LOWRANGE    SR      2,3                INDEX=INDEX − HALF
            B       MAKEHALF
HIGHRANG    AR      2,3                INDEX=INDEX+HALF
MAKEHALF    SRA     3,1                HALF=HALF/2
            B       SEARCH             SEARCH AGAIN
FOUND       LA      4,STOCKTBLE−4      LOAD ADDRESS OF ONHAND
            AR      2,4                POINT TO ONHAND QUANTITY
            MVC     ONHAND,0(2)        STORE ONHAND QUANTITY
            .
            .
PARTTBLE    DS      100F               TABLE CONTAINING PART NO
STOCKTBL    DS      100F               TABLE CONTAINING ON HAND
PARTNUM     DS      F                  SEARCH ARGUMENT
ONHAND      DS      F                  TABLE ARGUMENT
            .
            .
```

FIGURE 12.8. Binary Search.

Self Evaluation Quiz

1. Given a 200 word array, write a routine to count the number of zero words and place the count in a fullword COUNT. Use BXLE instruction for your loop.

2. Given a 20 word array, write a routine to arrange this array in ascending order. There may be multiple words containing the same value.

3. Is the instruction coded below valid? If not, give your reasons.

```
        LA      R3,5000(R3)        BUMP REG3 BY 5000
```

4. Assume that during a payroll program processing you have calculated the employee's earnings and various deductions. This information has been placed into 5 consecutive fullwords. The first word contains the gross pay while the remaining 4 contain the various *deductions*. Compute the net pay and place it in a word named NET. Use indexing approach.

5. Assume that the inventory in a particular store consists of 500 items, numbered 001 to 500. There are three 500 word long arrays in main storage into which the

values for the latest ONHAND, ISSUES and RECEIPTS have been read. (All entries are in ascending order by item number.) Write a routine which will update the ONHAND array by subtracting issues and adding receipts. Check the updated on-hand value and if it is equal to, or less than 300, print the following message:

ITEMbbNObbxx0bbbbREORDERbbPOINT

(b stands for a blank, xx0 format for item number indicates that this field should be zero suppressed.)

6. Read a card file and print address labels. The card records, instead of having the state's name punched, have a two-position code which ranges from 01 − 50. In the main storage there is a table consisting of 50 elements and each element is made up of 6 bytes; its format is:

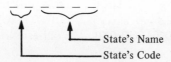

State's Name

State's Code

Write a routine to search and retrieve the proper state name for each card record and move it to print positions 10 − 13. If a card state code does not have a corresponding table entry, indicating an error condition, select the error record in pocket 2. All other cards go into pocket 1.

7. One of the subroutines of a program collects and places into 13 consecutive words the following information: The first 12 words contain monthly sales figures, 1 word for each month. The last word contains all ones to indicate the end of the information. However, if information is available for less than 12 months, the word containing ones will be shifted left accordingly. For example, if information is available for 8 months only, ones will be moved into the ninth word.

Write program steps to compute the average sale amount and place it in a word named AVERAGE.

$$AVERAGE = \frac{total\ of\ sales}{number\ of\ words}$$

[13]

Subroutines and Program Linkage

13.1 Subroutine Concept

A subroutine can be defined as a routine which is so arranged that control may be transferred to it from a main routine and at the conclusion of the subroutine, control flows back to the main routine. Usually control is transferred to a single subroutine from more than one place in a program to save programming time and conserve storage. Consider, for example, a program which requires a certain set of instructions (routine) to be performed many times. This routine may at times consist of hundreds of instructions and using the straight line method of coding we will be required to write the same routine in duplicate, triplicate or more, depending upon the number of times the operation is to be performed. Rather than writing these instructions over and over again, thus wasting programming time as well as core storage, it would be advisable to write one common routine and set up linkage to and from this routine whenever desired. Use of subroutines also helps in reducing the complexity of programs. As a program increases in size, the increase in its complexity is exponential rather than linear. Another advantage of using subroutines over the straight line coding method is the reduction in testing, debugging and maintenance time. Testing and debugging, to a large extent, can be done as the various subroutines become ready and in case of maintenance work, changes need to be made only to the subroutines involved.

Subroutine Linkage. Linkage logic for a subroutine is illustrated by Figure 13.1.

Calling Routine: The program that invokes a subroutine is usually referred to as the calling routine.

Called Routine: The subroutine which is being invoked by a calling routine is

349

known as the called routine.

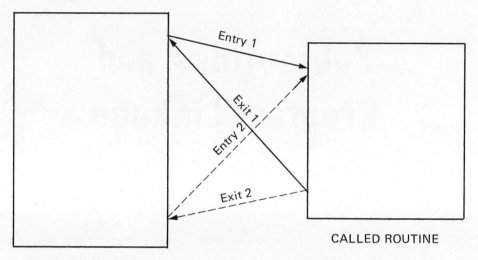

CALLED ROUTINE

CALLING ROUTINE

FIGURE 13.1. Subroutine Linkage Logic.

In this chapter, we will discuss the methods of handling communication between a calling routine and the called routine. This is also known as *subroutine linkage*.

Linkage Conventions. Communication between a calling and a called routine involves the following:

1. Providing the subroutine (called routine) with the return linkage, i.e., the address to which to return when execution of the routine is finished.
2. Supplying the subroutine (called routine) with the necessary information about the location of data and other facts which are needed by the subroutine for performing its functions. This is known as *passing of parameters.*

In certain cases, when subroutines are assembled separately but executed together, the assembler must also be informed that certain symbols will be defined only when the assembled routine(s) is loaded along with the main routine containing these symbols. The example coded below illustrates the basic logic of subroutine linkage (parameters are not being passed).

```
                    L        15,ADDRRTN  LOAD ADDRESS OF SUBROUTINE
                    BALR     14,15
                      .
                      .
                      .
ADDRRTN    DC        A(RTN)
                      .
                      .
```

We could have achieved the same result by coding this as follows:

```
        LA      15,RTN     LOAD ADDRESS OF SUBROUTINE
        BALR    14,15
        .
        .
        .
```

Another method of causing a branch to a subroutine would be:

```
        L       15,=A(RTN)
        BALR    14,15
        .
        .
        .
```

Figure 13.2 is an example of a program which invokes a subroutine, RTN, twice.

```
                START
BEGIN           BALR    9,0
                USING   *,9
                .
                L       15,ADDRRTN  LOAD ENTRY POINT OF RTN
                BALR    14,15               SET UP RETURN AND BRANCH
                .

                L       15,ADDRRTN  LOAD ENTRY POINT OF RTN
                BALR    14,15               SET UP RETURN AND BRANCH
                .

ADDRRTN         DC      A(RTN)
                .
                EOJ
RTN             .                   ENTRY POINT INTO ROUTINE
                .
                .

                .
                BR      14          EXIT FROM ROUTINE
                .
                END     BEGIN
```

FIGURE 13.2. Simple Subroutine Linkage Convention.

Note: 1. The L and BALR instructions in this particular example serve as linkage instructions, giving us the capability of setting up the entry to, and the return from, the subroutine.

2. Instead of using these two instructions to set up the return point and causing the branch to the subroutine, we could have used a single BAL instruction. For example:

```
          BAL        14,RTN
           .
           .
           .
          BAL        14,RTN
           .
           .
          EOJ
RTN        .
           .
          BR         14
```

However, if this approach is used, the address of the routine being branched to must be within the range of the current base register. This will not always be the case, especially when the subroutine is assembled separately.

Figure 13.2 shows us the basic logic of establishing linkage to the subroutine from different points of a main routine. The next example continues one step further and illustrates the logic of passing parameters from the main routine to the subroutine along with conventional linkage techniques.

Parameter: Parameter can be defined as a quantity in a subroutine whose value specifies the process to be performed. It may be given different values when linkage is established to a subroutine from different points of a main routine.

Example:

A program builds two arrays, ARRAYA and ARRAYB, and these have been defined as:

```
ARRAYA        DS        100F
ARRAYB        DS        100F
```

The count of the number of entries made in ARRAYA and ARRAYB is placed in 2 words named COUNTA and COUNTB respectively, which have been defined as:

```
COUNTA        DS        F
COUNTB        DS        F
```

Write program steps to sum the entries in ARRAYA and ARRAYB, placing the results in 2 words named RESULTA and RESULTB respectively. (We will use this example throughout the rest of the chapter.)

```
            START
BEGIN       BALR      9,0
            USING     *,9
            .
CALL1       LA        2,ARRAYA  SET
            LA        3,RESULTA  UP
            LA        4,COUNTA     PARAMETERS FOR ARRAYA
            L         15,
                      ADDRRTN  LOAD ENTRY POINT OF RTN
            BALR      14,15      SET UP RETURN LINKAGE AND BRANCH
            .

            .
CALL2       LA        2,ARRAYB  SET
            LA        3,RESULTB  UP
            L         4,COUNTB     PARAMETERS FOR ARRAYB
            L         15,
                      ADDRRTN  LOAD ENTRY POINT OF RTN
            BALR      14,15      SET UP RETURN LINKAGE AND BRANCH

            .
ADDRRTN     DC        A(RTN)
ARRAYA      DS        100F
RESULTA     DS        F
COUNTA      DS        F
ARRAYB      DS        100F
RESULTB     DS        F
COUNTB      DS        F

            .

            .

            .
            EOJ
*
*THIS IS THE START OF THE SUBROUTINE
*
            USING     *,15
RTN         SR        5,5        CLEAR ACCUMULATOR
ADD         A         5,0(2)     SUM ARRAYA OR ARRAYB
            LA        2,4(2)     POINT TO NEXT ELEMENT IN ARRAY
            BCT       4,ADD      IS ARRAY DONE
            ST        5,0(3)     STORE RESULTING SUM
            BR        14         EXIT
            END       BEGIN
```

FIGURE 13.3. Subroutine Linkage and Passing of Parameters.

From Figure 13.3 it is clear that a subroutine not only needs to know where to return when its work is finished; it also needs to know the location of the data on which it is to work. This information was passed to the subroutine via some general register. This method of passing parameters is not typical, and is certainly not always acceptable when we need to pass a large number of parameters. Thus, we need to look into a more flexible and versatile method of passing parameters. The most common technique of doing this is to write a *calling sequence.*

Calling sequence. A calling sequence is written immediately following the BALR instruction that causes the branch to the subroutine. It consists of data and/or data addresses that need to be passed on to the subroutine. Certain standard conventions exist for register usage in a calling sequence, which are as follows:

1. General register 15 contains the address of the entry point of the called program. This address is set up in the calling program and may be used as a base register in the called program.
2. General register 14 contains the return address.
3. If only one or two parameters are to be passed to the called routine, these values can be loaded into registers 0 and 1. If the number of parameters is large, a calling sequence is written to pass the values to the called routine.

```
              L         15,ADDRRTN
              BALR      14,15
              DC        A(ARRAYA)
              DC        A(RESULTA)
   COUNTA     DS        F
                  .
                  .
                  .
   ADDRRTN    DC        A(RTN)
   ARRAYA     DS        100F
   RESULTA    DS        F
                  .
                  .
```

Note: 1. The called routine, RTN, can use the address in register 14 to pick up the necessary parameters, as this register contains the address of the first word following the BALR instruction.

2. The branch instruction that will cause the exit from the subroutine will have to be coded somewhat like this:

```
              BC       15,12(14)    EXIT FROM THE SUBROUTINE
```

This is done to ensure that the return is made to a point *past the constants* in the calling sequence.

There is a great element of risk involved in writing a calling sequence in this way. What if the instruction before the BALR ended on a fullword boundary? The BALR, a 2 byte long instruction, will occupy the first 2 bytes of the next word. The assembler, since it automatically aligns on a word boundary an A-type constant for which no length is specified, would skip 2 bytes to perform boundary alignment for the A-type constant.

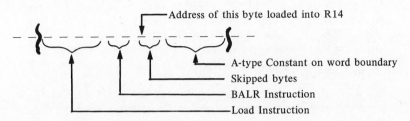

In this case the BALR instruction will load into register 14 the address of the first byte after BALR, which of course is not the address of the first byte of the A-type address constant. This would cause serious trouble as the subroutine counts on register 14 to contain the address of the A-type constant. This problem can very easily be solved by the use of the CNOP, a program control assembler instruction.

CNOP Conditional NO—Operation

This assembler instruction allows the programmer to align an instruction at a specific word boundary, i.e., halfword, word or doubleword boundary. If any bytes have to be skipped to achieve the specific boundary alignment, the assembler *ensures* an unbroken instruction flow by *generating* no-operation instructions. If the Location Counter is already properly aligned, the CNOP has no effect. The format of this instruction is:

Name	Op	Operand
symbol	CNOP	Two absolute expressions of the form b,w or not used

Both operands are written as self-defining decimal numbers. The second operand can be either 4 or 8. When 4 is specified for the second operand, the first operand can be either 0 or 2. If the second operand is specified as 8, the first operand may be either 0, 2, 4 or 6. Various valid combinations of the two operands for CNOP instructions are listed below.

b,w	Meaning
0,2	Beginning of a word
2,4	Middle of a word
0,8	Beginning of a doubleword
2,8	Second halfword of a doubleword
4,8	Third halfword of a doubleword (middle)
6,8	Fourth halfword of a doubleword

```
---------------------------------------------------------------
|                        DOUBLE WORD                          |
|-------------------------------------------------------------|
|          Word            |             Word                 |
|-------------------------------------------------------------|
| Half Word  |  Half Word  |  Half Word   |    Half Word       |
|-------------------------------------------------------------|
| Byte | Byte | Byte | Byte | Byte | Byte |  Byte  |  Byte     |
|-------------------------------------------------------------|
| 0,4          2,4          0,4             2,4                |
| 0,8          2,8          4,8             6,8                |
---------------------------------------------------------------
```

FIGURE 13.4. CNOP Alignment.

Example:

```
CNOP    6,8
BALR    14,15
```

The CNOP will cause three no-operations to be generated, thus aligning the BALR instruction at the last halfword in a doubleword. The instructions generated are listed below:

```
BCR     0,0
BCR     0,0
BCR     0,0
BALR    14,15
```

Example:

```
CNOP    2,4
BALR    14,15
```

If, when the assembler encounters the BALR instruction, the location counter is already set to a value that is two greater than a word boundary, the CNOP will have no effect. If, on the other hand, this is not the case, the assembler will generate one BCR 0,0 instruction, thus positioning the BALR instruction in such a way that the calling sequence will be located immediately after the BALR instruction. Consider the calling sequence, this time with a CNOP inserted before the BALR instruction.

```
          .
          .
          .
          L        15,ADDRRTN
          CNOP     2,4
          BALR     14,15
          DC       A(ARRAYA)
          DC       A(RESULTA)
COUNTA    DS       F
          .
          .
```

FIGURE 13.5. A Typical Calling Sequence.

Note: If, when the assembler reaches the BALR instruction, the location counter is already set to a value that is two greater than a fullword boundary, the CNOP instruction will be ignored.

Subroutine communication consideration

The *first* instruction at the entry point of a called routine should *store* the contents of the registers that will be used by the subroutine, and the instruction just *before* the exit point should *restore* these registers. This is a normal and very wise practice. Rarely, if ever, are registers assumed to be available to the subroutine without first saving their contents. Figure 13.6 illustrates the technique of passing parameters with the help of a calling sequence.

```
Name      Oper     Operand
          START
BEGIN     BALR     9,0
          USING    *,9

          .
          L        15,
                   ADDRRTN   SET UP ENTRY POINT TO RTN
          CNOP     2,4
          BALR     14,15        SET UP RETURN POINT AND BRANCH
          DC       A(ARRAYA) THE
          DC       A(RESULTA)  CALLING
                   (continued)
```

```
COUNTA      DS      F               SEQUENCE
              .
              .
            L       15,ADDRRTN
            CNOP    2,4
            BALR    14,15
            DC      A(ARRAYB)
            DC      A(RESULTB)
COUNTB      DS      F
              .
              .
ADDRRTN     DC      A(RTN)
ARRAYA      DS      100F
ARRAYB      DS      100F
RESULTA     DS      F
RESULTB     DS      F
              .
            EOJ
*
*THIS IS THE START OF THE SUBROUTINE
*
            USING   *,15
RTN         STM     2,5,SAVE        SAVE REGISTERS 2 TO 5
            L       2,0(14)         LOAD ADDRESS OF ARRAYA OR ARRAYB
            L       3,4(14)         LOAD ADDRESS OF RESULTA OR RESULTB
            L       4,8(14)         LOAD COUNTA OR COUNTB
            SR      5,5             CLEAR ACCUMULATOR
ADD         A       5,0(2)          SUM ARRAY
            LA      2,4(2)          POINT REG 2 TO NEXT WORD OF ARRAY
            BCT     4,ADD           IS ARRAY DONE
            ST      5,0(3)          STORE ARRAY SUM
            LM      2,5,SAVE        RESTORE REGISTERS
            BC      15,12(14)       EXIT POINT
SAVE        DS      4F
            END     BEGIN
```

FIGURE 13.6. A Program Containing Two Calling Sequences.

This method of passing parameters, with the help of a calling sequence, has one disadvantage. This is:

The programmer must write the unconditional branch instruction causing the exit from the subroutine in such a way that the control does not go back into the calling sequence itself. The programmer also has to make sure that the calling sequence is correctly positioned and this is generally done by writing a CNOP instruction.

An alternate method of passing parameters to a subroutine is to write the addresses of each variable in consecutive words in some area within the calling routine and, the starting address of this area is placed in register 1 by the calling routine. The called routine uses the address in register 1 to retrieve addresses and/or data it needs to perform its functions. Figure 13.7 illustrates this technique.

```
              START
BEGIN         BALR      9,0
              USING     *,9
                .
              L         15,ADDRRTN
              LA        1,PARMLSTA
              BALR      14,15
                .
                .
              L         15,ADDRRTN
              LA        1,PARMLSTB
              BALR      14,15
                .
                .
PARMLSTA      DC        A(ARRAYA)
              DC        A(RESULTA)
COUNTA        DS        F
PARMLSTB      DC        A(ARRAYB)
              DC        A(RESULTB)
COUNTB        DS        F
ARRAYA        DS        100F
ARRAYB        DS        100F
RESULTA       DS        F
RESULTB       DS        F
                .
              EOJ
*
*THIS IS THE START OF THE SUBROUTINE
*
              USING     *,15
RTN           STM       2,5,SAVE  SAVE REGISTERS
              L         2,0(1)      LOAD ADDRESS OF ARRAY
```

(continued)

```
            L         3,4(1)      LOAD ADDRESS OF RESULT WORD
            L         4,8(1)      LOAD COUNT
            SR        5,5         CLEAR ACCUMULATOR
ADD         A         5,0(2)      SUM ARRAY
            LA        2,4(2)      POINT REG 2 TO NEXT WORD OF ARRAY
            BCT       4,ADD       IS ARRAY DONE
            ST        5,0(3)      STORE RESULTING SUM
            LM        2,5,SAVE    RESTORE REGISTERS
            BR        14          EXIT
SAVE        DS        4F
            END       BEGIN
```

FIGURE 13.7. Passing of Parameters Via Register 1.

Program sectioning

When working with very large programs, it is often convenient and sometimes necessary to divide the program into several smaller sections in order to program each section separately. This approach facilitates testing and debugging, as the programmer can concentrate on one smaller part of a program at a time. After these various sections have been debugged and tested, they can be combined and executed as one program. The assembler provides the facilities for linking separately assembled control sections of a multisection program without reassembly of the entire program. When writing a multisection program, the programmer has the *responsibility* of providing section inkage and must ensure that the control passes properly from one section to another regardless of the relative position of the sections in core storage.

> Control Section: A control section can be defined as a unit of coding that can be relocated, independently of other coding, at program load time without affecting the operating logic of the program as a whole.

The assembler provides a separate Location Counter for each control section and, as such, control section contents can be intermixed. Different control sections are assigned starting locations consecutively, in the same order as they first occur in the program. The first control section of a program is usually established with the help of the START instruction and an absolute starting core location may be specified. Each subsequent control section is started with a CSECT instruction. The assembler establishes each control section subsequent to the first at the next available double-word boundary.

CSECT —— Identify Control Section

Format of this assembler instruction is:

Name	Oper	Operand
Symbol or not used	CSECT	Not used, must be left blank

The CSECT, a program control instruction, identifies the beginning or the continuation of a control section. The operand portion of this instruction is not used and, as such, *must* be left blank.

If a symbol is assigned to a CSECT, it is established as the name of the control section, otherwise the section is considered to be unnamed. It is permissible to have several CSECT statements with the same name interspersed in a program. The first of these is considered to identify the beginning of a control section and the rest, with the same name, identify the resumption of that section. During assembly time, the various segments of the same control section are assigned contiguous locations and assembled as one control section.

Unnamed Control Sections. If neither a START nor a named CSECT instruction appears at the beginning of a program, the assembler determines that it is to assemble an unnamed control section as the first (or only) control section. If a control section is unnamed and is followed by a named control section, any subsequent unnamed CSECT statements are considered to resume the unnamed control section.

Note: Sectioning of a program is optional and if a programmer desires to write an unsectioned program, he does not need to use a CSECT instruction.

Internal Linkage. If the various sections of a multisection program are assembled together, the setting up of linkage and passing of parameters is done in exactly the same manner as discussed previously in subroutine linkage. Figure 13.8 is an example of a program which has two control sections.

```
MAINPROG    CSECT
            BALR    9,0
            USING   *,9
              .
            L       15,ADDRRTN
            CNOP    2,4
            BALR    14,15
            DC      A(ARRAYA)
            DC      A(RESULTA)
COUNTA      DS      F
              .
              .
            L       15,ADDRRTN
```

(continued)

```
                    CNOP     2,4
                    BALR     14,15
                    DC       A(ARRAYB)
                    DC       A(RESULTB)
     COUNTB         DS       F
                    .
     ADDRRTN        DC       A(RTN)
     ARRAYA         DS       100F
     ARRAYB         DS       100F
     RESULTA        DS       F
     RESULTB        DS       F
                    .
                    .
                    EOJ
     *
     *THIS IS THE SECOND CONTROL SECTION
     *
     RTN            CSECT
                    BALR     12,0
                    USING    *,12
                    L        2,0(14)
                    L        3,4(14)
                    L        4,8(14)
                    SR       5,5
     ADD            A        5,0(2)
                    LA       2,4(2)
                    BCT      4,ADD
                    ST       5,0(3)
                    BC       15,12(14)
                    END      BEGIN
```

FIGURE 13.8. Program With Two Control Sections.

External Linkage. Separately assembled control sections can be joined together by the Linkage Editor at link edit time (for detailed discussion see Appendix 2). Before looking at an example of establishing external linkage, i.e., linkage between separately assembled control sections, it is necessary to introduce three assembler instructions which play an important role in establishing external linkage. These are ENTRY, EXTRN and V-type address constants.

ENTRY —— Identify Entry Point Symbol

The ENTRY instruction identifies linkage symbols that are defined in this control section but may be used by some other control section. The format of this assembler instruction is as follows:

Name	Oper	Operand
	ENTRY	One or more relocatable symbols separated by commas.

The symbols in the ENTRY operand field may be used as operands by other programs.

Example:

ENTRY   ARRAYA,ARRAYB,RESULTA,RESULTB

EXTRN —— Identify External Symbols

The EXTRN instruction identifies linkage symbols that are used by this program, but have been defined in some other program. Each external symbol being used by the control section must be identified except the ones established by V-type address constants. The format of this assembler instruction is as follows:

Name	Oper	Operand
	EXTRN	One or more relocatable symbols separated by commas.

Example:

EXTRN   ARRAYA,ARRAYB,RESULTA,RESULTB

Note: The symbols that are identified in the operand field of an EXTRN instruction may not appear as names of statements in this control sections.

V—Type Address Constant. This constant is used to reserve storage for the address of an external symbol that is used to establish linkage to other programs or control sections. The constant specified *does not* need to be identified by an EXTRN statement. The implied length of this type of constant is 4 bytes and boundary alignment is to a fullword. It is permissible to specify explicit length of either 3 or 4 bytes, but in such cases boundary alignment is not performed.

Example:

```
VCON1      DC      V(RTN)
VCON2      DC      V(RTN,RTNA,RTNB)
```

The first address constant, VCON1, will reserve 4 bytes and the second will reserve 12 bytes. Boundary alignment will be performed in both cases.

Note: A V-type address constant *must not* be used for external data reference.

The coding example that follows illustrates the linkage technique when two separately assembled control sections are used as one program. The main program builds four arrays named T1, T2, T3, and T4. The subprogram is to add the corresponding words of these four tables and places the result into a fifth table named TSUM.

```
MAINPROG    CSECT
            BALR    9,0
            USING   *,9
            ENTRY   T1
            .
            L       15,CONSTV
            BALR    14,15
            .
            .
            .
T1          DS      100F
T2          DS      100F
T3          DS      100F
T4          DS      100F
TSUM        DS      100F
CONSTV      DC      V(SUBRTN)
            END
SUBRTN      CSECT
            EXTRN   T1          IDENTIFY EXTERNAL SYMBOL
            STM     2,5,SAVE    SAVE REG 2 TO 5
            LM      2,5,AT1     LOAD PARAMETERS
ADD         A       5,0(3,2)    ADD ONE WORD OF T1
            A       5,400(3,2)  ADD ONE WORD OF T2
            A       5,800(3,2)  ADD ONE WORD OF T3
            A       5,1200(3,2) ADD ONE WORD OF T4
            ST      5,1600(3,2) STORE SUM IN TSUM
            LA      3,4(3)      POINT REG 2 NEXT WORD
            BCT     4,ADD       IS ARRAY DONE
            LM      2,5,SAVE    RESTORE REG 2 TO 5
            BR      14          EXIT
AT1         DC      A(T1)       SET UP ADDRESS OF T1
            DC      F'0'        INITIALIZE INDEX REG 3
            DC      F'100'      COUNT OF ENTRIES IN ARRAY
            DC      F'0'        INITIALIZE ACCUMULATOR
SAVE        DS      4F          SAVE AREA
            END
```

FIGURE 13.9. External Linkage Example.

[14]

Magnetic Tapes

14.1 Introduction to Magnetic Tapes

Until now the only input/output medium we have discussed has been the standard IBM card. The card files are not only slow in processing, they are also cumbersome to handle and require enormous amounts of storage space. The possibility and the probability of misplacing, missorting and leaving out a card(s) from a file is frighteningly high. Therefore, to speed up processing and to reduce the chances of human errors, other forms of input/output media were designed, e.g., magnetic tapes, drums, disks and data cell. In this chapter we will discuss the characteristics and use of the magnetic tapes.

A standard magnetic tape is approximately 2400 feet in length and 1/2" wide. Magnetic tape can be used both as an input and as an output medium. Information can be recorded in either true binary form or in EBCDIC code and a reel of tape can be read as many times as necessary. When the information recorded on a tape is no longer required, the same tape can be used to record new data (recording of new data *automatically* erases the old information on the tape).

Data can be recorded on tapes in two different densities. These are 800 characters per inch (CPI) or 1600 characters per inch. Data are not recorded from the physical beginning of the tape, approximately the first and the last ten feet[1] of the tape are left unrecorded. This is done in order to provide enough tape length for operator handling during mounting and unmounting of tape reels from tape units. To ensure that data recording and reading starts from the very same point, a *load point* marker is used to signify the beginning of the recording surface on the tape. This marker, a small

[1] This length varies from approximately three feet to ten feet.

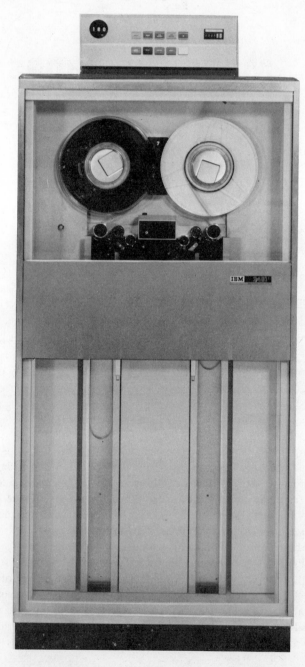

FIGURE 14.1. A Magnetic Tape Unit.

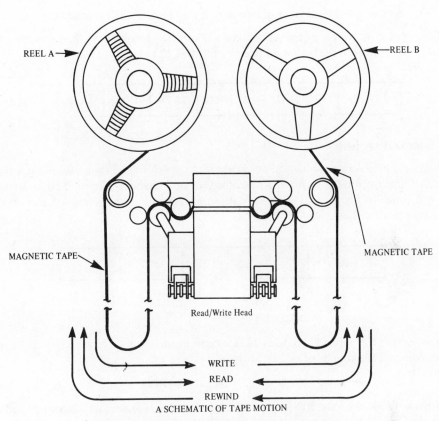

REEL A→

←REEL B

MAGNETIC TAPE

MAGNETIC TAPE

Read/Write Head

WRITE

READ

REWIND

A SCHEMATIC OF TAPE MOTION

FIGURE 14.1(a). A Schematic of Tape Motion.

aluminum strip, is sensed by a photoelectric cell in the tape unit during initial tape positioning. Similarly, an aluminum strip is affixed approximately ten feet from the physical end of the tape.

Theoretically speaking, we could have a single record extending from one end of the tape to another. This, however, will not be very practical as 2400 feet of tape with a recording density of 800 characters per inch will hold approximately 23 million bytes of data. It would be very difficult to find a computer capable of holding such a large I/O area.

Thus, the information on tapes is recorded in smaller size blocks. Each block is separated by an inter-block-gap[2] of 0.6 inch. The length of a block is generally governed by the amount of core storage available and the complexity of the programming techniques needed to process such records. The number of bytes between two successive inter-block-gaps constitutes a physical record.

---

[2]Same as Inter-record-gap.

Physical Record: The amount of data that is processed per I/O command.

The size of a record on a tape is not fixed and can vary according to the necessities of a problem. However, the *minimum* size of a block is 12 bytes.

| DATA | IRG | DATA | IRG | DATA | IRG | DATA |

Blocked records

Assume we have a card file and need to record the information contained in this file onto a tape in card-image form. At a density of 800 characters per inch, it will take only 0.1 inch of tape surface to record data from each card. In between each record on the tape there will be an IRG of 0.6 inch.

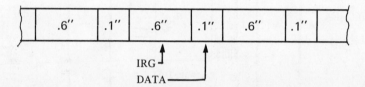

Suppose that the card file contains 24,000 cards in all. The total tape surface required to record this file would be:

$$(.1 + .6)/12 * 24000 = 1400 \text{ ft}$$

Of these 1400 feet only 200 feet are actually used for recording data from the cards, the remaining 1200 feet are taken up by the IRG. This seems to be an excessive waste of tape surface and it is. Now suppose that we group together four card records into one physical record on the tape, i.e., each physical record becomes 320 bytes long. The result would be that we will have only one IRG between every four records. In this way, the total surface required to record the entire card file would be:

$$(.4 + .6)/12 * 6000 = 500 \text{ ft}$$

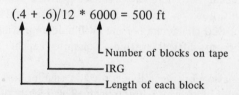

We have therefore saved tape by grouping four records together into one block. Note that we still have 200 feet of data; however, the IRG occupies only 300 feet instead of 1200 feet as was the case when each card image was separated by an IRG.

Blocking of records not only saves us tape but also increases the processing efficiency. Each I/O device requires a certain amount of time before it is ready to transfer data. This time is known as *startup time*. The startup time for a given I/O unit is fixed and *does not* depend on the physical size of the record being transferred. Thus, by blocking records together a great deal of startup time can be saved as the number of I/O commands will be reduced considerably. For instance, a file containing 24,000 records, where each record is separated by IRG will require a total of 24,000 I/O commands. The same file with four records to a block will require only 6000 I/O commands for reading the file into the storage. Secondly, we will be able to save some additional processing time, since it will take less time to pass a shorter tape. However, there is a penalty for blocking records together. With blocked tape records we have to have an I/O area large enough to contain the physical record. For example, a physical record containing 50 logical records where each logical record is 100 bytes long will require 5000 bytes of core storage for I/O area. At times, this much core space is not readily available.

Blocking Factor: The number of logical records contained in a physical record is known as the blocking factor. If a physical record contains 50 logical records, the blocking factor will be 50.

The logical record and the physical record may be the *same* entity, in which case the blocking factor is one and the tape is said to be *unblocked*.

From a programmer's point of view the processing of tape records, blocked or unblocked, is not very different than the processing of card records. For all practical purposes a tape can be compared to a number of cards strung together to form a continuous strip with spaces at appropriate places to separate one record or a group of records from another. The IOCS (PIOCS and LIOCS) makes it possible for a programmer to process blocked tape files in a simple way. Blocking and de-blocking is *performed* by the IOCS without much work on the programmer's part. The LIOCS routines generated by the DTF entries for a blocked tape file make available to the program one logical record at a time. For example, when a GET macro is issued to such a file, the first GET reads into the I/O area the entire physical record from the tape and also makes available to the program the *first* logical record. Each subsequent GET will make available the next logical record until all the records in the block have been processed. The GET macro issued after this completion of a block processing will again transfer a physical record from the tape to the storage and the first logical record of the block will be made available for processing. The same process takes place when PUT macro is used to write blocked tape records. Consider a tape with a blocking factor of 10. The first nine PUT macros issued will cause nine logical records to be blocked into the I/O area and the tenth PUT will complete the formation of the physical record in the core and *then* the completed block will be *transferred* to the appropriate I/O unit.

Note: When a physical record is read into core storage, each logical record is separated from the physical record and is made available for processing to the program as though only one logical record has been read. The same applies to the records that are to be written out on a tape.

Blocking: Grouping together of a number of logical records into a physical record.

De-blocking: Separation of the logical records from a physical record *after* it has been read into the I/O area.

At this time, we should distinguish between the types of record formats possible with tape files. These are: Fixed Length, often referred to as F; Variable Length, V; and, Undefined Length, U.

Fixed Length. In this case all logical records are identical in length and if the tape file is blocked, each physical record is identical in length to any other physical record. This is the easiest and the most common way of blocking tape files.

Variable Length. The size of the logical records and the physical records (if tape is blocked) may vary from record to record. This format, though complicated to process, has great merit. There are times when the length of individual records within a file may vary a great deal. For example, in case of a file of stockholders, some stocks may be held by one individual while others may be owned by a number of individuals. If all records were to be the *same* length they would have to be the length of the *largest* record possible. This way, much of the tape would be wasted. In cases like this, variable length records result in greater efficiency of processing and saving of tape as well.

Blocking and de-blocking of variable length records is certainly more involved than processing of fixed length records. Since the length of the logical and physical records can vary, it is necessary to have a *length identifying field* within each record. The standard convention is to add 4 bytes to the left of each logical record. The first 2 bytes of this word specify the length of the record in bytes and the low-order 2 bytes are always left blank.

L	L	b	b	LOGICAL RECORD

Variable Length Unblocked Record

If the variable length records are to be blocked, *additional* 4 bytes are placed to the left of the length field of the first logical record in each block. The high-order 2 bytes specify the length of the *physical record* in bytes and the low-order 2 bytes are left blank[3].

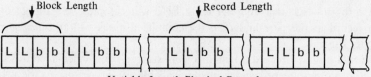

Variable Length Physical Record

[3]This is done to ensure that logical records start at a word boundary.

It is important to note that the blocking factor for variable length records may vary from block to block.

Undefined Length. These types of records do not have any length field to indicate the record length. The records are always considered as unblocked and blocking or de-blocking, if any, must be done by the programmer.

These three format types, F, V and U, which we have just discussed, are illustrated in Figure 14.1(b) below.

Logical Record

Format F Unblocked

L L b b	Logical Record

Format V Unblocked

Logical Record

Format U

Logical Record 1	Logical Record 2	Logical Record 3

Format F Blocked – Blocking Factor = 3

L L b b	L L b b	Logical Rec 1	L L b b	Logical Rec 2

Format V Blocked – Blocking Factor = 2

FIGURE 14.1(b). Blocked and Unblocked Tape Record Formats.

Tape labels

In the case of punched card or printed files, one could identify a file by visual inspection. However, the same is not possible with magnetic tape files as the data can not be read (unless of course you have a very magnetic personality). Thus, it is standard practice to record special identifying records on a tape along with the regular data records. In general, three types of records are used for this purpose. These are Volume Labels, Header Labels, and Trailer Labels. Certain standard label formats have been designed and, if adhered to, a programmer can save himself a great deal of programming effort as the manufacturer-supplied routines take care of the standard label processing. However, a programmer is at liberty to do these labels in any format he desires. In the rest of the text, we will *assume standard labels.*

Volume: A physical unit on which information can be recorded, e.g., tape, disk, and drum, etc.

File: A collection of related records. A file may occupy a part of a volume, one volume, or more than one volume. A file is also referred to as data set.

Volume Label. This is always the first record on the tape. Volume label is used to identify the tape as a whole and *does not* identify the data on the tape. The volume label is always the first record of each tape even if a file occupies more than one reel of tape. The format of the label is:

BYTES	FIELD
1 — 4	VOL 1
5 — 10	Volume serial number. This number is generally written when the reel is purchased. The number may contain alphabetic characters, but usually is numeric.
11 — 11	Security. A 0 in this field means that no further identification is required before this volume can be used. A 1 indicates that further identification is needed.
12 — 41	Always left blank.
42 — 51	Owner's name and address.
52 — 80	Always left blank.

Header Label. A header label follows the volume label and *precedes* the data on the tape. The format of the header label is:

BYTES	FIELD
1 — 4	HDR1
5 — 21	Identification. Any information which identifies the file.
22 — 27	File serial number. The volume serial number of the first volume on which the file is recorded.
28 — 31	Volume sequence number, i.e., 0001 for the first volume, 0002 for the second volume, 0003 for the third volume of a multi-volume file, etc.
32 — 35	Data Set sequence number. For example, it must be 0001

	for the first data set on the volume, 0002 for the second data set on the same volume, etc.
36 — 39	Generation Number. For files which are updated often, this field identifies the generation number, i.e., 0001, 0002, 0003, etc.
40 — 41	Version number of the generation. The number in this field indicates the stage in processing of this generation of the file.
42 — 47	Creation date. The date on which the data set was created. Its format is byyddd. When ddd= the day of the year.
48 — 53	Expiration date. Same format as the creation date. This field indicates the first date on which the data set on the tape may be over-ridden.
54 — 54	Security 0 or 1.
55 — 60	Always zeroes.
61 — 73	System Code
74 — 80	Blank

Trailer Label. Trailer label is the last label on a tape file and it is written *following* the data set. The trailer label format is the same as header label except in two fields, which are as follows:

BYTES	FIELD
1 — 4	EOF1 or EOV1
55 — 60	Block count. This is the number of blocks written on the file or on the volume

In case of multireel files, each trailer label except the last one will contain the identifying characters EOV1. The last reel's trailer record will contain EOF1. When processing multireel files, the IOCS on inspecting the first 4 bytes of the trailer label, can determine if additional reels have to be processed. Figure 14.2 illustrates these various labels and their arrangement on tape files.

It is possible to have more than one file on the same reel of tape. The arrangement and sequence of labels on such a reel of tape is illustrated in Figure 14.3.

VOL1, HDR1, EOF1 and EOV1 are required labels. There may be additional volume and data set labels but these are not processed by the IOCS. At the maximum, 8 labels of a type are permitted; however, a beginning programmer may do well to omit all the optional labels and use only the required ones, i.e., VOL1, HDR1, EOF1 and EOV1.

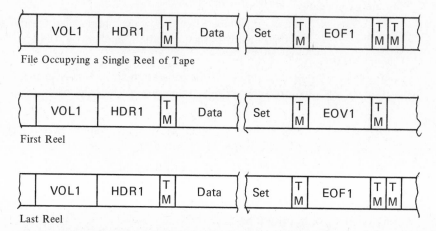

FIGURE 14.2. File Occupying More Than One Reel.

FIGURE 14.3. Label Arrangement on Multifile Tape Reel.

14.2 DTF Entries for Tape Files

The IOCS provided with System 360 operating systems provides *three levels* of input-output capabilities. These can be categorized into: Fundamental; Intermediate; and, High level.

When using fundamental level functions, the programmer has to write his own channel program (CCW) and must synchronize the completion of input/output operations with his program. This level, though quite involved and tedious, provides great flexibility. The intermediate level does not require the programmer to write the channel programs, although it still requires that the programmer provide synchronization between input/output operations and the program. The third level, the high level input/output functions, provides automatic blocking and de-blocking capabilities and a programmer is not required to write any channel programs at all. The necessary channel commands are constructed by the system, and all a programmer has to do is to supply certain information regarding the properties of the data set to be processed. This information is given to the system via DTF macro and its keyword entries. The third level of input/output functions, though very easy to program, is quite inflexible.

Magnetic Tape File (DTFMT). The rules regarding the header and detail cards and related DTF entries are the same as discussed in Section 4.2. Various keyword entries for DTFMT are given below.

Req'd	BLKSIZE=
	DEVADDR=
	EOFADDR=
	FILABL=
	IOAREA1=

Opt'l	ERROPT=
	HDRINFO=
	IOAREA2=
	IOREG=(nn)
	MODNAME=
	NOTEPNT=
	READ=
	RECFORM=
	RECSIZE=
	REWIND=
	TYPEFLE=
	WLRERR=
	WORKA=

Some of the entries listed above have already been discussed in previous chapters and to avoid repetition such entries will not be discussed in this section. Only the entries which are new or have expanded meaning or application are discussed here.

BLKSIZE=n

n stands for the number of bytes in I/O area.

The maximum allowable block size is 32,767 bytes and the minimum size is 12 bytes. A block of 11 bytes or less is considered as a noise record. In case the record format is undefined or variable, n specifies the length of the largest area.

Example:

Consider a tape file with blocking factor of 5 and each record of 100 bytes, the BLKSIZE entry for such a file would be:

BLKSIZE=500

EOFADDR=Name

This entry supplies to the IOCS the symbolic name of the end-of-file routine. On sensing the end-of-file condition, the IOCS will cause an automatic branch to this routine. In case of non-standard labels, it is the programmer's responsibility to test for and determine the end-of-file condition. This entry is *required* for input files only.

$$\text{ERROPT} = \left\{ \begin{array}{l} \text{IGNORE} \\ \text{SKIP} \\ \text{Name} \end{array} \right\}$$

The programmer may choose any one of the three entries specified. This entry applies only to input files and is used to specify the action to be taken in the event a tape read error (parity error) is detected. If a parity error is detected when a physical record is read from a tape, the IOCS automatically backspaces and rereads the tape 100 times. If at the end of the 100 read efforts the error still exists, the block is considered as an error block. The job is then automatically terminated unless ERROPT entry is included for the file. The functions of each of the three options are explained below.

Ignore: The error condition is completely ignored and the records are made available for processing.

Skip: Error block is skipped over and the next block is read into storage. The processing continues with the first record of the next block. The error block, however, is included in the block count for the file.

Name: IOCS causes a branch to the programmer's own routine. IOCS places the address of the error block in general register 1 and the return address in general register 14. In his routine the programmer must address the error block or the records in the error block via register 1. Furthermore, the programmer *must not* use any GET instructions to obtain any record from the error block. In case any other IOCS macros are to be used the programmer *must save and then restore* the contents of register 14. After completing his routine, the programmer *must* return to IOCS via register 14.

Note: This entry, ERROPT, does not apply to output files. The job is automatically terminated if parity error still exists after 15 attempts to write an output block. If both the ERROPT and WLRERR are omitted and wrong length record is encountered, the IOCS will assume the IGNORE option.

$$\text{FILABLE} = \left\{ \begin{array}{l} \text{STD} \\ \text{NO} \\ \text{NSTD} \end{array} \right\}$$

If this entry is omitted NO is assumed, which means that there are no labels. In case of a tape file with standard labels, STD is specified. IOCS automatically checks and processes labels. NO is specified if the tape file does not contain any labels. For tape files with non-standard labels, NSTD is specified. The programmer must program for checking or creating the non-standard labels.

Note: For input files with standard labels, which are not to be checked by IOCS, NSTD must be specified.

HDRINFO=YES

This operand, if specified with FILABL=STD, causes IOCS to print standard header information (fields $3 - 10$) on SYSLOG each time a standard label file is opened, and the filename, symbolic unit, and device address each time an end-of-volume condition is detected. If a programmer desires header information to be printed, he must specify both FILABL=STD and HDRINFO=YES entries.

IOAREA1=Name

This entry supplies to IOCS the symbolic name of the I/O area used by the file. When variable length records are to be processed, the size of I/O area must include 4 bytes for the block size.

IOAREA2=Name

This entry specifies the symbolic name of a second I/O area for the file. Rules for variable length records are the same as for IOAREA1.

IOREG=(r)

This entry is used if two input or output areas are used, or if blocked input or output records are processed in the I/O area, or if variable unblocked records are read. This entry specifies the register in which IOCS places the address of the record that is available for processing. IOCS places the absolute address of the current record in this register each time a GET or PUT macro is issued to the file. For output files the address placed in the register specifies the location where the programmer can build the output record(s). Any one of the registers from $2 - 12$ may be specified. (Note that this operand cannot be used if WORKA=YES is specified.)

$$\text{NOTEPNT} = \begin{Bmatrix} \text{POINTS} \\ \text{YES} \end{Bmatrix}$$

The parameter YES is specified if the NOTE, POINTR, POINTW, or POINTS macro instructions will be used in the problem program to process the *tape work* file. If POINTS is specified, only POINTS macro can be issued to the tape work file.

$$\text{READ} = \begin{Bmatrix} \text{FORWARD} \\ \text{BACK} \end{Bmatrix}$$

This entry applies to *input* files only. This entry specifies the direction in which the tape is to be read and if omitted, IOCS assumes FORWARD. This entry is generally omitted.

RECFORM=

This operand specifies the type of records in the input or output file. One of the following may be specified:

FIXUNB   for fixed-length unblocked records
FIXBLK   for fixed-length blocked records
VARUNB   for variable-length unblocked records
VARBLK   for variable-length blocked records
UNDEF   for undefined records.

In case the file contains fixed-length unblocked records, this entry may be omitted. Work files may use only FIXUNB or UNDEF.

RECSIZE = n or (r)

This entry must be included for tapes with fixed-length blocked record format. This entry specifies the number of characters in each logical record. In case of tape files with undefined record format, this entry is required for input files. It specifies a general register $(2 - 12)$ that contains the record length. In case of input files, IOCS will provide the length of the record transferred to main storage and for output files, the programmer must load the length of each record into the register before issuing the PUT for the file.

$$REWIND = \begin{Bmatrix} UNLOAD \\ NORWD \end{Bmatrix}$$

If this entry is not included, IOCS automatically rewinds the tape file on an OPEN or CLOSE instruction or on an end-of-volume condition but does not unload the file.

UNLOAD: To rewind the tape on OPEN or to rewind and unload on a CLOSE or end-of-volume condition.

NORWD: To prevent the rewinding of tape at any time.

$$TYPEFLE = \begin{Bmatrix} INPUT \\ OUTPUT \\ WORK \end{Bmatrix}$$

This operand is used to indicate whether the file is an input or output file. If INPUT is specified, the GET macro is used. If OUTPUT is specified, the PUT macro is used. If WORK is specified, the READ/WRITE, NOTE/POINT, and CHECK macros are used. (See the section Tape Work Files.)

WLRERR=Name

This entry applies to tape input files only. The symbolic name equated to WLRERR specifies the entry point into a programmer written routine. An error condition is recognized if a wrong length record is read from a tape file, and in such a case the IOCS causes a branch to the programmer written routine. The reasons for length error for various tape record formats are given below.

Fixed-Length Unblocked Records. If the DTF macro for a file includes the RECFORM=FIXUNB entry, a wrong length error condition is recognized if the length of the record read is not equal to that specified with BLKSIZE entry for the file.

Fixed-Length Blocked Records. An error condition is recognized if the physical tape record read into the core is not a multiple of the logical record length specified with RECSIZE parameter, up to the maximum length of the block that has been specified with BLKSIZE parameter.

Note: This stipulation permits us to read short blocks of logical records without any error condition.

Variable Length Records. An error condition is recognized if the length of the record read is not equal to the block length specified in the first 4 bytes of the block length field.

Undefined Records. An error is recognized if the length of the tape record read is greater than the size specified by the BLKSIZE parameter.

In case of an error condition, the IOCS causes a branch to the programmer written routine. IOCS places in register 1 the address of the error record. In his routine, the programmer must not issue any GET macro. If any other IOCS macro is used in this routine, the address in register 14 must be saved and then restored at the end of the routine. The programmer must return to the IOCS via the address in register 14.

If this entry is omitted, but a wrong length record is detected by the IOCS, one of the following actions will be taken by the system:

1. If the ERROPT entry has been specified for the file, the system will handle the length error condition the same way as the option specified with ERROPT entry (i.e., IGNORE or SKIP or programmer's routine).
2. In case both the WLRERR and the ERROPT entries are not included, IOCS will assume the IGNORE option of the ERROPT parameter.

Magnetic Tape Module (MTMOD). Listed below are the programmer supplied operands for MTMOD.

ERROPT=YES

$$\text{NOTEPNT} = \begin{Bmatrix} \text{YES} \\ \text{POINTS} \end{Bmatrix}$$

$$\text{READ} = \begin{Bmatrix} \text{FORWARD} \\ \text{BACK} \end{Bmatrix}$$

$$
\text{RECFORM} = \begin{Bmatrix} \text{FIXUNB} \\ \text{FIXBLK} \\ \text{VARUNB} \\ \text{VARBLK} \\ \text{UNDEF} \end{Bmatrix}
$$

$$
\text{TYPEFLE} = \begin{Bmatrix} \text{INPUT} \\ \text{OUTPUT} \\ \text{WORK} \end{Bmatrix}
$$

WORKA=YES

Recommended Module Name for MTMOD. Each name begins with a 3-character prefix (IJF) and consists of a 5-character field corresponding to the options permitted in module generation. In MTMOD there are two module classes for handling I/O: the module class for handling GET/PUT functions; and, the module class for handling READ/WRITE, NOTE/POINT, and CHECK functions (in case of work files).

Name List for GET/PUT Type of Modules.

MTMOD name = IJFabcde

a = F if RECFORM=FIXUNB (or FIXBLK)
    V if RECFORM=VARUNB (or VARBLK)
    U if RECFORM=UNDEF
b = B if READ=BACK is specified
    Z if READ=FORWARD, or if READ is omitted
c = C if CKPTREC=YES is specified
    Z if CKPTREC=YES is not specified

Note: This feature is not discussed in the text, thus Z should be specified.

d = W if WORKA=YES is specified
    Z if WORKA=YES is not specified
e = Z always

Name List for Work File Type Modules.

MTMOD name = IJFWabcd

a = E if ERROPT=YES is specified
    Z if ERROPT=YES is not specified
b = N if NOTEPNT=YES is specified
    Z if NOTEPNT=YES is not specified
    S if NOTEPNT=POINT is specified
c = Z always
d = Z always

Initialization of tape files

Prior to processing a file[4], it must be readied for use by issuing an OPEN macro. In case of tape files with standard labels, this macro checks or writes standard labels.

OPEN   Filename1,Filename2,......Filename n

The symbolic name of the file as specified in DTF macro is entered in the operand field. A maximum of 16 files may be opened with one OPEN macro instruction.

For an input file, OPEN rewinds the tape according to the specifications in the DTFMT entry REWIND. Both the volume (VOL1) and file header (HDR1) labels are automatically read and checked according to the information supplied by the job control cards. When the tape mark at the *end* of the label is read, IOCS opens the next file specified in the OPEN macro, or returns control back to the problem program if all files have been opened. The file(s) is then ready for processing.

For output files with standard label specification, the tape is rewound according to the specification in DTFMT parameter REWIND. When standard labels are to be written, the OPEN macro reads and checks the old volume (VOL1) and file header (HDR1) labels to make sure that the file on the tape is *no longer active* and may be destroyed.

If the file is *inactive,* the tape is then *backspaced* and the new file header (HDR1) label is written. The checking and writing of new labels is done in accordance with the information supplied by the job control cards. The file is then ready for processing.

Note: Only header labels are written and not the volume label. Generally, the volume label is written on a tape only once, at the time of its purchase.

I/O Operations for Tape Files. There are certain combinations of work areas and I/O areas that are possible. These are:

1. One I/O area with no work area.
2. One I/O area with a work area.
3. Two I/O areas with no work area.
4. Two I/O areas with a work area.

Work area: Work area can be defined as an area used for processing an individual record from a block of records.

GET Macro

There are two formats of GET macro. These are:

GET   Filename
GET   Filename,Workname

(GET macro *requires* the first operand)

---

[4]OPEN is not used with DTFCN files.

GET macro makes the next sequential logical record from an input file available for processing in either an input area or a work area.

Filename. The parameter value must be the same as specified in the header entry of the DTFMT for the file. For example:

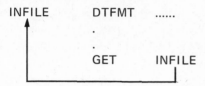

```
INFILE      DTFMT    ......
                .
                .
            GET       INFILE
```

Work area. This parameter is used if the logical records from a file are to be processed in a work area instead of the input area. The work area must, however, be defined by the programmer. If this operand is specified, all GET macros to the file must always use a workname. When workname option is used, each GET will move each logical record from the input area to the work area and then the record can be processed in the work area.

A programmer may use two input areas to allow for overlapping of data transfer and processing operations. The second area is always specified by the entry IOAREA2. In case of two input areas, the IOCS generated routines transfer physical records alternately to each area. This *flip-flop* is handled by the IOCS and is done in a manner so that the next sequential record from the file is always available for processing.

Processing in Input Areas. If a programmer wishes to process the logical records in the input area(s), he must specify the IOREG entry in the DTF macro if: tape records are blocked; or, two input areas are used (for blocked or unblocked tape records).
Note: If IOREG parameter entry is used for a file, workname *must not* be specified.

Processing of unblocked records

One I/O Area. When one input area is used, each GET to the file transfers a single logical record from the I/O device to the input area.

One Work Area. In case of a work area option, each GET macro issued to the file transfers a single record from the I/O device to the input area and then to the work area.

Two I/O Areas. Each GET macro makes the last record that was transferred to the main storage available for processing in either the input area or the work area depending upon the option used with the GET macro. The same GET also starts the transfer of the next logical record into the input area.

Processing of blocked records

In case of blocked[5] tape file records are handled as follows:

[5] The RECFORM entry for the files DTFMT must specify blocked record format.

1. The first GET issued to the file causes the transfer of a *physical* record from the tape file to the input area. If work area option is used, the first *logical* record is transferred to the work area and in case of IOREG option, the IOCS loads into the register the absolute address of the first logical record.
2. Each subsequent GET to the file either moves the next logical to the work area or adds an indexing factor (equal to the length of the logical record) to the register specified with the IOREG entry. This process continues until all the logical records in the block have been processed.
3. The next GET issued to the file transfers a *new* physical record into the main storage and depending on the option used with GET macro, it either initializes the register or moves the first logical record of the block to the work area.

The following two examples illustrate the use of work area and IOREG options.

Example:

Consider a blocked tape with blocking factor of 5, where each record is 100 bytes in length. Extract those records from the file which have I.D. code of either 78 or 76. I.D. code field is located in positions 11 − 12 of each record.

Name	Oper	Operand
	START	0
INFILE	DTFMT	IOAREA1=IN1,IOAREA2=IN2,WORKA=YES,....
	.	
	.	
READ	GET	INFILE,IN3
	CLC	IN3+10(2),=C'78'
	BE	FOUND
	CLC	IN3+10(2),=C'76'
	BE	FOUND
	B	READ
FOUND	.	
	.	
	.	
	.	
IN1	DS	5CL100
IN2	DS	5CL100
IN3	DS	CL100
	.	

Using IOREG.

Name	Oper	Operand
	START	0
INFILE	DTFMT	IOAREA1=IN1,IOAREA2=IN2,IOREG=(4),.....

(continued)

```
                      .
                      .

   READ        GET        INFILE
               CLC        10(2,4),=C'78'
               BE         FOUND
               CLC        10(2,4),=C'76'
               BE         FOUND
               B          READ
                      .
                      .

   IN1         DS         5CL100
   IN2         DS         5CL100
                      .
```

In the example coded above, each GET issued to the tape file will place into register 4 the absolute address of the record currently available. In the two compare instructions the first operand is:

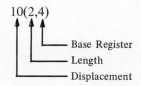

Each subsequent GET to the file will add an indexing factor of 100, the length of the logical record, to register 4, until all the records in the block have been processed. Then the *next* GET will make a new block available in main storage and will also *initialize* the register 4 with the absolute address of the *first* logical record in the block.

PUT macro

There are two formats of PUT macro:

```
                  PUT        Filename
                  PUT        Filename,Workname
```

(PUT macro requires the first operand)

Filename. The first operand of PUT macro must specify the same symbolic name as specified in the header entry of the DTFMT for the file.

Workname. This is an optional parameter and is used if the logical records from a file are to be built in a work area. The operand entry must specify the symbolic name of a work area which the programmer must set aside with perhaps a DS statement. If this operand is specified, all PUT macros issued to the file must always use a workname. When a PUT is used with the workname option, IOCS moves each record from the work area to the output area.

Note: Whenever a record is transferred from an output area or work area to the I/O device, the data remains in the area until it is cleared by the program or replaced by other data. IOCS does not clear the area.

The programmer may use two output areas to obtain overlapping of data transfer and processing operations. IOCS transfers the records to the output device alternately from each area and this *flip-flop* is handled completely by the IOCS routines. IOCS also makes available the proper output area for building next logical record.

Processing in output area(s)

When records for a file are built directly in the output area(s) *instead* of work area, a register must be specified by the IOREG entry, if: tape records are blocked; or, two output areas are used for either blocked or unblocked files. Each time a PUT is issued to an output file, the IOCS places the absolute base address of the currently available output record into the register specified by the IOREG entry. The output area must always be addressed by using the IOREG as the base.

Processing of Unblocked Tape Records. In case of unblocked tape records, each PUT issued to the file transfers one logical record from the output area to the file. If a work area is used to process records, each PUT instruction first transfers the work area to the output area and then to the file.

Processing of blocked tape records

In case blocked records are to be written on a tape, each PUT instruction either adds an indexing factor (equal to the length of the logical record) to the IOREG register or transfers the record from the work area to the output area. When the output block has been completely built, PUT macro transfers the complete block to the output unit and also initializes the IOREG register, if one is being used.

Notes: 1. Only one work area can be specified in any one GET or PUT instruction.

2. If work area option is used IOREG must not be used and the reverse holds true.

3. Individual records from a logical file may be processed in the same work area or a different record from the same file may be processed in different work areas.

Completion

After all the records for a file, input or output, have been processed, the file must be deactivated. This is accomplished by issuing the CLOSE macro and is generally done in the end-of-file routine.

Input Tape Files. On sensing a tape mark on an input file, the LIOCS determines whether it is EOV or EOF condition. In case of *end-of-volume* (EOV1) condition, IOCS after reading and checking the standard label either switches to an alternate tape drive or if no alternate drive is specified, a message is issued to the operator to change the tape reel and the system enters the wait state. After mounting the next tape of the file being processed, the operator issues a message to the system and processing resumes. IOCS then reads and checks the volume and header labels on the new reel and the file is made available for normal processing. In case of EOF condition, IOCS *branches* to the end-of-file routine for the file as specified by EOFADDR entry of the file.

Output Tape Files. When an end-of-reel condition (reflective spot) is sensed on an output file, LIOCS *prepares* the system for closing the file. If the programmer issues another PUT macro to the file (indication that more records are to be written on this file) the system *initializes* end-of-volume procedures as follows:

> Any record, or block of records, that has not been processed is written on the output file. Immediately following the last record, a tape mark is written. Following this the trailer label (EOV1) is written which in turn is followed by another tape mark. At this time the rewind option for the file is executed and then the system deactivates the file. In case of end-of-file condition, i.e., when there are no more records to be written on the file, the programmer issues a CLOSE macro and the system initiates end-of-file procedure.

CLOSE macro

Its format is:

> CLOSE   Filename1,Filename2,........Filename n

This macro is used to deactivate those files which have been opened *previously* by an OPEN macro.

Filename, the operand entry of the CLOSE macro, must specify the same symbolic name as assigned to the file with DTFMT header entry. A maximum of 16 files may be closed with one CLOSE macro instruction.

Input Tape Files. In case of tape input files, CLOSE is normally issued in the end-of-file routine for the file. This macro, when issued to an input file, initiates the rewind procedures for the tape file according to the specification of REWIND parameter entry.

Output Tape Files. In case of output files, this macro is issued when all the records for the file have been processed. Any record, logical or physical, that has not been already written on the output file is written out by the IOCS routines. In case a block is only partially filled at the time this macro is issued, IOCS writes a short block on the output tape file. After the last tape mark is written, the system checks and writes standard trailer label. After the trailer label two more tape marks are written and then the rewind option specified by the REWIND entry is executed, and the file is deactivated.

Notes: 1. It is possible that at times unfilled blocks of records (short blocks) may be written on EOV or EOF condition. When such a file is used for input, the IOCS has the capability of handling these short blocks and no error condition is given although the tape has been defined to have fixed-length blocked records.

2. If a CLOSE macro is issued to an input file before the end of data is reached, no label records are read or checked. The IOCS will simply execute the rewind option for the file and the file is then deactivated.

3. Whenever LIOCS are used to process output tape files, the block count for the trailer label is taken automatically by the LIOCS.

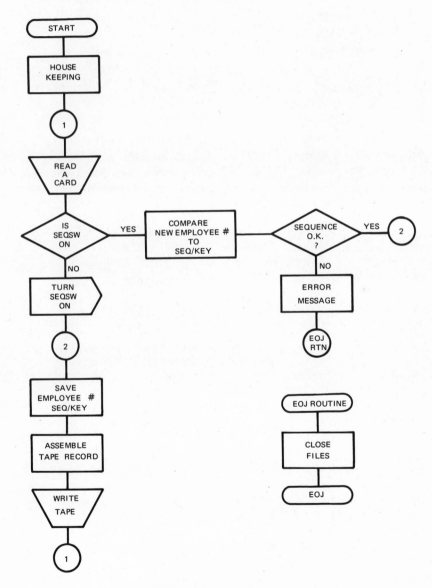

FIGURE 14.4. Suggested Flowchart.

Creating a tape file

Write program steps to read a card file and write each record on a tape file as 70 byte long logical records. The tape file is to be blocked with 15 logical records to a block. The card and tape record formats are given below.

Field Name	Card Columns	Tape Record
Employee Number	1 – 5	1 – 5
Employee Name	6 – 21	6 – 21
Street Address	22 – 47	22 – 47
City	48 – 60	48 – 60
State	61 – 65	61 – 65
Zip Code	66 – 70	66 – 70
Not used	71 – 80	

Figure 14.4 illustrates the block diagram for the problem and the coding is shown in Figure 14.5. The program is to check the sequence (ascending) of the input card file based on employee number. Checking of sequence is a usual and a very desirable practice when a tape file is being created. (See Figure 14.4 on page 387.)

Note: In Figure 14.4 the switch is *off* in the beginning

Name	Oper	Operand		
	START	0		
PRINTER	DTFPR	DEVADDR=SYS010,IOAREA1=LINE,		X
		BLKSIZE=14		
TAPE	DTFMT	DEVADDR=SYS011,BLKSIZE=1050,		X
		WORKA=YES,		X
		IOAREA1=BLOCK,RECFORM=FIXBLK,		X
		RECSIZE=70,TYPEFLE=OUTPUT		
INFILE	DTFCD	DEVADDR=SYS008,IOAREA=IN1,		X
		WORKA=YES,		X
		IOAREA2=IN2,EOFADDR=NOCARD		
BEGIN	BALR	2,0		
	USING	*,2		
	OPEN	TAPE,INFILE,PRINTER		
*			OPEN FILES	
F1	GET	INFILE,CARD	READ A CARD	
SWITCH	NOP	SEQCHK	SEQUENCE CHECK SWITCH	
	OI	SWITCH+1,X'F0'		
*			SET SWITCH ON	
F2	MVC	KEY,CARD	SAVE SEQUENCE KEY	

(continued)

```
            MVC        TAPEREC,CARD
*                                 ASSEMBLE TAPE RECORD
            PUT        TAPE,TAPEREC
*                                 WRITE TAPE RECORD
            B          F1
SEQCHK      CLC        CARD(5),KEY  COMPARE SEQ KEYS
            BNH        SEQERR       IF OUT OF SEQ, BRANCH
            B          F2
SEQERR      MVC        LINE,=C'SEQUENCE ERROR'
            PUT        PRINTER
NOCARD      CLOSE      TAPE,INFILE,PRINTER
            EOJ
LINE        DS         CL14         IOAREA FOR PRINTER FILE
BLOCK       DS         15CL70       BLOCKSIZE AREA FOR TAPE FILE
TAPEREC     DS         CL70         WORK AREA FOR TAPE FILE
IN1         DS         CL80         BUFFERS FOR
IN2         DS         CL80           THE CARD FILE
CARD        DS         CL80         WORK AREA FOR CARD FILE
KEY         DS         CL5
            END        BEGIN
```

FIGURE 14.5. Suggested Solution.

Processing a tape file

Write program steps to read the tape file created by the previous program and to print each tape record on a 1403 printer file.

```
Name        Oper       Operand
            START      0
TAPE        DTFMT      BLKSIZE=1050,DEVADDR=SYS011,          X
                       WORKA=YES,                            X
                       IOAREA1=BLOCK,RECFORM=FIXBLK,         X
                       RECSIZE=70,EOFADDR=TAPEEND
PRINTER     DTFPR      DEVADDR=SYS010,IOAREA1=LINE1,         X
                       BLKSIZE=70,IOAREA2=LINE2,             X
                       WORKA=YES
BEGIN       BALR       2,0
            USING      *,2
            OPEN       TAPE,PRINTER      OPEN FILES
            MVI        LINE,C'1'         CLEAR PRINT
```

(continued)

```
          MVC     LINE+1(69),LINE      AREA
READ      GET     TAPE,TAPEREC         READ TAPE FILE
          MVC     LINE,TAPEREC         ASSEMBLE PRINT LINE
          PUT     PRINTER,LINE         PRINT A LINE
          B       READ
TAPEEND   CLOSE   TAPE,PRINTER         CLOSE FILES
          EOJ
BLOCK     DS      15CL70               TAPE IOAREA
TAPEREC   DS      CL70                 TAPE WORK AREA
LINE1     DS      CL70                 PRINT FILE BUFFER 1
LINE2     DS      CL70                 PRINT FILE BUFFER 2
LINE      DS      CL70                 PRINT FILE WORK AREA
          END     BEGIN
```

FIGURE 14.6. A Suggested Solution.

Example of reblocking a tape file.

This example illustrates the technique of reblocking a tape file. The input tape file contains 15 logical records to a block and each logical record is 70 bytes in length. Write programming steps to create a tape file with a blocking factor of 25; the logical records are the same size as for the input tape file. Figure 14.7 below shows the coding for this problem.

```
Name      Oper    Operand
          START   0
TAPEIN    DTFMT   BLKSIZE=1050,DEVADDR=SYS011,          X
                  WORKA=YES,                            X
                  EOFADDR=ENDTAPE,IOAREA1=IN1,          X
                  IOAREA2=IN2,RECFORM=FIXBLK,           X
                  RECSIZE=70
TAPEOUT   DTFMT   BLKSIZE=1750,DEVADDR=SYS012,          X
                  WORKA=YES,                            X
                  IOAREA1=OUT1,IOAREA2=OUT2,            X
                  RECSIZE=70,                           X
                  RECFORM=FIXBLK,TYPEFLE=OUTPUT
BEGIN     BALR    4,0
          USING   *,4
          OPEN    TAPEIN,TAPEOUT
READ      GET     TAPEIN,AREA
          PUT     TAPEOUT,AREA
          B       READ
```

(continued)

```
ENDTAPE     CLOSE     TAPEIN,TAPEOUT
            EOJ
AREA        DS        CL70                COMMON WORK AREA
IN1         DS        15CL70              BUFFERS FOR
IN2         DS        15CL70                INPUT FILE
OUT1        DS        25CL70              BUFFERS FOR
OUT2        DS        25CL70                OUTPUT FILE
            END       BEGIN
```

FIGURE 14.7. Reblocking of Tape File.

[15]

Tape File Updating

15.1 Tape Update

The technique of updating files, one of the most common applications in business programming, will be examined in this chapter. There are numerous applications of file updating, such as:

1. Updating of existing data.
2. Addition of new records, e.g., records of new employees.
3. Deletion of obsolete records, etc.

The basic file updating logic[1] is explained below. Assume there are two magnetic tape files and both are in sequence by part number. One file is a master file; the other is a detail transaction file. Some quantity in the transaction record is to be added to the corresponding record on the master file and the updated master records are to be written on a new master file. There are three possible conditions that may arise in applying the detail transaction records to the master file records:

1. One or more detail records may match a single master record — active record.
2. There may not be a matching detail record for a master record — inactive record.
3. There may be detail records that do not match a master record — these are errors.

Note: In Figure 15.1 the switch is *off* in the beginning.

This logic of updating could be explained as follows:

Each detail record must be compared to a master record; if the identifying key fields match, the information from the detail record is applied to the matching master

---

[1] There are other and perhaps better methods but this is one of the basic and standard applications of tape file updating.

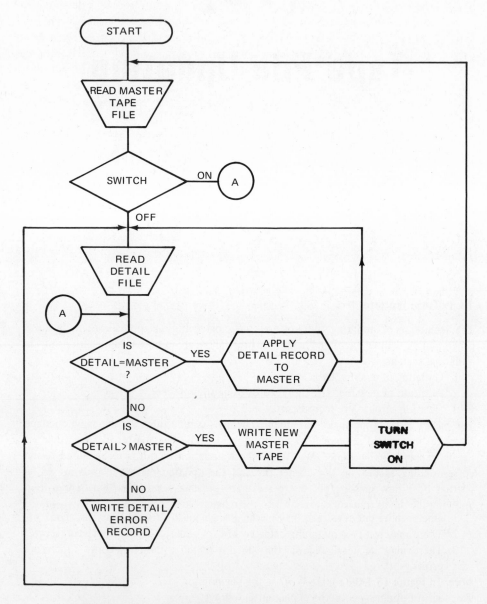

FIGURE 15.1. Tape Update Logic – A Generalized Flowchart.

record. If several detail records apply to the same master record, the program must continue reading the detail file without reading a new master record (of course, each detail record's information is to be applied to the master record).

On the other hand, if a master record is read without a corresponding detail record, the master record is written out on the new master tape without any change. The next step is to read in a new master record. If during processing we encounter a detail transaction record which is lower than the master record residing in core, it is written out on a separate unit, e.g., a tape file or printer, etc., as an error record and a new detail record is then read in.

Note: The update logic as explained here *assumes* that both files are in correct ascending sequence.

The example that follows illustrates the tape updating technique more specifically.

Example:

Write an update program which reads transaction cards and adds the quantity in cards to the corresponding records on the old master file (a magnetic tape file). Both files are in ascending order by customer number.

Note: If a detail record matches a master record, the quantity from the matching card record is added to the corresponding tape record's amount field. If a record on the tape file does have a matching detail record, indicating an inactive record, the tape record is written onto the new output tape without any alterations. In case of unmatched details, i.e., when a detail record does not have a matching master record (an error condition), the detail record is to be listed on a 1403 printer file. Figure 15.2 is the block diagram for this problem.

The block diagram shows that first a master record is read in. At this time, the switch is OFF (a NOP instruction) and as such a detail record is also read in. Next the key fields of the two records are compared. If the detail record is equal to the master record, the master is updated and the next detail record is read in. If the new detail record is not to be applied to the master record, it should be higher than the master (it is assumed that both files are in correct ascending order). At this time the updated master is written out on the new master tape, the program switch is turned ON, i.e., the NOP instruction is changed into an unconditional branch, and the program branches back to read a new master record. After reading the master record the control flows to the compare instruction. If the detail record at this time is lower than the master, an error condition, the detail record is written out on the printer file and a new detail record is read in.

End-of-File Routine. Entry to the end-of-file routine can be caused by one of two possibilities:

1. Detail file runs out before the master.
2. Master file runs out before the detail.

Figure 15.2 (Part 2) illustrates the logic for processing these possibilities.

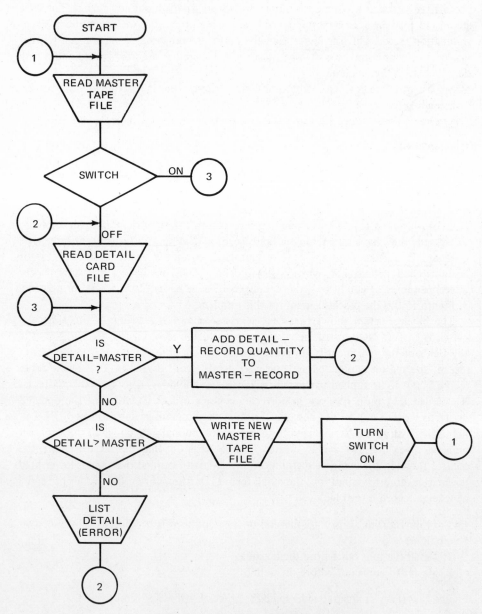

FIGURE 15.2. Tape Update Logic (Part 1).

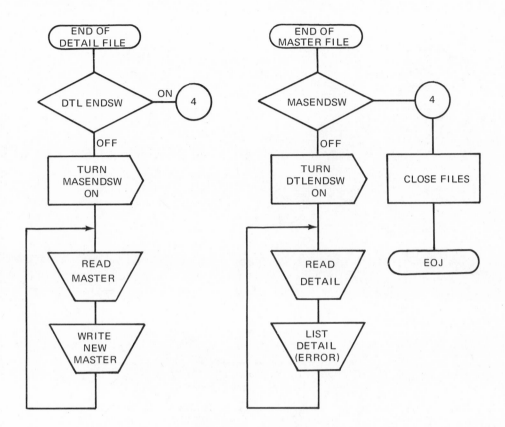

FIGURE 15.2. (Part 2).

Deletion of records

One of the common applications of file updates is to delete obsolete records from a file. In case of a card file the process is rather simple — remove the cards containing the obsolete records. The process is not that simple with tape files. One important point to note is that any time a tape file needs a change, the entire file has to be rewritten onto a new tape reel. In case of record deletions, we write all the records onto a new file except the ones that need to be deleted. The example that follows illustrates this process.

Example:

Write an update program that reads presorted customer transaction cards (sorted by customer number) and deletes the matching records from a master tape file. The new master file is to be written on tape. All deleted records are to be listed; and error records, i.e., a detail record without a matching master record, are to be written on an error tape file. Figure 15.3 illustrates a suggested solution for this problem.

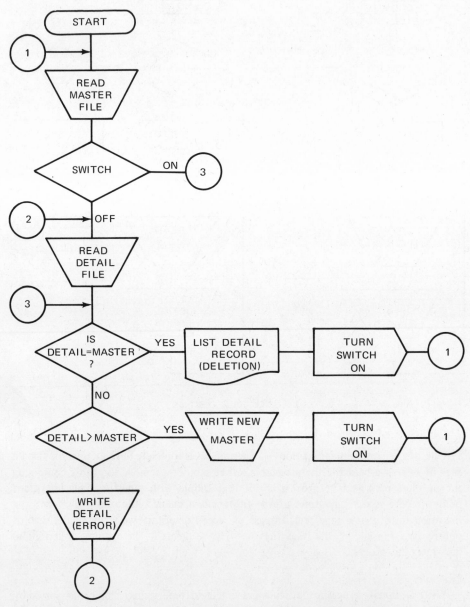

FIGURE 15.3. Flow Chart for Deletion of Records (Part 1).

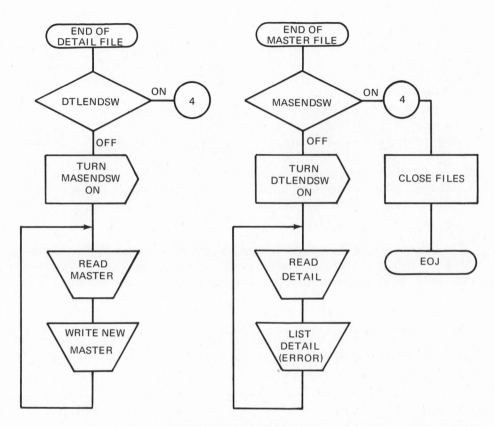

FIGURE 15.3. (Part 2).

As the switch is OFF to start with, the program reads a master and a detail record. The key fields are compared and one of the following three conditions may be encountered:

1. Key fields match, i.e., an equal compare.
2. Detail record is higher than the master record.
3. Detail record is lower than the master record.

For each of these conditions a different action needs to be taken. In case of an equal compare, indicating that a deletion is in order, we list the master record on the printer, turn the switch OFF and branch back to read another master and detail record. The two records just read are compared again and this time let us assume that the detail record is higher than the master. This means that the master record is to be written out on the new master file without any change. After issuing a PUT instruction for the new master we turn the switch ON and go back to read another master record. As the switch is ON the detail file will not be read, instead the program will branch to the compare instruction.

Note: Please note that at this point we read the master file and not the detail file. The reason for this is that we already have a detail record in core.

The other possibility is that the detail record is lower than the master record. This indicates an error condition. In such cases, write the detail record on the tape file for error records and then branch back to read another detail record. The logic for records can be summed up as:

1. If detail and master records match — do not write the master record on the new master file. This will delete the master record.
2. In case of unmatched master, i.e., a master record does not have a matching detail record, indicated by master-less-than-detail condition, the old master record is written on the new master file.
3. In case of unmatched detail record, indicated by detail-less-than-master condition, list the error detail record on an error file.

Addition of records to tape files

The following example illustrates the basic technique of updating a tape file by adding new records to the existing master file. It is important to point out again that with tape file updates we *always* have to *create* a new master file.

Note: In this type of tape updating application the error condition arises when we encounter a detail record that has a matching master record.

Figure 15.4 is a suggested flow chart for this problem.

Complete tape file update

In this chapter we have discussed three different updating possibilities and each was treated separately. More often than not, the programmer may be called upon to update a tape file with all three situations applying to the same file. Consider now a problem which will introduce this concept.

Example:

Detail file specifications:

Blocking factor = 15.
Record length = 70 characters.
Key field is located position 1 — 10.
There are three different types of records on the detail file and each is identified by a code in position 70. If the record type code is U, add the amount field (positions 65 — 69) to the corresponding field in the matching master record. There may be more than one detail record for a given master record. If the code is D, delete the corresponding master record and if the code is A, add the detail record on the new master file.

Old Master file specifications:

Blocking factor = 15.
Record length = 70.

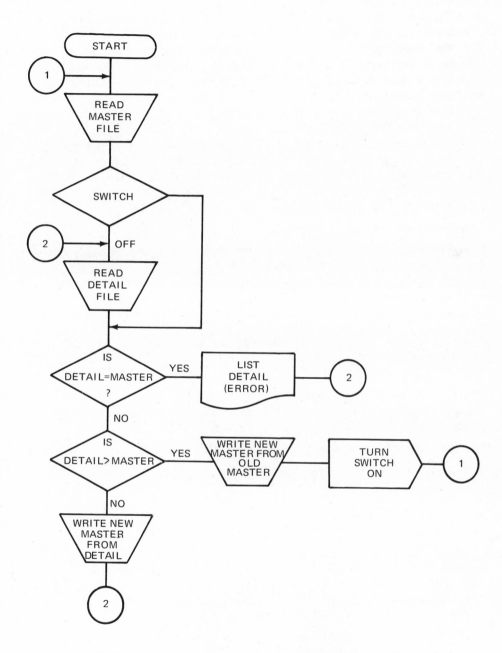

FIGURE 15.4. Tape Update Logic (Addition of Records) (Part 1).

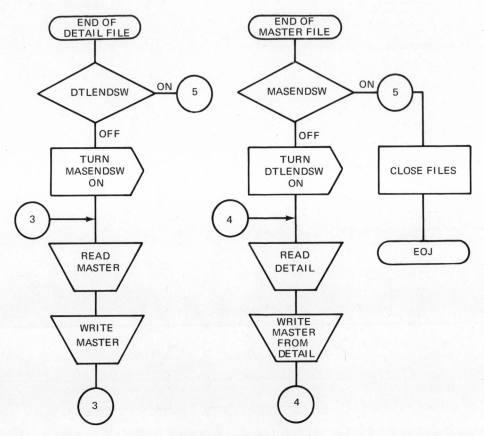

FIGURE 15.4. (Part 2).

New Master file specifications:

Same as the old master file.

Figure 15.5 is the flow chart for this problem. In this type of file updating there are two types of error conditions.

1. The first error condition results when a detail record that is to be added to the master file has a matching master record.
2. The second error condition results when we have a deletion record that does not have a matching master record.

The flow chart in Figure 15.5 shows that in case of an equal compare between a detail and a master record, the first step is to see if the detail record contains code U in position 70. If so, apply the amount field of the detail record to the corresponding

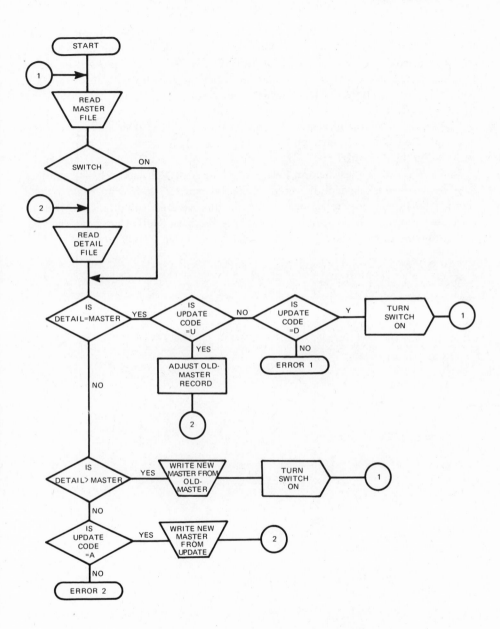

FIGURE 15.5. Complete Update of a Tape File.

master record and then branch back to read another detail record. If, on the other hand, the matching detail record contains a D in position 70, indicating that the matching master record is to be deleted, turn the switch OFF and proceed to read a new master and a new detail record. The third possibility is that the detail record is neither type D or type U. This means an error condition, which is identified by ERROR1 in the flow chart.

The second error condition arises when a detail record lower than the master record is encountered and it is not type A record. This error condition is identified by ERROR2 in the flow chart.

In the flow chart illustrated in Figure 15.5, the ERROR1 and ERROR2 routines have been left unexpanded. It would be a good practice for you to expand these routines taking appropriate actions on each of the two error conditions and then to code this problem. The end-of-file routines have also been omitted since they are very similar to those discussed in the previous update problems in this chapter.

[16]

Direct Access Storage Devices (DASD)

16.1 Introduction to Direct Access Storage Devices

A direct access storage device (DASD) is one on which each physical record has a definite location and a unique address. This allows us to store records on a DASD in such a way that any one record can be located without extensive searching. Records on a DASD can be accessed directly rather than serially.

Several DASDs are available for System 360. These devices differ in speed, capacity and physical appearance. However, they are very similar as far as recording of data, format of records and programming logic. DASDs available for System 360 are listed below.

1. Drive with removable disk packs: 2311 and 2314.
2. Drive with non-removable disk packs: 2302.
3. Drum: 2301 and 2303.
4. Data Cell drive: 2321.

In this chapter only the first two devices, i.e., 2311 and 2314 DASDs, will be discussed.

2311 Disk Storage Drive. The 2311 is a drive with removable disk packs. Each disk pack consists of six disks mounted on a vertical shaft. Each disk is 14 inches in diameter and is made of metal with magnetic oxide coating on both sides. The top surface of the top disk and the bottom surface of the bottom disk are *not* used for recording purposes, thus each pack contains *ten* recording surfaces.

FIGURE 16.1. 2311 Disk Storage Drive.

2314 Direct Access Storage Facility. The 2314 consists of nine different drives and a control unit. Any eight of the nine drives can be online at a time. The ninth drive is used as backup unit in case one of the other drives becomes inoperative or requires servicing. Each of these nine packs consists of eleven disks with a total of 20 recording surfaces (the top surface of the top disk and the bottom surface of the bottom disk are not used for recording). All nine disk packs are removable.

Recording of Data. The recording surface of each disk is divided into tracks. A track can be defined as a circumference of the recording surface.

FIGURE 16.2. 2314 Direct Access Storage Facility.

FIGURE 16.3. Disk Pack.

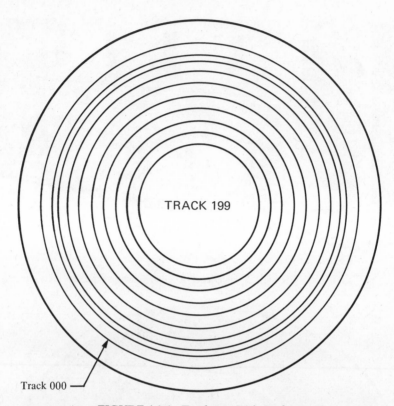

FIGURE 16.4. Tracks on Disk Surface.

Note: The tracks are numbered 000 (outermost) to 202 (innermost). Track numbers 200 − 202 are alternate tracks and are used only if any tracks (000 to 199) should become defective.

On 2311 and 2314 DASDs, data is recorded serially bit-by-bit, 8 bits per byte, along a track. The parity bit is not recorded. The number of tracks per recording surface and the capacity of a track for 2311 and 2314 disk packs are shown below. Each recording surface contains a fixed number of spare tracks, known as alternate tracks. These alternates are used by the system to store data in case one or more of the regular tracks become defective. Each track, in addition to regular data, contains some non-data information, such as: the address of the track, address of each record, length of each record, and gaps between records. This non-data information is used by the IOCS routines for proper processing of data records. The non-data information and the data record is usually referred to as a whole with the term *data record.*

Access Mechanism. Each DASD has some type of access mechanism which transfers data to and from the device. Basically, each device contains a number of read/write heads (one for each recording surface) that transfers data as the recording surface of the disk rotates past them. For 2311 and 2314, the access mechanism consists of a

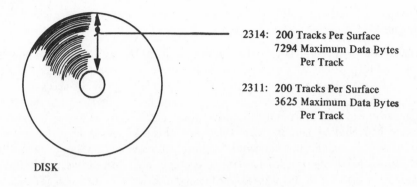

2314: 200 Tracks Per Surface
7294 Maximum Data Bytes
Per Track

2311: 200 Tracks Per Surface
3625 Maximum Data Bytes
Per Track

DISK

FIGURE 16.5. Track Capacities.

number of arms, each arm supporting two read/write heads. This comb-type mechanism moves horizontally, back and forth, to 203 different positions. The access mechanism for 2311 consists of five arms, each with two read/write heads, one for each surface. The mechanism for 2314 is very similar to that of 2311 except that it has ten arms each supporting two read/write heads.

FIGURE 16.6. Disk Pack With Mounted Heads

Note: Only one of the heads can be transferring data at a time. The access mechanism moves as a unit and all of the read/write heads are positioned in the same vertical plane.

Cylinder Concept. On a DASD the movement of the access mechanism represents a considerable portion of the time taken to locate and transfer data. If data was recorded in consecutive tracks (horizontally), the time taken by the access mechanism to move from one track to another would result in considerable time wastage. To minimize this wasted time and to improve the efficiency of the device, a very unique concept of recording data has been developed. This is known as the *cylinder concept.* The basic logic behind this concept of data recording is that instead of recording on consecutive horizontal tracks, the data is recorded in consecutive vertical tracks. For example, in the case of 2314 DASD all twenty read/write heads are positioned in the same vertical plane, thereby making all twenty tracks available for recording without any movement of the access mechanism. A cylinder of data can be defined as the amount of recording surface that is accessible with one positioning of the access mechanism. This allows us to store a large amount of data in a single cylinder, thereby minimizing the movements of the access mechanism.

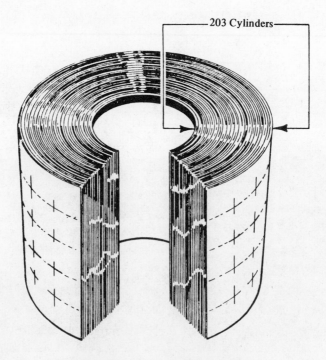

FIGURE 16.7. Cylinder Concept.

2314 Storage Capacity.

Capacity per track = 7,294.
Capacity per cylinder (20 tracks per cylinder) = 145,880.
Capacity per pack (200 cylinders per pack) = 29,176,000.
Capacity per 2314 facility (8 packs) = 233,408,000.

2311 Storage Capacity.

Capacity per track = 3,625.
Capacity per cylinder (10 tracks per cylinder) = 36,250.
Capacity per pack (200 cylinders per pack) = 7,250,000.
Capacity per 2311 drive (1 pack per drive) = 7,250,000.
Note: 1. All capacities are in bytes.
  2. All figures are based on one record per track.
  3. The capacities listed above do not include the alternate tracks.
  4. In the case of 2314 the figures for the facility do not include the capacity for the ninth back-up drive.

Track format

It was mentioned earlier that each track contains a certain amount of non-data information. This information is a function of, and is controlled by, the control unit. Each track has a home address, a track descriptor record (R0), followed by one or more data records (R1 – Rn). Each record has a count area, a key area (this field is optional), and a data record. A gap (identified as G in the figure below) separates each area on a track.

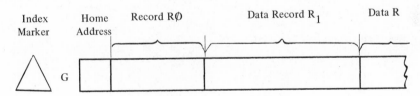

FIGURE 16.8. Track Format.

Index Point. For each pack of 2311 and 2314 DASD there is one index point (index marker). The beginning of a track is signalled when the index point is detected. It is important to note that there is only one index point per disk pack and all tracks on a pack are synchronized by the same index point.

Gaps. Gaps separate areas on tracks and contain no data. The length of the gap varies with the device, the location of the gap and the length of the preceding area.

Home Address (7 bytes). Home address, one on each track, defines the condition and location of the track. Home address is the first information area on a track following the index point. The format of the home address field is as follows:

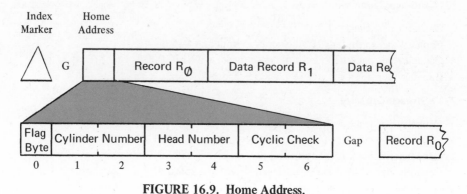

FIGURE 16.9. Home Address.

Flag (1 byte). The flag byte of the home address field indicates the track condition (operative or defective) and the use of the track (primary or alternate).

Cylinder Number (2 bytes). This 2 byte field indicates the number of the cylinder within which data is stored.

Read/Write Head Number (2 bytes). These 2 bytes specify the read/write head that services this track.

Cyclic Check (2 bytes). These 2 bytes are used for error detection.
Note: The combination of cylinder and read/write head numbers is used to locate a specific track.

Gap: The gap is generated by the control unit and serves to separate the home address from the following record.

Track descriptor record (R0)

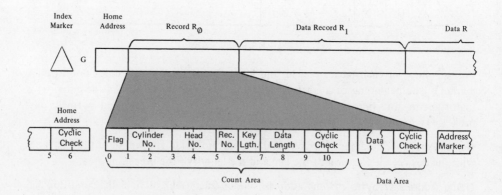

FIGURE 16.10. Track Descriptor Record.

The track descriptor record, sometimes referred to as R0, is the first record after the home address. The IBM programming systems use this area to store certain information about the track. The information stored in R0 record enables the system to move the entire contents of a track to alternate tracks if a portion of the primary track becomes defective.

Primary Track: A primary track is the original track on which data is stored.

Alternate Track: An alternate track contains data that has been repositioned from a primary (defective) track.

Count Area (11 bytes). The count area of R0 record, 11 bytes in length, is composed of the flag, cylinder number, read/write head number, record number, key length, data length and cyclic check bytes.

Flag (1 byte). The flag byte of R0 indicates the track condition (operative or defective) and the use of the track (primary or alternate).

Record Identifier (5 bytes). The record identifier (ID) field is composed of three sub-fields. These are: cylinder number; read/write head number; and, record number. The cylinder number field is 2 bytes in length and contains the cylinder number of the track on which R0 is written. In case of a defective track, the system stores, in this field, the cylinder number of the alternate track to which the information is moved. To serve as cross reference, the system also stores the cylinder number of the defective track in the cylinder number field of R0 of the alternate track. The read/write head number field (2 bytes) contains the read/write head number for the disk surface on which the record is stored. In case of a defective track, the head number that services the alternate track is stored in these 2 bytes. The head number of the defective track is stored in the head number field of the alternate track, thus providing a cross reference between the defective and the alternate track. The figure below illustrates this cross reference technique.

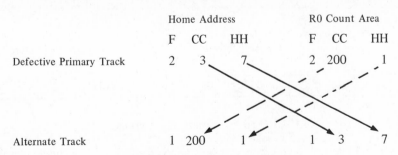

FIGURE 16.11. Cross-Referencing.

Note: 2 in the flag byte indicates a defective primary track.
    1 in the flag byte indicates an operative alternate track.
    0 in the flag byte indicates an operative primary track.

Record Number (1 byte). This byte, of the count area, designates the sequential number of the record on the track. For track descriptor record this field is always zero.

Key Length (1 byte). This byte specifies the number of bytes in the key area of the record (excluding cyclic check bytes). If the record has no key, this byte contains a zero. In case of R0 record, this byte is always set to zero (R0 records do not contain a key area).

Data Length (2 bytes). This field specifies the number of bytes in the data area of R0 record (excluding the cyclic check bytes). In the IBM programming system this field's value is set to eight.

Note: A data length of zero indicates the end of a logical file and upon reading end-of-file record the control unit sends a special indication to the CPU.

Cyclic Check (2 bytes). These 2 bytes are used for error detection.

Data Area (10 bytes). This area of the R0 record is used by the IBM programming systems for recording the identifier of the last record on the track and the number of bytes still available for writing new records. The last 2 bytes of data area field are used for cyclic check.

Data records (R1 — Rn)

One or more data records can follow R0 on a track. A data record, in addition to programmer-assigned data, contains certain non-data information used to specify the track address, record number and length of the key and data areas of the record. There are two possible data record formats: Count-Data Format; and, Count-Key-Data Format.

Note: These two types of records can not be intermixed in one DASD file. All records on a file must be of the same format.

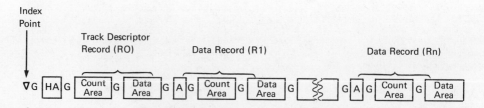

FIGURE 16.12. Count-Data Format.

Count Area (11 bytes). The count area is composed of the flag, cylinder number, read/write head number, record number, key length, data length and two cyclic check bytes. Bytes 1 through 8 are developed in the CPU by the IBM programming systems.

Flag Byte (1 byte). Same description as given earlier in this chapter applies to this field.

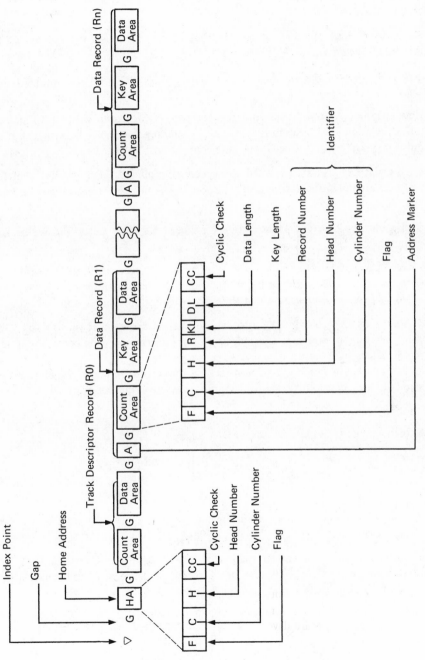

FIGURE 16.13. Count-Key-Data Format.

Cylinder Number (2 bytes). These 2 bytes contain the cylinder number in which this record is stored.

Read/Write Head Number (2 bytes). These 2 bytes contain the number of the read/write head that services this record.

Record Number (1 byte). This byte designates the sequential number of the record on the track.

Key Length (1 byte). In case the data records are formatted with keys, this byte specifies the number of bytes in the key field (excluding the cyclic check bytes). If the record is formatted without keys, this byte contains zero value.

Data Length (2 bytes). These 2 bytes specify the number of bytes (not including cyclic check bytes) in the data area of the record. A value of *zero* in this field *indicates* the end of a logical file.

Cyclic Check (2 bytes). These 2 bytes are used for error detection by the IBM programming systems.

Key Area (1 to 255 bytes). The key area (present only in records formatted with keys) can contain record identification information such as account number, policy number, etc. Two cyclic check bytes are added to the key area by the control unit.

Data Area. This area contains the information identified by the count and key areas. Data information of this area is arranged by the programmer. The control unit adds two cyclic check bytes to the data area.

If the data length field of the count area for the record contains zero, end-of-file is indicated. In such cases, the data area contains only two cyclic check bytes.

Record formats

As on magnetic tape files, records on DASD may be:

Fixed Length	(with or without key)
Variable Length	(with or without key)
Undefined	(with or without key)

If keys are used in formatting records, all records in the file must have keys and all keys must be the same length.

Fixed Length, Unblocked. This means that all records in the file are the same length and each data area contains only one logical record. If the records are formatted with keys, the key is usually not repeated in the data area.

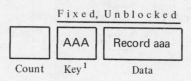

Fixed, Unblocked

Count   Key[1]   Data

Fixed Length, Blocked. All records in the file are the same length and each data area contains a block of more than one logical record. All blocks (physical records) in the file are the same length except for a possible short last block. The key area, if present, one for each block, usually contains the key of the highest record in the block. In addition, each logical record also contains a key so that records can be identified during processing.

Fixed, Blocked

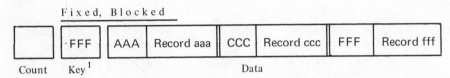

Count   Key[1]   Data

Variable Length, Unblocked. The records in the file are varied in length and unblocked, i.e., one logical record to a physical record. Records of this type, in addition to data information, contain two special fields — block length field (BL) and a record length field (RL). The BL is always the first 4 bytes of the block and indicates the number of bytes in the block including itself. The RL field is always the first 4 bytes of the logical record and designates the number of bytes in the logical record including itself.

Variable, Unblocked

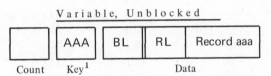

Count   Key[1]   Data

Variable Length, Blocked. Each data area on the file contains more than one logical record. The physical and logical records are of varying lengths. The BL and RL fields have the same significance as for the variable unblocked.

Variable, Blocked

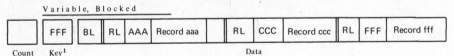

Count   Key[1]   Data

Undefined. This format is provided to permit handling of records that do not conform to the formats described above. Records of this type do not carry BL or RL fields.

Undefined

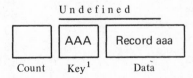

Count   Key[1]   Data

Track Capacity. Earlier in this section the maximum capacities for a track of 2311 and 2314 disk packs were given. This maximum can be achieved only when there is one data record per track (formatted without keys). As a track is divided to contain

[1] This field (Key) is optional.

multiple data records, the additional non-data information, such as address markers, count areas and gaps, reduce the number of bytes available for the data itself. The table in Figure 16.14 lists the number of records that can be contained in one track. It accounts for the bytes used up by home address, track descriptor record, address markers, count fields, gaps, etc. It shows the number of physical records (blocked or unblocked), of a given length, that can be contained on one track.

Maximum Bytes per Record Formatted Without Keys		Records per Track	Maximum Bytes per Record Formatted With Keys	
2311	2314		2311	2314
3625	7294	1	3605	7249
1740	3520	2	1720	3476
1131	2298	3	1111	2254
830	1693	4	811	1649
651	1332	5	632	1288
532	1092	6	512	1049
447	921	7	428	877
384	793	8	364	750
334	694	9	315	650
295	615	10	275	571
263	550	11	244	506
236	496	12	217	452
213	450	13	194	407
193	411	14	174	368
177	377	15	158	333
162	347	16	143	304
149	321	17	130	277
138	298	18	119	254
127	276	19	108	233
118	258	20	99	215
109	241	21	90	198
102	226	22	82	183
95	211	23	76	168
88	199	24	69	156
82	187	25	63	144
77	176	26	58	133
72	166	27	53	123
67	157	28	48	114
63	148	29	44	105
59	139	30	40	96

FIGURE 16.14. Track Capacity Table.

Example:

Device is 2311, records are unblocked and formatted without keys and data length is 125 bytes. Calculate the number of records that can be contained in one track. From the table in Figure 16.14, we see that a total of 19 records can be contained in one track.

Example:

Consider the same data length as in the previous example. In this case, however, assume that the blocking factor is 3. Now we have a physical record of 375 bytes. From the table in Figure 16.14, we see that 8 such records can be contained in one track or that 24 logical records can be contained in one track.

Records are blocked on DASD for the same basic reasons as on magnetic tape – to save storage space and to reduce data transfer time. However, in case of DASD blocking of records does not always save storage space. Consider, for example, a file containing 300 byte long unblocked records. From the track capacity table we find that 9 such records can be contained in one track of 2311 disk pack. Now consider the same records; however, this time they are blocked 4 logical records to a block. This gives us a record length of 1200 bytes. The table entries show that for the same device only 2 such records (8 logical records) can be contained on one track. From this it is clear that as the blocking factor is increased, DASD track utilization varies in efficiency. However, the foregoing is not a definite disadvantage of blocking. The main disadvantage occurs when blocked records are not processed consecutively. It takes no longer to locate a block than it does a logical record, but it definitely takes longer to transmit the block to and from storage.

In some cases the table in Figure 16.14 can not be used, for example, data records of 58 bytes or less in case of 2311 DASD. In such cases, the number of records that can be contained on a track must be calculated by using certain formulas. In this text we will restrict our applications to such records that can be taken care of by the track capacity table in Figure 16.14.

File organization

Until now we have discussed only sequential file organization. By their nature, card and magnetic tape files can not be organized any other way. Sequential organization, though easy to deal with, leaves much to be desired. In such files, records can be retrieved only sequentially. DASD facilities give us a better choice regarding file organization. Three different types of file organization methods can be used with System 360 DASD files. These are: Sequential; Indexed Sequential; and, Direct organization. Before discussing these three organization methods in detail, it is necessary to define a few terms.

Volatility. This term refers to the amount of additions and deletions of records from a file. A file with a high rate of additions and deletions is said to be a volatile file. On the other hand, a file with a relatively small number of additions or deletions is said to be a static file. Volatility of a file is of significant concern when choosing a particular file organization method. Additions and deletions to a file can be handled more efficiently by some methods of organization rather than others.

Activity: Activity can be defined as the amount of records that are processed in a given run. A file with low activity should be organized in such a way that any record can be located without a great deal of searching.

Size: The size of a file also has a great bearing in the selection of the file organization method. For example, a file so large that it can not be available to the system at one time must be given special thought.

In addition to the above-mentioned characteristics, the growth potential of a file must also be kept in mind.

DASD file organization methods

Sequential Organization. In a sequential file, records are organized solely on the basis of their successive physical location in the file. Tape files are always organized this way. The records are usually read or updated in the same order in which they appear on the file. For example, to read the seventieth record, it is necessary to read the first sixty-nine records. In this type of file organization, it is not possible to locate individual records easily. To add or delete records from a sequential file, it is usually necessary to rewrite the entire file. This becomes very inefficient in the case of low activity files. Generally, sequential organization is desirable if a file is highly active or extremely volatile or completely static (very few changes).

From a programmer's point of view, sequential DASD files are easiest to plan, program and process. Their overall logic is the same as discussed with tape files.

Direct (Random) Organization. In direct organization method, each record in the file is assigned a unique storage address, not usually in key sequence, but based on some predictable relationship between the key of the record and the address of that record on the DASD. This relationship is developed by the programmer. Direct organization is most useful when individual records must be located with a minimum of time delay.

Indexed Sequential Organization. This is one of the more desirable file organization methods, as it combines the facilities provided by sequential and direct organization methods without adding any great weaknesses. In indexed sequential organization method, records are stored sequentially by key, on one track after another. The IBM programming systems (Indexed Sequential Access Methods — ISAM) construct indexes for the various records and store these on the DASD. An indexed sequential file is very similar to a sequential file in that rapid sequential processing is possible. At the same time, it is possible to locate individual records in an indexed sequential file by referring to the indexes associated with the file. In this method of file organization, the programming system has control over the location of the individual records. The programmer, therefore, needs to do very little I/O processing. Most of the I/O is done by the system itself.

DASD file processing methods

The LIOCS routines support three types of processing for files on DASD. These are:

Sequential Access Methods	(SAM)
Direct Access Methods	(DAM)
Indexed Sequential Access Methods	(ISAM)

Sequential Access Methods (SAM). Sequential processing is used to read/write and process successive records of a logical file in a serial manner. DASD records are processed starting with a beginning address and then continuing serially through successive tracks and cylinders until the ending address.

A sequential file on DASD is created within one or more sets of limits (these limits are supplied by the job control extent cards). The records within each set must be adjacent to each other and contained within one disk pack. Different sets of a multiset file are not required to be adjacent or on the same volume. The IOCS routines automatically process each set as desired by the problem program. The LIOCS macros GET/PUT are used to process such files.

Direct Access Methods. The Direct Access Method (DAM) provides a method of processing records contained on 2311 or 2314 that are usually organized in a random manner. It is important to note that DAM is a method of processing records and not an organization method. In practice, random organization of data requires that the programmer have some method of determining the location of a given record in the file. To do this, the programmer supplies the IOCS with a record-location reference, which enables the IOCS to locate the particular record for processing. The location reference consists of two parts: a track reference; and, a record reference. The track reference specifies the track or the first of multiple tracks to be searched for locating the given record. The record reference may be the record key (if the records are formatted with keys), or the record identifier (ID). ID is in the count area of each DASD record.

The basic macros used for direct access method of processing are READ and WRITE. Various options that are available with these two macros permit records to be read, written, updated, replaced, or added to the file, thereby giving us the capability of maintaining a logical file in either random or sequential order.

Indexed Sequential Access Method (ISAM). DASD records contained in an indexed sequential file may be processed in random or sequential order by the use of control information. Both orders of processing use the control information of the records (such as employee number, policy number, etc.), which is located in the key area of each record. It is possible to process any record stored at any location in the file by using the random method. To accomplish this, the programmer supplies ISAM with the control information (key) of the desired record, enabling the ISAM to search for the particular record and make it available for processing by the problem program.

ISAM provides facilities to create an indexed sequential file and then add to, read from, and update records in that file. At the time of loading (creation) an indexed sequential file onto DASD, ISAM constructs and stores indexes for all of the records in the logical file. These indexes are created in such a way that records can be processed randomly or sequentially. In case of new additions to the file, ISAM updates the indexes to account for the new records.

The basic macros used for processing indexed sequential files are READ/WRITE and GET/PUT. READ and WRITE macros are used for random processing, and GET and PUT macros are used for sequential processing. For files organized in indexed sequential method, the programming system (ISAM) has control over the location of the individual records. Therefore, the programmer needs to do very little I/O programming; the ISAM does almost all of it for him.

Note: The random, or direct access method (DAM), is not discussed in any more detail in this text because of the fact that the majority of programming installations and programmers find the indexed sequential organization and processing methods as efficient and convenient, or more so. The indexed sequential organization and processing methods are discussed in Section 16.3.

DASD labels

DASD labels, like the labels for magnetic tape files, are used to identify the pack and the logical file(s) on it. The DASD labels follow the same general pattern as the labels for tape files. The standard DASD labels include one volume label for each pack and one or more file labels for each logical file. The following discussion will describe briefly the organization and formats of standard DASD labels.

Note: In the case of magnetic tapes, it is seldom that one uses one tape reel to hold more than one logical file. On the other hand, in case of DASDs it is a common practice to record multiple files on one pack.

Volume Labels. The standard DASD volume label identifies the entire volume and offers volume protection. The volume label, first label to be encountered, is usually the third record on the first track of the first cylinder, i.e., third record on track 0, cylinder 0. The first two records, 0 and 1, contain binary zeros. The reason for this is to make all packs compatible with SYSRES pack where the first two records are used as IPL (Initial Program Load) records.

A standard volume label consists of a count area, a 4 byte key area, and an 80 byte data area. The key area and the first 4 bytes of the data area contain the label identifier VOL1. The remaining 76 bytes of the data area are used for such identification information as the volume serial number and the address of the area where the file labels for this pack are stored. The volume label is generally written once, when the pack is received at the installation. IBM programming systems allow one to seven additional volume labels following the standard volume label. However, in the case of DOS processing, such labels are bypassed by the OPEN routines. For a complete breakdown of the different fields of the standard volume label, see Appendix 5.

Standard File Labels. The standard DASD file labels (five different formats) contain information that is used to identify the logical file, give its location(s) on the disk pack (it is possible for a logical file to be scattered over more than one area on a pack), and offer file protection. In the case of DASD, the labels for all logical files on a volume are grouped together and stored in a specific area of the pack known as the *Volume Table of Contents* (VTOC).

The number and format of labels required for any one logical file is governed by the file organization methods and the number of separate areas (also known as *extents*) of the pack used to contain the file.

Note: The data records for a logical file on DASD may be contained within one area of the pack, or may be scattered in different areas. The standard file labels of a logical file describe the limits (starting and ending addresses) of each area used by the file.

Standard File Label Formats. All standard file labels are formatted with count, key and data areas. The key and data area of a label consists of 140 bytes. Five different label formats are provided. The first four are used with DOS and the fifth is used only by Operation System 360 (OS/360).

Format—1. This format is used for all logical files with standard labels. It has a 44 byte key area and a 96 byte data area. Format—1 label is always the first standard file label. This label, in addition to file identification information, contains fields that provide the addresses of three separate DASD extents for the file. In case a logical file is scattered over more than three separate areas on one pack, the Format—1 label points to the second label set up for the file. If a logical file needs more than one pack, the Format—1 label is repeated for each additional DASD volume.

Format—2. This format is required only for files organized by the Indexed Sequential File Management System. If an indexed sequential file needs more than one volume, this type of label is used only on the volume containing the cylinder index.

Format—3. This type of label is used if a logical file is scattered over more than three separate areas (extents). The Format—3 label is pointed to by the Format—1 label for the file. In case a logical file is scattered over more than one volume, this type of label is repeated on each additional volume.

Format—4. This type of label is used to define the VTOC itself. It is always the first label in the VTOC. This type of label contains information regarding the location and number of available tracks in the alternate track area.

Format—5. This type of label is used by the Operating System/360 (OS/360).

Note: For a detailed breakdown of the different fields in these various labels, see Appendix 5.

16.2 Sequential Processing of DASD Files

The DTFSD macro instruction defines sequential processing for a file contained on a

DASD. The DTFSD macro can be used with both the 2311 and 2314 DASDs. The DTFSD macro, with its keyword operands, is included for each sequential DASD file (input or output) to be processed by the problem program. The rules for the DTFSD header and detail entries are the same as discussed earlier in the text.

A list of the DTFSD parameters is given below.

Req'd	BLKSIZE=
	EOFADDR=
	IOAREA1=

Opt'l	DEVADDR=SYSnnn
	DEVICE=
	ERROPT=
	IOAREA2=
	IOREG=(nn)
	MODNAME=
	RECFORM=
	RECSIZE=
	TYPEFLE=
	UPDATE=YES
	VERIFY=YES
	WLRERR=
	WORKA=YES

Note: Not all of the possible entries for DTFSD macro have been included in the list above. Some of the entries have been left out as this text does not include the functions supported by such entries. In the following pages, explanation is given only for those entries which have an expanded or different meaning than what has already been explained in the previous DTFxx macros.

BLKSIZE=n

This entry specifies the length of the I/O area. In case of variable or undefined record format, this entry is used to specify the length of the I/O area needed for the largest record.

DEVADDR=

This operand must specify the symbolic unit to be associated with this file if an extent statement specification is not provided (extent statement is not required for single volume input files). If an extent statement is provided, its specification over-rides a DEVADDR specification. This entry is used to specify the device on which data is located. If omitted, the 2311 is assumed.

DEVICE=2311 or 2314

ERROPT=IGNORE or SKIP or NAME

This operand is used to specify the action to be taken by the system in case a read or write error can not be corrected by the disk error routines of the IOCS. In the case of input files, the block is read at least 226 times before it is considered as an error block. If an error still exists after reading 226 times, the job is terminated unless ERROPT entry is included. If ERROPT entry is included, the system, after 226 read tries, takes the action specified by the ERROPT entry. For DASD input files, the action taken is the same as described in DTFMT macro's ERROPT entry. For DASD output files the only acceptable parameters are IGNORE or the name of the programmer error routine. In case UPDATE=YES is specified for the file, the ERROPT=SKIP causes write errors to be ignored. If WLRERR entry is not included for the file, the ERROPT entry applies to wrong length records as well.

IOAREA1=name

For input files this operand serves the same function as explained in previous DTFxx macros in the text. In the case of DASD output files, the first 8 bytes of the area must be alloted for IOCS to construct the count field for the record. The I/O area must begin on a halfword boundary.

IOAREA2=name

If two I/O areas are to be used by the GET or PUT macro, this operand is specified. The same rules as outlined for IOAREA1 apply to IOAREA2.

IOREG=(r)

This operand specifies one of the general purpose registers $(2 - 12)$ in which IOCS puts the address of the record that is available for processing. For output files, IOCS places the address of the area where the programmer can build a record.

The IOREG entry must be included if blocked input or output records are to be processed in the I/O area or if two I/O areas are being used and the records are processed in the I/O areas and not in work area.

Whenever this entry is included for a file, the DTF entry WORKA *must* be omitted.

UPDATE=YES

This operand is specified if DASD records are to be read, processed and then transferred back (PUT) to the same disk record location from which they were read.

A PUT for a DASD record must always be followed by a GET before another PUT is issued. GETs can be issued as many times in succession as desired. When updating a disk file, the record is not actually transferred with the PUT but with the next GET for the file.

VERIFY=YES

This entry is used if the programmer wants to check the parity of 2311 records after they are written. If this entry is omitted, any records written on 2311 are not verified.

Sequential DASD Module (SDMODXX)

Sequential DASD module generation macros differ from other IOCS module generation macros. The DASD file characteristics are separated into ten categories, and each category has a unique macro instruction associated with it.

SDMODFI: Sequential DASD Module, Fixed length records, Input file.
SDMODFO: Sequential DASD Module, Fixed length records, Output file.
SDMODFU: Sequential DASD Module, Fixed length records, Update file.
SDMODVI: Sequential DASD Module, Variable length records, Input file.
SDMODVO: Sequential DASD Module, Variable length records, Output file.
SDMODVU: Sequential DASD Module, Variable length records, Update file.
SDMODUI: Sequential DASD Module, Undefined records, Input file.
SDMODUO: Sequential DASD Module, Undefined records, Output file.
SDMODUU: Sequential DASD Module, Undefined records, Update file.
SDMODW: Sequential DASD Module, Work file.

The operands for these ten macros are listed below.

Name	Oper	Operand
	SDMODxx	CONTROL=YES
		ERROPT=YES
		UPDATE=YES

Recommended Module Name List for SDMODxx. Each name will begin with a 3-character prefix (IJG) and consist of a 5-character field corresponding to the options permitted in the generation of the module.

Name List for GET/OUT Type Modules for SDMODxx name = IJGabcde.

a = F if SDMODFx
   = V if SDMODVx
   = U if SDMODUx
b = U if SDMODxU
   = I if SDMODxI
   = O if SDMODxO
c = E if ERROPT=YES is specified
   = Z if ERROPT=YES is not specified
d = T if TRUNCS=YES is specified
   = Z if TRUNCS=YES is not specified
   TRUNC macro is not discussed in this text as such; Z should be specified.
e = C if CONTROL=YES is specified
   = Z if CONTROL=YES is not specified
   This facility of DASD files is not discussed in this text; therefore, Z should be specified.

Example:

Write a program to read a punched card file and to create a sequential file on 2311 DASD. The disk file records are to be unblocked and formatted without keys. The format of the disk records is the same as for the input card records.

Name	Oper	Operand	
	START	0	
CARDIN	DTFCD	DEVADDR=SYS008,IOAREA1=CARD1,	X
		EOFADDR=NOCARD,IOAREA2=CARD2,	X
		WORKA=YES	
DISKOUT	DTFSD	BLKSIZE=88,IOAREA1=DISK1,	X
		RECFORM=FIXUNB,RECSIZE=80,	X
		TYPEFLE=OUTPUT,WORKA=YES	
BEGIN	BALR	2,0	
	USING	*,2	
	OPEN	CARDIN,DISKOUT	
*		OPEN FILES	
READ	GET	CARDIN,CARDREC	
*		READ A CARD	
	MVC	DISKREC,CARDREC	
*		ASSEMBLE DISK REC	
	PUT	DISKOUT,DISKREC	
*		WRITE DISK	
	B	READ	
NOCARD	CLOSE	CARDIN,DISKOUT	
*		CLOSE FILES	
	EOJ		
CARD1	DS	CL80	BUFFER 1 FOR CARD FILE
CARD2	DS	CL80	BUFFER 2 FOR CARD FILE
CARDREC	DS	CL80	WORK AREA FOR CARD FILE
DISK1	DS	CL88	I/O AREA FOR DISK FILE
DISKREC	DS	CL80	WORK AREA FOR DISK FILE
	END	BEGIN	

Note: It is important to note that the IOAREA1 and BLKSIZE entries for the disk file specify a length value of 88 bytes each. The 8 extra bytes (high-order) are needed by the IOCS for constructing the count field for the record. However, the work area entry specifies a length value of 80 bytes only, the exact length of the disk data records. When a PUT is issued, the IOCS automatically transfers the contents of the work area to the low-order 80 bytes of the IOAREA.

In case only the I/O area was being used to build disk output records, the programmer would have to position the output data in the low-order 80 bytes of the I/O area.

Example:

Write a program to read a punched card file and to create a sequential file on 2311 DASD. The disk records are to be blocked. The blocking factor is ten and the records are to be formatted without keys. The format of the card and disk records is given below.

	Card Record	Disk Record
	1 − 70	1 − 70
	71 − 80 not used	

Name	Oper	Operand	
	START		
CARDIN	DTFCD	DEVADDR=SYS008,IOAREA1=CARD1,	X
		EOFADDR=NOCARD,IOAREA2=CARD2,	X
		WORKA=YES	
DISKOUT	DTFSD	BLKSIZE=708,IOAREA1=DISK1,	X
		RECFORM=FIXBLK,RECSIZE=70,	X
		TYPEFLE=OUTPUT,WORKA=YES	
BEGIN	BALR	2,0	
	USING	*,2	
	OPEN	CARDIN,DISKOUT	
*		OPEN FILES	
READ	GET	CARDIN, CARDREC	
*		READ A CARD	
	MVC	DISKREC,CARDREC	
*		ASSEMBLE DISK RECORD	
	PUT	DISKOUT,DISKREC	
*		WRITE A DISK RECORD	
	B	READ	
NOCARD	CLOSE	CARDIN,DISKOUT	
*		CLOSE FILES	
	EOJ		
CARD1	DS	CL80	BUFFER 1 FOR CARD FILE
CARD2	DS	CL80	BUFFER 2 FOR CARD FILE
CARDREC	DS	CL80	WORK AREA FOR CARD FILE
DISK1	DS	CL708	I/O AREA FOR DISK FILE
DISKREC	DS	CL70	WORK AREA FOR DISK FILE
	END	BEGIN	

Note: In the case of disk input files, the I/O area(s) for the file do not need the extra 8 bytes. The reason for this is that when a GET is issued, the IOCS transfers only the data record and the count field is not read into the main storage.

16.3 Indexed Sequential Access Method —— ISAM

The indexed sequential method of file organization combines the strong features of sequential and direct organization without incorporating many of their weaknesses. In indexed sequential type of organization the programming systems have control over the location of individual records. At the time an indexed sequential file is originally created, the records are stored sequentially by keys on one track after another and the programming system (ISAM) constructs indexes which it uses at I/O time to locate a desired record.

This type of organization makes it possible for a programmer to process records either in serial or random manner. A batch of sequenced transactions can be processed against an indexed sequential file just as efficiently as in sequential processing methods. In addition, it is possible to start sequential processing from any given record in the file without having to read all the preceding records. Indexed sequential organization, however, by the use of indexes associated with the file, makes it possible to quickly locate any given record for random processing. As with files organized sequentially, the indexed sequential organization method *does not* require the entire file to be *rewritten* when the records are updated, deleted or added. In case of indexed sequential files, a separate area (overflow area) is set aside for insertion of records; this alleviates the necessity for rewriting the entire file, a process that would usually be necessary when records are added to a sequential file.

It is important to note that in the case of indexed sequential files, the programming system has a great amount of control over the organization and location of records. The programmer supplies ISAM with the control information (key) of the desired record and ISAM searches, locates, and supplies the desired record to the problem program.

Record characteristics and types

All records of an indexed sequential file must be of count-key-data format and all *keys* must be the *same* length. Only fixed-length records, blocked or unblocked, are

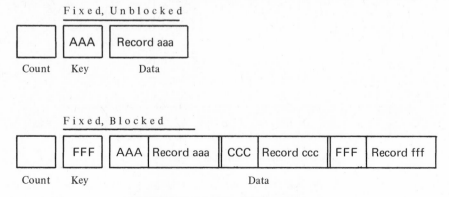

FIGURE 16.15. Record Formats.

permitted. The key may be any length and must occur as a separate record to the left of each block of data. Also, each individual record must also have a key. In case of blocked records, the key of the last record in the block is the key for the block itself. Therefore, ISAM stores it in the key area of the block. In case of unblocked records, the key that precedes the record is repeated within the record also.

Data records, when initially loaded on DASD by ISAM, are placed in a strict sequential order (from presorted input records) in an area of the disk called the *prime area*.

Prime area

Prime area can be defined as an area in which records are written when an indexed sequential file is originally created or subsequently reorganized. All the records in the prime area are in strict key sequence and may exist in blocked or unblocked format. The prime area of a file may occupy multiple volumes. There is another area in which data records may be placed and this is known as the *overflow area*.

Overflow area is used for containing addition records. It is important to note that at the time an indexed sequential file is originally created, no records are placed in the overflow area(s). There are two types of overflow areas that can be used and these are: cylinder overflow area and independent overflow area; either or both may be specified for a given file.

Cylinder overflow area

The programmer may direct the programming system (ISAM) to reserve a specific number of whole tracks in each cylinder for accommodating the overflow records from the prime tracks in that particular cylinder. When the cylinder overflow area is specified, the R0 record (track descriptor record) of each track index is used as a cylinder overflow control record (COCR). The COCR field contains the address of the last overflow record in the cylinder and also indicates the number of bytes left in the cylinder overflow area.

CYL 0	CYL 1	CYL 2	CYL 3	CYL 4	CYL 5	CYL 6
		Track Indexes				
		Prime Area				
		Cylinder Overflow Area				

FIGURE 16.16. Cylinder Overflow Area.

An advantage of using cylinder overflow area is that additional seeks are not required to locate overflow records. *Seek* can be defined as the movement of the access mechanism from one cylinder to another (each seek takes a small amount of time). Switching from one track to another within the same cylinder is practically instantaneous. Therefore, if possible, the prime and overflow tracks should be on the same cylinder. The main disadvantage of using the cylinder overflow area is that in case of unevenly distributed additions to the file, there will be some unused overflow space.

Independent overflow area

An independent overflow area is one in which overflow records from anywhere in the prime area are placed. The size and unit location of the independent overflow area is specified by the programmer; however, the area must be on the same type of DASD as the prime area. An advantage of this type of overflow area is that less space is required for overflow records. A disadvantage is that additional seeks are needed to access the overflow records.

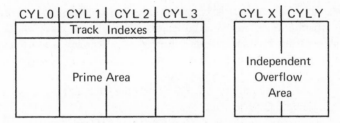

FIGURE 16.17. Independent Overflow Area.

A happy medium between the cylinder and independent overflow area is to reserve a large enough cylinder overflow area to accommodate the average number of overflow records. Also included is an additional independent overflow area that can be used when the cylinder overflow areas have been filled by additions to the file.

Characteristics of Overflow Records. The overflow records, like the prime data records, must be fixed-length and count-key-data format. However, ISAM writes records in the overflow area only in unblocked format. Each overflow record contains an additional 10 byte long field known as the *sequence link field*. The sequence link field is part of the data record and it occupies the first 10 bytes of data area of each record in the overflow area. See Figure 16.21 for sequence link field and its function. The sequence link field of each overflow record (except the last one) contains the address of the next overflow record. Therefore, we can say that the records in the overflow area are linked together by means of the sequence link field. The overflow records are not stored in physical key sequence but this does not reduce processing efficiency, as reference to records is made via indexes. The link field of the last overflow record points back to the track index.

Indexes

When a file is originally loaded (created) onto a DASD, ISAM builds and stores a set of indexes for the file. Up to three levels of indexes are created for a given file. These levels are: track index; cylinder index; and, master index. The first two indexes, track and cylinder, are *always* created for a given indexed sequential file. A master index is constructed only if a specific request is made by the problem program that creates the file.

The indexes, once constructed and stored, are used by ISAM for both random and sequential reference of records in the file. The indexes are made up of a series of records (index entries), each of which is composed of a key area and a data area. The key area of an individual index record is of the same length as that specified for the logical records for the file. The key field of each index record contains the highest key on the track or the cylinder. The data area of each index entry is 10 bytes in length and contains track address information.

Track Index. This is the lowest level index for an indexed sequential file and is always present. A separate track index is built for each cylinder used by the file and it contains index entries for that cylinder only. The track index is written starting with the first track of the cylinder it indexes. When a cylinder overflow area is used, record R0 of each track index is used as a cylinder overflow control record (COCR). There are three types of index entries that make up the track index. These are: normal; overflow; and, dummy index entries.

When a file is originally loaded onto a DASD, ISAM constructs two similar index entries, normal and overflow, for each track used to contain the logical file.

To begin with, both the normal and overflow index entries for a given track contain identical information, i.e., the key fields of both the normal and the overflow index entries for a given track contain the value of the last (highest) key on the track and the data fields contain the address of that particular track. These index entries are altered (updated) by ISAM if new records are added to the file.

The last entry of each track index is a dummy entry which indicates the end of the track index. The key field of the dummy entry contains all 1-bits and the data field is set to all 0-bits (null field). The remaining space, if any, on the index track is used to store prime data records. There are two important points that need to be mentioned here. These are:

1. No provision is made for records that have duplicate keys and it is assumed that every record has a unique key.
2. The data records to be loaded onto DASD by ISAM must exist in proper ascending sequence (by keys).

Note: The track indexes for the prime cylinders that do not yet contain data records are said to be inactive. The key areas of such index entries contain all 1-bits and the data areas are all 0-bits.

Cylinder Index. The next higher level of index is the cylinder index and it is always present. The cylinder index contains one entry for each cylinder taken up by the

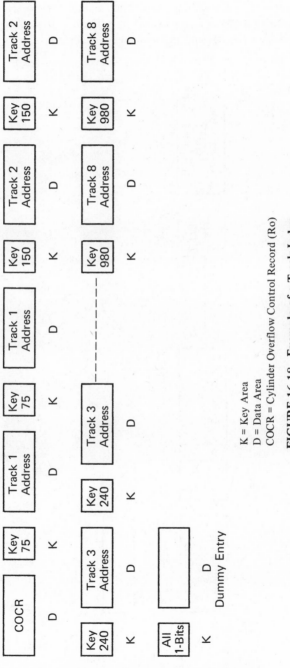

K = Key Area
D = Data Area
COCR = Cylinder Overflow Control Record (Ro)

FIGURE 16.18. Example of a Track Index.

logical file. There is a dummy entry following the last cylinder index entry. The basic structure of cylinder index entries is the same as that for the track index, i.e., each entry is made up of a key area and a data area. The key area contains the highest key associated with the cylinder, and the data area contains the address of the track index for that cylinder.

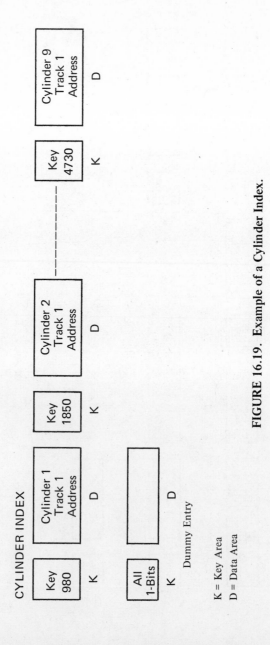

FIGURE 16.19. Example of a Cylinder Index.

The cylinder index for a given logical file may be located on one or more successive cylinders. A cylinder index must be contained within one volume and may not be continued from one volume to another. The cylinder index for a file must not be located on one of the cylinders that contain data records for that logical file.

Note: The space and location of the cylinder index for a file is specified by the programmer through the job control cards. It is possible to have the cylinder index located on a separate volume; however, this volume must be on-line whenever this logical file is processed.

Master Index. This is the highest level of index built for a logical file by DOS. This index is optional and is built only if a specific request is made by the programmer (through job control cards). Like the cylinder index, its location is specified by a job control extent statement and it may be located on the same volume as the logical file or on a different volume. The master index contains one entry for each track of the cylinder index. The key area of each entry contains the highest key on the cylinder index track, and the data area contains the address of that particular track. The number of entries in the master index is relatively small, as it contains only one entry for each track in the cylinder index. For example, a cylinder index that occupies seven tracks would require only seven entries in the master index.

The last record (entry) in the master index is the dummy entry. A master index, like the cylinder index, may occupy more than one cylinder and must be contained within one volume.

Note: A master index should be constructed only for large files, for which the cylinder index requires more than four tracks.

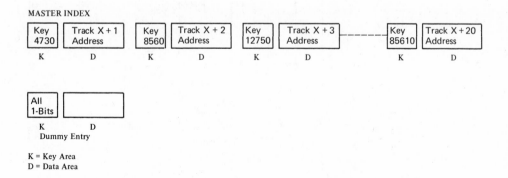

FIGURE 16.20. Example of a Master Index.

An example of an indexed sequential file on a DASD is shown in Figure 16.21.

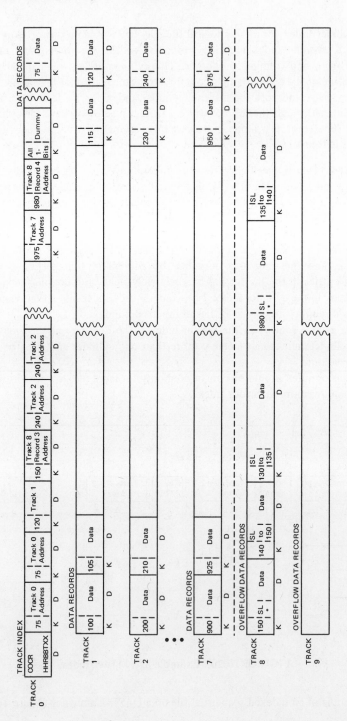

FIGURE 16.21. Example of an Indexed Sequential File (continued).

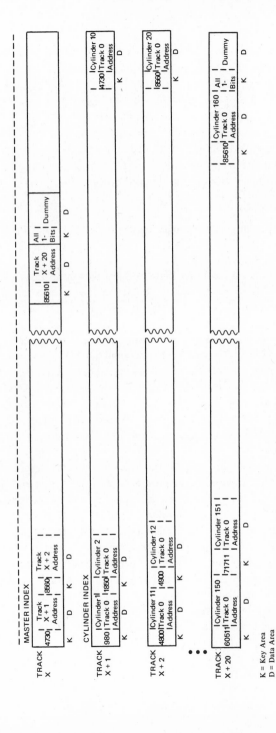

K = Key Area
D = Data Area
SL = Sequence Link   *SL Indicates the end of the overflow chain.
COCR = Cylinder Overflow Control Record (Contained in RO)

FIGURE 16.21. Example of an Indexed Sequential File.

Record search

The ISAM routines use the indexes to search for a given record. When a record is needed for processing, the programmer supplies the key of the desired record and ISAM searches the master index (if present), then the cylinder index, and then the track index. This search supplies ISAM with the address of the track on which the data record is located. Then ISAM searches that particular track to locate the desired record. Each index narrows the search by pointing to the next lower level index whose range includes the specified record. ISAM assumes that every record has a unique key and that all records in the prime area are arranged in strict ascending sequence by keys; as such, the search is made on a greater-than or equal-to basis.

Addition of records

Like any other file, an ISAM file may require updating from time to time. It may become necessary to add new records to the file or some of the existing records may need to be deleted.

The addition records may contain keys that are above the highest key presently in the file or the records may contain keys that fall between the existing records on the file. In case the new records have keys that are higher than the highest existing key in the file, the upper limits of the prime area can be extended (if necessary) and new records can be added by loading them onto the file. Or, the new records can be batched with other addition records (insertions) and added to the end of the file.

If the key of a new data record falls between records currently on the track, the very last record on the track is pushed off to the overflow area and the remaining data records are shifted one record location to permit insertion of the new record. This way the records on any one track are kept in proper sequence by keys. To maintain fast random and sequential retrieval of records, ISAM prefixes a sequence link field to each data record pushed off to the overflow area. The sequence link field, 10 bytes in length, contains the address of the record in the overflow area that has the next higher key. The sequence link field of the highest record indicates the end of the overflow records. All records in the overflow area are stored in *unblocked* format *regardless* of the format specified for prime data records.

When a data record is to be added (inserted) to the file, ISAM first searches the indexes to determine the track on which the given record must be placed (the keys of the last records on the tracks in the originally organized file determine the track where the given record belongs). After determining the proper track, ISAM searches the individual records on the track or the overflow area (if necessary) to determine the exact location for the data record. As a result of this search, the system may take either of the following two actions.

1. If the insertion record falls between two records presently on the track, ISAM inserts the record in proper sequence by shifting each succeeding record one record location higher until the last record is shifted off the track. The shifted record is moved to the overflow area and a sequence link field is prefixed to this record. At this time, the key field of the first index entry for the track is

updated to indicate the new last record located on the track. The track address field of the *second index* entry for the track is changed to point to the record that has been shifted off to the overflow area.

2. If the new record falls between the last record presently on the track and the last record originally on the track, the new record is placed in the overflow area. The record is written in the overflow area following the last record previously written. The sequence link field of the new record, and of the record preceding it by sequence key, are updated to point to the proper records.

Note: It is important to point out that the track index is adjusted with each insertion or addition to indicate which record is the last on each track, and which address in the overflow area has the original final record of each track.

ISAM provides facilities for creating an indexed sequential file, addition and insertion of new records and processing records sequentially or in random order. *No specific provision is made for *deletion* of obsolete records. Deletion of records from an indexed sequential file is explained later in this chapter.

Indexed sequential file (DTFIS)

The rules for DTFIS header and detail entries are the same as explained with earlier DTFxx macros. The detailed entries[2] that apply to the DTFIS macro are described below.

Req'd	DSKXTNT= IOROUT= KEYLEN= NRECDS= RECFORM= RECSIZE=
Opt'l	CYLOFL= DEVICE= IOAREAL= IOAREAR= IOAREAS= IOREG= KEYARG= KEYLOC= MSTIND= TYPEFLE= VERIFY= WORKL= WORKR= WORKS=

CYCLOFL=

This entry specifies the number of tracks on each cylinder that are to be reserved

---

[2]Not all of the possible entries are included in this text. Only the ones that are most commonly used are described.

for use as the overflow area. This operand must be specified if cylinder overflow areas are to be used.

DEVICE=2311, 2314 or 2321

If this entry is omitted, 2311 is assumed.

DSKXTNT=

This entry specifies the maximum number of extents for the file. Since an extent is a contiguous area on a cylinder, the minimum number which can be specified is 2, one extent for prime data area, and one for a cylinder index (master and cylinder indexes are treated as one area).

IOAREAL=name

This operand must be included when an indexed sequential file is first created (loaded) or when records are added to an existing file. This operand specifies the name of the area where ISAM constructs the record and then transfers it to the DASD. This area must provide enough space for containing the count area, key area, and the data area of the records. When records are added to an existing file, the area must also contain enough space for the sequence link field. Figure 16.22 illustrates the requirements for this area. Multiple IOAREAL areas are *not* permitted.

FUNCTION	OUTPUT AREA REQUIREMENTS (IN BYTES)			
	Count	Key	Sequence Link	Data
Load Unblocked Records	8	Key Length	—	Record Length
Load Blocked Records	8	Key Length	—	Record Length x Blocking Factor
Add Unblocked Records	8	Key Length	10	Record Length
Add Blocked Records	8	Key Length	— ─OR*─	Record Length x Blocking Factor
	8	Key Length	10	Record Length
* Whichever is Larger				

FIGURE 16.22. Area Requirements for Loading or Adding Records.

IOAREAR=name

This operand must be included if records are to be processed in random order. This operand specifies the symbolic name of the I/O area used for random retrieval and updating. This area must be large enough to contain the data area of the records. Figure 16.23 illustrates the requirements for this area.

FUNCTION	I/O AREA REQUIREMENTS (IN BYTES)			
	Count	Key	Sequence Link	Data
Retrieve Unblocked Records	—	Key Length for sequential unblocked records	10	Record Length
Retrieve Blocked Records	—	—	—	Record Length (including keys) x Blocking Factor
			——OR*——	
	—	—	10	Record Length
*Whichever is larger				

FIGURE 16.23. Area Requirements for Random or Sequential Retrieval.

IOAREAS=name

This entry must be included if records are to be processed sequentially by key. Figure 16.23 shows the length requirements for this area.

IOREG=(r)

This operand is specified if the records are to be processed directly in the I/O area instead of the work area. This entry specifies the number of the register $(2 - 11)$ which ISAM may use for supplying the address of the individual record that is available for processing. When this operand is included, WORK operand must *not* be specified.

IOROUT=

This is one of the required entries which specifies the type of function to be performed. The options are LOAD, ADD, ADDRTR or RETRVE.

LOAD: To build a logical file on DASD or to extend an existing ISAM file beyond the highest record presently on the file.

ADD: To insert new records into an existing file.

ADDRTR: If new records are to be inserted and existing records are to be retrieved for processing and/or updating.

RETRVE: To retrieve records from a file for either random or sequential processing.

KEYARG=name

This operand specifies the symbolic name of the main storage field in which the programmer must supply the record key. This operand must be included if random READ/WRITE operations are to be used and if sequential retrieval is to be initiated by key.

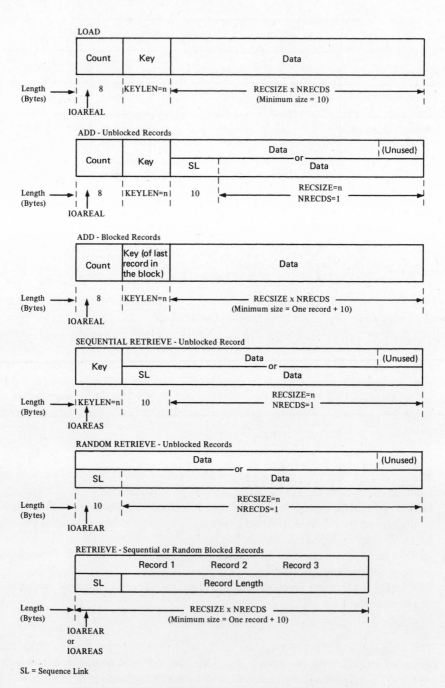

FIGURE 16.24. Schematic of I/O Area in Main Storage.

KEYLEN=

This operand is used to specify the length of the key (in bytes).

KEYLOC=

This operand must be specified if an add, load, or retrieve function is to be performed and the file is in blocked format. This field specifies the leftmost position of the key field within the records. For example, if the key is located in positions 30 – 34 of each record, this entry would specify 30.

MSTIND=YES

This operand must be included if master index is to be used for the file. The location of the master index is specified by a job control extent statement.

NRECDS=n

This operand is used to specify the blocking factor. If RECFORM=FIXUNB, n is assumed to be 1.

RECFORM=

This operand is used to specify the type of records in the logical file. The options are FIXUNB or FIXBLK.

RECSIZE=

This operand specifies the number of bytes in a logical record. It is important to note that this operand specifies *only* the length of the data area of each record.

TYPEFLE=

This operand must be specified when retrieval function is to be performed. One of the following specifications is entered.

RANDOM: Records to be retrieved in random order specified by key.

SEQNTL: This operand is specified for sequential processing. The problem program needs to specify the first record to be retrieved and thereafter ISAM retrieves records sequentially by key. The first record is specified by key, ID, or the beginning of the logical file.

RANSEQ: For both random and sequential processing.

Note: TYPEFLE entry is not required for loading or adding functions.

VERIFY=YES

The functions of this entry are the same as discussed with DTFSD macro.

WORKL=name

This operand must be specified whenever a file is to be loaded or records are to be added to an existing file. This operand specifies the symbolic name of the work area where the programmer builds the data records. This work area must provide space for

ADD, RETRVE, and ADDRTR

Bit	Cause	Explanation
0	DASD error	Any uncorrectable DASD error has occurred (except wrong length record).
1	Wrong length record	A wrong length record has been detected during an I/O operation.
2	End of file	The EOF condition has been encountered during execution of the sequential retrieval function.
3	No record found	The record to be retrieved has not been found in the data file. This applies to Random (RANSEQ) and to SETL in SEQNTL (RANSEQ) when KEY is specified.
4	Illegal ID specified	The ID specified to the SETL in SEQNTL (RANSEQ) is outside the prime data file limits.
5	Duplicate record	The record to be added to the file has a duplicate record key of another record in the file.
6	Overflow area full	An overflow area in a cylinder is full, and no independent overflow area has been specified, or an independent overflow area is full, and the addition cannot be made. The user should assign an independent overflow area or extend the limit.
7	Overflow	The record being processed in one of the retrieval functions (RANDOM/SEQNTL) is an overflow record.

LOAD

Bit	Cause	Explanation
0	DASD error	Any uncorrectable DASD error has occurred (except wrong length record).
1	Wrong length record	A wrong length record has been detected during an I/O operation.
2	Prime data area full	The next to the last track of the prime data area has been filled during the load or extension of the data file. The problem programmer should issue the ENDFL macro, then do a load extend on the file with new extents given.
3	Cylinder Index area full	The Cylinder Index area is not large enough to contain all the entries needed to index each cylinder specified for the prime data area. This condition can occur during the execution of the SETFL. The user must extend the upper limit of the cylinder index by using a new extent card.
4	Master Index full	The Master Index area is not large enough to contain all the entries needed to index each track of the Cylinder Index. This condition can occur during SETFL. The user must extend the upper limit, if he is creating the file, by using an extent card. Or, he must reorganize the data file and assign a larger area.
5	Duplicate record	The record being loaded is a duplicate of the previous record.
6	Sequence check	The record being loaded is not in the sequential order required for loading.
7	Prime data area overflow	There is not enough space in the prime data area to write an EOF record. This condition can occur during the execution of the ENDFL macro.

FIGURE 16.25. FilenameC — Status or Condition Code Byte.

the key and the data area, but need not provide space for the sequence link field or the count field.

WORKR=name

When records are to be read or written in random order, this entry must be specified if the individual records are to be processed in a work area rather than the I/O area. This work area must provide space for one logical record, but need not provide space for the key field or the count field. When this operand is specified, IOREG may not be used.

WORKS=YES

In case of sequential processing, this operand needs to be included if the records are to be processed in a work area instead of the I/O area. If the file contains unblocked records this area must be large enough for one logical record (data area) and the record key. In case of blocked records this area must be large enough for one logical record (data area). When WORKS operand is specified, IOREG must not be included.

Status or Condition Code Field. The DTF macro instruction provides a 1 byte field where ISAM places the condition codes after execution of each macro instruction. The status of this byte can be tested by referencing the field called filenameC. The file name should be the same as specified by DTFIS macro for this file. The values and meanings of filenameC byte are explained in Figure 16.25.

Initialization — OPEN macro

A maximum of 16 files may be opened with one OPEN macro instruction. OPEN macro checks all the labels in VTOC to make sure that the file to be created will not destroy an existing file if the expiration of the file is still pending. In case of a multi-volume index sequential file, all volumes must be on-line and ready when the file is first opened.

Creating (loading) or extending an indexed sequential file

The function of originally loading an indexed sequential file and the function of extending an existing file by adding new records that fall beyond the existing high record, are the same. Both of these functions are considered as LOAD operation and use the same macros. However, in case a file is to be created, the type field in DLAB card (job control card) must specify ISC and in case of load extension the specification must be ISE. During the load operation (creation and extension), ISAM builds the track, cylinder, and if specified, the master indexes.

Note: The input records must be presorted in ascending order by key.

Three macros are used to create or extend a logical file. These are explained below.

SETFL Macro

The SETFL (set file load mode) macro has only one operand, which is the name of the file as specified by DTFIS macro. If the SETFL macro specifies the name of a file that has not yet been loaded (new file), ISAM uses the disk area designated as being available by the XTENT job control card. If the disk area designated as being available already contains a file with the same name as specified by the SETFL macro, then ISAM gets the file ready for addition of high records.

WRITE Macro

The format of this macro is as follows:

Name	Oper	Operand
	WRITE	filename,NEWKEY

A WRITE macro, when issued between a SETFL and an ENDFL instruction, causes ISAM to load a record onto DASD. Both parameters of WRITE macro are required. Before issuing the WRITE macro instruction, the programmer must store the key and the data of the record in the area named by WORKL operand of DTFIS macro for this file. ISAM routines build the I/O area (see Figure 16.24) by moving the key to the key area, data record to data area, and building the count area. After completing this process, ISAM transfers the record to the DASD and constructs the count field for the next record. When loading or extending an indexed sequential file, ISAM also performs both a sequence check and a duplicate record check (both checks by key) before transferring the record to DASD.

After each WRITE is executed, ISAM makes the ID of that record or block available in an 8 byte field labeled filenameH. For example, if the filename specified by DTFIS macro for this file is NEWFL, the ID field is addressable by the symbolic name NEWFLH. By referencing this field, the programmer can obtain the ID of any given record for later use (this ID is needed if the programmer plans to retrieve records in sequential order starting with the ID of a particular record).

ENDFL Macro

The ENDFL macro (end file load mode) has only one operand, this is the symbolic name of the file. The ENDFL macro ends the mode initiated by the SETFL macro. The functions performed by this macro are somewhat similar to those performed by the CLOSE macro. It writes the last block of data records, if necessary, and then writes an end-of-file record. Any index entries that are needed and the dummy index entry for the unused portion of the prime area (if applicable) are also written. *Note:* The CLOSE macro must still be used.

Macros for adding records

Two macros, WRITE and WAITF, are available for adding new records to an organized indexed sequential file. If the file contains blocked records, the programmer must provide ISAM with the location of the key field (KEYLOC operand of DTFIS). The key field of all new records must be in the same location as the keys for the existing records.

WRITE Macro

Name	Oper	Operand
	WRITE	filename,NEWKEY

In case of unblocked records, before issuing the WRITE macro the programmer must position the record (key and data) to be added in the work area designated by the WORKL entry of DTFIS macro for this file. In case of blocked records, the programmer needs to store only the data as the key is assumed to be a part of the data.

WAITF Macro

Name	Oper	Operand
	WAITF	filename

This macro is used to ensure that the transfer of a record has been completed. It is required after each WRITE macro in order to give ISAM time to perform the building of index entries and other necessary operations. The WAITF macro posts any exceptional information in the DTFIS table at filenameC.

Deletion of records

ISAM provides no direct method for deletion of records from a logical file. However, there are two possible ways to achieve this goal. These are outlined below.
1. The most commonly used method of doing this is to insert a specific symbol (sometimes known as the purge code) in each record to be deleted. The most commonly used symbol is hexadecimal FF in the leftmost byte of the obsolete record. If the position used to store this purge code is part of the record key, none of the keys in the file should start with the purge code configuration. This method provides an easy way of deleting obsolete records when the file is reorganized at a later date.
2. The second method of deleting records is to copy the file, checking each record as it is read against a list of deletion records (this method is very similar to tape update logic discussed earlier in the text). This method requires that the entire file be copied each time records need to be deleted, thus making the process very time-consuming and inefficient.

Random processing

One of the main advantages of indexed sequential file is that records can be processed in either sequential or in random order. When invoking random processing procedures, it is necessary to specify IOROUT=RETRVE or IOROUT=ADDRTR and TYPEFLE=RANDOM in the DTFIS macro for the file. In the case of random processing the reference to individual records is by record key, and as such the problem program must supply the key of the desired record. This key must be stored in the main storage area named by the KEYARG entry. Three macros: READ;

WRITE; and, WAITF are used for random processing.

READ Macro

Name	Oper	Operand
	READ	filename,KEY

This macro causes ISAM to retrieve the specified record from the file. To locate a given record, ISAM searches the indexes to determine the track on which the record is stored, and then searches the track for the specific record. Upon locating the desired record, ISAM transfers it to the I/O area specified by IOAREAR entry and in case WORKR is also specified, the record is moved to the work area as well.

WRITE Macro

Name	Oper	Operand
	WRITE	filename,KEY

This macro causes ISAM to transfer a given record from a main storage location to DASD. ISAM rewrites the record previously retrieved (by a read instruction) from the same file. The record is written from the I/O area or from the work area. It is important to note that the key field of the record read into the main storage by the previous read instruction must not be altered in any way.

WAITF Macro

This macro must be used following each READ and WRITE instruction when using random processing. The functions of this macro were explained earlier in this section. *Note:* The WRITE macro, as explained above, can not be used to insert new records into an existing file as it provides no facilities for building indexes. If it becomes necessary to insert a new record into the file during record processing, it can be done by using the WRITE macro with NEWKEY as its second operand, The area being used for random processing must not be used for inserting or loading of new records.

Sequential processing

An indexed sequential file can be processed in sequential order (by keys). When such processing is desired, a programmer supplies ISAM with the key or the position of the record he wishes to process. From there on, ISAM takes the records one after the other in key or position sequence until the end of the file is reached. For sequential processing the programmer must include IOROUT=RETRVE and TYPEFLE= SEQNTL. The macros available for sequential processing are explained below.

SETL Macro

Name   Oper   Operand
              SETL   filename,idname
                                 ,KEY
                                 ,BOF
                                 ,GKEY

The SETL macro (set limits) initiates the mode necessary for sequential processing. The second operand of this macro specifies where processing is to begin. If the records are to be processed by record ID, the second operand specifies the symbolic name of the main storage area which contains the starting reference. The symbolic field's format is given in Figure 16.26.

Byte	Iden-tifier	Contents	Information
0	m	2-245	Number of the extent in which the starting record is located.
1-2	b,b	0,0 (disk)	Always zero for disk.
3-4	c,c	0, 1-199 (disk)	Cylinder number for disk.
5-6	h,h	0,0-9 (2311 disk) 0,0-19 (2314 disk)	Head position for 2311 and 2314 disk.
7	r	1-254	Record location.

FIGURE 16.26. Format of Field Containing First Record ID.

KEY: If sequential processing is to begin with a key, the second operand must be KEY. The programmer must supply the record key in the field specified by KEYARG entry of DTFIS macro for this file. In case the specified key is not present in the file, ISAM posts this indication at filenameC.

BOF: If the processing is to start at the beginning of the file, the second operand of SETL macro must be BOF.

GKEY: A selected group of records can be retrieved by the use of this operand. In this text we will not discuss the functions and applications of this operand in further detail.

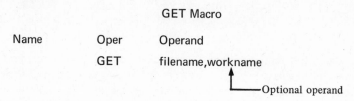

GET Macro

Name	Oper	Operand
	GET	filename,workname

When a GET is issued without the workname operand, ISAM transfers a record from the file to the I/O area and the record is available for processing. The key is located at the beginning of IOAREAS and the register designated by IOREG entry points to the data. In case of blocked records, ISAM supplies the address of each record in the register specified by IOREG entry. In this case, the key is assumed to be contained within the record.

Workname Option. When a work area is used with a GET macro, ISAM makes the record available in the area designated by the second operand of the GET macro. In case of blocked records, each GET that transfers a block of records to the main storage also may write the previously retrieved block back into the file in its original location (see PUT macro). The previously retrieved block is written back only if a PUT macro has been issued for at least one of the records in the block.

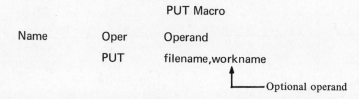

PUT Macro

Name	Oper	Operand
	PUT	filename,workname

This macro causes ISAM to transfer records to the file in sequential order. PUT returns a record that was *previously* obtained by a GET macro issued to the file (the PUT macro is used only for sequential update of data records; new records can *not* be *added* by this macro).

If the second operand is omitted, the records are processed in the area designated by IOAREAS entry. If the work area option is used, the records are processed in a work area instead of the I/O area. The workname operand may specify the same name as that specified in the preceding GET macro to this file. In case of unblocked records, each PUT issued to the file writes a record back onto the file in its original location. If some records do not require updating, a series of GET macros can be issued without embedding PUT instructions.

If blocked records are specified, the PUT macro does not transfer the block back to the file. Instead, each PUT informs ISAM that the block is to be written back after all the records in the block have been processed. Therefore, when a GET is issued to read the next block, that GET in addition to retrieving the new block also writes the previously retrieved block back on the file. If a PUT is not issued for any record in the block, the following GET does not transfer the block to the file.

Note: The ESETL macro (see below) writes the last block processed, if necessary, back on the file before the end-of-file.

ESETL Macro

Name	Oper	Operand
	ESETL	filename

This macro ends the sequential mode initiated by the SETL macro. In case of blocked records, this macro writes the last block back onto its original location on the file if a PUT was issued.

Note: CLOSE macro must still be used.

Figure 16.27 illustrates an example of the use of an indexed sequential file. The program reads a sequential disk file and creates an indexed sequential file. Both files are located on 2311 DASD.

Name	Oper	Operand	
	START		
INFILE	DTFSD	BLKSIZE=150,EOFADDR=DISKEND,	X
		IOAREA1=INAREA,ERROPT=SKIP,	X
		WLRERR=ERROR	
ERRFLE	DTFPR	DEVADDR=SYS010,IOAREA1=LINE,	X
		BLKSIZE=40	
OUTFL	DTFIS	DSKXTNT=4,IOROUT=LOAD,	X
		KEYLEN=10,	X
		RECFORM=FIXUNB,RECSIZE=150,	X
		CYLOFL=4,IOAREAL=LOADREC,	X
		VERIFY=YES,WORKL=WORKREC	
BEGIN	BALR	2,0	
	USING	*,2	
	OPEN	INFILE,OUTFL,ERRFLE	
*			
*		OPEN FILES	
	SETFL	OUTFL	
READ	GET	INFILE READ INPUT FILE	
	MVC	OUTKEY,INKEY	
*		POSITION RECORD KEY	

(continued)

```
                  MVC       OUTREC,INREC
    *                       POSITION DATA AREA
                  WRITE     OUTFL,NEWKEY
    *                       WRITE OUTPUT RECORD
                  B         READ
    DISKEND       ENDFL     OUTFL
                  EOJ
                  CLOSE     INFILE,ERRFLE,OUTFL
    ERROR         MVC       LINE(10),INKEY
                  PUT       ERRFLE  WRITE ERROR MESSAGE
                  B         READ
    LOADREC       DS        CL168    AREA FOR IOAREAL
    WORKREC       DS        0CL160   AREA FOR WORKL
    OUTKEY        DS        CL10     KEY FOR OUTPUT RECORD
    OUTREC        DS        CL150    DATA AREA FOR OUTPUT RECORD
    INAREA        DS        0CL150   AREA FOR INPUT RECORD
    INKEY         DS        CL10     KEY FOR INPUT RECORD
                  DS        CL140
    LINE          DS        0CL40    ERROR MESSAGE AREA
                  DC        CL15' '
                  DC        CL25'WRONG LENGTH INPUT RECORD'
                  END       BEGIN
```

FIGURE 16.27. Example of Loading an Indexed Sequential File.

[17]

Physical IOCS and
Tape Work Files

17.1 Processing with Physical IOCS

Records can be transferred to or from an input/output device by issuing physical IOCS macro instructions. These macro instructions communicate directly with the physical IOCS routines. When using physical IOCS to perform I/O operations, the programmer must provide any of the functions that are required for a problem program such as: blocking or deblocking (in case of tape or disk files) of records; performing wrong length record checks; switching I/O areas when two areas are used to achieve buffering; and, setting up Channel Command Words (CCW).

Three macro instructions are available to a programmer for direct communication with physical IOCS. These are:
1. CCB – Command Control Block.
2. EXCP – Execute Channel Program.
3. WAIT.

Whenever physical IOCS macro instructions are used, a programmer must also construct Channel Command Words (CCW) for the input/output operations.

CCB Macro

Name	Oper	Operand
Blockname	CCB	SYSnnn,Command-list-name

From the specifications in the CCB instruction, the macro sets up a 16 byte long Command Control Block. A CCB macro instruction must be specified in the problem program for each I/O device that is to be controlled by physical IOCS macro instructions.

Blockname. The CCB macro instruction must be assigned a symbolic name. This name can be used as the operand in the EXCP and WAIT macro instructions that refer to the Command Control Block.

SYSnnn. Two operands are required in this CCB macro instruction. The first operand, SYSnnn, specifies the symbolic unit for the actual I/O unit with which this control block will be associated. The possible names are SYSRDR, SYSLST, SYSIPT, SYSLOG, SYSPCH, SYSRES, SYS000–SYS244.

Command-list-name. The second operand of the CCB macro instruction specifies the symbolic name of the first CCW to be used with this CCB. This name must be the same as the name specified in the assembler CCW statement that constructs the Channel Command Word.

EXCP Macro

Name	Oper	Operand
	EXCP	Blockname

The EXCP (execute channel program) macro instruction requests physical IOCS to start an input/output operation for a particular I/O device. The Blockname of the CCB established for the device is the only operand required in this macro instruction. Physical IOCS determines the device concerned from the SYSnnn operand of the Command Control Block specified by the EXCP macro instruction. If the channel and the device are available, the channel program is started. Program control is then returned to the program.

WAIT Macro

Name	Oper	Operand
	WAIT	Blockname

This macro instruction is issued whenever the program requires that an I/O operation, started by an EXCP instruction, be completed before execution of the problem program continues. The Blockname of the CCB established for the I/O device is the only operand required in this macro instruction. This is also the same name as specified in the EXCP macro instruction for this device.

CCW   Define Channel Command Word

This assembler instruction generates an 8 byte Channel Command Word aligned on a doubleword boundary. Any bytes skipped to achieve alignment are set to zero. The CCW has the following format:

Command Code	Data Address	Flags	0 0 0		Count
0 7 8	31 32	36 37 39 40	47 48		63

FIGURE 17.1. CCW Format.

The fields in the CCW are allocated for the following purposes:

Command Code: Bits 0 − 7 specify the operation to be performed.

Data Address: Bits 8 − 31 specify the location of an 8-bit byte in main storage. It is the first location referred to in the area designated by the CCW.

Chain Data (CD) Flag: Bit 32, when this bit is one, it specifies chaining of data. It causes the storage area designated by the next CCW to be used with the current operation.

Chain Command (CC) Flag: Bit 33, when this bit is one, and when CD flag bit is zero, specifies chaining of commands. It causes the operation specified by the command code in the next CCW to be initiated upon normal completion of the current operation. By using this bit of the CCW, a programmer can obtain overlapping of I/O operations.

Flag Bits 34 − 36: These bits serve other special functions. Explanation of these bits is not included as their use and application is beyond the scope of this text. As such, these bits should be set to zeros.

Bits 37 − 39: These bits may be used in the future for the control of new functions and, as such, must be set to zeros.

Bits 40 − 47: The contents of these bits are ignored.

Count: Bits 48 − 63 specify the number of 8-bit byte locations in the storage area designated by the CCW (length of data to be processed).

A Channel Command Word can be defined in the Assembler Language by the CCW statement which has the format:

Name	Oper	Operand
	CCW	Operand1,Operand2,Operand3,Operand4

All four operands *must* be present. The CCW specifies the command to be executed, such as read or write and, for commands initiating I/O operations, the CCW also designates the storage area associated with the operation and the length (in bytes) of data to be transferred by the I/O operation. The various operands of the CCW statements are as follows:

Operand1: An absolute expression that specifies the command code. The command code for *read* is 2 and for *write* its value must be 1.

Operand2: An expression that specifies the address of the data area.

Operand3: An absolute expression that defines the flag bits and sets bits 37 through 39 to zeros.

Operand4: An absolute expression that defines the length of the storage area.

Example:

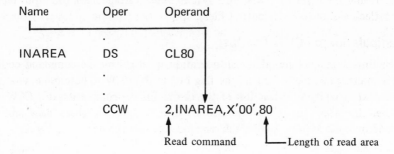

Name	Oper	Operand
INAREA	DS	CL80
	CCW	2,INAREA,X'00',80

Read command   └──Length of read area

Example:

Example of a program that uses physical IOCS and its associated macros. The program is to read a punched card file and to list all cards on a 1403 printer.

Name	Oper	Operand	
	START		
BEGIN	BALR	2,0	
	USING	*,2	
READ	EXCP	CARDFL	
	WAIT	CARDFL	
	CLC	CARD(2),=C'/*'	IF IT IS END—OF—FILE
	BE	ENDFL	BRANCH TO ENDFL
	MVC	LINE,CARD	
	EXCP	PRNTFL	
	WAIT	PRNTFL	
	B	READ	
ENDFL	EOJ		
CARDFL	CCB	SYS080,IOCARD	
IOCARD	CCW	2,CARD,X'00',80	CCW TO READ CARD
PRNTFL	CCB	SYS010,IOPRINT	
IOPRINT	CCW	1,LINE,X'00',80	CCW TO PRINT
CARD	DS	CL80	
LINE	DS	CL80	
	END	BEGIN	

FIGURE 17.2. Use of CCW.

EXERCISE:

Write a program using the physical IOCS to read a file of punched cards. The output of the program is: listing of each input card record; and, a punched card for each input card.

In the case of tape files, the end-of-file condition can be checked by testing the low-order bit of the fifth byte of the control block generated by the CCB for this file. This particular bit is set to 1 when the system detects a tape mark (on input tape file) or the reflective-spot (on tape output files).

Manipulation of CCW flag bits

Each time a channel completes an operation specified by the command code of a CCW, it interrogates the setting of the flag bits in the CCW to determine what action to take next. Therefore, the action of the channel at the completion of a CCW can be controlled by a programmer. The use of bits 32 and 33, chain data and chain command bits, will be discussed in the remainder of this chapter.

Use of Chain Data (CD) Flag Bit. When chain data flag bit, bit 32, of a CCW is 1, it causes the storage area designated by the next CCW to be used with current operation. The actual data chaining process is accomplished as follows:

> When the number of bytes specified by the count field of the current CCW have been processed, the I/O operation initiated by the CCW is not terminated. Instead, the operation continues and the area designated by the next CCW is used with the current operation.

Data chaining characteristic of the CCW can be utilized to read a contiguous data record into non-contiguous main-storage locations. When used with the write command, the process of data chaining is reversed, i.e., data from non-contiguous areas of main-storage can be written onto one contiguous record. The example that follows illustrates the use of the CD flag bit for reading a card record into four non-contiguous main-storage areas.

Example:
Write program steps to read a card record into four different main-storage locations.

Card Record Fields	Main-Storage Locations	
1 – 25	NAME	25 Bytes
26 – 49	ADDRESS	24 Bytes
50 – 69	CITYSTAT	20 Bytes
70 – 74	ZIP	5 Bytes

Name	Oper	Operand
	START	
	.	
READ	EXCP	CARDFL
	WAIT	CARDFL
	.	

(continued)

```
CARDFL      CCB     SYS080,IOCARD
IOCARD      CCW     2,NAME,X'80',25          CHAIN DATA
            CCW     2,ADDRESS,X'80',24       CHAIN DATA
            CCW     2,CITYSTAT,X'80',20      CHAIN DATA
            CCW     2,ZIP,X'00',5            NO CHAINING
NAME        DS      CL25
ADDRESS     DS      CL24
CITYSTAT    DS      CL20
ZIP         DS      CL5
               .
```

FIGURE 17.3. Chaining of Data Flag Bits.

Note: It is important to note that the last CCW does not specify data chaining; bit 32 of this CCW is set to 0.

Use of Chain Command (CC) Flag Bit. It is possible to chain commands of successive CCWs by setting the CC flag bit, bit 33, to 1. When this particular bit of a CCW is 1, it causes the operation specified by the next CCW to be initiated upon normal completion of the current operation.

Note: In case of data chaining, the successive CCWs apply to the same record. However, in case of command chaining, each CCW's command is interpreted separately and each applies to a different record.

The next example illustrates the use of command chain bit of the CCW.

Example:

Write program steps to read four tape records, each 80 bytes in length, and store these in a single 320 byte long area.

```
Name        Oper    Operand

            START
               .
            EXCP    TAPEFL
            WAIT    TAPEFL
               .
TAPEFL      CCB     SYS011,IOTAPE
IOTAPE      CCW     2,IN,X'40',80            CHAIN COMMAND
            CCW     2,IN+80,X'40',80         CHAIN COMMAND
            CCW     2,IN+160,X'40',80        CHAIN COMMAND
            CCW     2,IN+240,X'00',80
IN          DS      CL320
               .
```

FIGURE 17.4. Chaining of Command Flag Bits.

Note: This type of command chaining made it possible to read four tape records with a single tape movement.

It is possible to mix in one program both the data and command chaining. In fact, such a combination allows us to set up intricate programming logic. The next example illustrates one such combination.

Example:

Write a program to read two records from a tape without stopping the tape. Each record on the tape is 70 bytes in length and consists of Name (1 − 20), Address (21 − 50), and City & State (51 − 70).

Name	Oper	Operand	
	START		
	.		
	EXCP	TAPEFL	
	WAIT	TAPEFL	
	.		
TAPEFL	CCB	SYS011,IOTAPE	
	CCW	2,NAME1,X'80',20	CHAIN DATA
	CCW	2,ADDRS1,X'80',30	CHAIN DATA
	CCW	2,CITY1,X'40',20	CHAIN COMMAND
	CCW	2,NAME2,X'80',20	CHAIN DATA
	CCW	2,ADDRS2,X'80',30	CHAIN DATA
	CCW	2,CITY2,X'00',20	NO CHAINING SPECIFIED
NAME1	DS	CL20	
ADDRS1	DS	CL30	
CITY1	DS	CL20	
NAME2	DS	CL20	
ADDRS2	DS	CL30	
CITY2	DS	CL20	
	.		
	.		

FIGURE 17.5. Chaining of Data and Command Flag Bits.

Note: The various DS statements could have been set at non-contiguous main-storage locations.

Processing tape files using physical IOCS

When tape files with standard or user labels need to be processed by using the physical IOCS macros (EXCP, WAIT, etc.), the programmer must include DTFPH entries (DTF for a file handled by Physical IOCS) in his program.

DTFPH Macro

Name	Oper	Operand	
xxxxxxx	DTFPH	TYPEFLE=xxxxxx,	X
		CCWADDR=xxxxxxxx,	X
		DEVICE=xxxx,	X
		DEVADDR=SYSxxx,	X
		HDRINFO=YES,	X
		LABADDR=xxxxxxxx	

$$\text{TYPEFLE=} \begin{Bmatrix} \text{INPUT} \\ \text{OUTPUT} \end{Bmatrix}$$

This entry specifies the type of the file. This is a required entry and specifies whether this is an input file (create labels) or an output file (write labels).

CCWADDR=name

The symbolic name of the first CCW to be used with the CCB generated within the DTFPH macro. This must be the same name as specified in the CCW statement that constructs the channel command word.

DEVICE=TAPE

The parameter entry TAPE applies to any 2400-series tape drive.

DEVADDR=SYSxxx

This specification, or symbolic unit, represents an actual I/O address, and is used in the job control ASSGN statement to assign the actual I/O device address to this file.

HDRINFO=YES

Same as discussed in DTFMT macro.

LABADDR=

(This text does not include processing of user written labels, thus no explanation is included.)
Note: An OPEN to the tape file is necessary with EXCP when label checking is desired.

When using physical IOCS to process tape files, it is the programmer's responsibility to provide programming steps for such functions such as blocking or deblocking of records, performing programmed wrong-length record checks, and switching I/O areas when two areas are included.

Example:
Following is a program which reads a punched card file and creates an unblocked

tape file.

Name	Oper	Operand	
	START		
BEGIN	BALR	2,0	
	USING	*,2	
	OPEN	OUTTAPE	
READ	EXCP	CARDFL	
	WAIT	CARDFL	
	CLC	CARD(2),=C'/*'	CHECK FOR END OF FILE
	BE	FINISH	
	MVC	TAPEREC,CARD	
	EXCP	OUTTAPE	
	WAIT	OUTTAPE	
	B	READ	
FINISH	EOJ		
CARDFL	CCB	SYS080,IOCARD	
IOCARD	CCW	2,CARD,X'00',80	
CARD	DS	CL80	
IOTAPE	CCW	1,TAPEREC,X'00',80	
TAPEREC	DS	CL80	
OUTTAPE	DTFPH	TYPEFLE=OUTPUT,CCWADDR=IOTAPE, X	
		DEVICE=SYS011	
	END	BEGIN	

FIGURE 17.6. Example of Physical IOCS.

17.2 Tape Work Files

As the name implies, work files are used to contain intermediate results between successive phases or job steps. A work file can be used for tape and disk input, output or both. In this section, only the tape work files will be discussed. Work files can be written, read, and rewritten within a single phase without the necessity of additional OPEN or CLOSE processing. To designate a file as work file, TYPEFLE=WORK must be included in the DTFMT macro for the file. To process work files, DOS provides work file macro instructions READ, WRITE and CHECK. In addition, work file macro instructions NOTE, POINTR, POINTW and POINTS can also be used if the DTFMT macro for the file includes NOTEPNT=YES entry.

Note: Work files process fixed-length unblocked records and undefined-format records only.

The first time a work file is opened, the system opens it as an output file. OPEN macro examines the tape to determine whether the tape contains standard labels. (FILABL entry specified with DTFMT for the file is ignored by the system). In case the tape contains standard labels and the header label is expired, a new header label consisting of HDR1 and followed by 76 bytes is written. If the tape file does not contain standard labels, no labels are written. Trailer labels are not processed.

If a work file with standard labels is reopened, the IOCS determines from the header label that the file is a work file and does not rewrite the labels. Upon sensing a tapemark during a read operation or when end-of-file reflective spot is sensed during a write operation, the IOCS causes a branch to the address specified by the EOFADDR= entry in the DTFMT for the file.

Note: The job control label information cards are not required for the tape work files.

READ Macro

The READ macro instruction causes the next sequential physical record, or part of it, to be read from the file into the main-storage area designated by the third operand of the READ macro. It is necessary to use READ= entry in the DTFMT for the file to specify the type of read for the tape file, i.e., FORWARD or BACK. The format of the READ macro is:

Name	Oper	Operand	
	READ	Filename,SQ,Area,	$\left\{ \begin{array}{c} \text{Length} \\ \text{S} \end{array} \right\}$

Filename: This operand specifies the name of the file associated with the record to be read. This name is the same as specified in the DTFMT header entry for this file. This parameter is always required.

SQ: The parameter SQ (sequential) is always required with tape work files.

Area: This operand specifies the name of the input area used by this file. In case READ=BACK is specified, area operand must specify the address of the rightmost byte of the input area. This operand is always required.

Length: This parameter is used only for undefined type of records (RECFORM= UNDEF). In order to read only a portion of a record, actual length or a register containing the length is specified for the fourth operand. In case the entire physical record needs to be read, S can be specified.

In case the tape work file contains fixed-length unblocked records, this operand is not required. In such cases, the IOCS obtains the length from RECSIZE entry.

WRITE Macro

This macro instruction causes a record to be written from the indicated area into the file associated with the filename operand. The records are written sequentially. The format of this macro instruction is:

Name	Oper	Operand
	WRITE	Filename,SQ,Area, Length

The first three operands, Filename, SQ, and Area are always required. The fourth operand is used only with records of undefined format. The rules for these four operands are the same as described in the READ macro.

CHECK Macro

Name	Oper	Operand
	CHECK	Filename

This macro *must* be issued after *each* READ or WRITE to a work file. CHECK macro ensures that the control is not passed back to the problem program until completion of the I/O operation started by either a READ or a WRITE. If the I/O operation is completed without any errors, CHECK returns control to the next sequential instruction. In case of an error, the option specified by ERROPT= entry is processed. In case CHECK encounters an end-of-file condition, control is passed to routine identified by EOFADDR entry.

NOTE Macro

Name	Oper	Operand	
	NOTE	Filename	

This macro is used to obtain identification for the *last* physical record that was read or written on the tape file associated with the filename operand. The identification is the number of the physical records that have been read or written in the file from the load point marker. The number is returned in register 1 in the form 0bbb, where 0= eight binary zeros, and bbb = the physical record number in binary. This number may be stored in the 0bbb form and later used in conjunction with a POINTR or POINTW macro to locate this record.

POINTR Macro

Name	Oper	Operand
	POINTR	Filename,Address

This macro is used to reposition a tape file to read a record previously identified by a NOTE macro. The second operand of this macro specifies the address of the 4 byte main-storage location containing the required record identification. The 4 byte number must be in the form obtained from the NOTE macro.

Example:

Name	Oper	Operand
WORKFL	DTFMT	TYPEFLE=WORK,NOTEPNT=YES,

(continued)

```
            OPEN      WORKFL
              .
            WRITE     WORKFL,SQ,TEMP,80
            CHECK     WORKFL
            NOTE      WORKFL
            ST        1,IDENT          STORE IDENTIFICATION
              .

              .
            POINTR    IDENT
              .
IDENT       DS        F
TEMP        DS        CL80
              .
```

POINTW Macro

Name	Oper	Operand
	POINTW	Filename,Address

This macro instruction is used to reposition a work file to write a record *after* the one previously identified by a NOTE macro. The rules for the second operand specification are the same as described for POINTR macro above.

POINTS Macro

Name	Oper	Operand
	POINTS	Filename

This macro instruction is used to reposition a tape work file to the *beginning* of the file. The tape file is rewound; if any header labels are present, they are bypassed and the tape is positioned at the first record following the labels.

[Appendixes]

Appendix 1

Automatic Interrupt System

In this appendix we will discuss an overview of the System 360 interrupt system. The coverage will be limited to the basic structure and logic without going into detailed discussions.

System 360 has been designed to operate with a minimum of manual intervention, and as such, control programs and special hardware facilities have been provided to handle certain prescribed and/or unusual situations that may arise during program processing. Such situations may be the result of a malfunction in the computer system, an intervention by the operator, program error, a signal from an I/O device, unacceptable data, and so forth. If one or more of such conditions arise, the computer must be told what action to take. In System 360 an automatic interrupt system is provided to handle and process such conditions.

One of the reasons for using control programs is to reduce idle machine time during processing. Unlike the computers of the past, System 360 instruction set does not include a halt instruction; therefore a problem program cannot issue a halt command when it is finished processing. However, the finished program must pass control back to the supervisor. In System 360, this is accomplished by the Interrupt System. Other normal/abnormal conditions that may occur during problem program execution (such as an even number of bits in a byte, a halfword not aligned on integral boundary, a signal from an I/O device, etc.) also cause an automatic branch to the supervisor instead of stopping the computer. These automatic branches to the supervisor are known as *interrupts*, i.e., the current sequence of instructions is interrupted and an automatic branch is taken to a new set of instructions.

The heart of the interrupt system is the Program Status Word (PSW). To be able to understand the mechanism of the automatic interrupt system, it is necessary to take an expanded look at the PSW.

Program status word

The PSW is doubleword in length and consists of the following fields:

Bits 0 − 7: These 8 bits contain the System Mask. The system mask pertains to and controls I/O and External Interrupts.

Bits 8 − 11: These 4 bits contain the storage protection key. In case the storage protection feature is not installed on the computer or is not being used, these bits must be set to zeros.

Bits 12 − 15: This field contains 4 bits, each serving a different purpose.

Bit 12: If this bit is set to 1, the computer assumes that ASCII codes will be used; if the bit is 0, EBCDIC is assumed. (In this text we assume that this bit is set to 0).

Bit 13: If this bit is set to 1, a machine failure will cause an interrupt; if the bit is set to 0, machine failures are ignored. The usual state of this bit is 1 except when the customer engineer is servicing the machine.

Bit 14: The status of this bit, 0 or 1, tells us whether the computer is in RUN state or in WAIT state. When in WAIT state, the computer does not execute any instructions. (WAIT state, this bit is 1, RUN state the bit is 0.)

Bit 15: If this bit is set to 1, the computer is said to be in the problem state; if the bit is 0, the computer is in the supervisor state. Certain privileged and I/O instructions can only be executed when the computer is in supervisory state.

Bits 16 − 31: These bits contain the interruption code. At the time of an interruption, the system sets these bits and their contents help identify the cause of the interruption.

Bits 32 − 33: These 2 bits contain the Instruction Length Code (ILC). This field of the PSW indicates the length of the *last* instruction executed *prior* to the interrupt. Length codes and their meanings are:

Length Code	Meaning
01	1 Halfword
10	2 Halfword
11	3 Halfword

A code of 00 indicates that the computer did not determine the instruction length.

Bits 34 − 35: These 2 bits contain the condition code.

Bits 36 − 39: These 4 bits contain the program mask. Setting of these bits, 0 or 1, indicates whether certain unusual conditions will be allowed to cause an interrupt or not.

Bit 36: Fixed-point overflow.

Bit 37: Decimal overflow (Exponent overflow).

Bit 38: For Floating-point (Significance).

Bit 39: For Floating-point

To prevent interruptions caused by these exceptions, the corresponding program mask bits must be made zero.

Bits 40 − 63: These 24 bits contain the address of the next sequential instruction to be executed.

There are five distinct classes of interrupts. These are:

I/O: Can be caused by the end of an I/O operation.

Machine: Caused by a machine check, such as even number of bits in a byte.

Supervisor: Caused by a supervisor call instruction.

External: Can be caused by pressing an interrupt key on the operator's console.

Program: Caused by a program check, such as locating a halfword operand on an odd byte address.

For each of these five classes of interrupts, there is a distinct location for *new* and *old*

PSWs. These locations are as follows:

Interrupt	Old PSW	New PSW
External	0024	0088
Supervisor	0032	0096
Program	0040	0104
Machine	0048	0112
I/O	0056	0120

Note: The *old* and *new* PSWs reside in main-storage. There is only one *current* PSW, and it resides in the control section of the CPU. When an automatic interrupt occurs, the *current* PSW is automatically placed in the main-storage where it becomes the *old* PSW, and a *new* PSW is automatically fetched out of main-storage and becomes the *current* PSW.

The PSW location chart above indicates that a program check will cause the *current* PSW to be stored in location 0040 and a *new* PSW will be fetched from location 0104. When an interrupt occurs, the actual storing and loading of the PSWs is done automatically by the internal circuitry of the machine.

Interrupt action

When an interrupt occurs, the machine first determines the general cause of the interrupt, and then proceeds to take the following actions.

1. Stores the current PSW in the old PSW location for this class of interruption. The old PSW reflects the general status of the program, gives the reason for the interrupt (Interruption Code bits $16 - 31$) and also contains the address of the next instruction of the problem program. This process is done automatically by the internal circuitry of the computer.
2. Fetches a new PSW for this class of interrupt from the main-storage and loads it as the current PSW. This new PSW points to the first instruction of the interrupt handling routine. The interrupt handling routines are generally part of the supervisor, but at times can be written by house programmers.
3. The interrupt routine now proceeds to analyze the cause of the interrupt, stored in the old PSW, and then takes the necessary action required for the type of interrupt. Depending on the cause of the interrupt, this may consist of initiating an I/O operation, branching to a fix-up routine to correct the problem, or calling for a dump program to dump core, etc.

After the interrupt has been serviced, the instruction sequence of the original program may be resumed from the point of interruption, if possible. This is accomplished by the last instruction of the interrupt handling routine. This instruction (Load PSW — LPSW) loads the old PSW into the current PSW location and the control is back in the problem program.

Of the five different types of interrupts, we will discuss the conditions that cause

Program Interrupts in a little more detail. The remaining interrupts will not be discussed, as a detailed knowledge of these is not required of a beginner programmer.

Program Interrupts. A program interrupt causes the old PSW to be stored at location 40 and a new PSW to be fetched from location 104. Program interrupts are caused by various programming errors and other unusual conditions, such as: incorrect operands or specifications; and, exceptional results. In all, there are 15 possible conditions that can cause a program interruption. However, a program interrupt can occur only when the corresponding mask bit is one. If the mask bit is zero, the interrupt is ignored. As there are 4 program mask bits, 36 − 39, 4 of the 15 interruption causes can be masked. The actual cause of a program interruption is identified by the 4 low-order bits of the interruption code field of the old PSW (bits 28 − 31), the remainder of the bits (16 − 27) are made zero.

Number	Interrupt Code	Cause
1	0001	Operation
2	0010	Privileged operation
3	0011	Execute
4	0100	Protection[1]
5	0101	Addressing
6	0110	Specification
7	0111	Data
8	1000	Fixed-point overflow
9	1001	Fixed-point divide
10	1010	Decimal overflow
11	1011	Decimal divide
12	1100	Exponent overflow[1]
13	1101	Exponent underflow[1]
14	1110	Significance[1]
15	1111	Floating-point divide[1]

A description of the individual program exceptions follows.

Operation Exception. When an operation code is not assigned or the assigned operation is not available on the particular model, an operation exception is recognized. The operation is suppressed. The instruction length code is 1, 2, or 3.

Privileged-Operation Exception. When a privileged instruction is encountered in the problem state, a privileged operation exception is recognized. The operation is suppressed. The instruction length code is 1 or 2.

Execute Exception. When the subject instruction of an EXECUTE instruction is another EXECUTE, an execute exception is recognized. The operation is suppressed.

[1]Exceptions numbered 4, 12, 13, 14, and 15 are not discussed in any more detail in this text.

The instruction length code is 2.

Addressing Exception. When an instruction's address operand specifies any part of data or an instruction outside the available storage for the particular computer, an addressing exception is recognized. In most cases, the operation is terminated for an invalid data address. In a few cases, an invalid data address causes the instruction to be suppressed (NI, XI, OI, MVI, CVD, EX, ST, STC, STH). In case of invalid instruction address the operation is always suppressed. The instruction length code is normally 1, 2, or 3; but may be 0 in the case of a data address.

Specification Exception. A specification exception is recognized when:
1. A data or instruction does not specify an integral boundary for the unit of information.
2. R1 field of an instruction specifies an odd register address for a pair of general registers that contain a 64 bit operand.
3. The multiplier or divisor in decimal arithmetic exceeds 15 digits and sign.
4. The first operand field is shorter than, or equal to, the second operand field in decimal multiplication or division.

The operation is suppressed. The instruction length code is 1, 2, or 3.

Data Exception. A data exception is recognized when:
1. The sign or digit codes of operands in decimal arithmetic or editing operations or CVB are incorrect.
2. Fields in decimal arithmetic overlap incorrectly.
3. The decimal multiplicand has too many high-order significant digits.

The operation is terminated. The instruction length code is 2 or 3.

Fixed-Point-Overflow Exception. When a high-order carry occurs or high-order significant bits are lost in fixed-point add, subtract, shift, or sign control operations, a fixed-point-overflow exception is recognized. The operation is completed. The interruption may be masked by PSW bit 36. Instruction length code is 1 or 2.

Fixed-Point-Divide Exception. A fixed-point-divide exception is recognized when a quotient exceeds the register size in fixed-point divide operation, including division by zero, or the result of CVB instruction exceeds 31 bits. Division is suppressed. Conversion is completed by ignoring the information placed outside the register. The instruction length code is 1 or 2.

Decimal-Overflow Exception. When the destined field is too small to contain the result field in a decimal operation, a decimal-overflow exception is recognized. The operation is completed by ignoring the overflow information. The interruption may be masked by PSW bit 37. The instruction length code is 3.

Decimal-Divide Exception. When a quotient exceeds the specified data field size, a decimal-divide exception is recognized. The operation is suppressed. The instruction length code is 3.

Return to problem program

The last instruction of the interrupt-handling routine returns control to the problem program in those cases where it is possible and desirable to recover the error and continue the problem program from the point of interrupt. The instruction that accomplishes this is known as the Load PSW instruction. Its main function is to resume problem program processing after a supervisor call, an I/O, or external interrupt has been serviced. The Load PSW instruction fetches the old PSW from the designated doubleword location and loads it as the current PSW. The CPU now is able to resume the problem program processing from the point of interruption.

Masking of interrupts

At times it may be desirable, or even necessary, to prevent automatic interrupts, or at least postpone recognizing them until a later time. Preventing an interrupt, or keeping it pending until later, is known as *interrupt masking*. Masking is achieved by manipulating certain bits in the PSW. Three specific fields are provided by the PSW for the purpose of masking. These are: system mask; machine check mask; and, program mask. The system mask field is used to mask (prevent) I/O and external interrupts, while machine check mask bits are used to mask machine interrupts, and program mask bits are used to mask 4 of the 15 possible program exceptions.

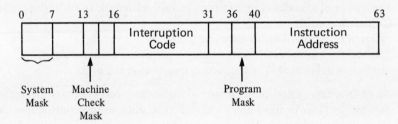

Whenever the mask bits for particular types of interrupts are made zero, the corresponding interrupts are said to be masked. On the other hand, when mask bits are set to one, the CPU can be interrupted for the corresponding type of interrupt. In this appendix we will discuss *only* the program mask bits, their manipulation and uses.

Programmer Use of Interrupts. Normally the processing of interrupts is controlled by a control program. The programmer at times may wish to have control, or partial control, of certain types of interrupts. Program mask bits 36 and 37 of the PSW, if made zero, will prevent program interruptions caused by fixed-point-overflow and decimal overflow respectively.

Set Program Mask Instruction.

Name	Oper	Operand	
	SPM	R1	RR Type Instruction

This instruction permits setting of the condition code and the program mask bits in either the problem or supervisor state. Bits 2 − 7 of the general register specified by R1 operand replace the condition code and the program mask bits of the current PSW. Bits 0, 1, and 8 − 31 of the register are ignored. The contents of the register remain unchanged.

Example:

Suppose that a program loops to repeat an arithmetic operation on a data field (fixed-point or decimal) until the field overflows. Instead of checking the magnitude of the result field each time through the loop, a programmer written overflow routine could be used to handle the overflow condition.

Name	Oper	Operand	
	SR	2,2	SET REGISTER 2 TO ZERO
	SPM	2	MASK OUT PROGRAM INTERRUPT
	L	3,X	
	A	4,Y	
	BC	14,ALLOK	CONTINUE IF NO OVERFLOW
	BAL	7,OVERFL	ELSE GO TO OVERFL ROUTINE
ALLOK	A	4,Z	
	BC	14,OUT	
	BAL	7,OVERFL	

Appendix 2

Job Control Statements (DOS)

In this appendix we will briefly discuss the job control statements necessary for: compiling a program; and, compiling, link editing, and executing a program.

When a program is first written, the normal practice is to only compile it as there is little chance of its successful execution (due to coding and keypunch mistakes). During compilation, the source program is translated into machine language and error messages, if any, are listed. After correcting the errors, the program is ready for the test run (compile, link-edit, and execute). In the following pages we will explain the job control statements to achieve the objectives listed above.

Job card

The JOB card has the following format:

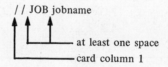

Columns 1 − 2 must contain / / followed by at least one blank, then the word JOB, and this must again be followed by at least one blank. Following the last blank, the programmer enters the name of the job to be compiled. The jobname operand is composed of from 1 to 8 characters and provides a name by which this program can be referenced. Example,

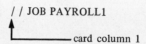

OPTION card

When the system for a given installation is generated, certain options are selected as standard options. Some of the options are: catalog the program on SYSRES for future reference; punch the object deck on SYSPCH; dump core in case of abnormal program end; etc. The format of the OPTION card is as follows:

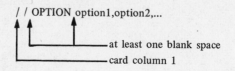

The options most commonly used are:

LOG: Control statements to be listed on SYSLST.

DUMP: In case of abnormal program end, dump registers and main-storage on SYSLST.

LINK: Output from assembler is written on SYSLNK for linkage-editing.

DECK: Output from assembler is punched on SYSPCH.

LIST: Source program is listed on SYSLST.

SYM: Print the symbol table on SYSLST and/or punch symbol deck on SYSPCH.

XREF: Print the cross reference table on SYSLST.

CATAL: Catalog the object module in the core image library immediately after completing the link-edit step. CATAL implies LINK option.

Note: If the name of an option is preceded by NO, then that particular option is suppressed. Thus NODECK means suppress DECK option.

The option card is used to override the standard options selected and included in the system at system generation time. Once an OPTION card is read, the specified option(s) applies until the end of the job or until another option card containing a contrary option is read.

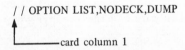

/ / OPTION LIST,NODECK,DUMP

————card column 1

ASSGN card

This job control command is used to relate the symbolic names (used in the program to address I/O devices) to the physical I/O devices available at program execution time. The symbolic names used in the program are of the form SYSnnn. Where nnn can be any number between 000 – 244 inclusive or nnn=RDR, IPT, LST, PCH, RES, or LNK.

SYSRDR: Refers to system reader from which the control cards are read (usually a card reader but it is possible to use a tape unit as SYSRDR).

SYSIPT: Refers to the system input unit from which data is read. SYSIPT may be the same unit as SYSRDR.

SYSLST: Refers to the printer used for listing normal printed output.

SYSPCH: Refers to the system punch, usually a card punch unit, but a tape unit could also be used. SYSPCH may be the same unit as SYSLST.

SYSLOG: Refers to the console typewriter or the line printer on which operator messages are to be logged.

SYSRES: Refers to the system residence disk unit.

SYSLNK: Refers to the disk unit used as input by the linkage editor.

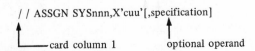

/ / ASSGN SYSnnn,X'cuu'[,specification]

————card column 1   optional operand

nnn specification can be RDR, IPT, PCH, LST, LOG, or any number from 000 to 244. X'cuu' operand specifies the address of the physical unit which is to be related to the symbolic name specified by SYSnnn operand. The values that can be assumed by X'cuu' are:

c = 0–6   (channel number), and uu = 00–FF (in hex, the address of
the unit on the channel).

The third operand, specification, is optional and its value can be either of the following:

X'CO'	set tape to 1600 bpi.
X'C8'	set tape to 800 bpi.
USC	block 1403 data check
ALT	alternate tape unit

The tape density specification can be used only if the tape unit can operate at either of the two densities. USC can be used only if the printer is equipped with universal character set. If ALT is specified, then the associated device is used as alternate when the tape on the original device has been completely processed. This specification can be used only for tape files occupying more than one reel of tape.

// ASSGN SYS020,X'180'
// ASSGN SYS020,X'181',ALT

With the above assignment the processing will start with the tape on unit 180; when EOV is encountered, the system will automatically switch to device 181. By using this type of arrangement, considerable tape mounting and dismounting time can be saved.

EXEC card

This card has the same format as the job card.

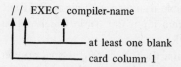

For Assembler Language programs, the compiler name is ASSEMBLY.

// EXEC ASSEMBLY

Another example of the EXEC card is:

// EXEC LNKEDT

In this command the specification is for calling the linkage-editor program for editing the object module which has been placed on SYSLNK unit by the assembly program. This step is necessary because the object module produced as a result of assembly process (// EXEC ASSEMBLY) does not have absolute core addresses assigned to it. The linkage-editor assigns absolute core addresses to the object module and stores it in the core image library.

The execute card needed to execute the object program (after link-edit step) is of the following format:

$$// \text{ EXEC}$$

The net effect of this command is to bring the edited object module from the core image library into the main storage and begin execution of the program. Listed below are the job control cards required for compilation only.

Job control cards for compile only

JOB card.
OPTION card(s) if needed.
EXEC card for assembly.
The source deck goes here.
/* card to indicate the end of the source deck.
/& card to indicate the end of the job.

Job control cards for compile, link-edit, and go

JOB card.
ASSGN cards (if needed).
OPTION card for link-editing option.
EXEC card for compilation.
The source deck goes here.
/* card.
EXEC card for link-edit step.
EXEC card for go step.
Data cards go here (if any).
/* card.
/& card.

Following is an example of JCL for compile, link-edit, and go

```
// JOB PRACTICE
// ASSGN SYS012,X'182'
// ASSGN SYS014,X'01F'
// ASSGN SYS010,X'181'
// OPTION LINK
// EXEC ASSEMBLY
The source deck goes here
/*
// EXEC LNKEDT
// EXEC
```

Data cards (if any) go here
/*
/&

If the problem program uses tape or disk files with standard labels, additional control cards are required. For each tape file and disk file with standard labels, a volume card is used. The format of this card is:

/ / VOL SYSnnn,filename

The filename may consist of 1 to 8 alphameric characters and is the same name that is used by the problem program to reference this file.

/ / VOL SYS018,PAYFILE

The volume card must be followed by a TPLAB card (for a tape file) or by a DLAB card (for a DASD file). The format of TPLAB card is as follows:

/ / TPLAB 'label fields 3–10'

The label fields 3 − 10 occupy 49 bytes (refer to Appendix 5 for standard tape label format). The information supplied in the TPLAB card must be the same as in the label for this tape file. DOS provides no facilities for processing fields 11 − 13 (security, block count, and system code fields). However, by continuing the TPLAB card and by starting with column 16 of the second card, a programmer may place fields 11 − 13 and these fields will be placed in the label of the output tape file.

Note: The VOL and TPLAB job control commands have been replaced by a single job control command − TLBL. However, VOL and TPLAB commands can still be used. See IBM Manual C24−5036 for details.

In case of the disk files, the VOL card must be followed by a DLAB card. Its format is:

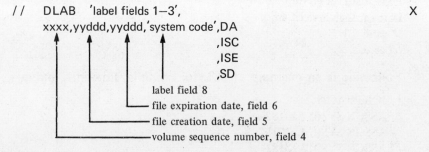

(In case of input files, the system code operand is ignored.)

The *last operand is optional* and if omitted, SD is assumed. Meaning of these four specifications are listed below.

SD: specifies a sequential file.
DA: specifies a direct file.

ISC: specifies loading or extending an IS file.

ISE: specifies an existing IS file.

In case of disk files, an extent job control card is needed for each extent of the file. The format of this card is:

/ / XTENT type,sequence,lower,upper,'serial',SYSnnn

The specifications given below apply to 2311 DASD only. The type field may occupy from 1 to 3 columns.

1 = data area, not part of split cylinder.

2 = overflow area for indexed sequential file.

4 = index area for indexed sequential file.

128 = data area for split cylinder file.

The sequence field may contain any number (decimal) between 0 − 255 inclusive. For a master index used with an IS file the sequence number is 0; the cylinder index is sequence numbered 1; and the data areas are numbered starting with 2. In case a master index is not used with a file, there is no 0 sequence number for the file. In case of non−IS files, the numbers for data extents start with 0.

The lower (lower extent limit) operand is a nine column field and the information punched in this field is of the form BSSCCCKHH. Where,

B = cell number, 0 for 2311 DASD.

SS = sub-cell number, 00 for 2311 DASD.

CCC = cylinder number, 000−199.

K = block position, 0 for 2311 DASD.

HH = head, 00−09.

The upper (upper extent limit) operand has the same format as the lower operand.

The serial number, which must always be enclosed in quotation marks, specifies the volume serial number. This must be the same number as specified in field 3 (file serial number field) of the format−1 label for this file. This field occupies six columns.

Note: The VOL and DLAB statements for disk files have been replaced by a single job control command − DLBL. However, VOL and DLAB commands still are used. The XTENT job control statement has been replaced by EXTENT (XTENT can still be used). Refer to IBM Manual C24−5036 for details.

Appendix 3

Assembler Listing Description

The assembler listing consists of five sections; these are: external symbol dictionary items; the source and object program statements; relocation dictionary items; symbol cross-reference table; and, diagnostic messages. The following sample program illustrates an actual assembler listing run on IBM System/360 under DOS. Several errors have been included to show their effect on an assembly.

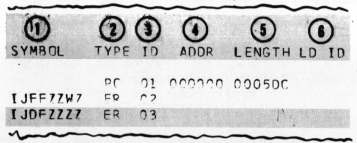

SYMBOL	TYPE	ID	ADDR	LENGTH	LD ID
	PC	01	000000	0005DC	
IJFFZZW7	ER	02			
IJDFZZZZ	ER	03			

FIGURE A.3.1. External Symbol Dictionary.

External symbol dictionary (ESD)

This section of the listing contains the external symbol dictionary information passed to the linkage-editor in the object module.

1. This column contains symbols that appear in the name field of CSECT or START statements, as operands of ENTRY and EXTRN statements, or in the operand field of V-type address constants.
2. This column contains the type designator for the entry, as listed below:
   SD: names section definition. The symbol appeared in the name field of a CSECT or START statement.
   LD: the symbol appeared as the operand of an ENTRY statement.
   ER: external reference. The symbol appeared as the operand of an EXTRN statement, or was defined as a V-type address constant.
   PC: unnamed control section definition.
   CM: common control section definition.
3. This column contains the external symbol dictionary identification number (ID). It is used by the LD entry of the ESD and by the relocation dictionary to cross reference to the ESD.
4. This column contains the address of the symbol (hexadecimal notation) for SD and LD type entries, and zeros for ER type entries. For PC and CM type entries, it indicates the beginning address of the control section.

480

5. This column contains the assembled length, in bytes, of the control section (hexadecimal notation).
6. This column contains, for LD type entries, the identification (ID) number assigned to the ESD entry that identifies the control section in which the symbol was defined.

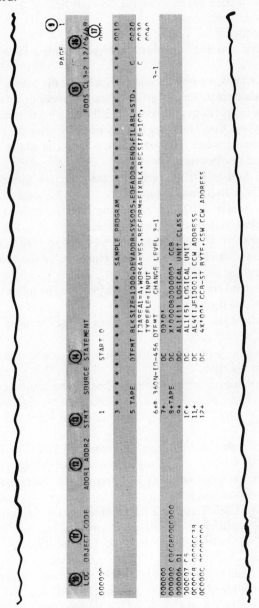

FIGURE A.3.2. Source and Object Program.

Source and object program

This section of the assembly listing documents the source statements and the resulting object program.

7. It is the symbol that appears in the name field of the first TITLE statement.
8. This is the information taken from the operand field of a TITLE statement. (Items 7 and 8 have been omitted.)
9. Listing page number.
10. This column contains the assembled address (hexadecimal notation) of the object code.
11. This column contains the object code produced by the source statement. The notation is hexadecimal. Entries are machine instructions or assembled constants. Machine instructions are printed in full with a blank inserted after every four digits (2 bytes). Constants may be only partially printed.
12. These two columns contain effective addresses (result of adding together a base register value and displacement value):

    The column header ADDR1 contains the effective address for the first operand of an SS or an SI instruction.

    The column header ADDR2 contains the effective address of the second operand of any instruction referencing storage.
13. This column contains the statement number. A plus sign (+) to the right of the number indicates that the statement was generated as the result of a macro instruction processing.
14. This column contains the source program statement. The following items apply to this section of the listing:

    a. Source statements are listed, including those brought in by macro statements.

    b. The statements generated as the result of a macro instruction follow the macro instruction.

    c. Diagnostic messages are not listed in-line in the source and object program section. An error indicator, ***ERROR***, appears following the statement in error. The message appears in the diagnostic section of the listing.

    d. Literals will appear in the listing following an LTORG or the END statement or both. Literals are identified by the equal (=) sign preceding them.

    e. If the END statement contains an operand, the transfer address appears in the location column (LOC).

    f. In the case of CSECT and DSECT statements, the location field contains the beginning address of these control sections, i.e., the first occurrence.

    g. For a USING statement, the location field contains the value of the first operand.

    h. For LTORG and ORG statements, the location field contains the location assigned to the literal pool or the value of the ORG operand.

    i. For an EQU statement the location field contains the value assigned.

15. This field indicates the assembler level and version number.
16. Current date obtained from SET card.
17. Identification-sequence field from the source statements.

(18) POS.ID	(19) REL.ID	(20) FLAGS	(21) ADDRESS
01	01	0C	000008
01	02	18	000011
01	01	08	000025
01	01	08	000039
01	01	0C	000040
01	01	0C	000078
01	03	18	000081
01	01	0C	000088
01	01	08	000099
01	01	0C	0000AC
01	01	0C	000080
01	01	0C	0000E4
01	01	0C	0000E8
01	01	0C	000500
01	01	0C	000504
01	01	0C	000508

FIGURE A.3.3. Relocation Dictionary.

Relocation dictionary

This section of the listing contains the relocation dictionary information passed to the linkage editor in the object module. The entries describe the address constants in the assembled program that are affected by relocation. For a detailed explanation of these four columns consult IBM System Reference Library Manual C24–3414, Assembler Language.

Cross reference

This section of the assembly listing gives information regarding symbols — where they are defined and used in the program.
22. This column contains the symbols.
23. This column gives the length (decimal notation), in bytes, of the field occupied by the symbol value.
24. This column contains either the address the symbol represents, or a value to

which the symbol is equated.

25. This column gives the statement number of the statement in which the symbol was defined.

26. This column contains the statement numbers of statements in which the symbol appears as an operand.

㉒ SYMBOL	㉓ LEN	㉔ VALUE	㉕ DEFN	㉖ REFERENCES			
A	00100	0000F0	00106	0028	0029		
B	00132	0005BC	00108	0058	0063	0085	
BEGIN	00002	0000A0	00066	0109			
END	00004	000CDC	00096	0023			
IJF10001	00008	000038	00028	0011			
IJF20001	00004	000044	00030				
IJJC0006	00004	0000F0	00098				
IJJD0002	00004	0000A8	00074				
IJJZ0002	00001	0000A0	00064				
PRINT	00006	000070	00047	0076	0088	0100	0114
READ	00004	0000B6	00081	0091			
TAPE	00006	00000C	00008	0075	0081	0099	0112
WRK	00130	0004D8	00107	0082	0085	0113	

FIGURE A.3.4. Cross-Reference.

Diagnostics

This section contains the diagnostic messages issued as a result of error conditions encountered in the program.

27. This column contains the number of the statement in error.

28. This column contains the message identifier.

29. This column contains the message.

A message indicating the total number of statements in error is printed following the cross reference table. If no statements are in error, the message: NO STATEMENTS FLAGGED IN THIS ASSEMBLY is printed following the cross reference table and no diagnostic section is printed.

See page 485 for Figure A.3.5. on Diagnostics.

STMT	ERROR CODE	MESSAGE	
67	IJY016	NEAR OPERAND COLUMN	5--INCORRECT REGISTER SPECIFICATION
73	IJY025	NEAR OPERAND COLUMN	15--ADDRESSABILITY ERROR
74	IJY035	NEAR OPERAND COLUMN	14--ADDRESSABILITY ERROR
81	IJY035	NEAR OPERAND COLUMN	11--ADDRESSABILITY ERROR
82	IJY035	NEAR OPERAND COLUMN	10--ADDRESSABILITY ERROR
85	IJY035	NEAR OPERAND COLUMN	5--ADDRESSABILITY ERROR
85	IJY035	NEAR OPERAND COLUMN	14--ADDRESSABILITY ERROR
85	IJY016	NEAR OPERAND COLUMN	18--INCORRECT REGISTER SPECIFICATION
88	IJY035	NEAR OPERAND COLUMN	12--ADDRESSABILITY ERROR
91	IJY035	NEAR OPERAND COLUMN	8--ADDRESSABILITY ERROR
97	IJY035	NEAR OPERAND COLUMN	15--ADDRESSABILITY ERROR
98	IJY035	NEAR OPERAND COLUMN	14--ADDRESSABILITY ERROR

10 STATEMENTS FLAGGED IN THIS ASSEMBLY

FIGURE A.3.5. Diagnostics.

Appendix 4

Number System

In day-to-day life the number system most commonly used is the decimal number system. In this system, numbers of any magnitude can be represented by using ten different symbols, and when necessary, the decimal point. In this system, the first digit to the left of the decimal place represents the value written down. As we proceed to the left, the next digit represents ten times the value of the digit; the next, a hundred times the value of the digit, and so on.

For example, in the number 222 the rightmost digit represents the value=2, the next digit to the left represents the value 20 and the leftmost digit represents 200. This number representation system was invented by Arabs. Cash registers, calculators, speedometers, etc., use this number system to record data. Computers, on the other hand, can be built most economically to function in binary mode. As such, the decimal number system becomes impractical for use by computers.

> Binary Mode: This means that computers function on quantities which can have only two possible states; usually referred to as ON and OFF or 1 and 0 status.

The number system most adaptable to this type of indicator is the Binary Number System. This number system uses only two digits, and these are 0 and 1. Any binary number can be represented by using a combination of the binary digits 0 and 1.

Digital computers have the capability of converting decimal numbers to binary notations and vice versa, but it is of great importance that a student of data processing be able to understand the basic principles of number systems. In this section we will present the basic principles and methods of representing data in the following number systems:

1. Decimal Number System.
2. Binary Number System.
3. Hexadecimal Number System.

Before going into detailed study of these different number systems, let us familiarize ourselves with the basic principles of all number systems.

Common principles

Decimal number system will be used to illustrate most of the basic principles of numbering systems. In the decimal number system each symbol or digit is given a fixed value. The string of numbers or symbols is used to represent any decimal number. The symbols used are 0, 1, 2, 3, 4, 5, 6, 7, 8, 9. The value of each symbol in this string is one higher than that of the symbol before it, from the smallest to the largest. Any decimal number can be expressed by a combination of these 10 digits. The value of the number so created depends upon two factors. These are: the digits used; and, the relative position of the individual digits in the number. This is also termed as the *place value* of the digit.

In decimal system, the rightmost place is called the units or ones position. Proceeding to the left, the place values are *tens, hundreds, thousands* and so on. From this we can say that the place value represented by each place increases by a power to ten, from right to left.

This increase in the place value is in direct relation to the Radix or the Base of a number system.

Base: The number of symbols used in a number system. In the decimal system ten symbols are used. Therefore, the base value of this system is 10. The example below illustrates the place values in the decimal number system.

10^4	10^3	10^2	10^1	10^0
10,000	1,000	100	10	1

Note: Any number raised to the power of 0=1.

Consider a decimal number and express it in terms of its place value. Decimal number 7434 could be expressed as:

$$7000 + 400 + 30 + 4 \qquad = 7434$$
$$7 \times 10^3 + 4 \times 10^2 + 3 \times 10^1 + 4 \times 10^0$$
$$7 \times 1000 + 4 \times 100 + 3 \times 10 + 4 \times 1$$
$$7000 + 400 + 30 + 4 \qquad = 7434$$

The value of the number is the sum of those place values which contain any digit other than zero. The zero digit functions as a place holder and when calculating the value represented by a number, the value represented by zero digit(s) is to be ignored. Electronic computers, due to the nature of their storage, use a numbering system with a base of two. This number system is known as *Binary Number System.*

Binary number system

This system uses only two symbols to represent numbers 0 and 1. Any binary number can be represented as a succession of zeros and ones. As the base value is two, the place value increases by a power of two from right to left.

Example:

2^5	2^4	2^3	2^2	2^1	2^0
32	16	8	4	2	1

Note: Any number raised to the power of zero is always 1.

Example:

Binary Number 1101

$$1 \times 2^3 + 1 \times 2^2 + 0 \times 2^1 + 1 \times 2^0$$
$$1 \times 8 + 1 \times 4 + 0 \times 2 + 1 \times 1$$
$$8 + 4 + 0 + 1 = (13)_{10}$$

Note: Remember place values represented by zero are not counted.

To avoid confusion when dealing with different numbering systems, it is customary to write the base number in subscript form:

$$(1101)_2 = (13)_{10}$$

or

$$1101_2 = 13_{10}$$

(Being easier, the former is more commonly used.)

The table below gives some decimal numbers and their binary equivalents.

DECIMAL	BINARY
0	0000
1	0001
2	0010
3	0011
4	0100
5	0101
6	0110
7	0111
8	1000
9	1001
10	1010
11	1011
12	1100
13	1101
14	1110
15	1111

Binary to Decimal Conversion. There are two different ways this can be accomplished.

1. Adding up the place values of the binary digits.
2. Double and Add method.

Method 1: Adding up the place values.

Binary number	1	1	0	1	1	0	1	1
Place values	128	64	32	16	8	4	2	1

So the number will be $128+64+16+8+2+1 = (219)_{10}$

Remember that the place values held by 0 digit(s) are not counted.

EXERCISE:
Convert the following binary numbers to decimal by using Place Value Method.

A.		1011
B.		1001111
C.		10000001
D.		1111000011110001

From example D above, it is clear that with large binary numbers it becomes quite cumbersome to calculate the place values. In such cases the second method, Double and Add, is more commonly used.

Method 2: Double and Add. Starting from left to right, follow the following steps.
1. Multiply the high-order digit of the binary number by its base value (2).
2. Add the next right-hand digit to the product.
3. Multiply the sum by the base value (2).
4. Repeat steps 2 and 3.
5. Stop when the extreme right-hand binary digit has been added.

Example:
Convert binary number 1101 to decimal.

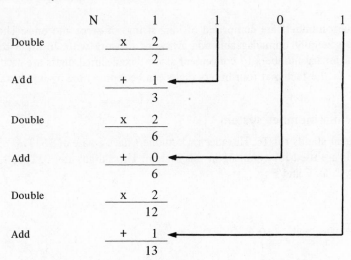

Conversion of Decimal Numbers to Binary.

Rules:
1. Divide the decimal number by the base value of the binary system.
2. The remainder, either 0 or 1, represents the rightmost digit of the binary number.
3. Divide the quotient obtained, in step 2, by the base value of the binary system.

4. The remainder will be the next digit of the binary number.

5. Repeat steps 3 and 4 until the quotient is zero.

Note: The first remainder represents the rightmost digit of the binary number and the last remainder represents the leftmost digit of the binary number.

Example:

Convert 15 to binary.

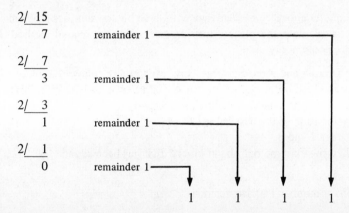

Large binary numbers are comprised of long strings of zeros and ones. These large numbers are generally unmanageable and awkward to work with. In order to reduce the length of binary numbers to convenient sizes, hexadecimal digits are used. This is possible due to the fact that four binary digits can be represented by one hexadecimal number.

Hexadecimal number system

Hexadecimal stands for 16. Hexadecimal numbers have a base of 16. This means 16 distinct digits are used for counting in this system. These digits are: 0, 1, 2, 3, 4, 5, 6, 7, 8, 9, A, B, C, D, E and F

Where

A	=	Decimal	10
B	=		11
C	=		12
D	=		13
E	=		14
F	=		15

It may be a little confusing to see alpha characters in a number system, but after a while it will become quite easy to interpret hexadecimal characters.

The table below shows Decimal, Hexadecimal and Binary Numbers.

DECIMAL	HEX	BINARY
0	0	0000
1	1	0001
2	2	0010
3	3	0011
4	4	0100
5	5	0101
6	6	0110
7	7	0111
8	8	1000
9	9	1001
10	A	1010
11	B	1011
12	C	1100
13	D	1101
14	E	1110
15	F	1111

Examine some of the place values in the Hex system.

16^3	16^2	16^1	16^0
4096	256	16	1

Some Hexadecimal numbers.

DBEF   FFF   00F   123   17A   1F7

Any of the 16 hex digits can be used to write a hex number.

The base value of the binary number system is 2 and it could be expressed as 2^1. The base value of the hexadecimal number system is 16, and this could be expressed as 2^4.

Binary Base	Hexadecimal Base
$2^1 = 2$	$2^4 = 16$

The ratio of 1:4 makes it possible for one hexadecimal digit to represent four binary digits. For example:

BINARY	HEXADECIMAL
1111	F
1010	A
1100	C etc.

Note: All information in storage is represented by binary numbers. Hex numbers are used primarily to display information on console and for indicating long binary codes in certain printed material.

Conversion from Decimal to Hexadecimal.

Rules.

1. Divide the decimal number by the base value of the hexadecimal number system, i.e., 16.
2. The remainder represents the low-order digit of the hex number. In case the remainder is 10 or more, it has to be converted to a hex number.
3. Divide the quotient so obtained by 16.
4. The remainder becomes the next digit of the hex number.
5. Repeat steps 3 and 4 until a quotient of 0 value is obtained.

Note: 1. First remainder represents the rightmost digit and the last remainder represents the leftmost digit of the hexadecimal number.

2. Any remainder which is greater than 9 has to be converted to its hexadecimal equivalent digit.

Example:

Convert Decimal 1792 to Hex.

```
16/  1792
      112      remainder 0 ─────────────────────┐
16/   112                                       │
        7      remainder 0 ───────────┐         │
16/     7                             │         │
        0      remainder 7 ──┐        │         │
                             ▼        ▼         ▼
                             7        0         0
```

Conversion from Hexadecimal to Decimal.

Rules.

1. Convert each hex digit to its equivalent decimal number.
2. Multiply the leftmost number by 16.
3. Add the next digit to the product.
4. Multiply the sum by 16.
5. Repeat steps 3 and 4.
6. Stop when the rightmost number has been added.

Example:
Convert Hex AC9 to decimal.

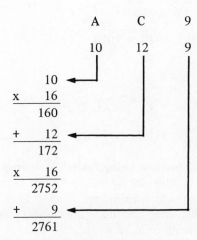

$$
\begin{array}{ccc}
A & C & 9 \\
10 & 12 & 9
\end{array}
$$

$$
\begin{array}{r}
10 \\
\times \quad 16 \\
\hline
160 \\
+ \quad 12 \\
\hline
172 \\
\times \quad 16 \\
\hline
2752 \\
+ \quad 9 \\
\hline
2761
\end{array}
$$

Conversion from Binary to Hexadecimal. Earlier in this chapter, we discussed how each Hex digit was capable of representing 4 Binary digits. This principle is used for converting Binary numbers to Hex.

Rules.
1. Starting from the rightmost digit (Binary or Bit Point) of the binary number, separate the numbers into groups of 4 digits. In case the leftmost group does not consist of 4 digits add the necessary high-order zeros.
2. Convert each 4 binary digits to their equivalent hex digit.

Example:
Convert Binary 1101101101110110011 to Hex.

Groups	0011	0110	1101	1101	1011
Hex	3	6	D	D	B

Example:
Convert Binary 10110001011111000011 to Hex.

Groups	0010	1100	0101	1110	0011
Hex	2	C	5	E	3

Conversion from Hexadecimal to Binary.

Rule.
Convert each Hex digit to 4 bit Binary Number.

Example:
Convert Hex 86AC to Binary.

8	6	A	C
1000	0110	1010	1101

Example:
Convert Hex FFF to Binary.

F	F	F
1111	1111	1111

Decimal and Hexadecimal Conversion Using Tables. To convert a decimal number to its equivalent hexadecimal number, locate the next lower decimal number and trace horizontally to find its equivalent hexadecimal number. Each difference is used to obtain the next hexadecimal number until the entire number is developed.
Note: The first hex digit takes the leftmost position.

To convert a hexadecimal number to its equivalent decimal number, locate the hexadecimal number and its decimal equivalent for each position. Add these to obtain the decimal number.

BYTE				BYTE				BYTE			
0123		4567		0123		4567		0123		4567	
HEX	DEC	HEX	DEC	HEX	DEC	HEX	DEC	HEX	DEC	HEX	DEC
0	0	0	0	0	0	0	0	0	0	0	0
1	1,048,576	1	65,536	1	4,096	1	256	1	16	1	1
2	2,097,152	2	131,072	2	8,192	2	512	2	32	2	2
3	3,145,728	3	196,608	3	12,288	3	768	3	48	3	3
4	4,194,304	4	262,144	4	16,384	4	1,024	4	64	4	4
5	5,242,880	5	327,680	5	20,480	5	1,280	5	80	5	5
6	6,291,456	6	393,216	6	24,576	6	1,536	6	96	6	6
7	7,340,032	7	458,752	7	28,672	7	1,792	7	112	7	7
8	8,388,608	8	524,288	8	32,768	8	2,048	8	128	8	8
9	9,437,184	9	589,824	9	36,864	9	2,304	9	144	9	9
A	10,485,760	A	655,360	A	40,960	A	2,560	A	160	A	10
B	11,534,336	B	720,896	B	45,056	B	2,816	B	176	B	11
C	12,582,912	C	786,432	C	49,152	C	3,072	C	192	C	12
D	13,631,488	D	851,968	D	53,248	D	3,328	D	208	D	13
E	14,680,064	E	917,504	E	57,344	E	3,584	E	224	E	14
F	15,728,640	F	983,040	F	61,440	F	3,840	F	240	F	15
6		5		4		3		2		1	

Example:

Convert $(347)_{10}$ to hexadecimal.

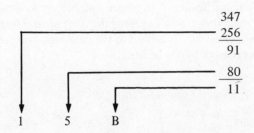

Example:

Convert decimal 1723 to hexadecimal.

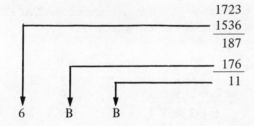

Example:

Convert $(F12)_{16}$ to Decimal.

F = 3840
1 =   16
2 =   2
     3858   Decimal equivalent

Example:

Convert $(FFF)_{16}$ to Decimal.

F = 3840
F = 240
F =   15
     4095   Decimal equivalent

Binary addition

Binary addition is very similar to decimal addition in that the carry-overs are done in the same way as with decimal addition. In binary number system, there are only two symbols, 0 and 1, meaning that 1 plus 1 exceeds the limit of counting and a carry of 1 is developed. The carry, as always, is carried to the next high-order position. The table below gives the various rules of binary addition.

Binary Addition Table

$$0 + 0 = 0$$
$$0 + 1 = 1$$
$$1 + 0 = 1$$
$$1 + 1 = 0 \text{ with a carry of } 1.$$

(The last result could also be written as 10, but is pronounced *one,Zero*.)

The examples below illustrate the rules of binary addition.

```
                              1 ◄──── carries ────► 1 1
    1 1 0 1 0       1 1 0 1 1 0          1 1 1
  +   0 1 0 1      +0 0 0 1 0 1         +0 1 1
  ───────────     ─────────────       ───────
    1 1 1 1 1       1 1 1 0 1 1         1 0 1 0
```

The example on the right (above) illustrates the expansion of the binary addition rules, i.e., 1+1+1=1 with a carry of 1. This may also be written as 11 and is pronounced as *one,one*. The following three examples illustrate this process.

```
      1 1 1 ◄───────── carries ─────────► 1 1 1
    1 0 1 1 1 0                          1 1 1 1
   +0 0 1 1 1 0                         +1 1 1 1
   ───────────                         ─────────
    1 1 1 1 0 0                          1 1 1 1 0
```

At times we may have to add several binary numbers together and more than one carry may develop to a single column.

```
                      ┌ 1 1 1 1
          carries ──► ┤ 1 1   1 1
                      └
                       0 0 0 1 =  1
                       1 0 1 1 = 11
                       1 1 0 1 = 13
                       1 0 1 0 = 10
                       1 0 0 1 =  9
                     ──────────────
                    (1 0 1 1 0 0)=(44)
```

Binary subtraction

The conventional direct method of subtraction involves borrowing from next high-order digit whenever necessary. The rules of direct binary subtraction are given in the table below:

Binary Subtraction Table

$$0 - 0 = 0$$
$$1 - 1 = 0$$
$$1 - 0 = 1$$
$$0 - 1 = 1 \text{ with a borrow of } 1.$$

In terms of *borrowing*, the last rule could be stated as:

$$10 - 1 = 1$$

which is the same as decimal $2 - 1 = 1$.

Some examples of binary subtraction are:

```
                                                    10
                                                   Ø 10
       0 1 1 1            0 1 1 1                 1 1 Ø 1
     − 0 1 0 1          − 0 0 1 1               − 0 1 1 1
     ─────────          ─────────               ─────────
       0 0 1 0            0 1 0 0                 0 1 1 0
```

From the last example we see that borrowing is necessary whenever the subtrahend (the number on the bottom) is larger than the minuend (the number on the top). Borrowing consists of subtracting a 1 from the next high-order digit to the left in the minuend and placing it to the left of the digit in the minuend. For example:

```
        10
        10
       − 1
      ──────
        01
```

An alternative, and certainly a better method of subtraction, is the *pay back* method. According to this method, the 1 borrowed from the minuend digit is carried back into the subtrahend digit immediately beneath the minuend digit from which we borrowed a 1. For example:

```
              1 1      Decimal value
     1 0 1 1 0 = 22
   − 1 0 0 1 1 = 19
         1 1
   ─────────────   ────
     0 0 0 1 1 =    3
```

Hexadecimal addition

Basic rules for hexadecimal addition are the same as for decimal and binary addition. However, working with alphameric symbols may appear strange and a bit awkward at first. For example, $1 + 8 = 9$, $1 + 9 = A$ and $8 + 7 = F$ in hexadecimal notations. The highest counting digit in hexadecimal number system is F, thus whenever the sum of 2 digits exceeds F, a carry of 1 is developed and taken into the next high-order digit position. For example:

$$
\begin{array}{r}
8 \\
+\,2 \\
\hline
\end{array}
$$

0 with a carry of 1 (or it could be expressed as 10)

$9 + 9 = 12$ (that is, 2 with a carry of 1), $A + B = 15$, and so on. More examples of hexadecimal addition are given below to familiarize you, as a programmer, with this addition process.

	1 1 ◄—— carries ——►1	
9 6 4 2	7 A B	A 3
+ 4 5 2 A	+ 1 F 7	+ 1 D
D B 6 C	9 A 7	C 0

Hexadecimal subtraction

Basically hexadecimal subtraction follows the same rules as binary and decimal subtraction, the only difference being that the borrow of 1 represents decimal 16. There are three different methods available to us for performing subtraction.
1. Conventional borrow method.
2. Pay back method.
3. Table look-up method, usually the easiest.

A 16	
7 B 6	Minuend
− 1 A 7	Subtrahend
6 0 F	

Payback Method.

1	
7 B 6	
− 1 A 7	
1	
6 0 F	

1 1			1	
F 8 D 4		F A A		Minuend
− E B 5 6		E D D		Subtrahend
1 1		1		
0 D 7 E		0 C D		Result

Self Evaluation Quiz

1. Convert the following decimal numbers to hexadecimal and binary numbers.
   a. 183
   b. 703
   c. 63
   d. 91
   e. 27
   f. 950

2. Convert the following hexadecimal numbers to decimal numbers.
   a. ABCD
   b. 12CE
   c. 201
   d. AAA

3. Convert the following binary numbers to decimal numbers.
   a. 11010010
   b. 11000001
   c. 00110011
   d. 00010101

4. What is the largest decimal number which can be represented 20 and 26 bits?

5. Convert the following binary numbers to hexadecimal numbers:
   a. 110110101101
   b. 110000100010
   c. 000100111011
   d. 100000100001

6. Convert the following hexadecimal numbers to binary numbers:
   a. FFED
   b. FEAD
   c. BAD
   d. EEFF

When solving the following problems use the conversion table.

7. Convert the following decimal numbers to hexadecimal numbers:
   a. 173
   b. 1,024
   c. 4,321
   d. 277

8. Convert the following hexadecimal numbers to decimal numbers:
   a. BEE
   b. 3A2B
   c. 4623
   d. 17AF

9. Add the following binary numbers:

$$
\begin{array}{r} 11011 \\ + \ 01110 \\ \hline \end{array}
\qquad
\begin{array}{r} 11011001 \\ + \ 11100111 \\ \hline \end{array}
\qquad
\begin{array}{r} 11001 \\ + \ 11111 \\ \hline \end{array}
$$

10. Subtract the following binary numbers:

$$
\begin{array}{r} 11011 \\ - \ 01101 \\ \hline \end{array}
\qquad
\begin{array}{r} 1011101 \\ - \ 0111110 \\ \hline \end{array}
\qquad
\begin{array}{r} 111111 \\ - \ 101011 \\ \hline \end{array}
$$

11. Add the following hexadecimal numbers:

$$
\begin{array}{r} FAAD \\ + \ DEAF \\ \hline \end{array}
\qquad
\begin{array}{r} AA99 \\ + \ 5CAF \\ \hline \end{array}
\qquad
\begin{array}{r} EEA \\ + \ AEE \\ \hline \end{array}
$$

12. Subtract the following hexadecimal numbers:

$$
\begin{array}{r} DA7F \\ - \ A72E \\ \hline \end{array}
\qquad
\begin{array}{r} FFA \\ - \ AFD \\ \hline \end{array}
\qquad
\begin{array}{r} DCAB \\ - \ CCDF \\ \hline \end{array}
$$

Appendix 5

Label Formats

Standard tape file label

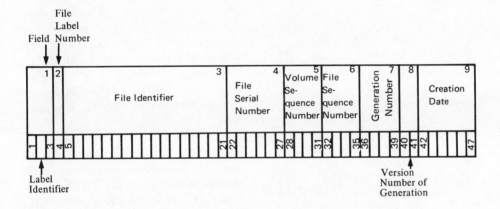

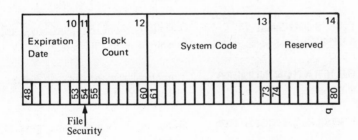

FIELD	NAME AND LENGTH	DESCRIPTION
1	**LABEL IDENTIFIER** 3 bytes, EBCDIC	identifies the type of label HDR = Header — beginning of a data file EOF = End of File — end of a set of data EOV = End of Volume — end of the physical reel

FIELD	NAME AND LENGTH	DESCRIPTION
2	**FILE LABEL NUMBER** 1 byte, EBCDIC	always a 1
3	**FILE IDENTIFIER** 17 bytes, EBCDIC	uniquely identifies the entire file, may contain only printable characters.
4	**FILE SERIAL NUMBER** 6 bytes, EBCDIC	uniquely identifies a file/volume relationship. This field is identical to the Volume Serial Number in the volume label of the first or only volume of a multi-volume file or a multi-file set. This field will normally be numeric (000001 to 999999) but may contain any six alphameric characters.
5	**VOLUME SEQUENCE NUMBER** 4 bytes	indicates the order of a volume in a given file or multi-file set. This number must be numeric (0000 - 9999). Multiple volumes of an output file will be numbered in consecutive sequence.
6	**FILE SEQUENCE NUMBER** 4 bytes	assigns numeric sequence to a file within a multi-file set.
7	**GENERATION NUMBER** 4 bytes	numerically identifies the various editions of the file.
8	**VERSION NUMBER OF GENERATION** 2 bytes	indicates the version of a generation of a file.
9	**CREATION DATE** 6 bytes	Indicates the year and the day of the year that the file was created:

Position	Code	Meaning
1	blank	none
2–3	00–99	Year
4–6	001–366	Day of Year

(e.g., January 31, 1965, would be entered as 65031).

FIELD	NAME AND LENGTH	DESCRIPTION
10	**EXPIRATION DATE** 6 bytes	indicates the year and the day of the year when the file may become a scratch tape. The format of this field is identical to Field 9. On a multi-file reel, processed sequentially, all files are considered to expire on the same day.
11	**FILE SECURITY** 1 byte	indicates security status of the file. 0 = no security protection 1 = security protection. Additional identification of the file is required before it can be processed.
12	**BLOCK COUNT** 6 bytes	indicates the number of data blocks written on the file from the last header label to the first trailer label, exclusive of tape marks. Count does not include checkpoint records. This field is used in trailer labels.
13	**SYSTEM CODE** 13 bytes	uniquely identifies the programming system.
14	**RESERVED** 7 bytes	Reserved. Should be recorded as blanks.

Standard DASD file label, format 1

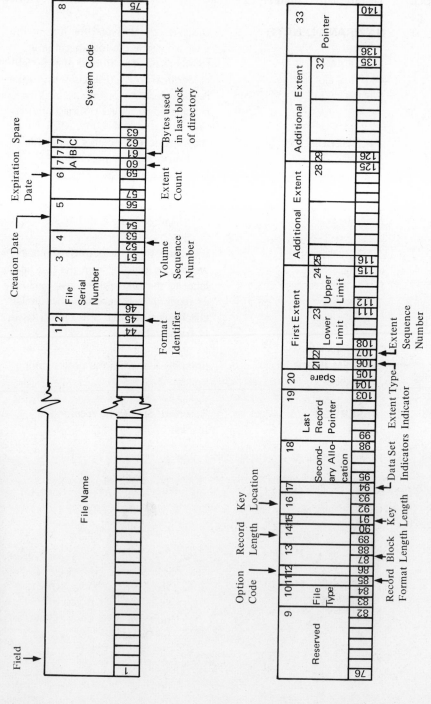

Format 1: This format is common to all data files on Direct Access Storage Devices.

FIELD	NAME AND LENGTH	DESCRIPTION
1	**FILE NAME** 44 bytes, alphameric EBCDIC	This field serves as the key portion of the file label.

Each file must have a unique file name. Duplication of file names will cause retrieval errors. The file name can consist of three sections:

1. **File ID** is an alphameric name assigned by the user and identifies the file. Can be 1-35 bytes if generation and version numbers are used, or 1-44 bytes if they are not used.

2. **Generation Number.** If used, this field is separated from File ID by a period. It has the format Gnnnn, where G identifies the field as the generation number and nnnn (in decimal) identifies the generation of the file.

3. **Version Number of Generation.** If used, this section immediately follows the generation number and has the format Vnn, where V identifies the field as the version of generation number and nn (in decimal) identifies the version of generation of the file.

Note: The Disk Operating System compares the entire field against the file name given in the DLAB card. The generation and version numbers are treated differently by Operating System/360.

The remaining fields comprise the DATA portion of the file label:

FIELD	NAME AND LENGTH	DESCRIPTION
2	**FORMAT IDENTIFIER** 1 byte, EBCDIC numeric	1 = Format 1
3	**FILE SERIAL NUMBER** 6 bytes, alphameric EBCDIC	Uniquely identifies a file/volume relation-ship. It is identical to the Volume Serial Number of the first or only volume of a multi-volume file.
4	**VOLUME SEQUENCE NUMBER** 2 bytes, binary	Indicates the order of a volume relative to the first volume on which the data file resides.
5	**CREATION DATE** 3 bytes, discontinuous binary	Indicates the year and the day of the year the file was created. It is of the form YDD, where Y signifies the year (0-99) and DD the day of the year (1-366).
6	**EXPIRATION DATE** 3 bytes, discontinuous binary	Indicates the year and the day of the year the file may be deleted. The form of this field is identical to that of Field 5.
7A	**EXTENT COUNT**	Contains a count of the number of ex-tents for this file on this volume. If user labels are used, the count does not in-clude the user label track. This field is maintained by the Disk Operating System programs.
7B	**BYTES USED IN LAST BLOCK OF DIRECTORY** 1 byte, binary	Used by Operating System/360 only for partitioned (library Structure) data sets. Not used by the Disk Operating System.
7C	**SPARE** 1 byte	Reserved.
8	**SYSTEM CODE** 13 bytes	Uniquely identifies the programming system. The character codes that can be used in this field are limited to 0 - 9, A - Z or blanks. (OS/360 only)

FIELD	NAME AND LENGTH	DESCRIPTION

9   **RESERVED**
       7 bytes

Reserved.

10   **FILE TYPE**
        2 bytes

The contents of this field uniquely identify the type of data file:

Hex 4000 =	Consecutive organization
Hex 2000 =	Direct-access organization
Hex 8000 =	Indexed-sequential organization
Hex 0200 =	Library organization
Hex 0000 =	Organization not defined in the file label.

11   **RECORD FORMAT**
        1 byte

The contents of this field indicates the type of records contained in the file:

Bit Position	Content	Meaning
0 and 1	01	Variable length records
	10	Fixed length records
	11	Undefined format
2	0	No track overflow
	1	File is organized using track overflow (Operating System/360 only)

FIELD	NAME AND LENGTH	DESCRIPTION

Bit Position	Content	Meaning
3	0	Unblocked re-cords
	1	Blocked records
4	0	No truncated records
	1	Truncated records in file
5 and 6	01	Control character ASA code
	10	Control character machine code
	00	Control character not stated
7	0	Records have no keys
	1	Records are written with keys

| 12 | **OPTION CODES** 1 byte | Bits within this field are used to indicate various options used in building the file. |

Bit

0 = If on, indicates data file was created using Write Validity Check.

1 — 7 = unused

FIELD	NAME AND LENGTH	DESCRIPTION
13	**BLOCK LENGTH** 2 bytes, binary	indicates the block length for fixed length records or maximum block size for variable length blocks.
14	**RECORD LENGTH** 2 bytes, binary	indicates the record length for fixed length records or the maximum record length for variable length records.
15	**KEY LENGTH** 1 byte, binary	indicates the length of the key portion of the data records in the file
16	**KEY LOCATION** 2 bytes, binary	indicates the high order position of the data record.
17	**DATA SET INDICATORS** 1 byte	Bits within this field are used to indicate the following:

BIT

0 If on, indicates that this is the last volume on which this file normally resides. This bit is used by the Disk Operating System.

1 If on, indicates that the data set described by this file must remain in the same absolute location on the direct access device. (OS/360 only)

2 If on, indicates that Block Length must always be a multiple of 8 bytes. (OS/360 only)

3 If on, indicates that this data file is security protected; a password must be provided in order to access it. (OS/360 only)

4—7 Spare. Reserved for future use.

FIELD	NAME AND LENGTH	DESCRIPTION

18   **SECONDARY ALLOCATION** 4 bytes, binary — indicates the amount of storage to be requested for this data file at End of Extent. This field is used by Operating System/360 only. It is not used by the Disk Operating System routines. The first byte of this field is an indication of the type of allocation request. Hex code C2 (EBCDIC B) blocks (physical records), hex code E3 (EBCDIC T) indicates tracks, and hex code C3 (EBCDIC C) indicates cylinders. The next three bytes of this field is a binary number indicating how many bytes, tracks or cylinders are requested.

19   **LAST RECORD POINTER** 5 bytes discontinuous binary — points to the last record written in a sequential or partition-organization data set. The format is TTRLL, where TT is the relative address of the track containing the last record, R is the ID of the last record, and LL is the number of bytes remaining on the track following the last record. If the entire field contains binary zeros, the last record pointer does not apply. (OS/360 only)

20   **SPARE** 2 bytes — Reserved.

21   **EXTENT TYPE INDICATOR** 1 byte — indicates the type of extent with which the following fields are associated:

HEX CODE

00   Next three fields do not indicate any extent.

01   Prime area (Indexed Sequential); or Consecutive area, etc., (i.e., the extent containing the user's data records.)

FIELD	NAME AND LENGTH	DESCRIPTION
		02 Overflow area of an indexed Sequential file.
		04 Cylinder Index or master Index area of an Indexed Sequential file.
		40 User label track area.
		8n Shared cylinder indicator, where n = 1, 2, or 4.
22	**EXTENT SEQUENCE NUMBER** 1 byte, binary	indicates the extent sequence in a multi-extent file.
23	**LOWER LIMIT** 4 bytes, discontinuous binary	the cylinder and the track address specifying the starting point (lower limit) of this extent component. This field has the format CCHH.
24	**UPPER LIMIT** 4 bytes	the cylinder and the track address specifying the ending point (upper limit) of this extent component. This field has the format CCHH.
25-28	**ADDITIONAL EXTENT** 10 bytes	These fields have the same format as the fields 21-24 above.
29-32	**ADDITIONAL EXTENT** 10 bytes	These fields have the same format as the fields 21-24 above.
33	**POINTER TO NEXT FILE LABEL WITHIN THIS LABEL SET** 5 bytes, discontinuous binary	the address (format CCHHR) of a continuation label if needed to further describe the file. If field 10 indicates Indexed Sequential organization, this field will point to a Format 2 file label within this label set. Otherwise, it points to a Format 3 file label, and then only if the file contains more than three extent segments. This field contains all binary zeros if no additional file label is pointed to.

Standard DASD file label, format 2

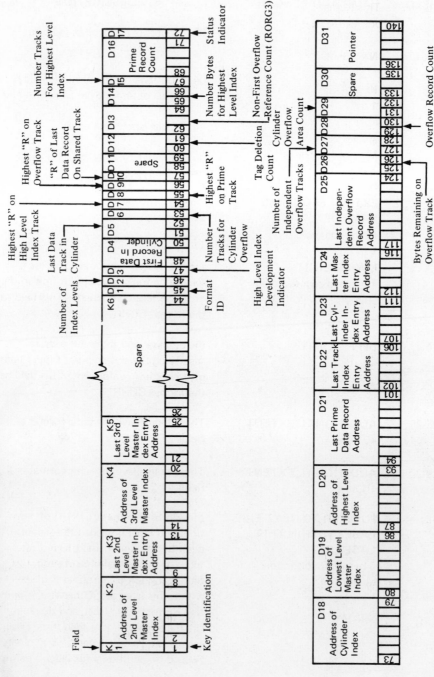

Format 2: This format is applicable only to Indexed Sequential data files. It is always pointed to by a Format 1 label.

FIELD	NAME AND LENGTH	DESCRIPTION
K1	**KEY IDENTIFICATION** 1 byte	This byte contains the Hex Code 02 in order to avoid conflict with a file name.
K2	**ADDRESS OF 2ND LEVEL MASTER INDEX** 7 bytes, discontinuous binary	This field contains the address of the first track of the second level of the master index, in the form MBBCCHH. (OS/360 only)
K3	**LAST 2ND LEVEL MASTER INDEX ENTRY** 5 bytes, discontinuous binary	This field contains the address of the last index entry in the second level of the master index, in the form CCHHR. (OS/360 only)
K4	**ADDRESS OF 3RD LEVEL MASTER INDEX** 7 bytes, discontinuous binary	This field contains the address of the first track of the third level of the master index, in the form MBBCCHH. (OS/360 only)
K5	**LAST 3RD LEVEL MASTER INDEX ENTRY** 5 bytes, discontinuous binary	This field contains the address of the last entry in the third level of the master index, in the form CCHHR. (OS/360 only)
K6	**SPARE** 19 bytes	Reserved.
D1	**FORMAT IDENTIFIER** 1 byte, EBCDIC numeric	2 = Format 2
D2	**NUMBER OF INDEX LEVELS** 1 byte, binary	The contents of this field indicate how many levels of index are present with an Indexed Sequential file.
D3	**HIGH LEVEL INDEX DEVELOPMENT INDI-CATOR** 1 byte, binary	This field contains the number of tracks determining development of Master Index. (OS/360 only)

FIELD	NAME AND LENGTH	DESCRIPTION
D4	**FIRST DATA RECORD IN CYLINDER** 3 bytes	This field contains the address of the first data record on each cylinder in the form HHR.
D5	**LAST DATA TRACK IN CYLINDERS** 2 bytes	This field contains the address of the last data track on each cylinder, in the form HH.
D6	**NUMBER OF TRACKS FOR CYLINDER OVER-FLOW** 1 byte, binary	This field contains the number of tracks in cylinder overflow area. (OS/360 only)
D7	**HIGHEST "R" ON HIGH-LEVEL INDEX TRACK** 1 byte	This field contains the highest possible R on track containing high-level index entries.
D8	**HIGHEST "R" ON PRIME TRACK** 1 byte	This field contains the highest possible R on prime data tracks for form F records.
D9	**HIGHEST "R" ON OVERFLOW TRACK** 1 byte	This field contains the highest possible R on overflow data tracks for form F records.
D10	**"R" OF LAST DATA RECORD ON SHARED TRACK** 1 byte	This field contains the R of the last data record on a shared track.
D11	**SPARE** 2 bytes	Reserved.
D12	**TAG DELETION COUNT** 2 bytes, binary	This field contains the number of records that have been tagged for deletion.
D13	**NON-FIRST OVERFLOW REFERENCE COUNT** (RORG3) 3 bytes, binary	This field contains a count of the number of random references to a non-first over-flow record.
D14	**NUMBER OF BYTES FOR HIGHEST-LEVEL INDEX** 2 bytes, binary	The contents of this field indicate how many bytes are needed to hold the highest-level index in main storage.

FIELD	NAME AND LENGTH	DESCRIPTION
D15	**NUMBER OF TRACKS FOR HIGHEST-LEVEL INDEX** 1 byte, binary	This field contains a count of the number of tracks occupied by the highest-level index.
D16	**PRIME RECORD COUNT** 4 bytes, binary	This field contains a count of the number of records in the prime data area.
D17	**STATUS INDICATOR** 1 byte	The eight bits of this byte are used for the following indications:

bit	description
0	last block full
1	last track full
2-7	must remain off

FIELD	NAME AND LENGTH	DESCRIPTION
D18	**ADDRESS OF CYLINDER INDEX** 7 bytes	This field contains the address of the first track of the cylinder index, in the form MBBCCHH.
D19	**ADDRESS OF LOWEST-LEVEL MASTER INDEX** 7 bytes	This field contains the address of the first track of the lowest-level index of the high level indexes, in the form MBBCCHH.
D20	**ADDRESS OF THE HIGHEST-LEVEL INDEX** 7 bytes	This field contains the address of the first track of the highest level master index, in the form MBBCCHH.
D21	**LAST PRIME DATA RECORD ADDRESS** 8 bytes	This field contains the address of the last data record in the prime data area, in the form MBBCCHHR.
D22	**LAST TRACK INDEX ENTRY ADDRESS** 5 bytes	This field contains the address of the last normal entry in the track index on the last cylinder in the form CCHHR.
D23	**LAST CYLINDER INDEX ENTRY ADDRESS** 5 bytes	This field contains the address of the last index entry in the cylinder index in the form CCHHR.

FIELD	NAME AND LENGTH	DESCRIPTION
D24	**LAST MASTER INDEX ENTRY ADDRESS** 5 bytes	This field contains the address of the last index entry in the master index in the form CCHHR.
D25	**LAST INDEPENDENT OVERFLOW RECORD ADDRESS** 8 bytes	This field contains the address of the last record written in the current independent overflow area, in the form MBBCCHHR.
D26	**BYTES REMAINING ON OVERFLOW TRACK** 2 bytes, binary	This field contains the number of bytes remaining on current independent overflow track. (OS/360 only)
D27	**NUMBER OF INDEPENDENT OVERFLOW TRACKS (RORG2)** 2 bytes, binary	This field contains the number of tracks remaining in independent overflow area.
D28	**OVERFLOW RECORD COUNT** 2 bytes, binary	This field contains a count of the number of records in the overflow area.
D29	**CYLINDER OVERFLOW AREA COUNT (RORG1)** 2 bytes, binary	This field contains the number of cylinder overflow areas full.
D30	**SPARE** 3 bytes	Reserved.
D31	**POINTER TO FORMAT 3 FILE LABEL** 5 bytes	This field contains the address (in the form CCHHR) of a Format 3 file label if more than 3 extent segments exist for the data file within this volume. Otherwise, it contains binary zeros. (OS/360 only)

Standard DASD file label, format 3

Format 3: This format is used to describe extra extent segments on the volume if there are more than can be described in the Format 1 (and Format 2 if it exists) file label. This file label is pointed to by a Format 1, Format 2, or another Format 3 file label.

FIELD	NAME AND LENGTH	DESCRIPTION
1	**KEY IDENTIFICATION** 4 bytes	Each byte of this field contains the Hex Code 03 in order to avoid conflict with a data file name.
2-17	**EXTENTS** (in KEY) 40 bytes	Four groups of fields identical in format to fields 21 - 24 in the Format 1 label are contained here.
18	**FORMAT IDENTIFIER** 1 byte, EBCDIC numeric	3 = Format 3
19-54	**ADDITIONAL EXTENTS** 90 bytes	Nine groups of fields identical in format to fields 21 - 24 in the Format 1 label are contained here.
55	**POINTER TO NEXT FILE LABEL** 5 bytes	This field contains the address (in the form CCHHR) of another Format 3 label if additional extents must be described. Otherwise, it is all binary zeros.

Standard DASD file label, format 4

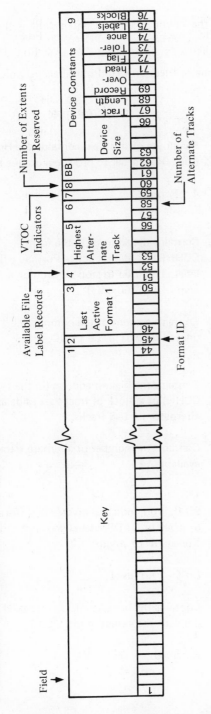

Format 4: This format is used to describe the Volume Table of Contents and is always the first file label in the VTOC.

There must be one and only one of these Format 4 file labels per volume.

FIELD	NAME AND LENGTH	DESCRIPTION
1	**KEY FIELD** 44 bytes, binary	Each byte of this field contains the Hex Code 04 in order to provide a unique key.
2	**FORMAT ID** 1 byte, EBCDIC numeric	4 = Format 4
3	**LAST ACTIVE FORMAT 1** 5 bytes	Contains the address (in the form CCHHR) of the last active Format 1 file label. It is used to stop a search on a file name. (OS/360 only)
4	**AVAILABLE FILE LABEL RECORDS** 2 bytes, binary	Contains a count of the number of unused records in the VTOC.
5	**HIGHEST ALTERNATE TRACK** 4 bytes	Contains the highest address (in the form CCHH) of a block of tracks set aside as alternates for bad tracks.
6	**NUMBER OF ALTERNATE TRACKS** 2 bytes, binary	Contains the number of alternate tracks available.
7	**VTOC INDICATORS** 1 byte	Bit 0, if on, indicates no DADSM (format 5) label, or DADSM label does not reflect true status of volume. Bit 1 - 7 not used.
8A	**NUMBER OF EXTENTS** 1 byte	Contains the hexadecimal constant 01, to indicate one extent in the VTOC.
8B	**RESERVED** 2 bytes	Reserved.

FIELD	NAME AND LENGTH	DESCRIPTION
9	**DEVICE CONSTANTS** 14 bytes	This field contains constants describing the device on which the volume was mounted when the VTOC was created. The following describes each of the sub-fields.

Device Size (4 bytes) — The number of cylinders (CC) and tracks per cylinder (HH).

Track Length (2 bytes) — The number of available bytes on a track exclusive of home address and record zero (record zero is assumed to be a non-keyed record with an eight byte data field).

Record Overhead (3 bytes) — The number of bytes required for gaps, check bits, and count field for each record. This value varies according to the record characteristics and thus is broken down into three subfields.

    I — Overhead required for a keyed record other than the last record on the track.

    L — Overhead required for a keyed record that is the last record on the track.

    K — Overhead bytes to be subtracted from I or L if the record does not have a key field.

Flag (1 byte) — Further defines unique characteristics of the device.

bits	meaning
0-5	reserved
6	CC and HH must be used as 1-byte values, as in the case of the 2321. A
7	tolerance factor must be applied to all but the last record on the track.

Tolerance (2 bytes) — A value that is to be used to determine the effective length of the record on the track. The effective length of a record is calculated in the following manner:

    1. Add the key length to the data length of the record.

    2. Test bit 7 in the flag byte:
        a. if 0 go to 3
        b. multiply value from 1 by the tolerance factor
        c. shift result 9 bits to the right

    3. Add overhead bytes to the result.

NOTE: Step 2 is not required if the calculation is for the last record on the track.

Labels/Track (1 byte) — A count of the number of labels that can be written on each track in the VTOC. (Number of full records of 44-byte key and 96-byte data lengths that can be contained on one track of this device).

Directory Blocks/Track (1 byte) — A count of the number of directory blocks that can be written on each track for an Operating System/360 partitioned data set. (Number of full records of 8-byte key and 256-byte data lengths that can be contained on one track of this device.)

The following illustrates the device constants field for the various direct access devices:

Device	CC	HH	Track Length	I	L	K	Flag	Toler-ance	Labels/ Track	Dir Blk/ Track
2311	203	10	3656	82	55	20	1	537	16	10
2321	20 10	5 20	2027	101	47	16	3	537	8	5
2301	0	200	20616	186	186	53	0	512	63	45
2302	250	46	5070	82	55	20	1	537	22	14
7320	0	400	2129	111	43	14	1	537	8	5

NOTE: CCHH for the 2321 above are separate 1 byte quantities.

10	**RESERVED** 29 bytes		Reserved.
11-14	**VTOC EXTENT**		These fields describe the extent of the VTOC, and are identical in format to fields 21 - 24 of the Format 1 file label. Extent type 01 (prime data area).
15	**RESERVED** 25 bytes		Reserved.

Appendix 6

Reference Data

List of instructions

NAME	MNEMONIC	TYPE	CODE	OPERAND
Add	AR	RR	1A	R1, R2
Add	A	RX	5A	R1, D2 (X2, B2)
Add Halfword	AH	RX	4A	R1, D2 (X2, B2)
Add Logical	ALR	RR	1E	R1, R2
Add Logical	AL	RX	5E	R1, D2 (X2, B2)
AND	NR	RR	14	R1, R2
AND	N	RX	54	R1, D2 (X2, B2)
AND	NI	SI	94	D1 (B1), I2
AND	NC	SS	D4	D1 (L, B1), D2 (B2)
Branch and Link	BALR	RR	05	R1, R2
Branch and Link	BAL	RX	45	R1, D2 (X2, B2)
Branch on Condition	BCR	RR	07	M1, R2
Branch on Condition	BC	RX	47	M1, D2 (X2, B2)
Branch on Count	BCTR	RR	06	R1, R2
Branch on Count	BCT	RX	46	R1, D2 (X2, B2)
Branch on Index High	BXH	RS	86	R1, R3, D2 (B2)
Branch on Index Low or Equal	BXLE	RS	87	R1, R3, D2 (B2)
Compare	CR	RR	19	R1, R2
Compare	C	RX	59	R1, D2 (X2, B2)
Compare Halfword	CH	RX	49	R1, D2 (X2, B2)
Compare Logical	CLR	RR	15	R1, R2
Compare Logical	CL	RX	55	R1, D2 (X2, B2)
Compare Logical	CLC	SS	D5	D1 (L, B1), D2 (B2)
Compare Logical	CLI	SI	95	D1 (B1), I2
Convert to Binary	CVB	RX	4F	R1, D2 (X2, B2)
Convert to Decimal	CVD	RX	4E	R1, D2 (X2, B2)
[1]Diagnose		SI	83	
Divide	DR	RR	ID	R1, R2
Divide	D	RX	5D	R1, D2 (X2, B2)
Exclusive OR	XR	RR	17	R1, R2
Exclusive OR	X	RX	57	R1, D2 (X2, B2)

[1]These instructions not included in this text.

523

NAME	MNEMONIC	TYPE	CODE	OPERAND
Exclusive OR	XI	SI	97	D1 (B1), I2
Exclusive OR	XC	SS	D7	D1 (L, B1), D2 (B2)
Execute	EX	RX	44	R1, D2 (X2, B2)
[2]Halt I/O	HIO	SI	9E	D1 (B1)
Insert Character	IC	RX	43	R1, D2 (X2, B2)
Load	LR	RR	18	R1, R2
Load	L	RX	58	R1, D2 (X2, B2)
Load Address	LA	RX	41	R1, D2 (X2, B2)
Load and Test	LTR	RR	12	R1, R2
Load Complement	LCR	RR	13	R1, R2
Load Halfword	LH	RX	48	R1, D2 (X2, B2)
Load Multiple	LM	RS	98	R1, R3, D2 (B2)
Load Negative	LNR	RR	11	R1, R2
Load Positive	LPR	RR	10	R1, R2
[2]Load PSW	LPSW	SI	82	D1 (B1)
Move	MVI	SI	92	D1 (B1), I2
Move	MVC	SS	D2	D1 (L, B1), D2 (B2)
Move Numerics	MVN	SS	D1	D1 (L, B1), D2 (B2)
Move with Offset	MVO	SS	F1	D1 (L1, B1), D2 (L2, B2)
Move Zones	MVZ	SS	D3	D1 (L, B1), D2 (B2)
Multiply	MR	RR	1C	R1, R2
Multiply	M	RX	5C	R1, D2 (X2, B2)
Multiply Halfword	MH	RX	4C	R1, D2 (X2, B2)
OR	OR	RR	16	R1, R2
OR	O	RX	56	R1, D2 (X2, B2)
OR	OI	SI	96	D1 (B1), I2
OR	OC	SS	D6	D1 (L, B1), D2 (B2)
Pack	PACK	SS	F2	D1 (L1, B1), D2 (L2, B2)
Set Program Mask	SPM	RR	04	R1
[2]Set System Mask	SSM	SI	80	D1 (B1)
Shift Left Double	SLDA	RS	8F	R1, D2 (B2)
Shift Left Single	SLA	RS	8B	R1, D2 (B2)
Shift Left Double Logical	SLDL	RS	8D	R1, D2 (B2)
Shift Left Single Logical	SLL	RS	89	R1, D2 (B2)
Shift Right Double	SRDA	RS	8E	R1, D2 (B2)
Shift Right Single	SRA	RS	8A	R1, D2 (B2)
Shift Right Double Logical	SRDL	RS	8C	R1, D2 (B2)

[2]These instructions not included in this text.

NAME	MNEMONIC	TYPE	CODE	OPERAND
Shift Right Single Logical	SRL	RS	88	R1, D2 (B2)
[3] Start I/O	SIO	SI	9C	D1 (B1)
Store	ST	RX	50	R1, D2 (X2, B2)
Store Character	STC	RX	42	R1, D2 (X2, B2)
Store Halfword	STH	RX	40	R1, D2 (X2, B2)
Store Multiple	STM	RS	90	R1, R3, D2 (B2)
Subtract	SR	RR	IB	R1, R2
Subtract	S	RX	5B	R1, D2 (X2, B2)
Subtract Halfword	SH	RX	4B	R1, D2 (X2, B2)
Subtract Logical	SLR	RR	1F	R1, R2
Subtract Logical	SL	RX	5F	R1, D2 (X2, B2)
[3] Supervisor Call	SVC	RR	0A	I
[3] Test and Set	TS	SI	93	D1 (B1)
[3] Test Channel	TCH	SI	9F	D1 (B1)
[3] Test I/O	TIO	SI	9D	D1 (B1)
Test Under Mask	TM	SI	91	D1 (B1), I2
Translate	TR	SS	DC	D1 (L, B1), D2 (B2)
[3] Translate and Test	TRT	SS	DD	D1 (L, B1), D2 (B2)
Unpack	UNPK	SS	F3	D1 (L1, B1), D2 (L2, B2)

Decimal feature instructions

Add Decimal	AP	SS	FA	D1 (L1, B1), D2 (L2, B2)
Compare Decimal	CP	SS	F9	D1 (L1, B1), D2 (L2, B2)
Divide Decimal	DP	SS	FD	D1 (L1, B1), D2 (L2, B2)
Edit	ED	SS	DE	D1 (L, B1), D2 (B2)
Edit and Mark	EDMK	SS	DF	D1 (L, B1), D2 (B2)
Multiply Decimal	MP	SS	FC	D1 (L1, B1), D2 (L2, B2)
Subtract Decimal	SP	SS	FB	D1 (L1, B1), D2 (L2, B2)
Zero and Add	ZAP	SS	F8	D1 (L1, B1), D2 (L2, B2)

[3] These instructions not included in this text.

Basic instruction formats

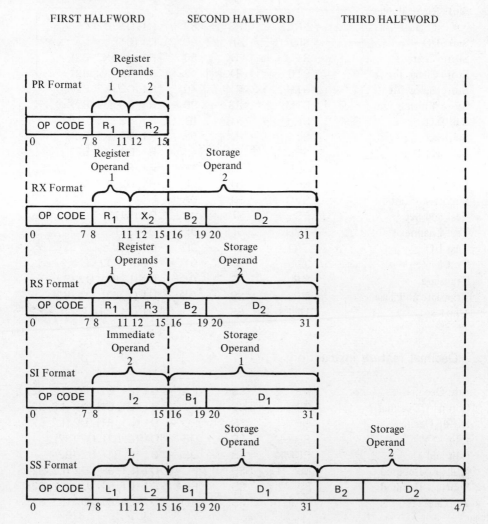

Characteristics for constants

Code	Type	Machine Format
C	Character	8-Bit Code for each Character
X	Hexadecimal	4-Bit Code for each Hexadecimal Digit
B	Binary	Binary Digits (ones and zeros)
F	Fixed-point	Signed, Fixed-point Binary Format; Normally a Full Word
H	Fixed-point	Signed, Fixed-point Binary Format; Normally a Half Word
P	Decimal	Packed Decimal Format
Z	Decimal	Zoned Decimal Format
A	Address	Value of Address; Normally a Full Word
V	Address	Space Reserved for External Symbol Addresses; Each Address Normally a Full Word
S	Address	Address in Base Displacement Form
Y	Address	Value of Address; Normally a Half Word

Extended mnemonic instructions

GENERAL

Extended Code		Machine Instruction		Meaning
B	D2 (X2, B2)	BC	15, D2 (X2, B2)	Branch Unconditionally
BR	R2	BCR	15, R2	Branch Unconditionally
NOP	D2 (X2, B2)	BC	0, D2 (X2, B2)	No Operation
NOPR	R2	BCR	0, R2	No Operation (RR)

AFTER COMPARE INSTRUCTIONS (A:B)

BH	D2 (X2, B2)	BC	2, D2 (X2, B2)	Branch on A High
BL	D2 (X2, B2)	BC	4, D2 (X2, B2)	Branch on A Low
BE	D2 (X2, B2)	BC	8, D2 (X2, B2)	Branch on A Equal B
BNH	D2 (X2, B2)	BC	13, D2 (X2, B2)	Branch on A Not High
BNL	D2 (X2, B2)	BC	11, D2 (X2, B2)	Branch on A Not Low
BNE	D2 (X2, B2)	BC	7, D2 (X2, B2)	Branch on A Not Equal B

AFTER ARITHMETIC INSTRUCTIONS

BO	D2 (X2, B2)	BC	1, D2 (X2, B2)	Branch on Overflow
BP	D2 (X2, B2)	BC	2, D2 (X2, B2)	Branch on Plus
BM	D2 (X2, B2)	BC	4, D2 (X2, B2)	Branch on Minus

(continued)

AFTER ARITHMETIC INSTRUCTIONS (continued)

BZ	D2 (X2, B2)	BC 8,	D2 (X2, B2)	Branch on Zero
BNP	D2 (X2, B2)	BC 13,	D2 (X2, B2)	Branch on Not Plus
BNM	D2 (X2, B2)	BC 11,	D2 (X2, B2)	Branch on Not Minus
BNZ	D2 (X2, B2)	BC 7,	D2 (X2, B2)	Branch on Not Zero

AFTER TEST UNDER MASK INSTRUCTIONS

BO	D2 (X2, B2)	BC 1,	D2 (X2, B2)	Branch if Ones
BM	D2 (X2, B2)	BC 4,	D2 (X2, B2)	Branch if Mixed
BZ	D2 (X2, B2)	BC 8,	D2 (X2, B2)	Branch if Zeros
BNO	D2 (X2, B2)	BC 14,	D2 (X2, B2)	Branch if Not Ones

CNOP alignment

Double Word							
Word				Word			
Half Word		Half Word		Half Word		Half Word	
Byte	Byte	Byte	Byte	Byte	Byte	Byte	Byte
0,4		2,4		0,4		2,4	
0,8		2,8		4,8		6,8	

Edit and edit & mark symbols

Mask	Meaning	Mask	Meaning
hex 40	blank	hex 22	field separator character
hex 21	significance start character	hex 20	digit-select character

Condition codes

	0	1	2	3
Condition Code Setting	0	1	2	3
Mask Bit Position	8	4	2	1

Fixed-Point Arithmetic.

Add H/F	zero	< zero	> zero	overflow
Add Logical	zero, no carry	not zero, no carry	zero, carry	not zero, carry
Compare H/F (A:B)	equal	A low	A high	— —
Load and Test	zero	< zero	> zero	— —
Load Complement	zero	< zero	> zero	overflow
Load Negative	zero	< zero	— —	— —
Load Positive	zero	— —	> zero	overflow
Shift Left Double	zero	< zero	> zero	overflow
Shift Left Single	zero	< zero	> zero	overflow
Shift Right Double	zero	< zero	> zero	— —
Shift Right Single	zero	< zero	> zero	— —
Subtract H/F	zero	< zero	> zero	overflow
Subtract Logical	— —	not zero, no carry	zero, carry	not zero, carry

Decimal Arithmetic.

Add Decimal	zero	< zero	> zero	overflow
Compare Decimal (A:B)	equal	A low	A high	— —
Subtract Decimal	zero	< zero	> zero	overflow
Zero and Add	zero	< zero	> zero	overflow

Logical Operations.

AND	zero	not zero	— —	— —
Compare Logical (A:B)	equal	A low	A high	— —
Edit	zero	< zero	> zero	— —
Edit and Mark	zero	< zero	> zero	— —
Exclusive OR	zero	not zero	— —	— —
OR	zero	not zero	— —	— —
Test Under Mask	zero	mixed	— —	one
Translate and Test	zero	incomplete	complete	— —

Hexadecimal and decimal conversion

To find the decimal number, locate the Hex number and its decimal equivalent for each position. Add these to obtain the decimal number. To find the Hex number, locate the next lower decimal number and its Hex equivalent. Each difference is used to obtain the next Hex number until the entire number is developed.

BYTE				BYTE				BYTE			
0123		4567		0123		4567		0123		4567	
HEX	DEC	HEX	DEC	HEX	DEC	HEX	DEC	HEX	DEC	HEX	DEC
0	0	0	0	0	0	0	0	0	0	0	0
1	1,048,576	1	65,536	1	4,096	1	256	1	16	1	1
2	2,097,152	2	131,072	2	8,192	2	512	2	32	2	2
3	3,145,728	3	196,608	3	12,288	3	768	3	48	3	3
4	4,194,304	4	262,144	4	16,384	4	1,024	4	64	4	4
5	5,242,880	5	327,680	5	20,480	5	1,280	5	80	5	5
6	6,291,456	6	393,216	6	24,576	6	1,536	6	96	6	6
7	7,340,032	7	458,752	7	28,672	7	1,792	7	112	7	7
8	8,388,608	8	524,288	8	32,768	8	2,048	8	128	8	8
9	9,437,184	9	589,824	9	36,864	9	2,304	9	144	9	9
A	10,485,760	A	655,360	A	40,960	A	2,560	A	160	A	10
B	11,534,336	B	720,896	B	45,056	B	2,816	B	176	B	11
C	12,582,912	C	786,432	C	49,152	C	3,072	C	192	C	12
D	13,631,488	D	851,968	D	53,248	D	3,328	D	208	D	13
E	14,680,064	E	917,504	E	57,344	E	3,584	E	224	E	14
F	15,728,640	F	983,040	F	61,440	F	3,840	F	240	F	15
6		5		4		3		2		1	

POWERS OF 16		POWERS OF 2	
16^n	n	2^n	n
1	0	512	9
16	1	1 024	10
256	2	2 048	11
4 096	3	4 096	12
65 536	4	8 192	13
1 048 576	5	16 384	14
16 777 216	6	32 768	15
268 435 456	7	65 536	16
4 294 967 296	8	131 072	17
68 719 476 736	9	262 144	18
1 099 511 627 776	10	524 288	19
17 592 186 044 416	11	1 048 576	20
281 474 976 710 656	12	2 097 152	21
4 503 599 627 370 496	13	4 194 304	22
72 057 594 037 927 936	14	8 388 608	23
1 152 921 504 606 846 976	15	16 777 216	24

Appendix 7

IBM FLOWCHARTING TEMPLATE

Symbols on this diagram—reflecting additions and changes—conform to
the International Organization for Standardization (ISO) Draft Recom-
mendation on Flowchart Symbols for Information Processing, and are
consistent with the fewer symbols adopted by the U.S.A. Standards Insti-
tute (USASI). ISO usages beyond USASI specifications are identified
(ISO). IBM usages beyond ISO specifications are three symbols—offpage
connector, transmittal tape, keying—identified IBM.

✳ Composite Symbols (preceded by a star) are those drawn by adding
to or combining shapes provided by cutouts in the template.

On this diagram, symbols are in three groups: (1) basic symbols; (2)
processing and sequencing symbols related to programming; (3) input/
output, communication link, and processing symbols related to systems.

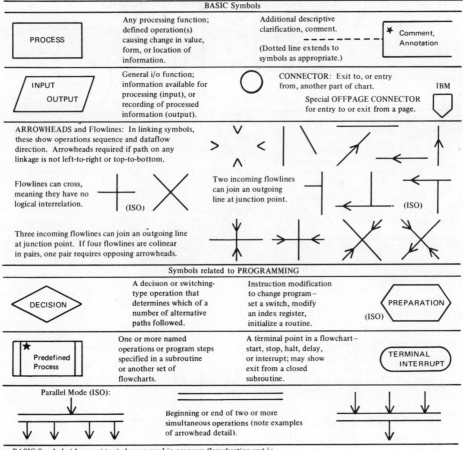

BASIC Symbols

PROCESS — Any processing function; defined operation(s) causing change in value, form, or location of information.

Additional descriptive clarification, comment.

(Dotted line extends to symbols as appropriate.)

✳ Comment, Annotation

INPUT OUTPUT — General i/o function; information available for processing (input), or recording of processed information (output).

CONNECTOR: Exit to, or entry from, another part of chart.

IBM — Special OFFPAGE CONNECTOR for entry to or exit from a page.

ARROWHEADS and Flowlines: In linking symbols, these show operations sequence and dataflow direction. Arrowheads required if path on any linkage is not left-to-right or top-to-bottom.

Flowlines can cross, meaning they have no logical interrelation. (ISO)

Two incoming flowlines can join an outgoing line at junction point. (ISO)

Three incoming flowlines can join an outgoing line at junction point. If four flowlines are colinear in pairs, one pair requires opposing arrowheads.

Symbols related to PROGRAMMING

DECISION — A decision or switching-type operation that determines which of a number of alternative paths followed.

Instruction modification to change program—set a switch, modify an index register, initialize a routine. (ISO)

PREPARATION

✳ **Predefined Process** — One or more named operations or program steps specified in a subroutine or another set of flowcharts.

A terminal point in a flowchart—start, stop, halt, delay, or interrupt; may show exit from a closed subroutine.

TERMINAL INTERRUPT

Parallel Mode (ISO):

Beginning or end of two or more simultaneous operations (note examples of arrowhead detail).

BASIC Symbols (shown at top) also are used in program flowcharting and in
systems flowcharting.

Symbols related to SYSTEMS

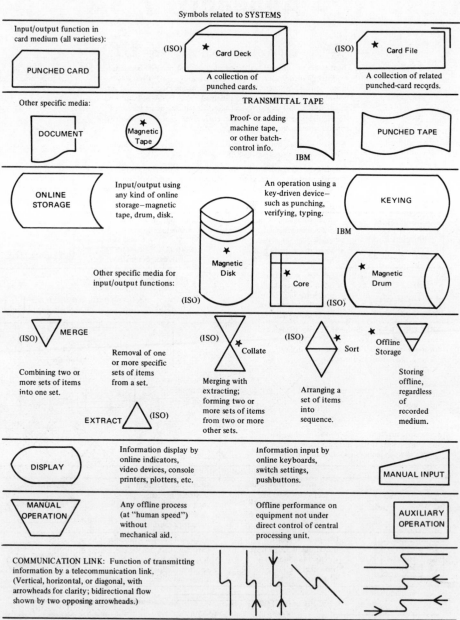

Input/output function in card medium (all varieties):

PUNCHED CARD

(ISO) ★ Card Deck

A collection of punched cards.

(ISO) ★ Card File

A collection of related punched-card records.

Other specific media:

DOCUMENT

★ Magnetic Tape

TRANSMITTAL TAPE

Proof- or adding machine tape, or other batch-control info.

IBM

PUNCHED TAPE

ONLINE STORAGE

Input/output using any kind of online storage—magnetic tape, drum, disk.

An operation using a key-driven device—such as punching, verifying, typing.

IBM

KEYING

★ Magnetic Disk

(ISO)

Other specific media for input/output functions:

★ Core

(ISO)

★ Magnetic Drum

(ISO)

MERGE

Combining two or more sets of items into one set.

Removal of one or more specific sets of items from a set.

EXTRACT (ISO)

(ISO) ★ Collate

Merging with extracting; forming two or more sets of items from two or more other sets.

(ISO) ★ Sort

Arranging a set of items into sequence.

★ Offline Storage

Storing offline, regardless of recorded medium.

DISPLAY

Information display by online indicators, video devices, console printers, plotters, etc.

Information input by online keyboards, switch settings, pushbuttons.

MANUAL INPUT

MANUAL OPERATION

Any offline process (at "human speed") without mechanical aid.

Offline performance on equipment not under direct control of central processing unit.

AUXILIARY OPERATION

COMMUNICATION LINK: Function of transmitting information by a telecommunication link. (Vertical, horizontal, or diagonal, with arrowheads for clarity; bidirectional flow shown by two opposing arrowheads.)

BASIC Symbols also are used in systems flowcharting.

Converting doubleword binary number to decimal

Routine coded below is one of the methods of converting a doubleword binary number to decimal.

```
Name          Oper      Operand


*   ASSUME THAT THE BINARY NUMBER IS CONTAINED IN
*   REGISTERS 6 AND 7

              CVD       6,DOUBLE+8
              SR        6,6
              SLDA      6,31
              CVD       6,DOUBLE1
              MP        DOUBLE1,=P'2'
              LTR       7,7
              BC        8,AROUND
              AP        DOUBLE1,=P'1'
AROUND        MVC       DOUBLE(8),ZERO
              MP        DOUBLE(16),CONST
              AP        DOUBLE(16),DOUBLE1
              .
CONST         DC        PL6'4294967296'      VALUE OF 2 ** 32
DOUBLE        DS        2D
DOUBLE1       DS        D
ZERO          DC        XL8'00'
```

Appendix 8*

Introduction to IBM System/370

This appendix presents a brief introduction to the System/370 computer system (Models 155 and 165).

The IBM System/370 is a data processing system based on the IBM System/360, which extends the concepts and capabilities of that system. The System/370 is a general purpose system for both scientific and commercial applications. Model 155 retains and extends the capabilities of System/360 Models 40 and 50; while Model 165 retains and extends the capabilities of System/360 Models 65 and 75. At the same time, both of the System/370 models are compatible with each other.

Transition from the System/360 to System/370 has been made possible and easy because most current System/360 user programs, I/O devices, and programming systems are upward compatible. Some of the more important highlights of this new system are as follows:

1. Internal performance of Model 155 is approximately 3½ to 4 times that of Model 50 for a typical instruction mix. Internal performance of Model 165 is approximately 2 to 5 times that of the Model 65.
2. The System/370 Models 155 and 165 standard instruction sets include new general purpose instructions in addition to the System/360 instruction set. These instructions enhance decimal arithmetic performance, eliminate the need for multiple move or compare instructions or move subroutines, and facilitate record blocking and deblocking, field padding, and storage clearing.
3. A time of day clock has been added in addition to the interval timer.
4. The system also provides for overlapping of instruction execution with instruction fetching to improve the internal performance.

Other improvements include extended precision floating point, an interval timer of 3.3 milliseconds resolution as opposed to 16.6 milliseconds resolution on System/360 Models 40, 50, and 65, and extended channels including the 2880 Block Multiplexer Channel. The extended channel feature increases the total system throughput by allowing more data to enter and leave the system in a given time.

System/370 provides for a two level memory system, consisting of a fast, large size main storage and a smaller, very high speed buffer storage. The CPU works mostly with the buffer thereby reducing the effective access time for data. The use of this two level memory system drastically reduces the effective storage cycle of System/370 and greatly contributes to the fact that the internal performance of the Model 155 is

---

*The material in this appendix is excerpted by permission, in part and with or without modifications from publications copyrighted by International Business Machines Corporation in 1970 as GC20–1729 and GC20–1730.

approximately 3½ to 4 times that of the Model 50. The internal performance of the Model 165 is approximately 2 to 5 times that of the Model 65.

The main processor storage available on Model 155 is from 256K to 2048K and on Model 165 from 512K to 3072K. This is a significant increase of storage over System/360 Models 40, 50, and 65. Model 155 provides 4 times the maximum main storage available on the System/360 Model 50, and 165 provides 3 times the maximum storage available on the System/360 Model 65.

The high speed buffer storage available on the Model 165 is 8K or 16K; 8K being the standard. On the Model 155, 8K buffer has been implemented.

PROCESSOR (MAIN) STORAGE			
SYSTEM/370	MODEL 165	SYSTEM/370	MODEL 155
I	512K	H	256K
J	1024K	HG	384K
JI	1536K	I	512K
K	2048K	IH	768K
KJ	3072K	J	1024K
		JI	1536K
		K	2048K

Error checking and correction (ECC) hardware provides automatic detection and correction of all single-bit processor storage errors and detection (but not correction) of all double-bit and most multiple-bit errors.

The System/370 also supports a byte boundary alignment facility for processor storage. The presence of the byte-oriented operand function allows the *storage operands* of unprivileged instructions (RS and RX formats) to appear on *one byte boundary* without causing a specification program interrupt. Without this facility, operands must be aligned on integral boundaries, that is, on storage addresses that are integral multiples of operand lengths (as is the case with System/360). Byte orientation is standard and *does not* apply to alignment of instructions or channel command words (CCW's).

Use of byte alignment reduces the instruction execution performance. However, byte alignment can be used effectively in commercial processing to eliminate the padding bytes added within records and to blocked records to insure binary and floating-point field alignment. The smaller physical record that results from the elimination of padding bytes requires less external storage and increases effective I/O data rates. I/O-bound commercial programs, in which throughput is in almost direct proportion to the I/O data rate, can achieve performance improvement by using byte alignment for binary and floating-point data.

A program written to use byte boundary alignment will not necessarily run on a System/360 model that does not have the feature. Therefore, programs that are to run on both the Model 165, 155 and on System/360 models without byte orientation should be written to adhere to integral boundary rules.

The general advantages gained by the larger main processor storage gives the user the ability to:

1. Execute more jobs concurrently.
2. Add and expand such applications as graphics, teleprocessing, time sharing, remote job entry, and manipulation of extremely large data bases.
3. Ability to execute larger problem programs without the use of overlay structures.
4. Allocate larger main storage to language translators and sorts to improve their execution time.
5. Use more and larger I/O buffers to speed up input/output operations and optimize use of direct access storage space.
6. Include those system generation options that help improve control program performance and support additional functions.

Most of the I/O devices currently announced for System/360 Models 40 and 50 can be attached to Model 155 and devices announced for Models 65 and above can be attached to Model 165. In addition, certain new I/O devices are available for System/370. These are:

1. The 3330 Disk Storage which provides up to 800 million bytes of fast direct access storage and an 806 KB data transfer rate. The average access time is 30 milliseconds.
2. The 2305 Fixed Head Storage facility is available in Model 1 and Model 2. Model 1 has a maximum capacity of 5.4 million bytes, data transfer rate of 3 megabytes and an average access time of 2.5 milliseconds. Model 2 has a maximum capacity of 11.2 million bytes, data rate of 1.5 megabytes and an average access time of 5 milliseconds.
3. The 3211 Printer with a tapeless carriage and an alphanumeric speed of 2000 lines per minute. The tapeless carriage reduces operator intervention by eliminating carriage tape loading and unloading.

Inclusion of these new I/O devices (3330 and 2305), which provide for larger storage capacities and faster data transfer rate, has helped to improve the overall system efficiency. The 3211 printer provides for faster print-out rate thereby reducing printing time.

The 3330 disk drive

The 3330 facility is a modular, large capacity, high performance direct access storage device. The 3330 facility consists of a 3830 Storage Control and from 1 to 4 3330 Disk Storage modules. A 3330 module contains a pair of independent disk storage drives. The new, removable 3336 Disk Pack is used for data storage.

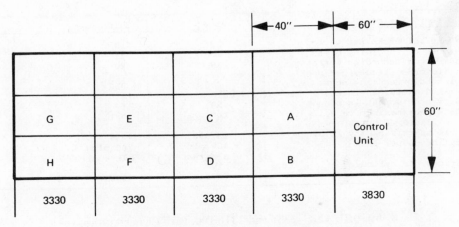

FIGURE A8.1. The 3330 Facility.

The configurations and maximum capacities of the 3330 facility, using full track records, are as follows:

3830 Storage Control + one 3330 Module	200 megabytes
3830 Storage Control + two 3330 Modules	400 megabytes
3830 Storage Control + three 3330 Modules	600 megabytes
3830 Storage Control + four 3330 Modules	800 megabytes

Individual drives are mounted in powered drawers that are opened and closed by a switch on the operator control panel on the 3330 module.

Functionally, the 3330 facility provides more capabilities than the 2314, especially in the area of performance. The 3330 facility supports all the standard 2314 commands (except the file scan command). The removable 3336 Disk Packs are interchangeable across 3330 disk drives but cannot be interchanged with the 2316 Disk Packs used on a 2314 facility. The table in Figure A8.2 compares disk pack characteristics of the 3336 and 2316 packs.

The increase in capacity achieved by using a 3330 facility over a 2314 or a 2321 depends upon the block size chosen for the data on the 3330 facility. For example, if a block size of 7294 bytes (full track capacity of 2314) is used on the 3330, the result is an increase of 91% in full track capacity. On the other hand, if data is reblocked to a full block of 13,030 bytes (full track capacity of 3330), the result is a 242% increase in full block capacity.

If a 3330 facility is used instead of a data cell drive, 6 full track blocks of data from the 2321 can be placed on each track of 3330 (if full track blocking is used). This means that slightly over four 3336 packs provide the capacity equivalent to 10 data cells or a full 2321 drive.

Characteristics	3336	2316
Number of disks per pack	12	13
Number of recording disks	10	11
Number of recording surfaces (recorded tracks per pack)	19	20
Disk thickness in inches	075	.050
Disk diameter in inches	14	14
Disk pack weight in pounds	20	15
Disk pack maximum capacity in millions of bytes	100	29.1
Full track capacity in bytes	13,030	7294
Cylinders per pack	404 plus 7 alternates	200 plus 3 alternates
Tracks per cylinder	19	20
Tracks per pack	7676	4000

FIGURE A8.2. 3336 and 2316 Disk Pack Characteristics.

Characteristics	3330	2314	2321
Capacity in bytes truncated to the nearest thousand (full track records)			
Pack or cell	100,018,000	29,176,000	39,200,000
Facility or Data Cell Drive			
2 drives/cells	200,036,000	58,352,000	78,400,000
4 drives/cells	400,073,000	116,704,000	156,800,000
6 drives/cells	600,109,000	175,056,000	235,200,000
8 drives/cells	800,146,000	233,408,000	313,600,000
10 cells	–	–	392,000,000
Access time in ms			
Maximum	55	130	600 (for strip select and load)
Average	30	60	175 (minimum for strip select and load)
Average cylinder to cylinder	10	25	95 (on a strip)
Rotation time in ms	16.7	25	50 (strip on drum)
Rotation speed (rpm)	3600	2400	1200
Data transfer rate (KB)	806	312	55

FIGURE A8.3. Capacity and Timing of the 3330, 2314 and 2321.

Some of the highlights of the 3330 storage system are:
1. Provides fast access to up to 800,000,000 bytes of on-line storage.
2. Average access time is 30 milliseconds, with a minimum of 10 and a maximum of 55 milliseconds.
3. Capacities of from 200,000,000 to 800,000,000 bytes in increments of

200,000,000 bytes are available.

4. Data rate is 806,000 bytes per second.
5. Powered drawers and frontal pack loading and unloading facility.
6. The 3330 storage facility also incorporates new error detection, correction and logging features.

The 3336 Disk Pack, which is used in the 3330 facility, contains 12 disks. Top and bottom disks protect the 10 disks used for recording. The system uses 19 of the recording surfaces, the twentieth surface contains the prerecorded data that controls seeking, track following, rotational position sensing and data clocking. Each pack offers 100,000,000 bytes of direct access storage and operates at 806,000 bytes per second data rate.

The 2305 fixed head storage module

The 2305 storage module provides faster access, higher data rate transfer and increased capacity direct access storage for the large System/370 computers. The 2305 is available in 2 models (Model 1 and Model 2). Each consists of a Storage Control Unit (IBM 2385 Storage Control) and 2 fixed-head storage modules.

Each module contains 6 nonremovable rotating disks on which data is recorded. Read/Write heads, called recording elements, are fixed in position to access each track on the 12 recording surfaces. As such no arm motion is required.

The 2835 control unit contains new error correction facilities similar to those of the 3830 control unit.

Data tracks on the Model 2 are formatted in the same manner as on System/360 direct access storage devices except for the absence of a home address on each track. There are 768 recording tracks and 96 spare tracks in 1 module. Each track is serviced by 1 fixed recording element. Each of the 12 surfaces contains 72 tracks, 64 recording surfaces and 8 spare. The spare tracks are interspersed among the 72 tracks so that every ninth track is spare. Data is recorded serially bit by bit on each track.

Four nonmovable access mechanisms are positioned around the rotating disks. Each access mechanism contains 2 groups of 9 recording elements per surface (a total of 16 recording and 2 spare elements). Each access mechanism accesses one-quarter of the tracks on each surface. A group of 8 recording elements accesses every other track.

In the case of Model 1, the data is recorded on the disks in a unique way in order to achieve faster data access. The Model 1 module contains the same number of recording elements as the Model 2, but they are so arranged as to double the data transfer rate and halve the average access time. The capacity of Model 1 is less than that of the Model 2 because of the following:

1. Only 384 recording tracks and 48 spare tracks are used.
2. There are 2 R0 records present on each physical track.
3. The gaps between data areas on a Model 1 track are larger than those of the Model 2 because of the higher data rate of Model 1.

An addressable recording track on a Model 1 occupies a 180-degree arc on a disk surface rather than a 360-degree arc as on a Model 2. A recording track in a Model 1

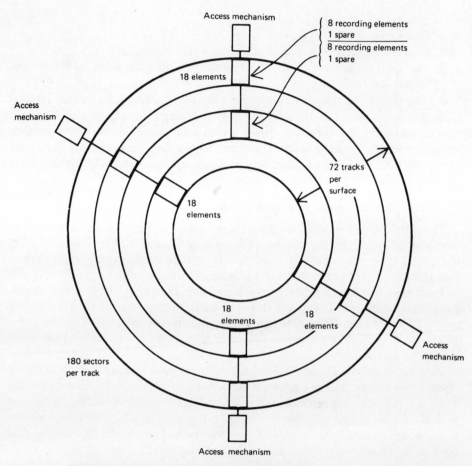

FIGURE A8.4. Top View of a 2305 Model 2 Disk Surface.

consists of 2 logical track segments. One track segment occupies a 180-degree arc on the top surface of a disk, while the other track segment occupies a 180-degree arc on the bottom surface of the same disk directly underneath the top segment. Two recording elements are paired to access each addressable track in parallel. One element records data on the top of the disk surface while the other element records data on the track segment on the bottom of the disk surface. Data is recorded in parallel, 2 bits at a time, 1 bit on each segment. Only half a rotation is required to record a full track of data. All odd track addresses occupy the same half of a disk, while all even track addresses occupy the remaining half. There are 64 recording and 8 spare tracks on each of the 6 disks in a module.

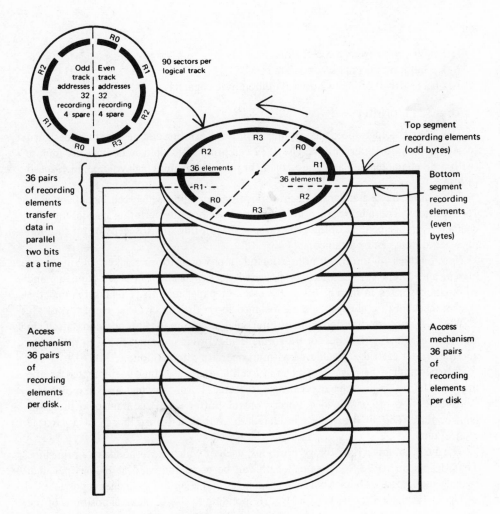

64 recording tracks/disk x 6   =   384 recording tracks/module
8 spare tracks/disk x 6   =   48 spare tracks/module
216 pairs of recording elements (read/write heads)/access mechanism

FIGURE A8.5. 2305 Model 1 Module

Some of the highlights of the IBM 2305 Storage facility are:

Model 1

1. 2.5 millisecond average access time.
2. 3 million bytes per second data rate.
3. 5.4 (1 drive) or 10.8 (2 drives) million bytes capacity.

Model 2

1. 5 millisecond average access time.
2. 1.5 million bytes per second data rate.
3. 11.2 (1 drive) or 22.4 (2 drives) million byte capacity.

The 3211 printer

The 3211 is a high-speed line printer with front printing and new features designed to reduce operator intervention. The 3211 can print 2000 alphameric lines per minute (with a 48-character set) and is designed for jobs that require high volume, high-speed printing.

The printer has a standard 132 print-position print line which can be expanded to 150 positions. The number of print positions does not alter printing speed. When the character arrangement is optimized for specific printing loads, speeds of up to 2500 lines per minute can be attained.

New features of the 3211 printer include a powered forms stacker, an automatic platen, and a tapeless carriage. The powered stacker mechanism is self-adjusting and automatically rises in increments as the stack of paper mounts. This insures that the stacker mechanism is always the same distance above the top of the stack of forms.

When forms are inserted, the printer platen automatically positions itself in accordance with the thickness of the forms. Thus correct clearance between the platen and the printer cartridge is achieved without operator intervention.

The need for a carriage control tape loading and unloading is eliminated by the implementation of a tapeless carriage feature. Form spacing and skipping are controlled by a program-loaded Form Control Buffer (FCB) contained in the 3811 control unit. The FCB can be considered to contain a storage image of a carriage control tape.

The FCB contains 180 storage positions, each of which corresponds to a print line. Thus, forms up to 22.5 inches in length can be accommodated at 8 lines per inch spacing and in case of 6 lines per inch spacing, a total length of 24 inches is possible.

Up to 12 channel codes (1 − 12), corresponding to the 12 channel positions of the paper carriage tape used on a 1403 printer, can be stored in the appropriate buffer line positions to control carriage skipping.

A carriage control address register is used to address the FCB and maintain correct line position with respect to the form. This register is incremented as space and skip commands are issued. When a skip to channel command is executed, the carriage control address register is incremented and the form moves until the channel specified by the command is sensed. If the requested channel number is not found in the FCB, the form's movement stops after address position 1 (line 1) has been sensed twice. *This feature prevents runaway form skipping.*

System/370 expanded instruction set

The instruction set of System/370 consists of the System/360 instruction set plus new instructions that support System/360 architecture and provide additional functions. The Model 165 standard instruction set includes all general purpose and I/O instructions and all binary, decimal, floating-point, and extended precision floating-point arithmetic instructions. In the case of the Model 155, all instructions outlined for the 165 are standard except those that are part of the extended precision optional feature. Storage protect and time of day clock instructions are also standard. The new STORE CPU ID instruction permits a program to determine the model upon which it is operating and provides the system serial number. The new STORE CHANNEL ID instruction can be used to identify the types of channels present in the system. Other new instructions are:

Extended Precision Floating Point (Optional on Model 155). This feature is provided for use in application areas in which the precision provided by the standard floating-point feature is not large enough. Precision of up to 28 hexadecimal digits, approximately equal to 34 decimal digits, is provided by the extended precision data format. Extended precision is achieved by using two doublewords to represent an extended precision floating-point number instead of using 1 doubleword as is done in long form representation.

Seven floating-point instructions are included in the extended precision feature. They provide addition, subtraction, and multiplication operations for extended precision data, using a pair of floating-point registers, and the ability to round from long to short form or from extended to long form.

General Purpose Instructions. Six general purpose instructions have been added to the System/370 instruction set.

＊ SHIFT AND ROUND DECIMAL, using a single instruction, provides right or left shifting of packed decimal data. This instruction can save 6 to 18 bytes of instruction storage and instruction execution time for each decimal shift and round operation performed in commercial processing.

MOVE LONG provides for movement of up to 16 million bytes from one location in storage to another with a single instruction, thereby removing the current limitation of 256 bytes per move. This instruction can eliminate the necessity of multiple move instructions or the inclusion of move subroutines.

COMPARE LOGICAL LONG can be used to compare logically 2 fields of up to 16 million bytes in length, thus removing the current 256-byte limit on byte compares. In addition, when an unequal compare occurs, the 2 characters that caused the inequality are identified.

COMPARE LOGICAL, STORE, and INSERT CHARACTERS UNDER MASK instructions provide byte addressability within the general purpose registers and permit nonword-size data that is not on a word boundary to be compared to data in a register, loaded into a register, and stored from a register. These 3 instructions can be of most benefit to control program programmers, compiler writers, and to those who must manipulate processor storage addresses.

The Model 165 CPU contains an instruction unit and an execution unit that overlap instruction fetching and preparation with instruction execution. The Model 165 instruction unit is controlled by logic circuits and can process several instructions concurrently while the execution unit is executing a single instruction.

In the case of the Model 155, instruction processing performance is improved by the fact that most instruction fetching is overlapped with instruction execution. Three one-word instruction buffers are provided in the I—Fetch area of the CPU for prefetching of instructions.

Two alterations have been made to the system action taken during the execution of certain instructions common to both System/370 and System/360 models. The first pertains to all instructions that check the validity of operands involved in packed decimal operations. In the case of System/370 (Models 155 and 165) an invalid sign in an operand causes the instruction to be suppressed (never executed) rather than terminated during execution as is done on System/360 models. Suppression, rather than termination, of an instruction when an invalid sign occurs insures that the data fields involved remain unchanged. Therefore, when a program check occurs, a routine can be executed that inspects the field that has the invalid sign.

For example, when an invalid sign results from packing an entirely blank field, the sign can be corrected by programming, and transaction deletion or program termination is avoided.

The second alteration concerns the recognition of a storage protection exception during the execution of an EDIT or an EDIT AND MARK instruction.

This appendix has been included to familiarize the reader with the basics of the System/370 from a problem programmer's point of view. Before attempting to code programs for this new system the student should consult the appropriate System Reference Library (SRL) publications for the Model 155 or 165 computer.

Index